Nelson's Annual

Preacher's Sourcebook

Nelson's Annual

Preacher's Sourcebook

Volume 3

THOMAS NELSON

Since 1798

NASHVILLE DALLAS MEXICO CITY RIO DE JANEIRO

Published in Nashville, Tennessee, by Thomas Nelson. Thomas Nelson is a registered trademark of HarperCollins Christian Publishing, Inc.

Typesetting by Kevin A. Wilson, Upper Case Textual Services, Lawrence, Massachusetts

Thomas Nelson, Inc., titles may be purchased in bulk for educational, business, fund-raising, or sales promotional use. For information, please e-mail SpecialMarkets@ThomasNelson.com.

9781401675769

Printed in the United States of America

1718[RRD] 65

CONTENTS

Articles

INTRODUCTION

There is no higher calling in life than to open the book of God to the people of God. In our increasingly godless culture the question asked of the ancient prophet has never rung more true in the hearts of those who come to here us preach—"Is there any word from the Lord?" The contributors in this volume are all Bible believers, not necessarily Bible beaters. They are young and old, well known and hardly known, widely published and unpublished, black and white, traditional and contemporary. Some of them preach in a coat and tie, others in jeans and open collars. But the one common characteristic they all hold is an insistence upon the trustworthiness of scripture and the knowledge that without a personal faith in Christ alone our hearers are in route to a godless eternity.

As a preacher myself for over four decades I want to raise a warning flag up the flagpole of a volume such as this. It is not designed to provide an "easy fix" for late Saturday night sermon preparation. Volumes such as this should never be used as the only tool on the work bench of your personal study. This sourcebook is designed to lay alongside all your other tools of word studies, exegesis, commentaries, prayer and analytical thought that goes into a fully developed and crafted sermon. Then filtered through your own personality and experience, along with windows of personal illustrations, it is the editor's prayer that the finished product will exhort, encourage and edify those who will hear it.

Perhaps there are no greater opportunities for the "preacher" to become the "pastor" than through the ministry of funerals and weddings. Our friends may soon forget some of our most thought provoking and well prepared sermons, but they will never forget who stood by their side at the open grave of a loved one or who shared in the joy of officiating when they became "one in Christ" at a wedding altar. Because weddings and funerals go a long way in legitimizing and earning a pulpit hearing much is devoted to these two ministries in this volume.

So, let's begin the journey, confidant that it still . . . and will always . . . please God "by the foolishness of preaching to save them that believe" (1 Cor. 1:21).

CONTRIBUTORS

Dr. O. S. Hawkins, General Editor

President, GuideStone Financial Resources
Former Pastor, First Baptist Church
Dallas, TX

Daniel L. Akin

President, Southeastern Baptist Theological Seminary
Wake Forest, NC

Dr. Mark L. Bailey

President and Professor of Bible Exposition
Dallas Theological Seminary

Dr. Phillip R. Bethancourt

Executive Vice President, The Ethics & Religious Liberty Commission
Nashville, TN

Matt Carter

Pastor of Preaching & Vision, Austin Stone Community Church
Austin, TX

Steve Dighton

Senior Pastor, Lenexa Baptist Church
Lenexa, KS

David Epstein

Senior Pastor, Calvary Baptist Church
New York, NY

J. D. Greear, Ph.D.

Lead Pastor, the Summit Church
Author of *Stop Asking Jesus Into Your Heart* and *Gospel.*

Jim Henry

Pastor Emeritus First Baptist Church
Orlando, FL

Dr. Jeff Iorg

President, Golden Gate Seminary
Mill Valley, CA

Dr. James MacDonald

Senior Pastor, Harvest Bible Chapel
Chicago, IL
www.harvestbiblechapel.org

Dr. Russell D. Moore

President, Ethics & Religious Liberty Commission
Nashville, TN | Washington, DC

Dr. Adrian Rogers (1931–2005)

Pastor Emeritus, Bellevue Baptist Church
Memphis, TN

Steve Rogers

Executive Editor, Adrian Rogers Sermon Library
www.adrianrogerslibrary.com

Steven Smith

Dean, Professor of Communication, The College at Southwestern
Fort Worth, TX

K. Marshall Williams, Sr.

Pastor, Nazarene Baptist Church
Philadelphia, PA

THE GOSPEL OF THE SERVANT KING

The Kingdom of God Marches On

Mark 1:35–45

Daniel L. Akin

Introduction

Jesus has just had an incredible day of teaching the Scriptures, casting out demons, and healing the sick. And even though the day is drawing to a close, there is more to be done for the kingdom to advance against the powers of darkness and the forces of evil. Three clear aspects emerge in our text, and it is instructive that we find the essential elements of prayer and preaching. Without both, the advance of the kingdom would have stopped dead in its tracks.

The Kingdom Advances through Prayer

Though He had been up late, Jesus still rose "very early" the next morning, "while it was still dark" (v. 35 HCSB). He left Peter's home alone, going to a place of solitude and privacy. A place for restoration and fellowship with His Father was what He needed and desired. Peter and those with him sent out a search party. Apparently the crowds had returned for more miracles. Peter's words almost have the sound of a rebuke: "Everyone's looking for You!" We are so much like Peter, not understanding the ways of God and how His kingdom will come. Yes, there will be healings and exorcisms. But, there must also be prayer.

The Kingdom Advances through Preaching

Jesus, as He so often does, responds to Peter in a different and surprising manner than we expect. He will not return to those who are looking for Him. Rather, He says, "Let's move on. Let's go to the next town. I will preach there also. This is why I came" (see v. 38). Neither the crowds nor the disciples understood why He had come into the world. But He knew! Jesus came to preach, to herald, to proclaim the gospel of salvation, a message that is both *by* Him and *about* Him. Indeed, He is the gospel!

The Kingdom Advances through Cleansing

As He was traveling and ministering, Jesus was met by a leper. This encounter is startling, provocative, and even offensive. In that culture, a leper was considered an outcast, a man deemed by the law as unclean and by the people as cursed by God. That he came near to Jesus, so close that Jesus could touch him, was to do the unthinkable. The touch of Jesus speaks more loudly than any words ever could, and His words must have thrilled this man's soul: "I am willing" (v. 41 HCSB). Unlike any ordinary man, the Lord Jesus is not polluted by the leper's disease when He touches him. Instead, the leper is cleansed by the gracious touch and contagious holiness of the Son of God.

Conclusion

Jesus's life illustrates the advancement of God's kingdom in the world through the ministries of prayer, proclamation, and the healing of the hurting. It is why Jesus came. He will take on Himself our sin, our sorrow, and our shame. In return He gives us His forgiveness, His holiness, and His righteousness—praise the Lord! What an exchange!

THE GOSPEL OF THE SERVANT KING

When Man-Made Rules Get in the Way of God's Gracious Plans

Mark 2:23–28

Daniel L. Akin

Introduction

Few things are more destructive, seductive, and deceptive to a relationship with God than the deadly poison of legalism. It is *destructive* because it breeds death rather than life. It is *seductive* because it has a natural allurement for the flesh that causes us to look to ourselves rather than to Christ for our spiritual status before God. It is *deceptive* because it makes us think we are the spiritual elite when actually we are spiritual slaves.

Do Not Let Man-Made Rules Make You a Spiritual Slave (Mark 2:23–24)

As Jesus and His disciples were walking, the disciples began to pick a few heads of grain. In the eyes of the Pharisees, they were guilty of *reaping*.

1. The Pharisees had constructed a man-made mountain of rules that enslaved those who tried to follow them. No one could live up to the expectations, nor should it have been expected that they would.
2. In a reversal of Genesis 50:20, what God had meant for good they had turned to evil. The clash is not over the rules, but over who makes the rules.

Remember That the Lord's Day Is to Be a Blessing, Not a Burden (Mark 2:25–27)

Jesus completely ignores the Sabbath question and turns to an event in the life of King David. Jesus's point is simple.

1. While it was not normal or lawful for David and his men to eat the showbread, it was even more the case that God did not want them to starve. He was primarily concerned with protection and provision for His servant David, the anointed king of Israel.
2. Jesus concludes with the principle that should have guided Jewish observance of the Sabbath all along: "The Sabbath was made for man, and not man for the Sabbath" (v. 27). Jesus had a liberating vision of the Sabbath that frees us from legalistic constraints instead of binding us with unbearable burdens.

Let the Lordship of Jesus Christ Be Your Anchor and Guide (Mark 2:28)

Modern readers cannot easily grasp the striking declaration of verse 28. Jesus weds the "Son of Man" title to that of "Lord of the Sabbath" and declares that He is both.

1. Jesus puts Himself in the place of and with the authority of God.
2. As the Lord of the Sabbath, He determines what is lawful and unlawful on the Sabbath day. He makes the call, and His Word is final! With one bold declaration, He silences His adversaries and all opposition.

Conclusion

The Pharisees relied on their own traditions for guidance, and in doing so, they missed the Law-giver entirely. Jesus Christ is our anchor for spiritual authority in all things. As God, He is Lord of the Sabbath! It is a fact, regardless of our permission. The question is, have you surrendered to Him as your God and the Lord of your life? Man-made rules will never get you to God! Only the Lord of the Sabbath, the Son of God, will get you there. Trust in His work and not your own.

THE GOSPEL OF THE SERVANT KING

It Is Always Right to Do Good

Mark 3:1–6

Daniel L. Akin

Introduction

In Mark 2:1–3:6 we see the build up to inevitable conflict. The hostility now reaches a climax, with anger and ill will on both sides. Jesus will not back down, though He understands where this will lead. Consumed with the will of His Father and emboldened by uncompromising conviction, He moves ahead with His face set toward the cross, convinced that "it is always right to do good!"

Doing Good for the Glory of God Will Invite Critical Scrutiny (Mark 3:1–2)

For Jesus, doing good for the glory of God is not restricted by date or location. This encounter occurs on the Sabbath in the synagogue. One cannot help but believe Jesus is deliberately provoking a confrontation with the religious leaders.

1. Be Sensitive to Those Who Need Compassion (Mark 3:1)

   Jesus sees a man with a withered hand. This man needed Jesus' attention, and his healing would be the occasion for God's power to be displayed. Jesus, with sensitivity and compassion, determined to act.

2. Be Ready for Those Who Always Criticize (Mark 3:2)

   The Pharisees had one goal: they sought to "accuse Him." They were enslaved to their own critical hearts, and they did their best to enslave others as well.

Doing Good for the Glory of God Will Require Personal Conviction (Mark 3:3–5)

There will be no retreat in His message and actions. With courage and conviction, He will press forward, obedient to the will of God regardless of consequences.

1. Be Right in What You Do (Mark 3:3–5)
   In this act of mercy, Jesus fulfills the Great Commandments. The Pharisees knew nothing of this love, thus were far from fulfilling the law of Moses.
2. Be Right in What You Say (Mark 3:4)
   Jesus raises the right question, and it is shocking and sad that the Pharisees could not respond. Their silence condemns them, and reveals a tragic flaw in their theology concerning the nature of the God of grace and mercy, love and compassion.
3. Be Right in What You Feel (Mark 3:5)
   Jesus is angered and grieved at their hardness of heart. Pride is dangerously deceitful, and it provoked our Lord to righteous anger.

Doing Good for the Glory of God Will Encourage Hostile Opposition (Mark 3:6)

For some, it is not enough to do the right thing. If you do not arrive at the "correct" destination by the "correct" route, you get criticized and misrepresented.

1. The Enemy of My Enemy Is My Friend
   The Pharisees and Herodians hated each other. However, their common disdain for Jesus united them. They "immediately" conspired together.
2. The Enemy We Fear Most We Will Seek to Destroy
   The Pharisees and Herodians wanted to destroy Jesus. Their hatred was coupled with fear, and this would lead to unspeakable evil: the murder of Messiah.

Conclusion

Jesus did a good thing in healing this man, and He did a good thing in saving our souls. Through word and deed, He teaches us well: it is always right to do good!

THE GOSPEL OF THE SERVANT KING

Do You Have Ears That Hear?

Mark 4:1–20

Daniel L. Akin

Introduction

Mark 4 teaches us there is a spiritual connection between the heart and the ear. Four times in this text Jesus makes this connection clear. What is Jesus' point in emphasizing our need to hear?

We Must Sow the Seed of the Gospel That People Might Hear the Word (Mark 4:1–9)

The text says "He taught them many things by parables" (v. 2). Just as Jesus opens the parable with an admonition to pay attention, so He closes it with one: "Anyone who has ears to hear should listen!" (v. 9 HCSB).

If We Do Not Listen to the Word, We Will Not Benefit from the Gospel (Mark 4:10–12)

The Word of the gospel hardens the resistant and the rebellious while it is enthusiastically received by the receptive. Those outside are not denied the possibility of belief, but if they persist in their unbelief they will not receive more evidence or revelation.

The Fruitfulness of the Seed of the Gospel Depends upon the Receptivity of the Hearer (Mark 4:13–20)

Jesus' words note the essential and foundational nature of the parable of the soils. If they do not understand this one, they will struggle to understand the others.

1. The Soil of Some Hearts Is Hard (Mark 4:14–15 [cf. 4:4])
   The sower in this story is Jesus, or anyone who shares the gospel. The seed is the Word of God. The path represents the hard-hearted individual. For whatever reason, these are hardened to the gospel. The book closes and the service ends, and so do their ears and hearts.
2. The Soil of Some Hearts Is Shallow (Mark 4:16–17 [cf. 4:5–6])
   The next soil is welcoming but not substantive enough to maintain the growth of the seed. The people to whom Jesus is referring with this soil are those who hear the Word and immediately receive it with joy. However, these people are shallow and have no roots. They are here today and gone tomorrow.
3. The Soil of Some Hearts Is Distracted (Mark 4:18–19 [cf. 4:7])
   This group of people undoubtedly hears and receives the Word better than the first two soils. However, they eventually get distracted by worry, wealth, and lust for other things. This life is more important to them than the life to come. Stuff is more important to them than the Savior.
4. The Soil of Some Hearts Is Fruitful (Mark 4:20 [cf. 4:8])
   The final soil is noticeably different than the first three. It represents those who hear the Word, accept it, and bear fruit. Their hearing is active, not passive. They aggressively pursue the Word, allow it to take root, and rejoice in its abundant growth.

Conclusion

Christianity is a religion of the Word and therefore of the ear. Hearing God's Word is a dangerous thing. What you do with it is critical to your soul. He who has ears to hear, let him hear.

Jesus Is the Great Physician

Mark 5:21–43

Daniel L. Akin

Introduction

This text has a "sandwich structure"—two stories wrapped in one big story. It makes comparisons and draws contrasts that are deeply personal to hurting people.

Jesus Hears the Cries of the Distressed (Mark 5:21–24)

Jesus cares for those in trouble. He is the omnipotent God. Disease and death surrender completely and immediately to His sovereign authority.

1. We Can Come to Jesus with Our Request (Mark 5:21–23)
   Jairus is a man of distinction with great humility. He comes to the only one he believes can save his little girl.
2. We Must Come to Jesus in Faith (Mark 5:23–24)
   Jairus's request was straightforward, delivered in dependency and urgency.

Jesus Responds to the Pain of the Diseased (Mark 5:24–34)

Jesus is not too busy to stop and help someone else who is hurting, especially one who is determined, humble, and hopeful in Him.

1. We Can Approach Jesus in Our Suffering (Mark 5:24–27)
   A woman sick for twelve years believes if she could just touch Him or His clothing she could be healed. Her theology may be weak, but her faith is strong.

2. We Must Approach Jesus in Faith (Mark 5:28–34)

    Though hundreds throng about, only one connects with Jesus in faith. She experiences physical and spiritual salvation.

Jesus Has Authority over the Power of Death (Mark 5:35–43)

Consider Jairus and the woman: (1) each knows only Jesus could help him or her, (2) each knows he or she is unworthy, (3) each falls down, and (4) each believes Jesus can heal.

1. We Can Believe in Jesus in Spite of the Circumstances (Mark 5:35–36)

    Jairus's daughter is dead. Jesus responds as if to say, "Despite all appearances I am neither distracted nor disinterested in your need. Believe and watch what I do."

2. We Can Believe in Jesus Regardless of the Skeptics (Mark 5:37–40)

    Hard-core realists and skeptics will always be with us. Have faith in the omnipotent sovereign Lord Jesus whose absolute authority and power knows no rival.

3. We Can Believe in Jesus because He Can Be Trusted (Mark 5:41–43)

    Gender, namelessness, uncleanness, and impossible condition did not stop the girl from experiencing the healing touch of Jesus. We can believe no matter what.

Conclusion

What does this text teach about God? God honors the faith of all who come to Him through Jesus, regardless of social status, gender, or other distinction.

What does this text teach about sinful humanity? Our world is filled with pain and sorrow, and desperately needs the touch and grace of God mediated through Jesus.

What does this text teach about Jesus Christ? Jesus cares and willingly loses/gives up power for those who have none.

What does God want us to know? God honors imperfect faith from a sincere heart when the object of faith is Jesus.

What does God want us to do? God wants us to come with any request regardless of circumstances, because He can be trusted.

THE GOSPEL OF THE SERVANT KING

What Do You Get for Faithful Service to God?

Mark 6:14–29

Daniel L. Akin

Introduction

What are the blessings for a life of devotion to King Jesus? We see an example in John the Baptist of one who lived such a life. We also see in his life that a servant is not greater than his master. If they treated Jesus with cruelty, they will do the same to His followers.

Expect That Some Will Fear You (Mark 6:14–16)

When doing the work of God, we can anticipate a variety of responses from those around us. Some may rejoice (Matt. 5:16). Others may oppose and reject us (Mark 6:11). Still others may actually fear us, not liking what we say or do, but being unable to deny God's work. How do we respond when others fear and resent us?

1. Let Your Good Works Honor You (Mark 6:14–15)
2. Let Your Good Works Haunt Them (Mark 6:16)

Expect That Some Will Try to Stop You (Mark 6:17–20)

Herodias would stop at nothing to get her way, even if it meant prostituting her daughter and taking the life of the man of God. In the midst of all the wickedness of the Herod family, we see a man consumed with a guilty conscience that will continue to haunt him for not doing the right thing.

1. Guilt Will Drive Some to Oppose You (Mark 6:17–18, 20)
2. Hatred Will Drive Others to Oppose You (Mark 6:19)

Expect That Some Will Attempt to Destroy You (Mark 6:21–29)

John had condemned Herodias as a treacherous and adulterous woman, and she will now have her revenge, showing what followers of Jesus may have to endure this side of eternity.

1. Accept That the Ungodly Will Use Ungodly Means to Get You (Mark 6:21–23)
2. Accept That the Ungodly May Get Your Head on a Platter (Mark 6:24–29)

Isn't it amazing that Jesus had declared John the Baptist to be the last and greatest prophet? And yet, John died in his early thirties, never performed a single miracle, and had a public ministry that lasted only about a year. Bad things do happen to good people. Life is often unfair. The righteous do suffer. And yes, sometimes good things happen to bad people. But never forget, God sees. He knows!

Conclusion

Death cannot silence a life. Murdering someone will not put an end to their witness and testimony. Remember the saying, "Being dead, yet he still speaks." Throughout history the message of the martyrs continues to ring loud and clear, none more so than John the Baptist. Herod and Herodias may have received his head on a platter, but our Lord received his soul into heaven for all eternity. John lost his head, but Herod and Herodias lost their souls. In the end, there is no question who won and who lost!

THE GOSPEL OF THE SERVANT KING

The Deadly Lures of Legalism

Mark 7:1–23

Daniel L. Akin

Introduction

God hates pride because human pride is in direct opposition to God's glory. It thinks more of itself than it should, and it may be lurking in unsuspecting locations like religion and legalistic bondage to the traditions of men. It is the deadly lure of legalism.

Legalists Honor God with Their Lips, Resulting in False Worship (Mark 7:1–8)

Pharisees and scribes, teachers of the Torah (Law), come again from Jerusalem amidst the growing popularity of Jesus (Mark 7:1), determined to take Him down. Under the guise of religious devotion, they set about exalting themselves and tearing down their enemies.

1. They Love to Compare Themselves to Others (Mark 7:1–5)
2. They Actually Play the Hypocrite with a Distant Heart (Mark 7:6–8)

Legalists Make Void the Word of God, Resulting in Spiritual Disobedience (Mark 7:9–13)

Not all traditions are bad, but they do become bad when we put them on the same level as Scripture or in the place of Scripture. A "Bible-plus" kind of religion practically nullifies the Bible's power in our lives (Mark 7:13).

1. They Reject the Commandments of God and Establish Their Own (Mark 7:9)

   Man-made rules and regulations became the object of obedience while God's commandments get set aside, left behind, kicked to the curb. First, they teach the commandments of men (v. 7). Then they leave the commandments of God (v. 8). Next they reject the commandments of God (v. 9). And finally they make void the Word of God (v. 13). And if we are not careful, we will fail to see our own hypocrisy in this progression.

2. They Manipulate God's Word to Their Own Advantage (Mark 7:10–13)

   They had placed their traditions in the place of Scripture and themselves in the place of God. The heart truly is an idol factory, and religious traditions are some of its best tools.

Legalists Are Confused Concerning the Source of Defilement, Resulting in a Lack of True Understanding (Mark 7:14–23)

The fruit of sin has its root in every human heart. Every human heart has the root of every human sin in it. You see, it is entirely possible to look nice on the outside while being dead on the inside. The most deadly contamination is not what I touch. The most deadly contamination is what is in my heart.

1. Defilement Has Its Root on the Inside (Mark 7:14–20)
2. Defilement Reveals Its Fruit on the Outside (Mark 7:21–23)

Conclusion

There are basically only two approaches to religion, each of which can be summed up in a single word: *do* or *done*. The world says the problem is out there and the solution is to answer the question, "What can I do?" The Bible says the problem is inside of us and the answer is what Christ has done! In legalism we think better of ourselves than Jesus does. But in salvation, we think of ourselves as Jesus does: hopeless, helpless sinners in desperate need of a Savior.

THE GOSPEL OF THE SERVANT KING

The Normal Christian Life: Following and Serving the King

Mark 8:27–38

Daniel L. Akin

Introduction

In contrast to the dangerous and seductive approach to Christianity that values health, safety, and comfort above all else, Jesus informs His followers and us what the normal Christian life looks like and what it means to follow and serve the King—a King who came to die and serve, a King who calls His followers to die and serve as well.

You Must Know and Personally Confess Who Jesus Is (Mark 8:27–30)

As Jesus brought gradual physical sight to the blind man of Bethsaida (Mark 8:22–26), He also brought gradual, spiritual sight to the disciples concerning who He is and what kind of Messiah He will be.

1. There Is an Inescapable Question (Mark 8:27–28)
2. Who Is Jesus?
3. There Is One Acceptable Answer (Mark 8:29–30)

    At the center of Mark's gospel we have the one and only acceptable answer concerning the identity of Jesus. Peter and the Twelve reject the prevailing opinions of the crowds and religious leaders (note their negative evaluation in 3:22), and so must we! He is Christ the Lord.

You Must Learn and Affirm the Ways of God and Not of Man (Mark 8:31–34)

This begins the second half of Mark's gospel, which focuses on what Jesus came to do. Jesus tells us here that He came to die. A King who dies is not what they *expected*. It is not what they *wanted*. It is, however, what they and we all desperately *needed*.

1. God's Ways Are Often Hard but Usually Clear (Mark 8:31–32)
2. God's Will Is Often a Challenge but Always Perfect (Mark 8:32–33)

You Must Understand and Accept That Jesus Calls You to Deny Yourself and Die for His Sake and the Gospel's (Mark 8:34–38)

Now, how must we respond? Confident that God's will is perfect, even if it might not be safe, we embrace the call of Jesus to follow Him and to die in order that we and others might truly live!

1. The Self-Centered Life Must Be Put to Death (Mark 8:34)
   Deny yourself. Give up the right to self-determination. Live as Christ directs. Treasure and value Jesus more than yourself, your plans, your comforts, your goals, and your aspirations. Put to death the idol of "I"! Say no to you and yes to Jesus!
2. The Safe Life Must Be Put to Death (Mark 8:35)
   Save or treasure your life, your soul, above all else, and you will lose it. The one who plays it safe and considers his existence more important than Jesus will lose both Jesus and eternal life.
3. The Self-Serving Life Must Be Put to Death (Mark 8:36–38)
   You are set free to live the normal/radical Christian life when you see death as reward and when you can say with Paul, "For me, living is Christ and dying is gain" (Phil. 1:21 HCSB).

Conclusion

May all of us learn how to die for Christ and the gospel so that we, and others, may truly live. May all of us learn what is and how to live the normal Christian life.

THE GOSPEL OF THE SERVANT KING

Lessons Learned in the Fires of Failure

Mark 9:14–29

Daniel L. Akin

Introduction

Failure is never fun and defeat is seldom something we take delight in. It can be painful, embarrassing, and humiliating. And our response can be life changing, altering our destiny. In this story of a father with a suffering son, Mark shows us that we can do nothing at all that really matters without Jesus, but also that this drives us continually to Him for help. We need to let our weakness drive us to His strength. We need to let our impotence drive us to His omnipotence. We need to let our limitations drive us to His unlimited resources. We need to let our humility drive us to His sufficiency.

We Never Advance Beyond Our Need for Jesus (Mark 9:14–19)

Mountaintop experiences are wonderful, and we need them from time to time for spiritual nourishment and the recharging of our spiritual batteries. However, God never intended for us to stay there. He wants us "down here" preaching the gospel to and ministering among the hurting and suffering. He wants us living with and serving real people devastated by the ravages of the fall and of sin. As Jesus's agents of redemptive love, we go in His name and with the promise of His presence. His disciples forgot this and opened themselves up to great pain and humiliation.

1. We Need Christ When Criticized by Our Detractors (Mark 9:14–16)
2. We Need Christ When Confronted with the Demonic (Mark 9:17–18)

3. We Need Christ When Corrected in Our Defeats (Mark 9:19)

We Never Advance Beyond Our Need for Faith (Mark 9:19–27)

How much belief—how much faith—do we need? A lot? Must it be perfect? No. Faith the size of a tiny mustard seed will do just fine (Matt. 17:20). The key to finding healing in Christ is not the *depth* of our faith but the *direction* of our faith. What is important is not the *potency* of our faith but the *person* our faith is in. A little faith in a great Savior gets amazing results!

1. The Key Is Direction (Mark 9:19–22)
2. The Key Is Dependency (Mark 9:23–27)

We Never Advance Beyond Our Need for Prayer (Mark 9:28–29)

It has been quite an interesting time for the disciples. They should have learned a lot. For the lowly disciples, it is time to stop, think, and evaluate. What went wrong? Why didn't their attempt at "binding the strong man" (cf. Mark 3:27) work?

1. Failure Should Lead Us to Ask Questions of Ourselves (Mark 9:28)
2. Failure Should Drive Us to God in Humility (Mark 9:29)

Conclusion

Lessons learned in the fires of failure may hurt us, but they can hurt us in a good way if they drive us to Jesus, increase our faith, and humble us in prayer. Today we do not have Jesus with us in the flesh, but through the gift of prayer He is only a word, a thought, away. Let us all remember what Jesus said to Thomas: "Because you have seen Me, you have believed. Those who believe without seeing are blessed" (John 20:29 HCSB). We believe, Lord. Help us in our unbelief.

THE GOSPEL OF THE SERVANT KING

Sent to Serve (Why Did Jesus Come?)

Mark 10:32–45

Daniel L. Akin

Introduction

Service is the ultimate reason Jesus came. It gets at the heart of the gospel. It is the pattern for all who would follow Christ. We are sent to serve, even laying down our life if God ordains it, just as He ordained it for His Son.

You Must Consider the Cost of Being a Servant (Mark 10:32–34)

Jesus the Savior leads the way going before them, His face set for the destiny that awaits Him. He has counted the cost and nothing will stop Him on His march to the cross. Nothing!

1. The Road of Service Invites Misunderstanding (Mark 10:32)
2. The Road of Service Involves a Mission (Mark 10:32–34)

You Must Consider the Challenge to Being a Servant (Mark 10:35–40)

Being a servant doesn't come easy, especially for those who have been trained to lead, and especially for those who dream of being served. James and John get one thing right but everything else wrong. They are correct that Jesus is headed for glory (10:37). They believe that in the end, He wins and will reign as King Jesus. But as for the rest, and in particular, how the glory would come, they don't have a clue.

1. Being a Servant Goes Against Our Human Inclinations (Mark 10:35–37)

2. Being a Servant Is Ordained by Divine Revelation (Mark 10:38–40)

You Must Consider the Conflict in Being a Servant (Mark 10:41–44)

Jesus steps into the midst of the strife among the Twelve and uses the occasion for His greatest and most powerful lesson on being a servant, on being great in God's kingdom. It is a hard lesson to learn. By earthly standards it just doesn't make sense. But Jesus reverses all human ideas of greatness, turning the world's philosophy on its head.

1. You Must Say No to the Ways of the World (Mark 10:41–43)
2. You Must Say Yes to the Work of a Slave (Mark 10:43–44)

You Must Consider Christ When Being a Servant (Mark 10:45)

Here, Jesus tells us *why* He came to die, making a promise no other religious leader in the world has made or could make. And in making it, He declares for all to hear that He came to serve you and me, not just as our example, but as our ransom! Here ransom speaks, and speaks clearly, of Jesus' substitutionary atonement—His sacrificial death on the cross as the price paid to purchase the release from guilt and bondage for sinners who would trust and believe in Him. *Righteousness* demanded this ransom. *Love* provided it.

1. Follow Christ in Service
2. Follow Christ in Sacrifice

Conclusion

The greatest person who ever walked on this earth was a humble servant. He got down low so that He might lift others up. He considered others as more important than Himself (Phil. 2:3), all the way to the death of the cross. And now He calls us to believe the same.

THE GOSPEL OF THE SERVANT KING

God Sent His Son and We Killed Him

Mark 12:1–12

Daniel L. Akin

Introduction

In the Holy Scriptures there are a number of biblical truths that we need to keep together so that we do not run the risk of distorting them, of understanding them out of balance. This is especially important when it comes to two central moments in the life of Jesus Christ: His *incarnation* and His *crucifixion*. Christmas must always be celebrated in light of Easter. The cradle in a stable providing a resting place for a little baby must always be viewed in tandem with a bloody man hanging on a cross at Calvary.

In our text, Jesus tells a story of which the meaning can scarcely be doubted: God sent His Son and we killed Him. There was a murder in the vineyard and we know who committed the crime. The story that Jesus tells is really an allegorical parable, and the identity of the central characters is not in question. It is drawn from a very familiar Old Testament passage: Isaiah 5:1–7. The *Man* who plants the vineyard is God the Father. The *vineyard* is Israel (cf. Isa. 5:1–7). The *tenants* are the religious leaders of Israel. The *servants* are the faithful prophets. And the *beloved Son* is Jesus.

God Is Incredibly Patient, Even When Sinners Resist His Gracious Wooing (Mark 12:1–5)

A parable is defined as "an earthly story or analogy with a heavenly meaning." This parable is a story of Israel's relationship to God and is a reminder of His incredible patience (cf. 2 Peter 3:9). God planted a nation called Israel as a special vineyard. In spite of the fact that He planted her, put in place some protective fencing and a tower, she did not produce good things, but bad. The landowner had made an agreement with the tenant farmers whom He believed could be trusted and would be reliable caretakers of His vineyard. They would work the vineyards, benefit from the produce, and pay a percentage of the harvest to Him as rent.

In order for a landowner to retain legal rights to his property, he had to receive produce from his tenants. However, as C. H. Dodd said, the tenants "pay their rent in blows."[1] In verses 2–3 harvest time has arrived and so the landowner sends a servant to collect what rightly belongs to the owner. They beat the servant and sent him away empty handed. In verse 4, the owner sends a second servant, who was treated even worse. In verse 5, the gracious and long-suffering landowner sends yet a third servant and the response of the tenants escalates—they kill him. And on and on it would go with many others. Some they would beat. Some they killed.

These faithful servants represent the faithful prophets sent by the Lord time and time again (cf. Jer. 7:25–26; 25:4–7; Heb. 11:35–38). God's gracious patience was extended repeatedly, but rebellious sinners like you and me resisted His wooing. We took what was His and in rebellion said it was ours!

When the Father Sent His Son, He Sent the One He Loves and We Should Honor (Mark 12:6–8)

The parable takes a remarkable turn in verse 6. It continues the theme of the amazing patience and long-suffering of God with humanity. Jesus is talking at this moment to the religious leaders of Israel and yet, I must confess, I see all of us in this crowd as well.

The landowner now becomes a father. In one final attempt, He sends on a mission "a beloved son." The phrase "beloved son" is filled with biblical and theological significance. It was idiomatic for "an only son" (cf. Mark 1:11; 9:7; also Gen. 22:2).

If verses 1–5 convey the *hope* of God for His people, verse 6 conveys the *loving-kindness* of God for His people. The Father sent His Son as an act of grace. Seeing the son may have led the tenants to wrongly conclude that the landowner was dead. They foolishly and with evil intent surmised that if they assassinate the son, then they could claim His property as their own. John 1:11 rings in our ears: "He came to His own, and His own did not receive Him." To reject the Son is to reject the One who sent Him. It is nothing less than an act of spiritual insanity.

Even Though People Believe They Can Escape It, God's Judgment Will Certainly Come (Mark 12:9–12)

The one rejected and murdered will be vindicated, and how we now respond to this radical change of events could not be more important. Historically, God judged the religious leaders and the nation for their rejection of His Son. In AD 70, Jerusalem was destroyed and the nation of Israel was brought to ruins. Today that same judgment falls on all who have "trampled on the Son of God, regarded as profane the blood of the covenant by which He was sanctified, and insulted the Spirit of grace" (Heb. 10:29 HCSB).

Jesus quotes Psalm 118:22–23, changing the metaphor from a vineyard to a building. The stone rejected would become a well-known symbol for the Messiah. The Jewish leaders rejected Jesus. They rejected the stone and cast it aside as worthless and of no value. They beat Him and crucified Him. God, however, in a marvelous reversal, takes what man rejects and makes it the cornerstone (literally, "the head of the corner"), the key stone, the most important stone to the whole structure that would ensure its stability and symmetry.

Jesus's rejection, humiliation, and crucifixion is an apparent tragedy, but God will use it all for a greater purpose that can only be described as, "This came from the Lord and is wonderful in our eyes!"

Conclusion

In *The Last Battle* by C. S. Lewis, Queen Lucy says to Lord Digory, "In our world too, a stable once had something inside it that was bigger than our whole world."[2] To this we might add, "In our world there once was also a cross and hanging on it was someone greater and more wonderful than our whole world." It was the Lord's doing. And it is marvelous in our eyes!

THE GOSPEL OF THE SERVANT KING

Two Great Commandments/Two Great Loves

Mark 12:28–34

Daniel L. Akin

Introduction

Humans love to ask what I call "mega" or "greatest" questions. Interestingly, these "mega" questions are not new. They go back even to the time of Jesus, when a religious leader asked our Lord about the greatest, "the most important" of all the commandments (Mark 12:28). Surprisingly, our Lord did not give him one. He gave him two, telling him, as Matthew 22:40 records, "All the Law and the Prophets depend [NIV: "hang"] on these two commands" (HCSB). And both commandments are grounded in our responsibility to love. First, we are to love God supremely, and second, we are to love our fellow humans genuinely.

We Are Commanded to Love God Supremely (Mark 12:28–30)

A scribe, a religious lawyer, asked Jesus a question that was often bantered about in religious circles: "Which command is the most important of all?" (Mark 12:28 HCSB). The rabbinic tradition had identified 613 commandments in the first five books of the Bible, the Torah. Of these, 365 were negative and 248 were positive. Some were "light," making less demand, while others were viewed as "heavy" with severe repercussions for disobedience.

Jesus responds quickly and to the point: He quotes what Israel called the "Shema," found in Deuteronomy 6:4–5. This confession was recited by every devout Jew morning and evening. James Edwards explains, "It was and is as important to Judaism as is the Lord's Prayer or the Apostles' Creed to Christianity."[1]

The context of the Shema is quite instructive. To love God is to obey His commandments and statutes "all the days of your life" (Deut. 6:2 HCSB). To love God means you will teach these commandments to your children and grandchildren (Deut. 6:2), when you sit, walk, lie down, and rise up (Deut. 6:7), remembering He is the God "who brought you out of the land of Egypt, out of the place of slavery" (Deut. 6:12 HCSB). To love God supremely means you shall "not follow other gods, the gods of the peoples around you, for the LORD your God [*Yahweh* your *Elohim*], who is among you, is a jealous God" (Deut. 6:14–15 HCSB).

The repetition of the word "all" (four times in Mark 12:30) is significant, as it emphasized the comprehensive nature of how we are to love *Yahweh* our *Elohim*, the Lord our God. What is called for is a total response of love and devotion to our great God. Indeed the four-fold use of heart, soul, mind, and strength is not intended as a "psychological analysis of human personality," but a call to love God wholly and completely.

We Are Commanded to Love Others Genuinely (Mark 12:31–34)

As is so often the case, Jesus gives us more than we ask for! The religious lawyer wants to know what commandment is the most important. Jesus responds by telling him there are two that go together. Why? Because how you respond to the first (loving God) will determine how you respond to the second (loving your neighbor). And, when you obey the second, it will give evidence that you have embraced the first.

Jesus adds Leviticus 19:18 as a complement to Deuteronomy 6:4–5. Growing out of my love for God I love those who have been created by God in His image. "Neighbor" is not used here in a restrictive sense. All of humanity, even my enemies, are in view (Luke 10:25–29).

Now, there is a healthy kind of self-love that is cognizant of the truth that we are the objects both of the "creating" and "redeeming" love of our God. To hate myself is actually an offense to God and calls into question His wisdom and goodness. Furthermore, the love a person naturally has for himself is now "turned out" toward others. The object of my affection and concern moves from me to others (cf. Phil. 2:3–5). In a mysterious paradox, the more I truly love myself, the more I will deny myself and love others. However, only by loving my God supremely will I be able to love others—all others—genuinely.

Examine the context surrounding Leviticus 19:18. It shows us that loving your neighbor as yourself means a lot! Among other things, it means that you will care for the poor (Lev. 19:10), not steal (Lev. 19:11), not lie (Lev. 19:11), be fair in business dealings (Lev. 19:14), care for the deaf (Lev. 19:14), care for the blind (Lev. 19:14), deal justly with all (Lev. 19:15), avoid slander (Lev. 19:16), not "jeopardize" the life of your neighbor (Lev. 19:16 HCSB), not "harbor hatred against your brother" (Lev. 19:17 HCSB), rebuke your neighbor when necessary for his and your good (Lev. 19:17), and not take revenge or bear a grudge against others (Lev. 19:18). God does not leave it to our imaginations as to what He means when He tells us to love our neighbors as ourselves.

The scribe responded with delight to our Lord's answer. First, he affirmed Jesus' creedal confession of the exclusive monotheism of the one true God (Mark 12:32). Second, he affirmed the comprehensive love, devotion, and worship our God is worthy to receive (Mark 12:33*a*). Third, he adds an insight that verse 34 reveals drew the praise and applause of Jesus (Mark 12:33*b*).

To love God supremely and our neighbor genuinely "is far more important than all the burnt offerings and sacrifices" (Mark 12:33 HCSB). He now sees that "real religion" ultimately is a matter of the heart. Even the most sacred of religious rituals and services do not trump my love for my God and others.

Conclusion

Mark informs us that Jesus was pleased with the scribe's answer ("Jesus saw that he answered intelligently"). Jesus then said, "You are not far from the kingdom of God" (Mark 12:34 HCSB). What did Jesus mean by this? It is not, "You are close, so try harder!" Rather, the man has come to see that ultimately eternal life, entering the kingdom of God, is a matter of the heart and not of ritual. It is a matter of heart devotion, not hard duty. I need to draw near to the One who has brought the kingdom of God near (Mark 1:15). I need to draw near to Jesus. One draws near and enters the kingdom not by religion. One draws near and enters this kingdom by a relationship with Jesus, a relationship that results in loving God supremely and others genuinely.

THE GOSPEL OF THE SERVANT KING

A Sacrifice of Extravagant Love

Mark 14:1–11

Daniel L. Akin

Introduction

Let me ask you a question that I hope you will be brutally honest in answering: Have you in your life as a follower of King Jesus ever made a sacrifice of extravagant love? Can you recall a time when you did something that really cost you? A time when you actually went without something you really wanted because of a sacrifice of extravagant love for Jesus? The sad fact is that we are good at giving Jesus our leftovers and hand-me-downs.

In Mark 14:1–11 we see something truly remarkable: an indisputable sacrifice of extravagant love. And we also see the tale of two lives that could not stand in greater contrast when it comes to true and unreserved devotion to our Lord: a woman who gave her very best and a man named Judas who betrayed the Son of God. Of the woman Jesus said, "Wherever the gospel is proclaimed in the whole world, what this woman has done will also be told in memory of her" (Mark 14:9 HCSB). Of the man Judas our Lord said, "It would have been better for that man if he had not been born" (Mark 14:21 HCSB).

Extravagant Acts of Love Will Be Public (Mark 14:1–3)

The backdrop of this story is the Jewish feast of Passover and Unleavened Bread (Mark 14:1). Jewish persons were flocking to Jerusalem to celebrate, but in the shadows of secrecy the Sanhedrin ("the chief priest and scribes") were seeking to arrest Jesus and kill Him. Mark says they hoped to arrest Him in "a treacherous way" (Mark 14:1 HCSB; NIV: "some sly way") but felt they must wait until after the feast because "there may be rioting among the people" (Mark 14:2 HCSB). However, things would proceed on God's timetable, not theirs, and Christ the Passover Lamb would be sacrificed for us right on time (cf. 1 Cor. 5:7).

Suddenly the scene shifts (Mark 14:3) to a home in Bethany of a man named Simon. Jesus apparently had healed him of leprosy. John 12:1 (HCSB) tells us the event happened "six days before the Passover," so Mark's account is something of a flashback. John's gospel also informs us that the lady who anointed both Jesus's head (Mark 14:3) and feet (John 12:3) was Mary, the sister of Martha and Lazarus, "the one Jesus had raised from the dead" (John 12:1 HCSB). Mark says, "She broke the jar and poured it on His head" (Mark 14:3 HCSB). What she did was done in full display of a room full of people. It was done against cultural convention, as a woman normally would not approach a man in this setting except to serve him food. Mary cared not one wit for any of this. Jesus was her Lord and Master. She deeply loved Him and would have done anything for Him. And, she did not care who heard or saw. Her devotion to Him trumped all other concerns.

Extravagant Acts of Love Will Often Be Criticized (Mark 14:4–5)

The woman's act of astonishing, radical devotion did not go unnoticed. It also did not go without significant criticism. Led by Judas (John 12:4) and in self-righteous pride, they questioned both her motive and her action. "Why has this fragrant oil been wasted? For this oil might have been sold for more than 300 denarii [a year's salary] and given to the poor" (Mark 14:4–5 HCSB).

Several important observations can be made at this point. *First*, the disciples demeaned not only the woman but also Jesus. *Second*, some are willing to be poor in their possessions in order to be rich in their devotion to Jesus. *Third*, the world, and sadly many in the church, will never have a problem with moderate, measured devotion to Christ. They will have little or no problem with a comfortable and convenient Christianity.

Extravagant Acts of Love Will Be Remembered (Mark 14:6–9)

"Leave her alone," Jesus commands them (Mark 14:6 HCSB). "Why are you bothering her?" Why do you harass her, harangue her, give her a hard time? "She has done a noble thing for me." She has done something wonderful and incredibly important to Me. Indeed, Jesus makes three striking observations about her in verses 8–9. *First*, "She has done what she could." She held nothing back. *Second*, her act of extravagant love had prophetic and symbolic significance: "She has anointed My body in advance for burial." *Third*, Jesus makes a promise that her sacrifice of extravagant love will never be forgotten as the gospel advances throughout "the whole world" (Mark 14:8–9 HCSB). Wherever the good news of salvation is proclaimed, what this lady has done will be told again and again in memory of her.

Extravagant Acts of Love Will Stand in Stark Contrast to Those of Betrayal (Mark 14:10–11)

Some people find Jesus useful because of what they think they can get from Him. Others find Jesus beautiful because they get *Him*. This woman found Jesus beautiful and gave all she had to Him. In contrast, Judas found Jesus useful and sought to get all he could for Him. Judas takes the initiative in going "to the chief priests to hand [Jesus] over to them" (Mark 14:10 HCSB). The leaders of the Sanhedrin were glad to hear this and promised Judas money. Matthew informs us it was for thirty pieces of silver (Matt. 26:15; cf. Zech. 11:12–13), "the value of a slave accidentally gored to death by an ox (Ex. 21:32)."[1] Judas then "started looking for a good opportunity to betray Him" (Mark 14:11 HCSB).

Conclusion

What a contrast we so clearly see in Mary and Judas. A comparison is most instructive.

Mary	Judas
A woman of no real standing	A man and one of the apostles
Gave what she could to Jesus	Took what he could get for Jesus
Blessed her Lord	Betrayed his Lord
Loved her Lord	Used his Lord
Did a beautiful thing	Did a terrible thing
Served Him as her Savior	Sold Him like He was his slave
Memorialized forever for her devotion	Memorialized forever for his betrayal

Oh, how I want to be like Mary. But oh, how often it is that Judas so readily appears when I look in the mirror. Only the gospel of my Savior is sufficient for my sin-sick soul.

GREAT MOMENTS IN GREAT PLACES

The Hill of the Beatitudes: A Life Well Worth Living

Matthew 5:1–12

Dr. Mark L. Bailey

Introduction

Harry S. Truman was quoted as saying, "I do not believe there is a problem in this country or the world today which could not be settled if approached through the teaching of the Sermon on the Mount."

Not only could the sermon as a whole solve every potential problem, what is often overlooked are the positive qualities of life Jesus promises if people would only adopt the worldview with which He introduces the Sermon on the Mount in the section called the Beatitudes.

If you asked a group of people what would make living life really worth the effort, you would get a list that might include success, significance, and security. All of these and more are ours if we will only allow Him to develop the character qualities He desires in His disciples.

Even Jesus' enemies said, "No man ever spoke like this!" (John 7:46 HCSB). While this referred to all that Jesus taught, it goes without saying that the Sermon on the Mount was the greatest message ever delivered. The Beatitudes form the introduction of that message as recorded in Matthew 5:1–12 and together stress the theme that heart righteousness is far more valuable than hand ritual.

Those who listened to Jesus' message on the north shore of the Sea of Galilee included both the broader audience of the curious crowd and the disciples who had attached themselves to the Galilean Messenger.

Jesus set heaven and earth in perspective when He talked about the blessings that can be anticipated when a series of heart attitudes are adopted. Bookending the list with the first and last beatitudes is the *present assurance*: "for the kingdom of heaven is theirs." In between the first and the last beatitudes are six that stress *future rewards* for present attitudes. While the kingdom is a present reality, its consummation comes only in the future. Blessings are promised for both the present and the future. The kingdom is a present possession (Col. 1:13–14) as well as a future realization. R. G. V. Tasker, professor of New Testament exegesis at the University of London, wrote, "The future tense ... emphasizes their certainty and not merely their futurity. The mourners will *indeed* be comforted, etc."[1]

The Beatitudes are too often memorized and too infrequently applied. The following is a suggested framework to see the attitude, the assurance, and an application for each. The first phrase contains the "be-attitude" Jesus desires; the second contains the blessed assurance" Jesus promises. Just as surely as all eight of the qualities should be part of the life of every Christian, so also should be the eight blessings.

The first four seem to emphasize one's vertical relationship with God. The second set has more to do with one's horizontal relationships with people.

Matthew 5:1–12

[1] When He saw the crowds, He went up on the mountain, and after He sat down, His disciples came to Him. [2] Then He began to teach them, saying: [3] "The poor in spirit are blessed, for the kingdom of heaven is theirs.	Application: You bring nothing of spiritual value to the table that can serve to merit your salvation. Therefore, be *humble* and enjoy a secure future.
[4] Those who mourn are blessed, for they will be comforted.	Application: Mourning throughout the Scriptures is almost always associated with the recognition of sin. Therefore be *repentant* and experience a calm heart.

5 The gentle are blessed, for
they will inherit the earth.

Application: People who are meek and gentle of heart share the character of Christ who described Himself by these same terms. Therefore, be *controlled* and make a real impact.

6 Those who hunger and thirst
for righteousness are blessed, for
they will be filled.

Application: The insatiable appetite for doing life according to the direction of God is the key to biblical success. Therefore be *teachable* and bask in a fulfilled life.

7 The merciful are blessed, for
they will be shown mercy.

Application: A reflection of the undeserved favor of God toward others is the human extension of the unconditional love of God. Therefore, be *gracious* and you will have great relationships.

8 The pure in heart are blessed,
for they will see God.

Application: The perfection of God's character is and always has been the standard of righteousness that will enable one to stand confident in the presence of God. Therefore be *holy* and one day you will share His glory.

9 The peacemakers are blessed,
for they will be called sons of
God.

Application: The reconciliation of sinners is the purpose of the redemptive work of Christ. Therefore be *fair*, thus demonstrating that you belong to the family of God.

10 Those who are persecuted
for righteousness are blessed, for
the kingdom of heaven is theirs. 11
"You are blessed when they insult
and persecute you and falsely
say every kind of evil against you
because of Me. 12 Be glad and
rejoice, because your reward is
great in heaven. For that is how
they persecuted the prophets
who were before you.

Application: Followers of Christ can expect to be treated very similarly to the Christ they follow. Therefore, be *patient* and you will be rewarded with ultimate justice.

Conclusion

C. S. Lewis said, "If you read history you will find that the Christians who did the most for this world were those who thought the most of the next. It is since Christians have largely ceased to think of the other world that they have become so ineffective in this."[2]

The character of any disciple is the foundation for his or her ability to impact their culture. While there is a crisis of leadership in this world, the crisis of leadership is really the absence of Christian character. If we would possess the *light* of Christ's character, we would become the *salt* of His savor to our generation.

GREAT MOMENTS IN GREAT PLACES

A Wadi Cave in the Wilderness: A Model of Integrity for Leadership

1 Samuel 24:1–22

Dr. Mark L. Bailey

Introduction

One of the greatest temptations I have observed in young leaders is the contempt allowed to grow in them toward those older leaders who seem to be standing in their way of promotion or influence. Youthful arrogance is immature, and too often humility that God could reward is lacking. The failure to wait for the timing of God is devastating. One young leader however models for us the integrity that God would use to lead a nation and earn him a reputation for having a whole heart for God.

Conflict with Leadership

The words stuck in Saul's craw, and his heart had grown to hate the tune; even worse, it was being sung by the women of his own kingdom. "As they celebrated, the women sang: "Saul has killed his thousands, but David his tens of thousands" (1 Sam. 18:7 HCSB). Because of the growing popularity of the young man from Bethlehem, within the political culture and within his own family clan, the insecurities of Saul the king of Israel had begun to take over his rationale. On a few occasions he had even elected David to be the chief javelin catcher on the track team of Israel.

Character in Leadership

David spent close to eight years in flight from Saul. According to 1 Samuel 24, on one occasion Saul and his men returned from fighting the Philistines and came across David and his men at the Spring of Goats, called En-gedi in Hebrew. David was hiding in the inner recesses of a cave when Saul came to rest or relieve himself. David was close enough to cut the edge of Saul's robe, and when Saul left the cave David came out and called after him. Contained in this conversation are four character qualities that distinguished David from Saul.

1. David was a man with a sensitive conscience.

In contrast to the opportunistic followers of David who thought the circumstances were the sovereign provision of God to take Saul's life, David's conscience bothered him for even cutting the corner off of Saul's robe. 1 Samuel 24:5 states, "Afterward, David's conscience bothered him because he had cut off the corner of Saul's robe" (HCSB).

Merriam-Webster's 11th New Collegiate Dictionary defines the conscience as "the sense or consciousness of the moral goodness or blameworthiness of one's own conduct, intentions, or character together with a feeling of obligation to do right or be good." God had developed within David a tender sensitivity to what was right in the sight of God.

2. David had a high regard for God's appointed leadership.

David recognized that God is the one who sets up kings and takes them down. While Samuel had anointed him to be the next king, he knew it was not yet his time to become the king of Israel. He stated this first to his men: "I swear before the LORD: I would never do such a thing to my lord, the LORD's anointed. I will never lift my hand against him, since he is the LORD's anointed" (1 Sam. 24:6 HCSB). Then he confronted Saul and said, "Why do you listen to the words of people who say, 'Look, David intends to harm you'? You can see with your own eyes that the LORD handed you over to me today in the cave. Someone advised me to kill you, but I took pity on you and said: I won't lift my hand against my lord, since he is the LORD's anointed" (1 Sam. 24:9–10 HCSB).

3. David worked hard to avoid a spirit of retaliation for the evil he had previously experienced.

David had no trouble exposing the error of the king while at the same time affirming his own innocence while resting in the justice of God for his vindication against Saul (1 Sam. 24:11–12). He even quoted a proverb to hold up a mirror of reflection for Saul: "Wickedness comes from wicked people" (1 Sam. 24:13). Saul was forced to admit on this occasion that David was more righteous than he since David did good to Saul while Saul had done evil to David. David caught that God is the only righteous judge and He alone has the insight necessary to judge the hearts and actions of men. Both Jesus and Paul would later extrapolate that vengeance is only appropriate for a holy and righteous God.

4. David was willing to trust the timing of God for his tour of duty.

Even Saul had to admit that the kingdom once given to him would one day be given to David. While not always thinking clearly, Saul caught the message of God for that day. The average man would not have acted with goodness to someone who had treated him with wickedness. Such a character quality even impressed David's antagonist, Saul, the current king of Israel. Saul asked David to extend this character of grace to spare his name and his family once David became the king. David made a promise on which he would later make good, especially when he cared for one called Mephibosheth from the house of Jonathan, Saul's son (2 Samuel 9).

Conclusion

The grace of David anticipates the grace of the Greater Son of David, Jesus Christ, as expressed by Julie Martin.

Grace in a Barren Place

I was that Mephibosheth
Crippled by my twisted pride and
Hiding from You in a barren place

Where You could not find me
Where You would not give me what I deserved.
But somehow You found me and
I don't understand why but You
Gave me what I do not deserve
You not only spared my desolate life but
You made it bountiful
And here at Your table
I will thank You, my King.

–Julie Martin

GREAT MOMENTS IN GREAT PLACES

A Bedrock of Stone at the Base of Mount Hermon: The Foundation of the Church

Matthew 16:13–17:13

Dr. Mark L. Bailey

Introduction

Nowhere else do history, geography, topography, and theology come together quite like they do at Caesarea Philippi. The Jordan River finds one of its sources from the snowmelt and underground springs flowing from the base of Mount Hermon and may explain why the site, later named Caesarea Philippi, was first founded. The city was known for its pagan worship of the nature god Pan, and later the Roman emperors were worshipped as deities. Rock niches for the idols can be seen to this day when one visits the site.

The visit of Jesus and the disciples provided a series of teachable moments beginning with His questions as to the perceptions of Him by the culture at large as well as that of the disciples. No less than five messianic moments can be observed in Matthew 16:13–17:13.

The Confession of Christ (Matt. 16:13–17)

In contrast to the inadequate answers the populace had suggested as to who Christ was, Peter got it correct when he confessed, "You are the Messiah, the Son of the living God!" (Matt. 16:16 HCSB). Jesus is the long-awaited Messiah of Israel, and is also God's Son who came in human flesh. That Jesus came from God would be the apostle John's litmus paper test of who is of the real Christ and who is of the spirit of Antichrist (see 1 John 4:3).

Principle: Christianity is confessional at its core and its core confession is the Person and Work of Jesus, the Messiah, the Son of God.

The Foundation of the Church (Matt. 16:18–20): The second teachable moment came with the role assigned to Peter and the disciples with the announcement of the church. Peter is called "petros" and upon a "petra" (16:18) Jesus promised to build His church. The former is a single stone and the latter is a bedrock of stones. While Roman Catholics tend to interpret Peter as the foundation of the church, Protestants advance either the content of Peter's confession or Jesus Himself as the foundation of the church. Actually, there is truth to both. Peter is a part of the foundation as one stone, but the apostles and prophets of the New Testament are said by Paul to be the foundation stones with Jesus being the cornerstone—the critical "direction-giving-Stone" to the whole building (Eph. 2:19–22). The "keys of the kingdom" represent the authority to act on earth in keeping with what God had already decided in heaven. This is the significance of the Greek tenses and the vocabulary of binding and loosing in these verses. The authority of God has been entrusted to the leadership of the church for this present age. The gates of hades is a term for the authority of hell itself. The devil himself will not be able to prevent the birth and growth of the church.

Principle: The work of the church is accomplished within the context of spiritual warfare.

The Revelation of the Cross (Matt. 16:20–23): Jesus takes the third moment to reveal His coming rejection and crucifixion at the hands of Israel's leaders. The command for secrecy concerning His messianic identity includes the avoidance of premature reaction by Israel's leaders, the development of His disciples, and the accomplishment of redemption through His death and resurrection. Like the leaders of Israel, Peter could not countenance that Messiah of Israel would have to die at the hands of His own people. Peter's rebuke of Jesus is seen to be Satan's influence in the wrongful thinking of Peter.

Principle: To think the thoughts of humanity in absence of God's control is to operate according to human wisdom that is always demonic at its core (cf. James 3:15).

The Dedication of the Christian (Matt. 16:24–26): For the fourth teachable moment, Jesus said to His disciples, "If anyone wants to come with Me, he must deny himself, take up his cross, and follow Me. For whoever wants to save his life will lose it, but whoever loses his life because of Me will find it. What will it benefit a man if he gains the whole world yet loses his life? Or what will a man give in exchange for his life?" (Matt. 16:24–26 HCSB). To deny oneself means literally "to say no to oneself." Making the condemned carry their own crosses displayed a forced submission to the Roman government. Jesus was asking the disciples to submit themselves to Him even if it meant their death. Every time Jesus announced His cross, He called for a dedication to committed discipleship for those who would follow Him.

Principle: To lose oneself in Christ is to find out what life is really intended to be.

The Expectation of the Crown (Matthew 17:1–13): The fifth teachable moment—the transfiguration—assured the doubting disciples that in spite of the necessary death of Christ, Jesus is nevertheless the King of Israel who will one day come again to consummate the kingdom. The presence of Moses as a representative of the Law and Elijah as one of the prophets, along with Jesus and the three disciples, shows the future kingdom will include the saints of all the ages. The glorious appearance of Jesus confirms His Messianic kingship, which will one day be known in all its glory.

Principle: If Jesus is the Son of God and the delight of His Father, His teaching is true and we ought to be obedient listeners.

Conclusion

What one believes about Jesus is the most important conviction anyone can have. Jesus and the apostles were the foundation stones of the church. One doesn't have to spend much time in ministry to know that church work comes with spiritual warfare. If we are not careful, we can go from being a channel of divine revelation to being the conduit of the enemy within a matter of minutes.

GREAT MOMENTS IN GREAT PLACES

A Spring in the Valley of Jezreel: The Development of Courage

Judges 6–7

Dr. Mark L. Bailey

Introduction

In William Shakespeare's *Julius Caesar*, the nobleman Cassius tries to persuade Brutus that, in the best interests of the public, Julius Caesar must be stopped from becoming monarch of Rome. Brutus is torn between his love of Caesar and his duty to the republic. His famous statement is often quoted, "The fault, dear Brutus, is not in our stars, but in ourselves."[1]

Paralyzing fear made Gideon cower in the winepress as he thrashed wheat. The Midianites were God's instrument of discipline for sinful Israel. When Israel cried out to God, His pick of the next delivering judge of Israel was an unlikely leader. The angelic messenger addressed Gideon with a most unusual ascription: "The Lord is with you, mighty warrior" (Judg. 6:12 HCSB). God knew He *would* use Gideon well before Gideon ever knew God *could* use him.

Go!

While Gideon would stumble and then succeed, the lessons Gideon learned that fateful night near the Spring of Harod in the Jezreel Valley are lessons we all need to learn if we would lead with godly courage. To his objection that God seemed to be absent or distant since He had brought them out of Egypt, God reminded him, "Go in the strength you have and deliver Israel from the power of Midian. Am I not sending you?" (Judg. 6:14 HCSB). The first lesson we need to learn is this: *wherever God sends you . . . go!*

Believe!

Judges 6:15–16 contain the second lesson. *Whatever God promises you . . . believe!* The same God who delivered Israel from Egypt would be the one who would deliver them from the Midianites. God was the one sending and God was the one staying with Gideon for the battle.

Trust!

Judges 7:1–8 gives us the next two lessons. God asked Gideon to trim the fighting forces from 33,000 to 10,000 based on their fear. God further tested Gideon by separating the lappers and kneelers at the spring called En Harod. The lappers were kept and the others sent home. "The LORD said to Gideon, "I will deliver you with the 300 men who lapped and hand the Midianites over to you. But everyone else is to go home" (Judg. 7:7 HCSB). Gideon needed to learn that it would not be him but God Himself who would deliver Israel. *Whenever God tests . . . trust!*

Take!

God in His grace continues to nurture courage by supernatural signs. He ultimately wins the war in the most unconventional of tactics. "When Gideon's men blew their 300 trumpets, the LORD set the swords of each man in the army against each other" (Judg. 7:22 HCSB). When God does give victory, remember: *Whatever God gives you . . . take.*

Conclusion

Spiritual battles cannot be won in the flesh. God's presence and power are the weapons of warfare in the arsenal of the believer. The arc of the Gideon narrative is a realistic journey from helplessness to victory, and from victory to defeat. On each end Gideon operated without relying on God.

GREAT MOMENTS IN GREAT PLACES

Between Two Pools in Jerusalem: The Relationship of Sin and Suffering

John 5 and 9

Dr. Mark L. Bailey

Introduction

John 5 and John 9 contain two separate healing miracles Jesus performed in His earthly ministry. Both reveal much to bring into balance the opposite extremes of spurious teachings that affect the church of Jesus Christ today. Some people believe that suffering is always the result of sin, and some believe that when one is sick, it is too cruel to consider sin to be the source.

John 5

In the account of John 5 we have the healing of the infirmed man at the Pool of Bethesda. When Jesus later found him in the temple complex, He said to him, "See, you are well. Do not sin anymore, so that something worse doesn't happen to you" (John 5:14 HCSB). For this man sin was the cause for his thirty-eight years of sickness. Not coincidentally, the pool is named Bethesda—house of mercy. Jesus brought merciful healing to an undeserving man whose sins had kept him in physical as well as spiritual bondage for so many years. Jesus took the opportunity through this event to teach two key claims: (1) Jesus is equal to the Father in authority and action, and (2) enough witnesses can be assembled to prove Jesus is who He proclaims Himself to be.

John 9

In the account of John 9 we have the disciples asking, "Rabbi, who sinned, this man or his parents, that he was born blind?" (v. 2 HCSB). Jesus answered, "Neither this man nor his parents sinned," Jesus answered. "This came about so that God's works might be displayed in him" (v. 3 HCSB). The sovereignty of God and His providential plan was served by this man's disability. The man was sent to the Pool of Siloam to be healed in its waters. The name *Siloam* means "sent." Jesus used the opportunity to teach the two purposes for which He was sent: (1) to give sight to those who recognized their need of spiritual blindness, and (2) to judicially blind those who thought in their self-righteousness they had no spiritual need for God's light. Jesus claimed to be the Light of the World in this passage.

Conclusion

The lack of healing in the first account is rooted in the pagan superstition that arose around the Pool of Bethesda that the first one to enter the pool when the waters were stirred would be healed. The lack of insight in the second account is rooted in the religious tradition that blessing is seen in wealth and health and the lack of either is evidence of God's displeasure and judgment. Both extremes are inadequate explanations of a God of truth and grace. Sin is serious and unbelief is reason enough to explain the absence of God's grace and restoration. God is also more sovereign that we would ever believe to accomplish His glorious work in the most unexpected of ways.

GREAT MOMENTS IN GREAT PLACES

The Guardhouse Beside the Mediterranean Sea: A Bold Witness for Christ

Acts 24:10–21

Dr. Mark L. Bailey

Introduction

In my youth I heard a challenge from a youth leader. He asked, "If you were arrested for being a Christian, would there be enough evidence to convict you?" When Paul was arrested in Jerusalem and then transferred to the coastal city of Caesarea, the administrative center for the Roman government, he was imprisoned in Herod's Praetorium, the guardhouse for the bodyguards of the emperor (Acts 23:35). Kept in prison there for at least two years, Paul faced trials at the hands of Felix, Festus, and Agrippa. The charges brought against him by the Jewish leadership from Jerusalem accused him of being "a plague, an agitator among all the Jews throughout the Roman world, and a ringleader of the sect of the Nazarenes!" (Acts 24:5 HCSB).

Courage Under Pressure

Paul's defense before Felix serves well as a model for a bold witness for Christ in front of a hostile audience both religious and political. First, Paul was *unashamed of his service for God.* In verse 14, Paul stated, "But I confess this to you: I worship my fathers' God according to the Way, which they call a sect" (Acts 24:14*a* HCSB). Paul was more than willing to identify with the believing community even though it was grossly misunderstood as a spurious sect.

Second, Paul was *uncompromising in his trust in God's Word.* Paul understood the continuity of the Jewish Scriptures and the Jewish Messiah. He affirmed his belief in "all the things that are written in the Law and in the Prophets" (Acts 24:14*b* HCSB). The faith of the Bible is truly a Judeo-Christian faith.

Third, Paul was *unwavering in his hope in the resurrection.* As was true of Paul when he spoke before the forum in Athens (Acts 17), Paul proclaimed his faith in Jesus and the resurrection. "And I have a hope in God, which these men themselves also accept, that there is going to be a resurrection, both of the righteous and the unrighteous" (Acts 24:15 HCSB). Contrary to even some so-called evangelicals today, the reality of eternal blessing for the saved and the conscious judgment of the unsaved are both critical components of the apostolic message.

Fourth, and finally, Paul evidenced his integrity of heart in that he was *untainted in his relationships with God and others.* Paul continued, "I always do my best to have a clear conscience toward God and men" (Acts 24:16 HCSB).

Conclusion

Here is a summary of the great commandments: a love for God and a love for others that comes from an undivided loyalty to God and an unconditional love for others. A bold witness for Christ is a witness that is thus rooted in both truth and grace. A commitment to the gospel and a compassion for those not yet believing in Christ are the character qualities from which effective evangelism and apologetics arise.

GREAT MOMENTS IN GREAT PLACES

A Community Near the Caves of Qumran: A Different Kind of Baptism

Matthew 28:19–20

Dr. Mark L. Bailey

Introduction

When one visits the archeological site of the ancient community of Qumran in the Judean wilderness at the edge of the Dead Sea, one is struck with efforts to which that community of religious separatists went to bring water into their compound that would serve for both their physical as well as their ritualistic needs. The community was known for their sacred meals as evidenced by the stoneware from which they would eat and drink. They undertook the copying of the biblical scrolls as well as composing the manuals of behavior for the community—collections that would become known in the last century as the Dead Sea Scrolls.

Bathing

What also calls for attention was their well-crafted water system that brought water winding from the hills, cascading over a step-stone designed for sediment filtration, flowing through channels into the cisterns for bathing and drinking, and on into the special ritual baths known as Mikveh baths. These baths were constructed for self-immersion whereby they sought to achieve spiritual cleansing and consecration.

Baptism

The site of Qumran becomes a great place for a great moment and visual aid to distinguish Jewish cleansing baths from Christian baptism. Jewish cleansing was active and self-initiated. Christian baptism is passive, in that another person performs the rite for the benefit of the recipient. Such a passive submission to the grip of another is a great reminder that we cannot save ourselves. We must in faith trust in the merit of Jesus Christ. It is a reminder that forgiveness comes from God and not something we can muster up by ourselves. Christian faith is exactly the opposite of self-reformation.

When rightly understood the ordinance signifies identification with Jesus Christ who both modeled and mandated it. He modeled it when Jesus asked John to baptize Him as an act of fulfilling righteousness and identifying with the remnant who were putting their faith in God. John preached the need to be baptized as evidence of the forgiveness of sin. Jesus mandated it in the Great Commission of Matthew 28:18–20 as the initiatory sign of the discipleship process. Such a baptism is triune in that it is to be done in the name of the Father, the Son, and the Holy Spirit.

The ceremony of baptism becomes a confession of faith in that baptism in the names of all three members of the Godhead expresses a faith that Jesus is equal to the Father and the Spirit and they to Him. *A belief in the doctrine of the* Trinity *is a core confession of faith that distinguishes Christianity from all the other religions and "isms" of the world.*

Conclusion

Water baptism is a one-time event that is followed by the continuous communication of the life and teachings of Jesus and the obedience that it should enjoin. The mandate to disciple the nations came with the accompanying promise of the presence of Him who said, "And remember, I am with you always, to the end of the age" (Matt. 28:20 HCSB).

GREAT MOMENTS IN GREAT PLACES

The Garden of the Olive Press on the Mount of Olives: A Commitment of Obedience

Matthew 26:36–46

Dr. Mark L. Bailey

Introduction

One writer has said it well: two of the greatest "battles" of human history were fought in gardens. In the Garden of Eden, the first Adam chose to disobey God, bringing sin to the human race. He did not resist temptation, but chose his will over the Father's.

In the Garden of Gethsemane, the Second Adam, Jesus Christ, chose the Father's will over His own (human) will. Although the pain and spiritual misery of the cross awaited Jesus,the internal battle was fought in the Garden. Just as Adam's decision in Eden affected all who are related to Adam, so Christ's decision in Gethsemane affects all who are related to Him by faith.

The Setting

The Gospels combine to pinpoint the place for this teachable moment in the life of our Lord. The site was located "across the Kidron Valley, where there was a garden" (John 18:1 HCSB) on the Mount of Olives (Luke 22:39) at a place called Gethsemane (Matt. 26:36; Mark 14:32).

The *company* included the eleven disciples with a concentration upon Peter, James, and John. The *conflict* Jesus faced was a level of incomparable spiritual and emotional suffering as both Matthew and Mark highlight. The *commands* for the disciples were to stay there and keep watch, and pray that they might not enter into temptation.

The Significance

The Gethsemane experience became for Jesus a lesson in *obedience*. Let me pose three observations. First, while Jesus was never disobedient, what He endured took Him to a level of fulfilling the Father's will that He had not yet experienced. Hebrews 5:8 states, "Though He was God's Son, He learned obedience through what He suffered" (HCSB). Second, His grief revealed the seriousness of sin. Jesus knew the cup of suffering awaited Him. His personal desire voiced a hesitancy to be separated from His Father—something that had not happened for all eternity. His submission to the will of the Father rather that satisfying His own independently from the Father becomes a model of obedience for us all.

The Gethsemane application for us as seen in how Jesus worked with His disciples is a lesson in *dependence*. First, the exhortation by Jesus shows that prayer is an effective weapon against temptation. Prayer reorients our hearts toward God and demonstrates a faith toward God to provide the power to resist temptation that we in ourselves do not possess. Second, the flesh is always an inadequate resource with which to fight the spiritual battles we face. Spiritual warfare requires the Spirit of God to win the war. Third, what ought to be encouraging to us is the fact that there is no sin in the struggle with God's will if the end result is obedience. Jesus faced temptation without sinning because He resisted the impulse to sin. Jesus faced the troubled soul of emotional conflict and yet God won the war of His will. Just because we face troubled hearts and tempting thoughts, we have not sinned as long as the end of that struggle results in obedience and dependence.

Conclusion

Billy Graham once wrote: "I watched the deck hands on the great liner *United States* as they docked that ship in New York Harbor. First they threw out a rope to the men on the dock then, inside the boat the great motors went to work and pulled on the great cable. But, oddly enough, the pier wasn't pulled out to the ship; but the ship was pulled snugly up to the pier. Prayer is the rope that pulls God and us together. But it doesn't pull God down to us; it pulls us to God. We must learn to say with Christ, the master of the art of praying: 'Not my will; but Thine be done.'"[1]

It was a prayer of surrender to His Father's will. And in that surrender, Jesus found the strength to overcome.

GREAT MOMENTS IN GREAT PLACES

An Altar at the Top of Mount Carmel: The Need to Make a Decision

1 Kings 18

Dr. Mark L. Bailey

Introduction

Former president Ronald Reagan once had an aunt who took him to a cobbler for a pair of new shoes. The cobbler asked young Reagan, "Do you want square toes or round toes?" Unable to decide, Reagan didn't answer, so the cobbler gave him one square-toed and one round-toed shoe! "This will teach you to never let people make decisions for you," the cobbler said to him. "I learned right then and there," Reagan said later, "if you don't make your own decisions, someone else will."[1]

The Battle of the Gods

Dr. Howard G. Hendricks wrote a book about Elijah called *The Battle of the Gods.* Elijah was a prophet God raised up to deal with Baal worship that had swept through the northern kingdom of Israel during the days of the divided monarchy. Baal was worshipped as a storm god who controlled nature and provided fertility to families, fields, and flocks. In the days of Ahab and Jezebel, Elijah issued a *great invitation* to the prophets of Baal to gather together at Mount Carmel for the "battle of the Gods." Elijah's *great accusation* was that the country was being destroyed because of forsaking God's commandments and following after the Baals (1 Kings 18:18). Elijah's *great question* was directed toward the people: "How long will you hesitate between two opinions? If Yahweh is God, follow Him. But if Baal, follow him" (1 Kings 18:21 HCSB).

Each side prepared their altars and each called upon their God to answer with fire from heaven. The prophets of Baal called from morning till evening with no effect. With great glee and irony Elijah challenged the prophets of Baal as to the impotence of their god who appeared to have all the humorous limitations of humanity as opposed to the power and authority of deity. When it is Elijah's turn, and after soaking the altar three times with water, the God of Israel sent an all-consuming fire.

Elijah's *petition* was pointed and God's response was prompt. "Answer me, LORD! Answer me so that this people will know that You, Yahweh, are God and that You have turned their hearts back" (1 Kings 18:37 HCSB). Then Yahweh's fire fell and consumed the burnt offering, the wood, the stones, and the dust, and it licked up the water that was in the trench. When all the people saw it, they fell facedown and said, "Yahweh, He is God! Yahweh, He is God!" (1 Kings 18:37–39 HCSB). Elijah's execution of divine justice resulted in slaying the prophets of Baal at the Wadi Kishon at the foot of Mount Carmel.

Conclusion

The following is a list of principles on which to rely and apply:

1. Hesitant commitment is no commitment at all (1 Kings 18:21).
2. The decision for God is the most important decision you can make (1 Kings 18:24).
3. Passionate worship in the wrong direction is still false worship (1 Kings 18:25–29).
4. Servants serve best when they serve according to God's Word (1 Kings 18:36–37).
5. Yahweh alone is God and He alone is worthy of our worship (1 Kings 18:39).

GREAT MOMENTS IN GREAT PLACES

A Stronghold by the Waters of the Dead Sea: A Rock of Refuge

Psalm 46

Dr. Mark L. Bailey

Introduction

Masada is an ancient fortification built on a rocky plateau high above the surrounding landscape. Though Herod built a fortress there as a testimony to his own power, it is remembered today as a symbol of the Jewish desire for freedom. Israeli soldiers take an oath there: "Masada shall not fall again."

According to the first-century Jewish historian Josephus, 960 Jews committed suicide there in AD 73 rather than succumb to the slavery and savagery of the Romans. While that incident is not in the Bible, the mountain may very well be the same stronghold to which David fled and was later pictured in many psalms.

The Stronghold of God

Psalm 46 falls into three sections, each concluding with the word *Selah*. In verses 1–4 God is our refuge in face of natural disasters. In verses 5–8 God is a refuge from the threats of enemy nations. In verses 9–12 the natural and the national threats are woven together, and God is still the best refuge we can find. The three stanzas are connected with the word *earth* (vv. 3, 7, 9, 10, 11) and ideas of refuge and stronghold (vv. 1, 7, 11).

Stanza One

> [1] God is our refuge and strength, a helper who is always
> found in times of trouble.[2] Therefore we will not be afraid,
> though the earth trembles and the mountains topple into

the depths of the seas, [3] though its waters roar and foam and the mountains quake with its turmoil.

Selah

1. God is the protection and power for those who will put their trust in Him.
2. Natural disasters are never a reason to doubt the existence and care of God.

Stanza Two

[4] There is a river—its streams delight the city of God, the holy dwelling place of the Most High. [5] God is within her; she will not be toppled. God will help her when the morning dawns. [6] Nations rage, kingdoms topple; the earth melts when He lifts His voice. [7] The LORD of Hosts is with us; the God of Jacob is our stronghold.

Selah

1. The presence of God is the secret of safety.
2. While God may not help immediately, He will help ultimately.
3. The work of God in the history of Israel guarantees the work of God in our lives.

Stanza Three

[8]Come, see the works of the LORD, who brings devastation on the earth. [9] He makes wars cease throughout the earth. He shatters bows and cuts spears to pieces; He burns up the chariots. [10] "Stop your fighting—and know that I am God, exalted among the nations, exalted on the earth." [11] Yahweh of Hosts is with us; the God of Jacob is our stronghold.

Selah

1. God is sovereign over nations and nature.

2. God alone is to be exalted and worshipped as the one and only God.

Conclusion

The geography and topography of Israel reveal much about the ancient culture. Water sources determined where villages would be located. Travel routes developed along the coast or on the ridges. Elevation on heights and rock walls were key for security. Such became images for the biblical authors to use as images for all that God supplies for the sustenance, safety, and security of the believer.

GREAT MOMENTS IN GREAT PLACES

A Lake in the Basin of Galilee: A Time for Trust

Selections from the Gospels

Dr. Mark L. Bailey

Introduction

While it is called a sea, the Sea of Galilee is a lake that measures approximately fourteen miles long and seven miles wide. The shallowness of this lake accounts for the sudden rise of dangerous waves when even a mild wind comes through the Galilean basin. The majority of the miracles of Jesus occurred on the north shore of the Sea of Galilee and a select few are associated with the lake itself. Contemplating those special moments in the ministry of Jesus on and around the lake allows us to travel with Jesus on the "High Cs" as He demonstrates His power, proving Himself to be the Messianic King and the Son of God.

With Christ on the "High Cs"

Miracles of crossing—an issue of security (Matt. 14:12–23; Mark 6: 45–52; John 6:16–21).

Jesus proved He was the Son of God by walking on the water. What threatened to undo the disciples, Jesus controlled under His feet. If Jesus can control nature, He is equal to the Father as the God of all creation. If He is equal to the Father, our security and salvation are found only in Him.

Miracles of catching—an issue of capability (Luke 5:1–11; John 21:1–11).

At the beginning and end of Jesus' ministry with His disciples, He reminds them that any success in their ministry would be because of the gracious provision of God. Only He knows where the fish are and only He can guarantee the catch. Evangelism is impossible without the powerful direction and provision of God.

Miracles of calming—an issue of responsibility (Matt. 8:23–27; Mark 4:35–41; Luke 8:22–25).

The humanity and the deity of Jesus are placed side by side in Matthew's account where we find Jesus sleeping after a tiring day and then awakening and stilling the storm on a threatening night. In Mark's account the word "rebuke" is repeated showing the power of Jesus as manifested in His words as well as His works.

Miracles of cleansing—an issue of eternity (Matt. 8:28–34; Mark 5:1–21; Luke 8:26–40).

In Jesus' confrontation with the demons, even they confess Him to be the Son of God. They also know that He will ultimately be the Judge who sends them to their eternal torment. Ironically, not even the pigs could tolerate the demons even though the people from that region had done so. And sadly, how unfortunate that some people today are dumber than demons in that they refuse to believe Jesus is the Son of God. That Jesus has the power to defeat Satan shows He is the Savior from Satan, sin, and death.

Conclusion

The miracles of Jesus manifest the *power* of God.
The parables of Jesus reveal the *wisdom* of God.
The discourses of Jesus unfold the *truth* of God.
The interpersonal relationships of Jesus show the *love* of God.
The crucifixion and resurrection of Jesus proclaims the *grace* of God.

GREAT MOMENTS IN GREAT PLACES

An Out-of-the-Way Stop in the Saddle of Lower Galilee: The Problem with the Prophet at Home

Luke 4:14–30

Dr. Mark L. Bailey

Introduction

"Humble beginnings" is a phrase used for everything from rock bands, tattoo parlors, and even the name of a church. There is a play on the words for "branch" (*nazar*) in the Old Testament that allows for the identification of Jesus as a Nazarene in Matthew 2:23. Jesus' hometown is Nazareth (the feminine plural of "Nazer" is "Nazeroth"). "Then a shoot will grow from the stump of Jesse, and a branch from his roots will bear fruit" (Isa. 11:1 HCSB). Jesus who has humble beginnings will one day rule the world.

Can Anything Good Come Out of Nazareth?

Two proverbial statements have been associated with the site of Nazareth. When Nathaniel is introduced to Jesus, he questioned, "Can anything good come out of Nazareth?" (John 1:46). Nazareth is isolated on a ridge away from the Via Maris, the main highway through the Valley of Jezreel. Nazareth had a poor reputation at the time of Christ, being despised by both the Romans and the Jews. Their lack of spiritual perception became quite evident in their response to Jesus at His appearance in the Nazareth synagogue. What began well ended poorly.

At the center of Jesus' address is His adaptation of Isaiah 61:1–2*a*, which can be written out to reflect its inverted parallel structure.

'The Spirit of the Lord is on Me,
because He has anointed Me
to *preach* good news to the poor.
He has sent Me
to proclaim *freedom* to the captives
and recovery of sight to the blind,
[He has sent Me] to *set free* the oppressed,
[He has anointed Me] to *proclaim* the year of the Lord's
favor. (HCSB)

No Prophet Is Accepted in His Hometown

Jesus concluded His message by claiming this Scripture was being fulfilled in front of them. Their initial response was one of marveling at His words of grace. Jesus then enunciated the second great proverb, "I assure you: No prophet is accepted in his hometown" (Luke 4:24 HCSB). He anticipated their rejection and illustrated the problem for which both freedom and forgiveness were still necessary. He recalled the help given to the widow of Zarephath in the days of Elijah and the healing of Naaman the Syrian. These two Gentiles responded to the prophets of Israel, whereas none in Israel had responded this well. Infuriated, the officials went from marveling to murder when they took Him out of the city and attempted to throw Him off the cliff.

Conclusion

How could they miss it? What is it that they missed that we dare not miss from this passage?

- Jesus is the God-appointed and Spirit-anointed Messiah.
- The message of the gospel of Jesus Christ is God's means for bringing salvation to the world.
- Only God can help and heal us in our deepest need.
- The toughest place to live the Christian life is at home.

GREAT MOMENTS IN GREAT PLACES

In Fields Near Bethlehem: A Night of Witness, Wonder, and Worship

Luke 2:1–20

Dr. Mark L. Bailey

Introduction

A sign is a miracle with a messianic punch. Signs in the New Testament were miracles that carried a message to prove that Jesus was the Messiah. The angels said to the shepherds, "Today a Savior, who is Messiah the Lord, was born for you in the city of David. This will be the sign for you: You will find a baby wrapped snugly in cloth and lying in a feeding trough" (Luke 2:11–12 HCSB). Why the emphasis on the "you"? You who?

The Shepherds

The significance of the shepherds who kept sheep in the fields of Bethlehem is that they were not ordinary shepherds. According to ancient Jewish sources like the Mishnah (*m. Šeqal.* 7:4), these shepherds were hired by the temple officials in Jerusalem to keep sheep that were destined for sacrifice at the temple in Jerusalem. Thus the announcement to these shepherds and the birth they announce becomes the first of the New Testament signs that Jesus is the Son of God.

The Sign

The sign to the shepherds has three major components. The first is their own identity as special shepherds. Second, they would find the baby wrapped in swaddling clothes. Both Jewish and Arab guides have told about a custom that a woman would never leave home without having a strip of linen cloth wrapped around her waist in case she died on the journey. They wanted to be buried in their own linens. Heavy with child, Mary would thus have a "ready made" linen swath suitable for a newborn baby who would one day by His own death become the Savior of the world. Thirdly, they would find the baby lying in a manger. Mangers were hewn out of rock or the side of the natural limestone caves that speckle the hillsides of the shepherd fields near Bethlehem. At night, baby animals were lifted up and placed safely above the trampling hooves of the larger animals. The Mishnah identified a sight called Migdal Eder, the Tower of the Flocks as a site on the road on the way into Bethlehem where the shepherds birthed and cared for lambs as they were charged with their sacred duty. If this is the scenario, we may well have a greater revelation of the Person and future work of the Son of God than we have known.

Conclusion

Revelation always demands a response. The response that we see from the shepherds adds to the significance of the incarnation. First, they gave *witness* to what they had seen and what had been told them about the Christ Child (Luke 2:17). Second, there was great *wonder* generated because of the testimony of the shepherds (Luke 2:18). Third, the shepherds went back to their places in an attitude of *worship* "glorifying and praising God for all they had seen and heard, just as they had been told" (Luke 2:20 HCSB).

GOSPEL SERMONS FOR THE CHRISTIAN LIFE

The Pursuit of a Sinner

Mark 2:14–17

Matt Carter

Introduction

Many of us have an improper view—an unbiblical view—of our own sinfulness, and in light of that, Jesus is going to show us that we have to have a proper view of our own sinfulness in order for us to really come to Him and be saved.

Some of us are deeply aware of our own sinfulness. But another group knows they're a sinner, and at the end of the day, they just don't think they're that bad. And as a result of that, grace just simply isn't that amazing to you.

Mark 2

In Mark 2:14 Jesus sees Matthew sitting in the tax collector booth and says to him, "Follow Me!" (HCSB). And Matthew gets up and follows Him. The Pharisees see that Jesus is eating with the sinners and tax collectors and they say to His disciples, "Why does He eat with tax collectors and sinners?" (Mark 2:16 HCSB).

And then Jesus makes one of the most difficult statements in the whole Bible: "And when Jesus heard it, He said to them, "Those who are well have no need of a physician, but those who are sick. I came not to call the righteous, but sinners" (Mark 2:17 ESV).

Matthew was literally in the act of living a sinful life. Think about that. He was right smack dab in the middle of his sin, and Jesus walks right up to him and says, "I want you to follow Me." The Bible says nothing about this guy having a crisis of conscience. Jesus didn't ask him to clean up his act before commanding Matthew to follow Him.

The picture the Bible is painting is a picture of God in the flesh walking on the earth, pursuing us and loving us and calling us into fellowship with Him and calling us to serve Him right in the midst of our sin. Make no mistake, Jesus calls the guy out of the tax booth. Jesus calls the guy out of the sin, but Jesus loves him, pursues him, and wants him right in the middle of his sin. You do not have to clean yourself up before you come to Jesus. You come to Jesus, and He will clean you up.

Here's the message to the other group of people: obedience is a good thing, but make sure in your obedience that you realize you still need a Savior. If you're saved today, you were the tax collector, and Jesus didn't save you because He looked at you and said that you have your act together.

Conclusion

Let me show you what I'm talking about. Romans 5:8 says, "But God shows us His love for us in that while we were still sinners, Christ died for us" (ESV).

You were a sinner, you were an enemy of God, and the wrath of God was coming your way. But Jesus saved you while you were still a sinner.

GOSPEL SERMONS FOR THE CHRISTIAN LIFE

Religion vs. the Gospel

Mark 1:14–15

Matt Carter

Introduction

For the last forty or fifty years in the American church, we have quit teaching the gospel for the most part. A lot of us grew up in churches where what we were taught was more of a works-based kind of follow-the-rules, Old Testament-law-following Christianity, rather than the gospel. It was not taught that our standing with God doesn't change based on how good we are or how bad we are on any given day, but rather our standing with God is based on the righteousness of Jesus.

And so the pastors of my generation are looking at the Bible, and they're saying that the Christianity they read about in the Scriptures is not the Christianity they were taught growing up.

If you wanted to be a good Christian, there was a "good" list, and the bad people did stuff on the "bad" list. And you wanted to make sure as a good Christian that you did more things on the "good" list than you did on the "bad" list. When you did stuff on the "bad" list, you'd think, *I must not be saved. How can a person that's saved struggle like I do with sin?* And when you were good, you'd think, *Hey, I've been good, so God must be pleased with me now.* So in those times we replaced that self-loathing with good old-fashioned self-righteousness.

That is not the picture of Christianity that the Bible paints. The essence of our faith, the essence of Christianity, is not a list of do's and don'ts that you do your best to follow. The essence of our faith is the truth that God loves you and accepts you and connects with you, not on the basis of what you've done, good or bad, but that God loves you, and accepts you, and connects with you on the basis of what Jesus has already done for you at the cross. That's the gospel.

Mark 1:14–15

Look at the very first sentence of Jesus' very first sermon. Mark 1:14–15 (NASB) says, "Now after John had been taken into custody, Jesus came into Galilee, preaching the gospel of God, and saying, 'The time is fulfilled, and the kingdom of God is at hand. Repent, and believe in the gospel.'" What Jesus did was separate Christianity from every single religion that has ever come in the history of this world with that one statement.

The first thing Jesus says is, "The time is fulfilled." Why does He say this? The Scripture says God is slow to anger, so we know that God is gracious toward our sin. In Exodus 34:6 it says God is "compassionate and gracious, slow to anger, and abounding in loving-kindness and truth'" (NASB).

But the Scripture tells us that God is not just gracious, but He is also just. God is a God of justice, and if God never punished sin, if He never dealt with sin, then it could be said of Him that He was gracious but not that He was a God of justice.

He will endure our sin, and endure our sin, and endure our sin, but there comes a time when justice has to be enacted for our sin. It says in Numbers 14:18 (NASB): "The Lord is slow to anger and abundant in loving-kindness, forgiving iniquity and transgression; *but He will by no means clear the guilty*" (emphasis added). In other words, He's going to punish our sin. When that time comes, when His gracious endurance of our sin is over, that time is called the time of fulfillment.

Imagine for a second that you are in the first century there and the first thing out of the prophet of God's mouth is this: "The time is fulfilled!" What goes through your mind when you hear "The time is fulfilled" is the story of the flood where God endured our sin, and endured our sin, and endured our sin, until He endured it no longer and took us out. You're thinking about Sodom and Gomorrah, where God endured our sin, and endured our sin, endured our sin, until there were none righteous that could be found, and He poured out fire and brimstone on the city and took them out. What's going through your mind is, God is done with our sin, and His wrath is coming on us.

And so if you're in the original audience, you expect Jesus to finish the sentence "The time is fulfilled!" with "The kingdom of God is at hand! Repent because the wrath of God is coming and He's going to take you out!" But that's not what Jesus said. He said He wanted everybody to know the time is fulfilled. Yes, God's patient endurance of your sin is over. But He said repent and believe the gospel. The time is at hand, and yes, you broke all the rules, every one of you.

The Scripture says that even our righteous deeds are like filthy rags in the sight of our God. All of us have fallen short of the glory of God. But Jesus walks up and says the time is fulfilled, and yes, God's wrath is coming. But Jesus said this time is different. Jesus said God's wrath is not going to be poured out on you. This time God's wrath, once and for all, is going to be poured out on Me. It's called the gospel.

Conclusion

Why does that statement right there distinguish Christianity from every other religion in history? Because every other religion in history is defined by this: a person doing their best to fulfill a list of qualifications and regulations and rules and dos and don'ts, hoping that they please God. A Christ-follower is very simply somebody who repents and believes the gospel.

GOSPEL SERMONS FOR THE CHRISTIAN LIFE

The Trinity

Mark 1:9–11

Matt Carter

Introduction

In telling the story of Jesus' baptism, Mark is tying Jesus directly back to the story of creation and giving us an amazing glimpse into the inner working of the eternal relationship of the Trinity.

Mark 1:9–11

"In those days Jesus came from Nazareth in Galilee, and was baptized by John in the Jordan. Immediately coming up out of the water, He saw the heavens opening, and the Spirit like a dove descending upon Him; and a voice came out of the heavens: 'You are My beloved Son, in You I am well pleased'" (NASB).

Now what makes this so powerful is that the baptism of Jesus is one of only two places in Scripture where all three persons of the Trinity manifest themselves at the same place, at the same time. You've got God the Son. He's in the water. All of a sudden, the heavens open up, and God the Spirit shows up on the scene and descends upon God the Son in power, and then lo and behold, you've got God the Father who says, "This is My beloved Son with whom I'm well pleased."

God the Father, God the Son, and God the Spirit are always together. They've always *been* together except at the cross, but this is one of only two places where they manifest themselves, where the Scripture actually describes them at the same place and the same time. The other place is Genesis 1.

If you're wondering where Jesus is in the creation story, in Genesis 1:3 (ESV) it says: "And God said, 'Let there be light,' and there was light." God spoke. John 1:1–5 (ESV) says: "In the beginning was the Word"—that's Jesus—"and the Word was with God, and the Word was God. He was in the beginning with God. All things were made through Him, and without Him not anyt hing made that was made. In Him was life, and the life was the light of men. The light shines in the darkness and the darkness has not overcome it."

Mark is deliberately pointing us back to creation. The same Father and Son and Holy Spirit that was active and present in creation, is the same Father and Son and Holy Spirit that has come back to us to renew and to restore creation from the destruction of our sin.

The Cross

When Jesus was hanging on a cross for six hours becoming your sin so that you could become the righteousness of God, something happened for that six hours that had never occurred in all of eternity. God the Father turned His back on God the Son, while He was bearing the burden of your sin.

And that's why He cried out, "My God! My God! Why have you forsaken me?" Imagine the pain He was experiencing. Every other time in eternity He called Him, "Daddy, Father, Abba," but not on the cross. He was forsaken from that divine, eternal, loving relationship for *you*.

Conclusion

If you go to Jesus and trust in Him, you will experience the unbroken relationship with God the Father that your sin has kept you from. And because of Christ, He accepts sinners with open arms.

GOSPEL SERMONS FOR THE CHRISTIAN LIFE

Hell

Matthew 7:13–14

Matt Carter

Introduction

We're going to talk about a place called *hell.* The first reason is Jesus taught on the subject of hell, and He taught on the subject of hell at length. The second reason is that we need to have a deep understanding of what it is that the gospel has saved us from. Third, our generation is more afraid of death than any other generation that I'm aware of and I think you can tie that directly back to a lack of understanding of the doctrines of heaven and hell.

Matthew 22

In Matthew 22:13 (ESV), when Jesus is talking about the parable of the wedding feast, He says this about hell: "Then the king said to the attendants, 'Bind him hand and foot and cast him into the outer darkness. In that place there will be weeping and gnashing of teeth.'"

You experience common grace in things like feeling a cool breeze against your face. You stand on a beach and you look out and you experience things like cool breezes and beauty. This is common grace, and even nonbelievers experience things like good friends and community and joy and pleasure. In hell, there will be no joy. None. There will be no pleasure. There will be no community. There will be no fellowship. There will be no beauty. There will be no cool breezes. Jesus simply called it a place of *outer darkness,* which I think means a place of loneliness, a place of joylessness, a place of utter isolation, and a place totally devoid of good.

How long is hell going to last? In Matthew 25:45 (ESV), Jesus gives us the answer. "'Truly, I say to you, as you did not do it to one of the least of these, you did not do it to me. And these will go away into eternal punishment, but the righteous into eternal life.'"

From a *human* perspective, this punishment seems like a *massive* divine overreaction. But when you sin against somebody, the punishment you receive is always proportionate to the authority of the person you have offended.

Let's say you lie to your friend. What's the punishment? Worst-case scenario, that person is no longer your friend. Let's take a judge in a court of law. He or she could put you in jail. The greater the authority, the greater the punishment. How big is the authority of almighty God?

Conclusion

If you don't trust in Jesus, enjoy the pleasures of this life, enjoy the warmth of the sunshine, enjoy the cool of the wind on your face. Enjoy good friends and good food and community and fellowship and love, because this earth is as close to heaven as you're ever going to get.

But for those of you who are in Christ today, endure this world. Endure its suffering, endure its pain, endure its loneliness, endure its sickness, endure its trials, because for those of you who are in Christ Jesus, this world is as close to hell as you're ever going to get.

GOSPEL SERMONS FOR THE CHRISTIAN LIFE

From Lifeless to Lordship

1 Corinthians 13:12

Matt Carter

Introduction

Have you ever been in an environment or situation in which something you had to do was so difficult you wanted to quit, but you hung in there because the result of enduring was worth it? In other words the pain was worth it because of the outcome. That is the point of this text.

1 Corinthians 13

In 1 Corinthians 13:8–10 (NASB) Paul wrote, "Love never fails; but if there are gifts of prophecy, they will be done away; if there are tongues, they will cease; if there is knowledge, it will be done away. For we know in part and we prophesy in part; but when the perfect comes, the partial will be done away." Verse 12 (NASB) says: "For now we see in a mirror dimly, but then face to face; now I know in part, but then I will know fully."

Paul is saying to exercise spiritual gifts in love because it's going to be hard loving the body of Christ, and enduring in the church. But, Paul says, heaven is coming, and it's going to be perfect. These spiritual gifts are necessary, but they're absolutely temporary, designed to show an eternal reality. You're not going to need the spiritual gift of prophecy in heaven. There is no sin in heaven and the Truth is sitting there on the throne.

If you have the spiritual gift of service and you choose to go and serve in a homeless shelter, the Scripture has taught us the Spirit starts showing up there. And what happens is all the people in that homeless shelter get this view of God. But what Paul just taught us there is that view is limited. There is only so much you are able to show of God to other people. There is a bigger view of God we eventually will see.

"For we know in part and we prophesy in part but when the perfect comes, the partial will be done away." He's saying there is coming a perfect reality in which our little partial views of God will no longer be needed. What's the perfect? It's heaven. When we're in heaven we will have an unobstructed view of God. When we're in heaven, we are no longer going to have a partial snapshot of God.

In heaven, we will have a front-row seat for all eternity to God pouring out His grace, kindness, and mercy toward us in Christ Jesus. But here on earth we see through a mirror dimly. We're getting a dim view of God as we walk through life and operate in our giftedness, but there is coming a day where that is going away and we will be standing there with Jesus Christ face to face.

Conclusion

Paul believes that it is better for him to depart from this world so he might be with Jesus. When other religions talk about heaven, what fires them up? They talk about virgins; they talk about earthly pleasures on steroids. But when the guys from this Book talk about it, they can't quit talking about Jesus.

GOSPEL SERMONS FOR THE CHRISTIAN LIFE

What Will Heaven Be Like?

Revelation 21:1–4

Matt Carter

Introduction

In 1 Corinthians 2:9 (ESV), the Scripture says: "But, as it is written no eye has seen, nor ear heard, nor the heart of man imagined what God has prepared for those who love Him." This verse is telling us that there are things about heaven that are so amazing we can't even understand them. And then it goes on: "These things God has revealed to us through His Spirit. For the Spirit searches everything, even the depths of God" (2:10 ESV).

This means that there are certain things about heaven that the Scripture has revealed to us by the Spirit of God, and so that's what we're going to concern ourselves with here. We're going to focus on the things that are really clear about heaven, things that we at least somewhat know about heaven. We're not going to spend a bunch of time in theory and in the debatable stuff.

Hebrews 9

Heaven, before Jesus returns, is going to be a different place than after He comes back. In Hebrews 9:27 (ESV), it says, "And just as it is appointed for man to die once, and after that comes judgment." Are you in Christ? The question is not about how good you were in this life. Not how bad you were in this life. Not how much you went to church or didn't go to church. The Scripture is clear as it can be. You're going to be judged on one thing at the moment of your death. Were you in Christ Jesus?

If you are in that moment found in Christ Jesus, not having a righteousness of your own but that which comes through faith in Him, you're going to go to a place immediately called heaven. The Scripture is crystal clear that when you are away from the body, you are at home with Jesus. Do not be afraid of death, Christian. Your eyes close in death, and you're home.

Jesus said this home is going to be pretty special. Luke 23:43 (ESV) says: "And [Jesus] said to him, 'Truly, I say to you, today you will be with me in Paradise.'"

After Jesus' Return

In Revelation 21, it says God re-creates the earth. Most theologians believe that this new earth that God creates is like earth but with heaven wrapped up in it. Verse 3 (NASB) says: "I heard a loud voice from the throne, saying, 'Behold, the tabernacle of God is among men, and He will dwell among them, and they shall be His people, and God Himself will be among them." God is going to be hanging out with us.

Some of you think that's going to be boring. Here is what Psalm 16:11 (ESV) has to say: "You make known to me the path of life; in your presence there is fullness of joy; and at your right hand are pleasures forevermore."

GOSPEL SERMONS FOR THE CHRISTIAN LIFE

True vs. False Repentance

Genesis 27:30–41

Matt Carter

Introduction

Isaac's son Jacob has coerced and tempted his brother, Esau, into giving him his birthright. At the same time, Jacob has lied and deceived his father, Isaac, into giving Jacob the blessing that should have gone to Esau. God tells us in the previous chapter that that was the plan from the beginning, that the younger, Jacob, would be blessed, and the younger would be served by the older.

Genesis 27

Isaac realizes that he doesn't like how this turned out, and he is going to become sorrowful. Isaac's sorrow is going to be birthed out of the fact that he has been fighting and rebelling against God's will. And so Isaac repents.

Esau is also going to realize that he has been deceived, and he is not going to like how all this happened. And he is going to be sorrowful also, but Esau is going to have a greater sorrow over the *consequences* that are going to happen to him. He is *not* going to truly repent, and we never see Esau truly resign himself to God's plan and God's will. And so what I think this story does through these two guys' responses to all this is it shows us the difference between real, true, godly repentance in our lives and the fake, false repentance of the world.

In 2 Corinthians 7:8–9 (NASB) we read: "For though I caused you sorrow by my letter, I do not regret it—for I see that letter caused you sorrow, though only for a while—I now rejoice, not that you were made sorrowful, but that you were made sorrowful to the point of repentance; for you were made sorrowful according to the will of God, so that you might not suffer loss in anything through us."

And so Paul makes it absolutely clear that when you are confronted with your sin, there are two kinds of sorrows that can come out of you. The first kind of sorrow that can come out of you when you are confronted with your sin is a sorrow that is from God, it aligns itself with God's will, and it will produce in you a real, true repentance. There's another kind of sorrow that can come out of your life when you're confronted with your sin, and it will lead you not to true repentance in God's will but to death.

Conclusion

Isaac is sorrowful but the sorrow came from the thought that *I'm rebelling against God.* Esau was sorrowful, but it was because of the consequences of his sin. Isaac was deceived, but he realized, *This is God's plan. I submit to God's plan.* Esau was deceived, but he views himself as a victim and becomes deeply bitter. Isaac humbles himself, submits himself to God, and you see peace settle over Isaac. Esau becomes enraged at God's plan and becomes murderous in his heart.

GOSPEL SERMONS FOR THE CHRISTIAN LIFE

Jacob I Loved, Esau I Hated

Genesis 25:19–26

Matt Carter

Introduction

The doctrine of election teaches that the work of salvation in our lives is ultimately catalyzed and accomplished not by you, but by God. And it's a doctrine that teaches that salvation is not a result of God offering salvation to you and then sitting back and hoping that you choose Him; it's because God pursued you.

Genesis 25

In Genesis 25, Abraham's son Isaac marries a woman named Rebekah. She can't have children, so Isaac prays, and she conceives twins. And while they're in the womb, they're struggling and beating each other, as brothers are prone to do. Rebekah asks God why these two children are beating each other, and God answers that it is because two nations are in her womb, and two peoples from within her shall be divided and "The one shall be stronger than the other, the older shall serve the younger" (v. 23*b* ESV).

In virtually all patriarchal ancient societies, the firstborn son had what was called the *birthright*. Second-born sons were an afterthought, but not here. God chooses Jacob, the second-born son, over Esau, the firstborn son. God chooses Jacob to be the heir of salvation. The line of the Messiah, the line of Jesus, the line of salvation goes through Jacob. It does not go through Esau for one reason: because God chose Jacob.

Romans 9

The idea of the older now serving the younger made no sense to the early Roman Christians, and so Paul begins to explain it in Romans 9:8 (ESV): "This means that it is not the children of the flesh who are the children of God, but the children of the promise are counted as offspring." In other words, his point is God's children are not saved because of earthly merit. They're saved because of God's work and God's promise.

Paul is trying to tell us that God is the author of salvation, not man. "For this is what the promise said: 'About this time next year I will return, and Sarah shall have a son'" (v. 9 ESV). And then in verses 10–12 (ESV) Paul writes, "And not only so, but also when Rebekah had conceived children by one man, our forefather Isaac, though they were not yet born and had done nothing either good or bad—in order that God's purpose of election might continue, not because of works but because of Him who calls—she was told, 'The older will serve the younger.'"

Conclusion

In Romans 9, Paul explained what was happening in Genesis. Paul is telling us that God was trying to show us when this happened that this older, deserving son was going to serve the younger, undeserving son, not because of works but because of Him who calls.

GOSPEL SERMONS FOR THE CHRISTIAN LIFE

Grace for Sodom and Gomorrah

Genesis 18:20–33

Matt Carter

Introduction

We've all probably heard the story of Sodom and Gomorrah. It's basically the idea that God looks down at these two cities, sees their wickedness, and makes the decision that "I'm going to destroy them." It's where we get the term *hell fire and brimstone*. But the main takeaway from the story of Sodom and Gomorrah is not that God punishes sinners, but that He is actually willing not to punish sinners. God won't give you and me what we deserve because of our sin if there can be found in our midst one that is righteous who can take our place.

Genesis 18:20–22

"Then the Lord said, 'Because the outcry against Sodom and Gomorrah is great and their sin is very grave, I will go down to see whether they have done altogether according to the outcry that has come to me. And if not, I will know.' So the men [that's the angels] turned from there and went toward Sodom, but Abraham stood still before the Lord" (ESV).

Abraham and God are talking. Abraham hears in just a second that God is going to destroy the city because of their great sin, and Abraham does something incredibly bold. Like a defense lawyer, Abraham comes and stands before the Great Judge, and he makes a case for why the accused should be pardoned.

"Then Abraham drew near to God and said, 'Will you indeed sweep away the righteous with the wicked? Suppose, God, there are fifty righteous within the city. Will you then sweep away the place and not spare it for the fifty righteous who are in it?" (Gen. 18:23–24 ESV).

Abraham's request was something that had never been asked of God before. "God, will You not punish sinners? Instead of bringing destruction because of the sin of the many, God, will You spare the many because of the righteousness of the few?"

There was also a big concept in ancient Near Eastern culture called *guilt by association* or guilt transference. It's the idea that because of the guilt of one, the consequences would be transferred to the many. Paul talks about it in Romans 5:12 (ESV): "Therefore, just as sin came into the world through one man, and death through sin, and so death spread to all men because all sinned." Paul is talking about this idea of guilt transference. You just have this one guy. His name is Adam, who sinned, and what the Bible says is because he sinned, the consequences spread to everybody.

But here, for the very first time, Abraham comes before the Lord and asks Him to consider enacting righteousness transference. And what's even more remarkable than Abraham asking that of God was that God said yes.

Genesis 18:26 (ESV) says: "And the LORD said, 'If I find at Sodom fifty righteous in the city, I will spare the whole place for their sake.'" There was a problem. And as soon as Abraham asked God that crazy question and God said yes, it hit Abraham like a ton of bricks. *There might not be fifty righteous in Sodom.* And so in verse 28, Abraham asks God if He would spare them for forty-five righteous people, and God says yes. Then forty righteous people. Thirty. Twenty. Ten.

What happens from here? God destroys the city. Why did He destroy it? The answer is very obvious. God obviously did not find ten righteous people in the city of Sodom or Gomorrah, and therefore He destroyed it. But what's crazy about the story is that you get the sense that Abraham could have kept asking and kept lowering the number, and God would have kept saying, "Yes."

You get the sense from the story that Abraham could have said, "God, will You save this city on behalf of five?" And God would have said, "Sure." "Will You save the whole place on behalf of one righteous?" You get the sense that God would have said, "Yes." Why didn't Abraham keep asking? He realized one of the central truths in Scripture, one of the most amazing truths, one of the scariest truths in Scripture, and one of the most awesome truths in Scripture: God is willing to not punish sinners if there is one righteous that can be found among them, but none of us are righteous.

In Romans 3:10 (ESV), Paul talks about this very truth. "As it is written: 'None is righteous, no, not one; no one understands; no one seeks for God. All have turned aside; together they have become worthless; no one does good, not even one.'"

Conclusion

And so, what is our hope? Our only hope to be pardoned for sin, because none of us are righteous, is that God will send to us One who is. What's so amazing about God's grace toward us is not that we were so wonderful. It's not that we were so worth it that God died for us and took our place. What's so amazing about grace is that we were so messed up and that we were so *not* worth it, and God came and died for us and took our place.

When you stand before God the eternal Judge and He asks you, "Why should I pardon you, sinner?" you'd better not say, "Because I was worth it." Instead, you point to the right hand of the Father. "God, why should You pardon me? Because of Jesus. And God, I know You pardon sinners if one righteous can be found. He was found righteous."

GOSPEL SERMONS FOR THE CHRISTIAN LIFE

In the Beginning Was Jesus

Genesis 1:1–3

Matt Carter

Introduction

"In the beginning God created the heavens and the earth. The earth was formless and void, and darkness was over the surface of the deep, and the Spirit of God was moving over the surface of the waters. Then God said, 'Let there be light'; and there was light" (Gen. 1:1–3 NASB).

Moses was writing the book to a before-the-common-era Jewish audience, thousands of years before Christ ever came on the scene. Now there are two main purposes for why Moses wrote the book of Genesis to that audience.

1. *He was trying to make a connection in the minds of the Jewish audience.* He was trying to connect the dots in their minds from the God of their fathers. That's what the second half of Genesis is all about. You see Moses trying to connect the dots in their minds from *that* God to the God who created the heavens and the earth. He wants to make that connection in the Jewish heart and the Jewish mind.
2. *He wanted to ensure in the minds of Jews that it was, in fact, the God of Israel, YHWH and Him alone, who created the heavens and the earth.* The God of Israel, YHWH, created the heavens and the earth. You see that purpose from the very first sentence of the book of Genesis. Moses says, "In the beginning God [the LORD, YHWH, was the One who] created the heavens and the earth."

The Jews, just like us, wanted to worship other gods all the time. Moses went up on the mountain to meet with the Lord and get the Ten Commandments, and when he came back down, the Israelites had built themselves a calf and were worshiping it. All the time the writers of the Old Testament have to remind the Jews that it's God, and God alone, who is Creator of the heavens and the earth.

The purpose of Genesis *is for you and me to understand that the earth was created and it was the God of Israel who did it.*

The Gospel

But there is another purpose for the book of Genesis. *Genesis, the very first book of the Bible, over and over again is a foreshadowing of the gospel.* From the very beginning, thousands of years before the name of Jesus would ever be spoken, thousands of years before Gabriel would come on the scene and knock on Mary's door and say, "Blessed are you because you will carry in your womb the Son of the living God and we will call His name *Emmanuel*, which means *God with us*," you begin to see in Genesis 1:3, a glimpse of the gospel.

Purpose number one can be found in Genesis 1:1 (NASB): "In the beginning [YHWH,] God created the heavens and the earth." Purpose two is hinted at immediately after: "The earth was formless and void, and darkness was over the surface of the deep, and the Spirit of God was moving over the surface of the waters. Then God said, 'Let there be light'; and there was light" (vv. 2–3 NASB). In the very second verse of the Bible, Moses uses specific words to describe the condition of the earth. He said *formless* and *void*.

The words *formless* and *void* in the Hebrew carry with them the idea of chaos. Just imagine that. It was just chaotic. It carries the idea of being uninhabitable, cold, dark, chaotic, lifeless.

Moses was describing this picture of earth as this cold, dark, chaotic, uninhabitable place, until something happened. What happened? God spoke. For the very first time that we know of in all eternity, God opened His mouth and spoke into this lifeless, void, formless, dark, and chaotic place, and when He spoke, light—not the sun, but light. What used to be chaotic was now order. What used to be lifeless now had life. What used to be ugly now was beautiful.

Do you hear the gospel in that? Do you hear the echoes of the coming Messiah in that? You should. Do you see there from the very beginning that God is orchestrating and setting the stage for greater purpose? The answer is *yes*.

What is the condition of our hearts before Jesus speaks into them and changes us? Genesis 6:5 (NASB) says, "Then the LORD saw that the wickedness of man was great on the earth, and that every intent of the thoughts of his heart was only evil continually."

Over and over and over again, in a hundred places, the Scripture says that our hearts are lifeless. They're without life, but then God looks at us and He speaks and He shines His light into your heart and into my heart and He gives us "the knowledge of the glory of God in the face of [Jesus] Christ" (2 Cor. 4:6 NASB).

Look at how Jesus, with His own words, would describe Himself and what He does. He says in John 8:12 (NASB), "Then Jesus again spoke to them, saying, 'I am the Light of the world." You remember the Old Testament saying, "Then God said, 'Let there be light'"? Jesus said, "I am the light of the world. Whoever follows me will never walk in darkness, but will have the light of life" (John 8:12 NIV).

Conclusion

In the very beginning, the very first time God spoke, light shattered the darkness, and we see that God was setting the stage for a day when He would send His Son, who would also speak and shine His life-giving light into the darkness and the chaos of your heart and change it. From the very first moments of creation, we see the echoes of the gospel.

GOSPEL SERMONS FOR THE CHRISTIAN LIFE

Is Church Membership Biblical?

Hebrews 13:17

Matt Carter

Introduction

For so many of us, church membership has come down to an issue of personal preference. But church membership is really not an issue of personal preference at all. Church membership is an issue of biblical obedience. As a culture, we have a serious problem with commitment and with authority. But we need to ask, *Are the principles behind church membership biblical?*

Hebrews 13:17

The Scripture says, "Obey your leaders and submit to them, for they keep watch over your souls as those who will give an account. Let them do this with joy and not with grief, for this would be unprofitable for you" (NASB).

The first thing you see in this Scripture is a *command.* He says, "Obey your leaders and submit to them." If there is no biblical requirement for you to belong to a local church, then to which leaders are you, as a believer, supposed to obey and submit?

The second thing this verse does is tell us *why* God gives us the command to submit to church leaders. In 1 Timothy 3, God begins to lay out the qualifications of these men He's going to call to shepherd and lead the church. So from the beginning, again, God's plan was that Christians would not live their lives separately, doing their own thing, but that believers would come together in a community of faith, and in that community of faith, God would raise up a group of men to care for, shepherd, and lead them. Here's why: "... for they keep watch over your souls as those who will give an account." They keep watch over your souls.

We Have an Enemy

Revelation 12:7–9 (NASB) tells us why you might need someone to keep watch over your soul: "And there was war in heaven, Michael and his angels waging war with the dragon. The dragon and his angels waged war, and they were not strong enough, and there was no longer a place found for them in heaven. And the great dragon was thrown down, the serpent of old who is called the devil and Satan, who deceives the whole world; he was thrown down to the earth, and his angels were thrown down with him." According to this scripture, Satan is on the earth, and his job is to go around deceiving the world, you and me.

Conclusion

Finally, Hebrews 13:17 (NASB) tells us *how* to obey and submit to these men who keep watch over our souls: "Let them do this with joy and not with grief, for this would be unprofitable for you." That doesn't mean you never question your elders. It doesn't mean you never push back. It doesn't mean you can't ever have problems. It just means you engage those men whom God has raised up in your life, and you do it in such a way that brings them joy, and not grief, because the Scripture says that would be unprofitable for you.

GOSPEL SERMONS FOR THE CHRISTIAN LIFE

The One Unforgivable Sin

Mark 3:28–29

Matt Carter

Introduction

The Lord will forgive you of any and all sins that you commit in your life. But Jesus said there is one sin that will not be forgiven.

Mark 3:28–29

Jesus says this: "Truly, I say to you, all sins will be forgiven the children of man, and whatever blasphemies they utter, but whoever blasphemes against the Holy Spirit never has forgiveness, but is guilty of an eternal sin" (ESV). Now, that statement is made in the context of Jesus having a conversation with the scribes of the Pharisees, and Jesus had just cast out a demon from a demon-possessed man.

He was casting out demons, so the scribes were saying that the reason Jesus has the power to cast out demons is because He is demon-possessed Himself. And then Jesus makes the famous statement to them: "If a house is divided against itself, that house will not be able to stand" (Mark 3:25 ESV). His whole point was if His power came from demons, then why in the world would He be casting out demons?

Mark 3:28 might be one of the most amazing articulations of the gospel in the entire Bible. What Jesus just said is that all sins will be forgiven the children of man. One of the words for *sin* in the Greek is called *hamartia*, and it means every single one of your sins. But Jesus is using the Greek word *pánta hamarteémata*, which means all your sins lumped together as a whole, all at one time. The word *forgiven* means to utterly and completely remove something from somebody's account forever so that it can never be charged against him again.

But then after He does that, Jesus gives us probably the strongest warning in the Scriptures. Jesus says that there is one sin you can commit, and that if you commit this sin, God will not lump all your sins together and remove them away from you. And Jesus calls this sin "the blasphemy against the Holy Spirit."

To understand what it means to blaspheme against the Holy Spirit, you have to understand what the Holy Spirit does. The Holy Spirit is going to convict you of your sin. He is going to convict you of your need for righteousness. He is going to convict you of the coming judgment. And then once He convicts you of those three things, Jesus said the Holy Spirit is going to take your heart, and He is going to lead you to Jesus.

Conclusion

If you reject the Holy Spirit's leading to repent, turn to Jesus, and be forgiven, then you have said *no* to Jesus and *no* to the Spirit; you've said *no* to the only place you can get forgiveness. And if you say *no* to the only place you can get forgiveness, you will not be forgiven. It's called blasphemy of the Holy Spirit, and your sins will not be forgiven.

GOSPEL SERMONS FOR THE CHRISTIAN LIFE

Why Did Jesus Speak in Parables?

Matthew 13:10–11; 16:13–17; Mark 4

Matt Carter

Introduction

A lot of times when Jesus would draw a crowd, He would teach in what was called *a parable*. We're going to answer the question, *Why did Jesus speak in parables?*

Mark 4:1–2

"He began to teach again by the sea. And such a very large crowd gathered to Him that He got into a boat in the sea and sat down; and the whole crowd was by the sea on the land. And He was teaching them many things in parables" (NASB).

A lot of preachers say that the reason Jesus taught in stories is because that was the most effective way to communicate a truth. Some pastors say that they only teach in stories because Jesus only taught in stories.

That can't be right. Watch the disciples' response after Jesus teaches the parable of the sower.

He just taught it, and in verse 10 it says, "As soon as He was alone, His followers, along with the twelve, began asking Him about the parables" (NASB). So He teaches the parable. He gets alone with them. The disciples start asking Him about the parables. The disciples' typical response after He taught a parable was not understanding.

Mark 4:34 says, "He did not speak to them without a parable; but He was explaining everything privately to His own disciples" (NASB). So Jesus would get up in front of a crowd, preach a story with a meaning that nobody had a clue about, and then would pull the disciples away and explain to them privately the meaning of the story.

Why did He not reveal the true meaning of the parable publicly to the crowds? Verses 9–12 give us the answer. In verse 9 He says, "And he was saying, 'He who has ears to hear, let him hear.'" It's an interesting way to end a sermon. And then in verses 10–11 it says, "As soon as He was alone, His followers, along with the twelve, began asking Him about the parables. And He was saying to them, 'To you has been given the mystery of the kingdom of God, but those who are outside get everything in parables'" (NASB).

In the very next verse Jesus explains why some people get revealed the truth of the Word of God and why some people just get parables: "So that 'they may indeed see but not perceive, and may indeed hear but not understand, lest they should turn and be forgiven'" (ESV). In the same story in Matthew 13:11: "Jesus answered them and said, 'To you it has been granted to know the mysteries of the kingdom of heaven, but to them it has not been granted'" (NASB).

Conclusion

Here's the whole point: if you believe the gospel today, it is because you have been granted by the Lord to know the gospel today. This should create in you both profound humility and incredible rejoicing as you begin to understand the kindness and severity of our God.

THE GOSPEL PROJECT

The Passion of Christ

Isaiah 53

Steve Dighton

Introduction

It has been nine years since *The Passion of the Christ* was released. It was a movie that captured the last twelve hours of Jesus' earthly life, taking us from the agony in the Garden of Gethsemane to the resurrection of our Savior. The movie grossed over $600 million as people flocked to see this reenactment of the crucifixion. Many found it agonizing to watch—as well it should have been. Our text this morning is about this very story—the passion of the Christ.

Isaiah 53 is a prophecy like no other that makes the destination of the Messiah crystal clear. From this side of the cross we see the fulfillment of this prophecy is undeniable—Jesus is the One Isaiah spoke of. His story has become our story; as believers, we too have experienced the cross (Gal. 2:20). The high price of redemption can only be understood in the suffering of our Savior.

His Rejection (vv. 1–3)

As Isaiah peered down the corridors of time, he saw the Savior coming not in celebration or grandeur, but in obscurity and humility.

His Birth

The description (v. 2) graphically describes the coming of our Savior—a helpless baby coming to an unaccepting, unpromising environment—the dry ground of barren, empty religion. His earthly life was one of rejection from before His birth to His death on the cross (Matt. 27:46).

His Beauty

He had no appearance that we should desire Him. Men were blind to His beauty. Many know the pain of rejection. You've been overlooked, dumped for someone else, ignored, and passed over. Jesus identifies and empathizes with your pain.

Our Redemption

Isaiah graphically revealed the coming agony, misery, and substitutionary nature of Calvary as he peered down the Via Dolorosa and foresaw what was coming.

The Vast Problem (v. 6)

Because of our inherent nature, we all have a heart problem. We're like sheep being scattered. Just as in Isaiah 64, our iniquities have taken us away from the presence of God.

The Violent Punishment (vv. 4–5, 7–8, 10*a*)

In these five verses we catch a glimpse of the punishment Jesus would endure. Isaiah sees the Via Dolorosa and sensed the high price of God's redemption.

His Vicarious Provision (vv. 6, 11)

Verses 5–6, 11*b*–12—His wounds were for us, our sins were upon Him, our judgment fell on Him, He was struck down because of our rebellion (2 Cor. 5:21).

He bore our punishment so we would not have to—to set us free from the judgment we deserve.

His Reward (vv. 11–12)

This plan of redemption was master-minded by God—it was His plan, His purpose. Jesus' death satisfied the Father. Not that God rejoiced in the suffering and death of Jesus, but He was pleased that the chasm had been spanned—reconciliation was accomplished; sin had been atoned for. In giving His Son He received many sons (Rom. 8:37).

Conclusion

The Suffering Servant of God can only find its prophetic fulfillment in Jesus of Nazareth.

THE GOSPEL PROJECT

Condemned to Die

Luke 23:13–25

Steve Dighton

Introduction

This story is mentioned in every one of the four gospels. It's the story of Barabbas, a secondary character in the story of Passion Week, but still a study worthy of our consideration because the truth is, if something is mentioned once in the Bible it's noteworthy; how much more if someone is mentioned in all four gospels. God's providential plan provides for us a substitutionary atonement for our sins through Christ's death on the cross. That is the story of Barabbas.

The Collaboration

Pontius Pilate's name has become synonymous with one who allowed Jesus' crucifixion. While he was simply attending to his duties as governor, he found himself in the most precarious, providential plot in the history of the world. But we know that he was merely a pawn in the hand of almighty God.

The Incident

Pilate had compromised when he should have stood strong and with cynicism and a lack of respect. His capacity to rule was being jeopardized. We see him display the abandonment of his own conviction of Jesus' innocence and give in to the will of the chief priests and leaders.

His Innocence

Pilate found no fault in Jesus because there was no fault to be found. He was the perfect, unblemished sacrifice of God (2 Cor. 5:21).

His Compliance

This dilemma regarding the fate of Jesus brought Herod and Pilate together (Luke 23:12). Neither one knew what to do about this predicament. They became like-minded friends because of this quagmire taking place in Jerusalem. Two things that bring people together are a common anger or a common devotion.

The Custom

At the Passover the governor was to release one prisoner whom the people wanted to be let go. Surely this would be his hold card to get Jesus vindicated.

The Criminal

Barabbas was a notorious criminal, one guilty of murder, insurrectionism, and being a political terrorist.

The Cry

First the crowd called for Jesus' crucifixion. When Pilate declared that he was innocent of the blood of this innocent man, they responded with, "His blood be on us and on our children!" (Matt. 27:25 HCSB). While Pilate sought to distance himself from the calamity of the cross, still he would be guilty—as well as the Jewish leaders and people of Jerusalem that day and you and me as well.

The Crucifixion

The culmination of this epic story continues with the mention of Simon of Cyrene, who carried the cross of our Savior.

The Criminals

Two anonymous thieves still clinging to life frame the centerpiece of redemption, the Lamb of God who has been led to slaughter. There He would die with the people He came to save.

Their Conversation

How different their perspectives (Luke 23:40–43). One taunted Jesus while the other, in contrition and belief, trusted in Jesus.

Conclusion

The story of Barabbas is our story. He was not only the first person who received Jesus' atoning sacrifice, but he became the prototype of all for whom Jesus would vicariously die.

THE GOSPEL PROJECT

Jesus' Message, His Men, and Their Ministry

Matthew 4:17–23

Steve Dighton

Introduction

Our text is about the early beginnings of Jesus' ministry—His simple message, the men He would select,

and the rapid spread of His ministry. God sovereignly chooses and uses unlikely men to accomplish extraordinary things.

His Simple Message (v. 17)

Matthew gives us the simple and concise message that Jesus was proclaiming. It was a simple, saving, and sobering message.

Repentance

The message of repentance was not a new and trendy message originating with Jesus. No, it was the message of all the prophets, and it was the mirror-image of the message of John the Baptist (Matt. 3:1). Repentance is not a once-for-all-time event. It's to be the continual, habitual practice of everyone who desires to live their life for God.

Recognition

The kingdom is now present tense. Jesus ushered in an age of righteousness—personifying God's rule and reign. He was and is looking for men and women who would humble themselves and turn from a life of pretense, of permissiveness and perversion and pride, and find rest and resolve in living their life for God in the protective and peaceful kingdom of God (John 3:6–7).

His Select Men (vv. 18–22)

These men would go on mission with Him to accomplish His agenda, His mission, and His mandate. The mission would be one of rescuing men from the fields of sin. His passion was evidenced in Matthew 23:27. His purpose was declared in Luke 19:10.

Their Similarities

We have two sets of brothers here. The similarities were that they were two brothers, same vocation and same response to Jesus' call. Both "immediately" began a journey that would shape their lives and the future of the Christian faith.

Their Significance

These men were rough and uncultured. Peter was impulsive and capricious. James and John were aggressive and short-tempered. The point is these were ordinary men who would do extraordinary things. These are the kind of people Jesus is looking for. He chooses "diamonds in the rough" and models them into something extraordinary for His purpose.

His Spreading Ministry (v. 23)

Jesus stayed in motion—traveling the entire region of Galilee.

Informational (teaching)

Jesus' teaching in the synagogue was basically expository, as He would take Scriptures and explain them section by section, precept by precept, and verse by verse with the purpose of teaching the truth. Hosea 4:6 speaks of our need for knowledge of the Word.

Inspirational (preaching)

The good news was the inspirational and transformational message that Christ had come. While the target of teaching is the head, the focus of proclamation is the heart. The gospel calls for life change—for recalibration. Not merely to think differently but to be different.

Incarnational (healing)

He made the blind see, the lame walk; He even raised the dead. Jesus had compassion and also was validating His deity—that He was the Son of God.

Conclusion

As Jesus called these select men for the purpose of propagating the gospel, He still sovereignly calls us to get engaged in His worldwide mission of redemption.

THE GOSPEL PROJECT

Look and Live

Numbers 21:4–9

Steve Dighton

Introduction

Moses records an incident when God's people were critical toward his leadership. God's displeasure led Him to bring judgment by sending poisonous snakes in retribution for their sins.

A Complaining People

These fickle followers of Moses were impatient and complaining. When reading about the wilderness wanderings, you see the people were habitually dissatisfied—quick to voice their displeasure. The twofold complaints—they didn't like the way they were led or fed.

They spoke against *Moses' leadership*. Truth is: rebelling against Moses was rebelling against God. Rejecting Moses was rejecting God.

Earlier (Num. 16) we read about Korah's rebellion that began with complaints and opposition to Moses. This incident caused God to kill fifteen thousand Israelites. This was obviously a serious offense before God. It can be very dangerous to speak against God's leader—God takes it personally. Every leader is vulnerable. Everybody's got an opinion. Everybody can do it better, but let's not be complainers. Give grace to our leaders.

They complained about the *miserable food*. The diet of manna and the lack of water caused them to lose their patience, and again a grievance was filed. I think manna may have gotten a better billing over the years than it deserved. We speak of manna from heaven like it's chicken fried steak with gravy. It was probably closer to a stale vanilla wafer. Manna means "What is it?" Rarely have I looked at an inviting entrée and responded by saying, "What is it?" These weary wanderers wanted to go back to Egypt, to their life as slaves. They'd lost perspective. Their discontentment bred more discontent.

God disdains complaining. He gives us much more than we deserve—but that's not enough for some people—ingratitude and entitlement result in boisterous complaint. Resolve to let your speech always be with grace.

Condemning Punishment

In retribution for their rebellion, God sent venomous snakes as a symbolic reminder to God's people—sin will not go unpunished. Its wages have always been spiritual death and, oftentimes, physical death. This condemning punishment was both *fiery* and *fatal.*

People were dying from the fiery, fatal fangs of their sin. The timeless reality is: while sin is attractive, alluring, and provocative, in the end, it will kill, steal, and destroy your life (Gal. 6:7–8).

A Contrite Plea

After God's punitive plot of poison serpents, He got the attention of His pouting people. They understood the reason for their punishment and began *their confession.* They had complained before (chap. 11) and God sent fire. This second verse was same as the first. They rebelled, God sent judgment, they repented and confessed, and God forgave—only to see this predictable cycle happen time and again.

Here's the promise of the New Testament (1 John 1:9). The acknowledgment of your sin is the first step in finding forgiveness and hope. Confession takes ownership—it doesn't blame circumstances, peers, parents, or problems. Someday you will give an account before God and answer for your sin.

Now we see *Moses' intercession* (Num. 21:7*b*). He laid hold of God on behalf of his people. What a picture of Jesus interceding on our behalf; shedding His own lifeblood that we might be forgiven. We see Moses' prayer brought an atypical solution—but God's ways are past finding out.

A Christ-like Pardon

God gave Moses a peculiar antidote for these suffering victims—a bronze serpent mounted on a pole. If the dying looked at it, they lived. That is bizarre, illogical, and irrational. But it's no more peculiar than God's ultimate antidote for sin—sending His own Son to hang on a cruel Roman cross in naked humiliation, to bear the sins of mankind (Prov. 14:12; John 3:13–14).

We observe three similarities in the requirement for those in Moses' camp to be saved and what's required for us today. The expected response was *effortless*. Nothing could have been easier. They didn't have to labor or attend any classes on the dangers of snake venom. It wasn't that they had to be good, healthy, or strong enough—they simply had to look.

There is not one thing you can do to deserve God's free gift of salvation—it's not about penance, joining church, or human effort. It's about God's grace through faith, a willingness to look at the one who paid your sin debt and put your trust in Him. Believe it, receive it, and be saved (Acts 16:29–31).

The way to healing was *exclusive*—simply look. There were hundreds of serpents, but the only way to receive healing was to look at the serpent on the pole. No one could look for you. There was one remedy. It was God's provision—His way. Today the prevailing notion is, any religion is as valid as the next—everyone finding their own way to God.

There was one *essential* hope of healing. The victims could not be nursed back to health or survive because they were in good cardiovascular shape. If they wanted to live, it was mandatory, not optional—look at the serpent.

Many who have been bitten by sin would rather look around and give their myriad of excuses for not looking. The only healing that day in the Sinai wilderness was to look at the serpent on the pole, today it's only in coming to Jesus. Let's imagine the scene with poisonous snakes covering the ground, people crying out in fear and screams of dying people. You see families grieving—a friend has died; a brother is gone. It's as if the death angel has returned and there is no blood for the doorposts. But during the chaos and confusion a man yells, "Moses has a remedy! You can be saved! Look and live!"

What will the responses be? "That's a stupid remedy. I won't do it" (see 1 Cor. 1:18). "I could look—maybe tomorrow." "I'll shake this off, then look." "I'm guilty—getting what I deserve."

Conclusion

People are dying on every hand, yet the healing is so near—just look and live. If you visit your doctor's office, you will see the symbol of a snake on a pole, known as Nehustan, a reminder from antiquity that our hope of healing comes from God.

THE GOSPEL PROJECT

The Ark of God's Salvation

Genesis 6–7

Steve Dighton

Introduction

The gospel—the precious treasure we possess as believers in Jesus Christ—the pearl of great price; worth selling all we have and forsaking all we possess to own. From Genesis to Revelation we find the scarlet thread of God's redemptive narrative being played out. It is promised in the Old Testament and personified in the New.

Genesis 6 chronicles one of the most well-known stories in all Christendom. It's usually portrayed as a children's story with cartoonish portrayals of a boat filled with smiling animals. This is hardly what's going on. This epic event is one of the most graphic pictures of the judgment of sin in the history of mankind when God poured out His unrestrained wrath on all creation. Yet, Noah found grace in the eyes of the Lord. Grace—God's unmerited favor, the essence of the gospel experienced by every man and woman who has ever been saved (Eph. 2:8–9).

The Depravity of Mankind

Moses revealed the decline of the morality of humanity. In Genesis 1 all God had made was "good"; after He created mankind—things were "very good." But five chapters later, the story became tragic. No longer "good"; things hit rock bottom and we see the depravity and decadence of mankind.

The depravity was *extensive*. They were "evil all the time." Every thought, idea, plan, and pursuit was twisted and wicked. They had turned their back on their Creator. What started with a seemingly innocuous act of disobedience, eating the forbidden fruit, had now resulted in every man and woman being consumed and obsessed with carnality (Ps. 14:2–3). All these acts of moral collapse revealed the source of the problem—the heart. The gospel promise is this: by grace through faith God will take a heart of stone—cold, indifferent, hardened, and calloused—and He'll change it into a heart of flesh—alive, forgiven and transformed.

There were *extraordinary* men. Genesis 6:1–4 tells the story of one of the acute anomalies of the ages—the sons of God having relations with the daughters of men. Their offspring, known as the Nephilim, were men of renown; legendary giants who lived on the earth. While this event defies explanation, still it tells of angelic beings copulating with human women (Jude 5–6). How deeply depraved things had gotten—affecting not only things on earth but things in heaven as well.

We see the *emotions* of God. The text says it grieved God's heart and He was sorry He had made mankind. Sometimes we lose sight of the fact that God has emotions—that His heart can be grieved. When you and I walk by faith, He is blessed. But here His emotions tell us of His displeasure and deep-seated disappointment.

God is omniscient—He knew of man's irreverence and perverse nature. That didn't keep it from hurting any less and it didn't cause Him to be cavalier about the wickedness of the human heart. Parents understand this if they've dealt with a rebellious child. While you knew that a disappointing event could happen, it wasn't any less painful when you experienced it.

The Decree from God

The wages of man's iniquities are about to be paid—God's wrath is about to go unrestrained toward the fallen world. While God is longsuffering and merciful, He will not tolerate blatant and blasphemous sin.

God's *response* was imminent judgment. The consequences of sin—He would blot out man and animals alike (Gen. 6:13). The destruction would be inclusive and without mercy, save for those who found safety in the ark.

God's *request*: Noah is to build an enormous ark. Since it had never rained and no coastline was near, this command was one that would test the faith and endurance of any man. It took 120 years to complete the task of cutting and shaping the gopher wood into this massive sea-going vessel. Noah was a preacher of righteousness and was building an object of rescue from God's coming judgment—but no one listened.

Noah, his family, and the animals entered the ark—the door was shut. All humanity was outside. Those who had mocked and harassed Noah were silenced as the fountains of the deep burst forth and rain rushed from the heavens until all mankind, all living things had died (Gen. 7:21).

Soon the stench of decay testified that God would not always contend with the heart of man. He would execute a harsh and grievous judgment against sin. For those who reject God's grace through Jesus, God's judgment will one day be equally as harsh and grievous. Through God's grace, Noah found deliverance and became the hope of the human race.

The Deliverance by Grace

God's mercy brought deliverance to a remnant of people. Now, we too are invited to come into the ark and find deliverance, forgiveness, and safety.

There was *salvation* in the ark. While the world was drowning in transgressions and unbelief, Noah and his family found salvation. Through faith they entered through the one door that led them to salvation; one way in—only one door to be saved (Matt. 7:13–14; John 10:9). There is urgency to the gospel—today the door is still open but soon the opportunity will be gone.

There was *security* in the ark from the storm. So it is with all who come to faith in Christ. He'll bring security, confidence, hope, and assurance. Say with the psalmist, "Lead me to the rock that is higher than I. For You have been a shelter for me" (Ps. 61:2*b*-3*a*).

There was *serenity* in the ark. While the world was perishing, God gave peace, comfort, security, and salvation to Noah and his family. This serenity is pictured by the dove that returned with a freshly plucked olive leaf: the symbol of peace and hope. You, too, will find peace and hope in your life when you come into the ark of God's salvation.

Conclusion

The gospel of grace is experienced by all who will walk through the door of the ark of God's redemptive love.

THE GOSPEL PROJECT

Jonah: The Gospel of a Second Chance

Jonah 1–3

Steve Dighton

Every person with a thimble full of biblical knowledge knows the story of Jonah. Three verses make mention of the phenomenal fish, while forty-five tell the heart and message of the book—our God is a God of mercy and grace; our failures are not final, our mistakes are not fatal, we can start over with Him. It's a book about the futility of running from God, about how prayer changes things and about beginning again. It's about the gospel—the message of hope that compels us to return to God and live our lives in obedience and faith.

A Rebellious Prophet (v. 1)

Jonah's story might be your story. Perhaps God has called you to salvation but you ignored Him. Perhaps it was a call to ministry or missions. Has God compelled you to do something difficult but you've cowered down in fear and turned a deaf and defiant ear? Who knows? There may be a lot of Jonah in all of us.

A call from God. While we are not told God's method of communication, rest assured Jonah got the message. The question is, how does God communicate to us? With Jonah, it might have been audible. God had spoken to Moses from a burning bush. Maybe a vision like Peter at Joppa or a gentle whisper like Elijah in 1 Kings 19. Generally we hear from God through His Word (Ps. 119:105). Sometimes we hear God through other people or circumstances—perhaps a trial, difficulty, or death and we hear God like never before. God is still speaking. He's still calling particular people to particular places for a particular purpose. So it was with Jonah. "Go to

Nineveh."

Jonah knew about this capital city and didn't want to go there. The residents were the meanest, vilest men in recorded history. They delighted in mutilating their adversaries. Jonah didn't like the prospects of what might await him.

The conduct of Jonah was to head in the opposite direction instead of heeding God's call. He clearly understood what God wanted him to do, but he deliberately chose to disobey. That choice got him in a precarious place.

The consequences for his disobedience. On a vessel headed to Tarshish, sinking amidst the storm, the problem wasn't with the cargo weight, but the rebellious prophet. The resolve was to make atonement to Jonah's God. Jonah declared, "Throw me overboard." They obliged him and the sea stopped raging. Jonah was learning a lesson—you can't escape God. Jonah knew better, but when you are on the run from God, you're delusional. You believe anything that justifies your behavior.

While there have been other Jonah's in the world, trying to run and hide from God, there are none who've escaped His presence. Some try to lose God in academics, while others seek to lose God partying, drinking, and wallowing in our crumbling, corrupted culture. Eventually there will be nowhere to hide—no place to run (Ps. 139:7–9). Jonah's decision was deliberate, dangerous, and delusional and God prepared a great fish to teach him a valuable lesson.

A Reverent Prayer (v. 2)

Prayer of Desperation (vv. 2–3, 5–6*a*). In chapter 2 we find a different Jonah—contrite, repentant; engaged in a reverent, heartfelt prayer. Jonah was quite aware of his dire situation and knew, unless God had mercy on his soul, he was a goner. Like the heart of desperation that drove David to cry out in

Psalm 142:6. Is anyone desperate enough to cry out to God? God does business with those who mean business.

Prayer of Determination (vv. 7, 9). Not only was Jonah demonstrating a repentant and contrite spirit, he was pursuing God with a new fervor. God heard his prayer—delivered him but not immediately. It was three days and three nights that Jonah stewed in the belly of the fish. Most of us give up if our prayer is not answered in fifteen minutes. Perhaps God wanted Jonah not only to ask but to keep on asking, to keep on seeking, to keep on knocking. Remember the promise of Jeremiah 29:13.

Jonah, in desperation, found determination resulting in devotion.

A Repentent Preacher (v. 3)

A few days in the great fish and Jonah saw things differently. He had a change of mind and attitude. His rebellious spirit was tempered and he repented.

A Second Chance (vv. 1–3). The most encouraging words in the book of Jonah are right here—"The word of the LORD came to Jonah the second time." God didn't abandon Jonah to find another prophet. The wonderful truth about God is—He makes a practice of giving us second chances. We can put our past failures behind us, start over—a new page can be added to our narrative.

Have you wondered if God could use you again? There are a litany of personalities who failed and later did something significant for God—Moses, David, Peter, Paul. Second chances are God's patented and promised possibility to all who call upon Him. The hope of the gospel is found in a second chance. Who hasn't needed one? It was a second chance that got Jonah on mission for God—to go to Nineveh and proclaim God's message.

A Short Sermon—"Yet forty days, and Nineveh shall be overthrown!" (Jonah 3:4). I guess there is something powerful about a short, concise sermon! The gospel message is a brief and succinct message. Believe on the Lord Jesus Christ and you will be saved. That clear message is the truth that has transformed tens of millions and still has the power to save.

A Shocking Revival (vv. 5–10). The people of Nineveh believed God and repented. This is arguably the greatest revival ever recorded. Jonah changed his ways and it changed his world. Hundreds of thousands turned to God in repentance and belief. This barbaric and belligerent people were transformed by faith that came from hearing God's word (Rom. 10:17).

It will convict, show the way of salvation and the second chance.

Conclusion

God will use us mightily if we come to Him in repentance and faith. God has plenty of "big fishes" awaiting all who run from Him, but He has forgiving, merciful grace to all who call upon Him in their time of need.

THE GOSPEL PROJECT

The Last Word Before the Living Word

Malachi 1:1–4

Steve Dighton

Introduction

The Gospel Project is about seeing God's loving and redemptive hand at work throughout the Bible. The scarlet thread of redemption runs from Genesis to Revelation.

One hundred years after the captives had returned, their love for God had grown cold. Malachi dealt with spiritual drought and indifference toward God from top to bottom—from priests to paupers, religious to reprobates. But God stepped in with a prophetic word of expectation and hope. The pieces of this prophetic puzzle are fitting together and the Blessed Hope is on the horizon. The sinful state of man's indifference toward God reveals the necessity of our redemption.

A Misguided People

God speaks in forty-seven of fifty-five verses in this book. As God's mouthpiece, Malachi had much to say. These people had abused and confused what many Christians are guilty of as well—with privilege comes responsibility.

These were God's chosen people. Yet they no longer honored God's name. They were self-centered, self-absorbed, and self-reliant. They no longer glorified the name of God. God was not pleased.

The Defilement of the Priests

There is a lack of reverence, fear, and awe. Instead of giving God their best, the priests were giving Him lame, sick animals of no value.

The Deceitfulness of the People

In their indifference, cynicism, and pragmatism the people thought it was vain to serve God. It didn't profit them. They were hypocritical and their faith was empty and pretentious.

The Displeasure of God

It is God's desire to make His name great among the nations. He has high expectations for all of us. His call on our lives is to live as a kingdom of priests, a holy nation (1 Peter 2:9).

A Memorable Principle

Chapter 3 contains the most well-known scripture in the book. It is tucked away in God's confrontation about the unfaithfulness of His people.

Robbery

They took what belonged to God and consumed it on themselves. Many see the biblical mandate of giving 10 percent as antiquated law, but God says refusing to give this is like armed robbery. God says that to be negligent is to steal from Him.

Reciprocation

Notice:

The Plan—Bring your tithe, as an act of worship.
The Place—The church.
The Promise—God will give to you in return (Luke 6:38; 2 Cor. 9:6–7).

Restoration

God will restore the wasted days, weeks, months, and years, as well as the wasted energy, money, and resources. He will forgive yesterday's rebellion and disobedience (Joel 2:12).

A Messianic Promise

The hope of the gospel resides in all the Old Testament books.

His Messenger

Malachi pulls back the drape on this coming incarnation to say in the days that precede His arrival, God's messenger will be sent before the One who is coming to bring redemption (3:1; 4:5).

His Motive

Jesus will provide a vicarious cleansing. Reconciliation will be the order of the day. He will heal our broken relationship with God (1 Peter 3:18) and peace will prevail on a horizontal plane.

THE GOSPEL PROJECT

The Essence of the Gospel

1 Corinthians 15:1–8

Steve Dighton

Introduction

The resurrection of Jesus Christ is the foundational truth of our faith and validation of the promises and claims of our Savior. There are many passages giving testimony of the resurrection—none are more clear and concise than 1 Corinthians 15. We must not overlook or underestimate the critical nature of the resurrection.

A Rightful Reminder (vv. 1–2)

We see the reemphasis of the resurrection and the personal responsibility of the believers.

Clarification

The clarification was relative to the gospel message.

Caution

They were to hold fast to their personal belief in the death and resurrection. This is a warning against a non-saving faith. This disingenuous faith could be because the object of their faith wasn't the resurrected Jesus, but was rules, rituals, and religious externals.

A Reflective Review (vv. 3–4)

Chronicled here we have the summary statement of the glories of the gospel of Jesus Christ.

Personal Experience

Paul reinforced these nonnegotiable components and validated them by his own personal experience. He understood them, embraced them, and had firsthand knowledge, not speculation.

Purposeful Event

Jesus had become the atoning sacrifice for sins by being crucified on a cross. Earlier in the epistle (1:18) we read that the message of the cross is what defines us as believers, as well as empowers us. If you take away the cross, you remove the hope of forgiveness and the promised redemption from God.

Precise Evidence

Paul becomes an apologist mentioning the third triad of the gospel—the resurrection and precise evidence of Jesus' claims. Beginning in Matthew 16, after Peter's confession at Caesarea Philippi, Jesus began to tell His disciples that He would go to Jerusalem, suffer, be killed, and rise again (Matt. 16:21). The resurrection was promised by Christ and personified in Him, and now it is being proclaimed by His body, the church. It is the centerpiece of the Christian faith—the linchpin of all the claims of Jesus. It validates and authenticates His ministry. It assures us that He defeated our last enemy—death—and now offers eternal life to all who believe (Rom. 6:5).

A Ratifying Resurrection (vv. 5–8)

Now Paul gathers the historical evidence surrounding the resurrection.

The Personalities

He first mentioned the people who witnessed the resurrected Christ. He singled out Peter and James then the five hundred (many of whom were still alive twenty-five years later at the writing of the epistle). He mentioned his own fateful encounter with Christ on the road to Damascus (Acts 9). We don't want to forget the other recorded post-resurrection appearances—to Cleopas and the unnamed disciple in Luke 24 or to Mary Magdalene and the women at the tomb.

The Proclamation

The remaining verses emphasize the proclamation regarding the resurrection and the fact that if Christ had not been raised both our claims and our faith have no foundation.

Conclusion

The Gospel Project is about the good news of what Christ has done in bringing salvation to a lost and dying world through the death, burial, and resurrection of Jesus.

THE GOSPEL PROJECT

Christ's Salvation and Our Obligation

Colossians 1:15–29

Steve Dighton

Introduction

Doctrine and duty go together like a ball and glove or salt and pepper. If you want to know someone's theology, look at their life. What they say with their mouth is what they want you to believe about them. What they say with their actions reveals what they believe. In chapter 1 we have the greatest Christological passage in the New Testament. Following that great discourse we see the apostle Paul make the shift from the person of Christ to how His work on the cross affects all mankind.

The Preeminence of Our Lord (vv. 15–20)

Christ is the image (*eikon*) of God. This is where we get our English word *icon*. He is God incarnate—the icon of our worship.

Creation

He is creator and the glue that holds everything together.

Church

He is the head of the church.

Cross

Peace is made available only through His blood.

The Pattern of Our Lives (vv. 21–23)

Paul begins to relate the depravity of mankind.

Past Alienation

He tells of our past—estranged from God because of our evil deeds, our attitudes, and our actions. We are guilty of being hostile in our mind. That's why repentance is critical for salvation. We first think differently, which results in our behavioral change.

Present Reconciliation

The result of our salvation is reconciliation. This happens because God took the initiative—loving us while we were yet sinners (Rom. 5:8). The emphasis here is on the physical body of Jesus and how it was nailed to the cross (1 Peter 2:24). The purpose of this reconciliation is to present us holy, pure, and blameless (*amomos*). This word is used in the LXX in Numbers 6 to speak of sacrificial animals. Christ our sacrifice was sinless and has now vicariously made us sinless (2 Cor. 5:21).

Future Glorification

Now we see the hope of the gospel—the blessed hope of the Lord's return.

The Proclamation of Our Lips (vv. 25–29)

As believers we are entrusted as stewards of the gospel message (1 Cor. 4:1–2). We are to rightfully manage this pearl of great price.

Mystery

The mystery (*musterion*) of the message means: that which was once concealed, now has been revealed. It is the term Paul often used to communicate how the Gentiles have been given the privilege to become a part of the family of God (John 1:11–12).

Mission

The mission was to present believers as mature in Christ. Paul did this by teaching them and warning them of the lies of false teachers, the heresy that was being propagated, angelic worship, ascetic practices, etc.

Might

The labor is to be done with all of our might. The word "labor" (*kopiao*) means to work to the point of exhaustion, striving in the strength of the Lord.

Conclusion

From a prison cell in Rome, Paul declares that while he is locked up he will not be shut up and will continue to share his faith.

THE GOSPEL PROJECT

Advancing the Gospel

Philippians 1:3–10

Steve Dighton

Introduction

The book of Philippians is about the advancement of the gospel. In essence the apostle Paul lays out the Gospel Project for us here, as it was his life to propagate the truth of redemption.

Our Partnership in the Gospel (vv. 3–5)

Paul clearly expresses his gratitude that comes from having a connectedness with like-minded believers. The apostle Paul had made a heart connection with the Macedonian believers. He declared that they had a "Koinonia" in the gospel, meaning they had things in common. So it is with us too; regardless of our differing ethnic, vocational, or educational backgrounds we are all one in Christ, brought together by the work of our Savior.

Prayer

This partnership caused Paul to remembering them in prayer.

Joy

This heart connection also brought Paul much joy. Paul used the word *joy* or *rejoicing* some sixteen times in this short epistle. It is evident that this joy is not because of favorable circumstances since he is writing this from a Roman prison cell. His joy is a by-product of knowing Christ (Phil. 3:10). The church has as its mission this "partnering together" to make the gospel known. Every program, every event, every meeting should be for the sake of the gospel.

The Promise of the Gospel (v. 6)

Paul reminds us of the facts of our salvation.

God Started

The gospel is from God. He began the work in us as believers. It didn't begin because of our initiative; it wasn't because we longed for it—it wasn't even our idea. Instead, God pursued us, He redeemed us, and we love Him because He first loved us.

God Sustained

He sustains His work of redemption to the end—until the day of our Lord Jesus (1 Cor. 1:8).

God Secured

He also secures it—it is God who completes it. This promise puts our confidence totally on Christ and not ourselves.

The Price of the Gospel (v. 7)

Now the apostle, in house arrest and chained to the palace guard, brings to light the sober reminder that there is a price for standing for the gospel.

His Prayers

They were for a continued love for one another. Paul prayed that love would win out in spite of the issues of conflict and strife within the church.

His Priority

Most important to the spread of the gospel was that the believers' lives would be marked by righteousness and goodness.

The Paradox

Paul's imprisonment has helped advance the gospel—not hinder its spread. God has proven once again that all things do work together for good to those who love God and are called according to His purpose (Rom. 8:28).

Conclusion

The gospel message defines our mission as believers. We partner together with other believers in our calling. We rest in the promise that God will complete what He began, and finally, we see that there is a cost in living for Jesus.

THE GOSPEL PROJECT

What It Means to Be "Born Again"

John 3:1–16

Steve Dighton

Introduction

John 3:16 is the gospel in one verse. It tells of God's unconditional love for mankind, the hope of forgiveness and life everlasting. Jesus teaches no one can come into right relationship with God until they are "born again." I am afraid there is much confusion about what it means to be "born again." Some believe it's about infant baptism; that this forgives their original sin problem. Others believe it is about baptismal regeneration of adults. Some believe being born again is not necessary at all. While others believe it's in understanding spiritual truths through Catechism or Confirmation classes. Let's unpack this text of Scripture that sheds divine light on this doctrinal enigma.

A Clandestine Encounter (vv. 1–2)

Nicodemus came at night because of what his colleagues might say. The Pharisees were out to prove Jesus as a fraud, a radical, and a charlatan. He didn't observe the Sabbath and was a friend of sinners. He challenged their rabbinical laws and was deemed a troublemaker.

His Esteem

Nicodemus was a Pharisee, respected in Jewish circles, a member of the Sanhedrin, and one of the richest men in Jerusalem. From a human perspective, he had it all. Even so, he needed what Jesus was promising.

His Emptiness

Something was missing in Nicodemus's soul—this emptiness caused him to reach out to Jesus. His fear caused him to seek the encounter that led to his salvation in the dark of night.

A Clarifying Exchange (vv. 3–15)

Jesus diffuses any notion that Nicodemus might have an upper hand on being a citizen of the kingdom by his position, his power, or his possessions.

The Confusion

Jesus' theme of being "born again" is confusing to Nicodemus. He relates it to a physical birth.

The Clarification

It doesn't matter who you are or what you've done (Matt. 7:13–14). The problem wasn't the acquisition of knowledge, but the application of truth.

His Comparison

Jesus relates the story of the brass serpent from Numbers 21. Jesus surely referred to what the church must do today regarding His preeminence. We need to simply show up, lift Jesus up, keep Him at the epicenter of all we do, and He will draw people to Himself.

A Captivating Explanation (v. 16)

This one verse both clarifies and crystallizes this dialogue. It is the promise of God's redemptive love and the hope of all who will believe.

God's Initiative

There is no one who seeks God. It is God's redeeming love that pursues us (Rom. 5:8).

God's Incarnation

Jesus didn't simply represent God—He was God. He was the Spirit of God in human flesh (John 1:1, 14).

God's Invitation

This matter rests with you. You can be born again and have everlasting life, or you can stay your course of trusting in religion, rituals, or rule-book faith, but these will not get you to God.

Conclusion

Nicodemus is a most religious man, one who had done all the religious rituals, had studied the Torah, taught in the synagogue, but who had a misguided faith. Sometimes people get just enough religion to inoculate them from the real thing.

THE GOSPEL PROJECT

Getting People to Jesus

Mark 2:1–12

Steve Dighton

Introduction

You and I are either compelling people or repelling people by our actions. Our responsibility is to make the gospel attractive. The call of the disciples was, first, to follow Jesus and, second, to fish for men. We have been saved for a purpose. We were created in Christ Jesus to do good works. Surely part of that mission is the responsibility to urgently labor to bring people to our Savior.

His Expected Disruption

When you read the Gospels you will notice Jesus' life was about disruptions. What transpires from these disruptions are some of the greatest personal touches in His ministry.

The Multitude

The popularity of Jesus is growing exponentially (Mark 1:28, 45). This magnetism attracted many then and is still attracting people today.

The Message

This is the Gospel Project. It is the word, the message—not just proclaimed by Jesus, but incarnate in Him. Here, the God-man is telling the God-story.

The Maimed

The man in our story was blessed to have four caring souls who were willing to get him the help he needed. That help was only found in getting him to Jesus.

An Eager Determination

It's rarely easy to get people we care about to Jesus. There are always obstacles, challenges, distractions, and reasons to give up. These men had a compelling commitment and a dedicated determination to help their friend.

Their Concern

They had genuine love for their friend. They were well acquainted with his hurts, pain, and agony.

Their Creativity

It was more than pity that prompted them. It was sacrificial love. It would have been easier to give up, but they made a plan and acted upon it. Our mission is to get people to Jesus any way we can. Every program we have in church serves as a stretcher to get people to Jesus.

Their Certainty

These men were bringing their friend to Jesus because they had a confident faith that Jesus could make all the difference in the crippled man's life.

An Effectual Demonstration

These determined friends got much more than what they had hoped for with their friend. That's the way it is with Jesus (Eph. 3:20).

God's Forgiveness

Jesus emphasized and prioritized the spiritual over the physical. It was a whole lot more important to get this man right with God than it was to get him back on his feet.

God's Favor

This man who did not have the strength to get himself to Jesus would now be able to walk by himself to his house fully justified.

Conclusion

Develop a caring, compassionate heart for others who are in need. Christian love has ears to hear the cries of the hurting and hands to help with their needs.

Develop a fresh passion to live for God. Remember the transforming power of the Lord Jesus Christ.

Bring someone to church with you to hear the gospel.

THE GOSPEL PROJECT

A Final Farewell

Acts 20:17–32

Steve Dighton

Introduction

Charles Schulz, writer of the *Peanuts* comic strip, wrote of the dread we all have of saying farewell. In the childrens movie *Snoopy Come Home*, a despondent Charlie Brown, upon saying good-bye to Snoopy, said, "Why can't we get all the people together in the world that we really like and then just stay together? I guess that wouldn't work. Someone would leave. Someone always leaves. Then we would have to say good-bye. I hate good-byes. You know what I need? I need more hellos."[1]

The apostle Paul finds himself in Acts 20 saying a final good-bye to the elders of Ephesus. These men were close to his heart. He had founded their church and appointed them to oversee the flock in his absence. On his departure He reminded them of what he stood for, what he clearly proclaimed, and how they must continue in these things.

Proven Reputation (vv. 17–23)

This proven reputation was demonstrated in three dimensions of his life.

Serving (v. 19)

The apostle had labored for some time with humility and tears.

Sharing (vv. 20–21)

He reminded them that he stayed tethered to the gospel of grace and that he declared it both in the public arena and from house to house.

Suffering (vv. 22–23)

He proclaimed his determination regardless of the suffering he was going to endure. A proven reputation has many facets, and since Paul brought evidence of his integrity and character, his message was readily received.

Personal Resolve (vv. 24–31)

While the struggles and challenges were trying, Paul would not be deterred from what God had called him to do. We see this personal resolve in three ways.

Perseverence (v. 24)

Paul resolved to finish the course and fulfill the ministry that he had "received" from the Lord. This wasn't Paul's ministry; it belonged to the Lord, and with determination, he would fulfill his calling.

Proclamation (v. 24)

He was not only determined to persevere but was also compelled to preach the gospel of grace that had saved and sanctified him. Paul would write, "Woe is me if I do not preach the gospel!" (1 Cor. 9:16).

Protection (vv. 29–30)

Paul warned them of their need to be protectors of doctrine and the flock. He told them to beware of those who worm their way into the church propagating false doctrine, as any compromise in truth will lead to certain disruption and destruction.

A Passionate Request (v. 32)

Paul prayed a heartfelt benediction for the saints he loved.

Faithfulness

He commended them to the Word of God's grace that would build them up and set them apart.

Future

He assured them of the hope of their future, the inheritance to all who are in Christ Jesus, the future hope of heaven.

Conclusion

This emotionally charged farewell gave Paul another chance to reinforce what he had spent years communicating in Ephesus. First, the message must be modeled to have validity. Second, the message of the gospel of grace must remain as it had been delivered to them. Finally, they must not lose heart as they await the inheritance that comes to all who know the Lord Jesus.

CLOSE ENCOUNTERS

New Age—Old Lies

Genesis 3:1–5

Dave Epstein

Introduction

In Genesis 3 we are confronted with a "close encounter of the third kind"—not an encounter with the living God but rather with Satan, the "god of this world"—the god who rules the *new age with the old lies.*

Up until the 1960s Satan staged a frontal assault on truth. He emphasized a "scientific atheism," which is making a comeback with Richard Dawkins and *The God Delusion* and Christopher Hitchens and *God Is Not Good*; but this is no longer Satan's primary tactic. Now the approach is more subtle, more sophisticated, more "spiritual." Satan loves to talk about "Jesus," God, harmony and peace, brotherhood, unity, light, love, hope, angels, and salvation.

The Greeks laid siege to Troy for ten years with no success. So they built a large wooden horse and apparently sailed away. The Trojans were curious and ignored the warning to "beware of Greeks bearing gifts." Therefore, Troy was captured, the people massacred, and the city burned. Beware of the god of the new age peddling old lies!

Five Lies Satan Loves to Tell

There are five lies Satan loves to tell in Genesis 3:1–5: the first two are meant to critically wound you and the last three will kill you forever.

1. You can't really trust the God of the Bible: His character is suspect.

He is an unfair God. He wants to make the rules and give moral commands and restrict many of your freedoms and privileges (v. 1). "Has God indeed said, 'You shall not eat of every tree of the garden'?" God is so unfair!

He is at best an ignorant and at worst a dishonest God (vv. 2–4). "God has said, 'You shall not eat it, nor shall you touch it lest, you die.' Then the serpent said to the woman, 'You will not surely die.'" Therefore, God is either ignorant and has no idea what He is talking about or He is a liar.

He is a selfish God (v. 5): "For God knows that in the day you eat of it your eyes will be opened, and you will be like God, knowing good and evil." God doesn't want to share His privileges and wisdom and deity with you. He is selfish and wants to keep it all for himself.

2. You can't really trust the Bible either.

If you can't trust the God who claims to have written the Bible, then how can you trust the Bible?

There are so many "uncertainties" in the Bible: "Has God *really* said . . . ?" It's all a matter of opinion. It's all a matter of interpretation. There are so many "contradictions" in the Bible. God says, "You will surely die" and Satan says, "You will not surely die." Who can you trust?

You can't really trust the Bible because of higher criticism and liberal theology: The Bible may *contain* the word of God somewhere, but the Bible *isn't* the word of God. We must first demythologize it, take the supernatural out, and reconstruct it.

You can't really trust the Bible because of Neo-orthodox theology: The Bible may *become* the word of God, but the Bible *isn't* always the word of God—"Has God *really* said . . . ?"

Now, if you have believed these first two lies, your spirit is already critically wounded! The next three lies will kill you forever.

3. There is no such thing as eternal death, final judgment, and hell.

Regardless of what the God of the Bible says, since you can't trust God or His book anyway, "you will not surely die." Haven't you ever heard of *universalism*? Everyone will be okay in the end, because "love wins." A loving God would never judge anybody or send anyone to hell forever. Haven't you ever heard of *reincarnation*? There are plenty of chances to overcome bad karma. God is the God of endless chances, not last chances. Haven't you ever heard of all those *near-death experiences?* What about those feelings of love, peace, joy, and that great light at the end of the tunnel? So forget the sinfulness of man, the holiness of God, and the atonement of Christ. Relax! There is no eternal death, final judgment, or hell.

4. You can be God!

You have the divine nature and life within you; you have just been so ignorant for so long. "For God knows that in the day you eat of it your eyes will be opened, and you will be *like God*, knowing good and evil" (v. 5, emphasis added). Haven't you ever heard of *pantheism*? Haven't you ever heard of *transcendentalism* and the *new age*? All is one, all is god, I am god.

5. There is secret (occult) knowledge available to you, superior to the Bible.

Haven't you ever heard of *Gnosticism*? Secret occult knowledge? "your eyes will be opened ... knowing good and evil ... desirable to make one wise ... then the eyes of both of them were opened" (vv. 5–7). Haven't you ever heard of *fortune telling*, *astrology*, *witchcraft*, *séances*, *crystals*? You can have secret knowledge superior to the Bible.

Conclusion

Do people really believe these lies? All the time! Look at Adam and Eve (vv. 7–10). And the consequences are devastating (vv. 11–24).

The only effective response to Satan's lies is God's truth. The God of the Bible is the only true God and fully trustworthy. Therefore, God's best-selling book *The Bible* is fully trustworthy also. There is eternal death, a final judgment, and a hell to come. We are not God and never can be. Neither can Satan be God. *Secret* knowledge is that which Satan provides and it will kill you. *Certain* knowledge is that which God provides and Jesus Christ will save you.

CLOSE ENCOUNTERS

When God Demands Our Very Best

Genesis 22:1–18

Dave Epstein

Introduction

What kind of God would tell a man to kill his own son? Who could imagine such a thing! There is nothing more precious in this world than the life of a child.

Genesis 12–21 tells us the interesting story of Abraham: how he obeyed the call of God and left his home in Ur of the Chaldees; how God promised him the blessings of the Abrahamic covenant; how Abraham's lineage included Ishmael and Isaac (Isaac being the son of the promise); and how God had ordered the sacrifice of Isaac.

What could God possibly be telling us in this historical passage of Scripture?

When God considers the life of a believer, He wants it all. He demands our very best. He wants all we have to give at whatever the price to us. But He promises a great reward.

A Drama in Three Acts

1. God's incredible test (vv. 1–2)

   Two characteristics of God's test:

   a. It was intentional.

      God doesn't make mistakes. What He does He does on purpose; what He allows He allows for a reason.

   b. It was severe.

      Because God owns us, spirit, soul, and body, He tests us thoroughly.

2. Abraham's amazing obedience (vv. 3–14)
   a. It was immediate (v. 3).
      Such instant obedience is an amazing thing, particularly with such a severe test. I would have expected questions, procrastination, pleas for mercy, and an appeal for reconsideration.
   b. It was worshipful (reverent) (vv. 4–5*a*).
      Abraham understood that obedience to God was an act of worship. God, in this severe test, was inviting Abraham to grow in his ability and commitment to worship the living God.
   c. It was trusting (faithful) (v. 5*b*).
      Abraham trusted that God was a God of His word; that He was a God who would keep His promise (Heb. 11:17–19).
   d. It was literal (vv. 6–10).
      Can you picture yourself literally obeying God in such a matter? If there was ever a time to spiritualize God's word, if there was ever a time for a symbolic, non-literal interpretation and application, surely it was now! Abraham's literal obedience is shocking and disturbing. What is God up to?
   e. It was prophetic (vv. 11–14).
      Abraham's obedience typified and foreshadowed the offering of Jesus Christ two thousand years later. God the Father, instead of requiring men and women to die for their own sins, would provide a perfect sacrifice—the Lamb of God who would take away the sins of the world. Jehovah Jireh—the Lord Himself will provide a sacrifice. God would send His only Son, whom He loved, to be the substitutionary sacrifice.

3. God's awesome reward (vv. 15–18)
   The reward was twofold:

a. Physical blessing: Abraham became the father of many nations.
b. Spiritual blessing: Abraham, through the Jewish people, brought forth the Messiah, who would bless all nations.

Conclusion

Why was Abraham a great man? Because he obeyed God immediately, reverently, faithfully, literally, and prophetically. When we offer God our own sacrificial obedience we, like Abraham, also point people to the Messiah. Our obedience becomes prophetic also. God demands our very best!

CLOSE ENCOUNTERS

Witness Lost

2 Samuel 11:1–12:14

Dave Epstein

Introduction

In his early years David had a genuine, powerful witness for God. He was actually called, by others and even by God Himself, "a man after God's own heart" (1 Sam. 13:13–14; 15:27–29; Acts 13:22).

David had become king over all Judah and Israel in 2 Samuel 5. His early reign was a great success. He even treated Saul and his other enemies with justice and compassion. He transported the ark of God to Jerusalem and received the Davidic covenant in 2 Samuel 7. He defeated all his military opponents in 2 Samuel 8–10 and adopted Mephibosheth, the crippled son of his deceased best friend, Jonathan. Then suddenly, in 2 Samuel 11, we find David committing adultery and murder! Witness lost.

What happened?

Five Major Conclusions Concerning David's Lost Witness

David committed a criminal act (2 Sam. 11:1–5)

Adultery is a sinful act, certainly. But why call it a crime? Because it violates the commandment of God; it breaks His moral law. Nathan asked David in 2 Samuel 12:9, "Why have you despised the commandment of the Lord to do evil in His sight?" Nathan is referring to the Ten Commandments, given by God to Israel through Moses 450 years earlier, and particularly the sixth commandment prohibiting murder and the seventh commandment prohibiting adultery (Ex. 20:13–14).

So it's not enough to understand David as a sinner. If we are to appreciate the lesson of his adultery and murder, we must see him as a criminal, guilty of a capital offense, because that is how God saw him. In this passage we are watching David being arrested, booked, fingerprinted, photographed, picked out of a lineup, and convicted. Notice the progression of this criminal act:

It began with *personal irresponsibility*. Second Samuel 11:1 indicates that the army went to fight the Ammonites, but David remained at Jerusalem. The implication is clear: David was *not* where he should have been.

It was *fueled by lust*. Second Samuel 11:2*b* says, "[David] saw a woman bathing, and the woman was very beautiful to behold." Lust is an overpowering stimulant. James wrote in James 1:15 that "when lust has conceived, it gives birth to sin; and when sin is accomplished, it brings forth death" (NASB).

It was *encouraged by abusive authority*. Second Samuel 11:3–4*a* says that "David sent and inquired ... and took her ... and ... lay with her" (NASB). David was guilty of the worst kind of sexual harassment: he abused his authority as king of Israel.

It resulted in *an illegitimate pregnancy*. Second Samuel 11:5 says, "The woman conceived and sent word to David, saying, 'I am pregnant'" (NIV).

David's criminal act encouraged a cowardly cover-up (2 Sam. 11:6–25)

Initially, David tried to cover his adulterous tracks with a clever alibi. In verses 6–13 he tries to get Bathsheba and her husband together so that everyone will assume that the child is a result of their sexual union, but Uriah's character and integrity frustrated David's attempt to create an alibi: "Shall I then go to my house and eat and drink, and to lie with my wife?" (v. 11*b*).

Eventually David got desperate. He decided to have Uriah murdered as a cover-up for adultery: "Set Uriah in the forefront of the hottest battle, and retreat from him, that he may be struck down and die" (v. 15).

David's cover-up did not prevent his criminal conviction (2 Sam. 11:26–12:9)

It was obvious a crime had been committed: Bathsheba was in mourning; her husband was dead (v. 26)! "The thing that David had done was evil in the sight of the LORD" (v. 27 NASB).

The Lord therefore initiated high court proceedings. He sent Nathan, a godly prophet, to David in 2 Samuel 12:1. Nathan shared a parable of selfishness and abuse of authority by a rich man who abused a poor man, and then Nathan watched as David's hypocritical self-righteousness rose to its full indignation in 2 Samuel 12:5: "As the LORD lives, the man who has done this shall surely die." Then Nathan said, "You are the man!" You, David, are the criminal, the adulterer and the murderer! You are the one guilty of death. (You have said it yourself.) "You have despised the commandment of the Lord and done evil in His sight" (see v. 9).

The most ingenious cover-up will never fool an all-knowing God.

David's conviction resulted in a criminal confession (2 Sam. 12:13)

"I have sinned against the LORD" (v. 13). It was a tardy confession, after the fact of discovery and conviction, but a sincere confession nevertheless. And in God's eyes, a sincere confession, however late, is always preferable to no confession at all. So Nathan can say in verse 13: "The LORD also has put away your sin; you shall not die!"

It is never too late to confess sin and repent.

David's confession did not stop the criminal consequences (2 Sam. 12:10–12, 14)

"The sword shall never depart from your house" (v. 10). Second Samuel 18 describes the murder of David's own son Absalom and records David's grief: "Oh my son Absalom, my son, my son Absalom—if only I had died in your place! Oh Absalom, my son, my son" (v. 33).

The Lord says, "You sinned secretly, but I will punish you publically" (see 2 Sam. 12:12). So Absalom, before he died, had sexual relations with his father's concubines, thus publically humiliating David (2 Sam. 16:20–23).

"However, because by this deed you have given great occasion to the enemies of the LORD to blaspheme, the child also who is born to you shall surely die" (2 Sam. 12:14).

Conclusion

Crimes, even confessed crimes, have horrible consequences. Witness lost! But God would use all of David's guilt and grief to turn his heart back again: "Have mercy upon me, O God, according to Your lovingkindness; according to the multitude of Your tender mercies, blot out my transgressions ... *then I will teach transgressors Your ways, and sinners shall be converted to You*" (Ps. 51:1, 13, emphasis added).

Witness found!

CLOSE ENCOUNTERS

Witness Found

Psalm 51

Dave Epstein

Introduction

Is there life for the believer after blatant sin? Is there a way back to God after willful disobedience? Once your witness is lost, can you ever find it again?

Psalm 51 is David's personal prayer response to his crimes of adultery and murder. It is an intimate self-portrait of "a man after [God's] own heart" (Acts 13:22) as he honestly faces the challenge of rebuilding his severely wounded relationship with God. Perhaps for some of us it is our task as well.

Three Important Steps in Reestablishing Your Witness and Relationship with God

1. A sinful believer's first order of business is **repentance** (vv. 1–6).

   God wants us to literally "change our minds." He wants us to begin to think differently about our relationship to Him and the people around us. He wants us to make a 180 degree turn in our understanding of how we are to live the Christian life.

   a. Notice first, that repentance depends upon a merciful and loving God—God can be appealed to (vv. 1–2).

   b. Notice second, that repentance requires confession—God has been offended (vv. 3–4).

   David tells us, "Against You, You only, have I sinned, and done this evil in Your sight" (v. 4). David abused his authority and pressured Bathsheba into adultery; he had Uriah murdered and now he says he had sinned *only* against God. Sin literally means to "miss the mark" of God's perfect, holy standard. To sin is to disobey the law of God, which is a reflection of His nature. Therefore, every human sin is ultimately sin against God.

   c. Notice third, that repentance produces a changed life—God expects "unnatural" behavior (vv. 5–6). Truthfulness is "unnatural" because by nature "I was brought forth in iniquity and in sin my mother conceived me."

2. A loving God's first order of business is **renewal** (vv. 7–11).

   When God sees our genuine repentance, He initiates for us personal renewal. He makes our life with Him fresh and new. He renews our relationship.

   a. Notice first, renewal results in a sense of cleanliness (v. 7).
   b. Notice second, renewal results in joy at sins forgiven (vv. 8–9).
   c. Notice third, renewal results in assurance concerning our relationship with God (vv. 10–11). Unlike the New Testament Christian, who is sealed with the Holy Spirit permanently, the Old Testament saints could lose their privilege of the presence of the Holy Spirit. Like us, however, they *could* lose the *assurance* of their salvation because of unrepentant hearts and unconfessed sin.

3. Finally, a renewed life always produces a restored testimony (vv. 12–19).
   a. First, David mentions his restored witness (vv. 12–13).
   b. Second, David mentions his restored worship (vv. 14–19).

   Restored worship depends upon a renewed heart and spirit—"the sacrifices of God are a broken spirit, a broken and a contrite heart" (v. 17).

Conclusion

Ultimately, God doesn't want my religious service and sacrifice—He wants my obedience! There is no sin too great for God to forgive. There is life after sin if we repent.

Witness lost—witness found!

CLOSE ENCOUNTERS

The Silence of the Lamb

Isaiah 53

Dave Epstein

Question

What if you were condemned to death for a crime you did not commit? Would you go quietly?

Introduction

Twenty-seven hundred years ago the Jewish prophet Isaiah predicted that a child would be born who would be known as the servant of the Lord (Isa. 42:1–9).

1. This child would be born to a virgin (Isa. 7:14).
2. This child would one day become the king of the world (Isa. 9:6).
3. But between His birth and His world government, this child would grow up, die a horrible death, and then rise from the dead. Isaiah refers to the death of this innocent servant of God as *the silence of the Lamb* (Isa. 53:7).

Three Reasons the Lamb Was Silent

Why would an innocent person go quietly and silently to his death? The answer is mind-boggling:

1. Because the Messiah *trusted His executioner* (vv. 4, 6, 10) (cf. John 10:17–18; Heb. 10:1–14).
   a. "Smitten by God, and afflicted … the LORD has laid on Him the iniquity of us all. … Yet it pleased the LORD to bruise Him, He has put Him to grief" (Isa. 53:4, 6, 10).
   b. And you thought all along that the Christ killer was one of the usual suspects: the Jews, the Romans, Judas, the

human race, or Satan!

c. The shocking truth is that the Christ killer is God!
d. "Father, 'into *Your hands* I commit My spirit'" (Luke 23:46, emphasis added).

2. Because the Messiah *loved the real criminals*, the sinful, guilty, condemned people, like you and me. Therefore, because of His love for us, He became:
   a. Our *substitute* (vv. 4–5)
   b. Our *scapegoat* (vv. 6–7)
   c. Our *sin offering* (v. 10)
   d. Our *sin bearer* (vv. 11–12)
   e. Our *intercessor, advocate* (v. 12)

3. Because the Messiah had been *given specific promises* that He knew God would keep:
   a. He would not die in vain.
      "He shall see His seed. . . . By His knowledge My righteous Servant shall justify many" (vv. 10–11). His death would be effective in redeeming His people (cf. John 10:11, 27–30).
   b. His death would not last forever.
      "He shall prolong His days . . ." (v. 10). (cf. John 10:17–18)
   c. His death would please God.
      "The pleasure of the Lord shall prosper in His hand" (v. 10).

Conclusion

1. Did Jesus really consider Himself to be this Lamb of God? In Luke 22:37 He directly quotes Isaiah 53 in speaking of Himself: "For I say to you that this which is written must still be accomplished in Me: 'And he was numbered with the transgressors.' For these things concerning Me have an end [a fulfillment]."
2. Did Jesus die in vain? Ask the thief on the cross (Luke 23:39–43).

3. Did the death of Jesus please God? It is finished—mission accomplished (Luke 23:39–43; John 19:30)!
4. Did Jesus die forever (Luke 24:1–8)?
5. Does His death continue to change lives today? Ask the Ethiopian eunuch (Acts 8:26–39). "He was led as a sheep to the slaughter, and as a sheep before its shearers is silent, so He opened not His mouth" (Isa. 53:7–8). *The silence of the Lamb . . .*

CLOSE ENCOUNTERS

For Such a Time As This . . .

Esther 4:1–17

Dave Epstein

Introduction

Do you believe in destiny? Jesus was destined for the cross; David for the throne in Israel; Daniel to speak truth to power in Babylon; Joshua to take his people into the promised land; Mary to bear the Messiah and Esther to deliver the Jewish people from a holocaust—a fifth-century BC Persian final solution to the Jewish problem.

Why was Esther successful in fulfilling her destiny, and how can her example teach me about God's destiny for my life?

Four Elements in God's Destiny for Esther

1. First, God revealed Esther's destiny through a *gigantic problem* (vv. 1–9).
   a. A man named Haman had promised to pay into the king's treasuries to destroy the Jews (v. 7*b*).
   b. We are all too familiar with the twentieth-century Jewish Holocaust: the Nazi "final solution."
   c. When you read Esther 1–3, you find that Esther was Jewish; her Jewish name was Hadassah. She had won the most famous beauty pageant in history, the Miss Persia Pageant, and had become the wife and queen of King Ahaseurus, the ruler of the Persian empire. His Greek name was Xerxes, and he ruled from India to Ethiopia! His empire was the largest and strongest the world had ever known.
   d. Mordecai was Esther's cousin, but had raised her as

his own daughter. He warned her to keep her Jewish identity secret. Haman, an official of the king, hated Mordecai but couldn't touch him because the king favored him. Therefore, the Scripture says in Esther 3:6, "Instead, Haman sought to destroy all the Jews who were throughout the whole kingdom of Ahaseurus, the people of Mordecai."

   e. So Queen Esther's people, the Jews, now faced a holocaust; and out of the crucible of this overwhelming problem, Esther would embrace her destiny.

2. Second, Esther threatened her destiny with a *protective excuse* (vv. 10–12).
   a. Self -defense, self-preservation, and self-protection are highly developed and deeply rooted responses, not easily challenged and not easily resisted.
   b. It's risky to serve God in a world full of hate and danger, but discovering God's destiny is a high-risk adventure!

3. Third, Mordecai clarified Esther's destiny with an *unacceptable alternative* (vv. 13–14).
   a. Our excuses will not prevent the judgment of God.
   b. Our excuses will not prevent the will of God from being accomplished. He will simply use someone else who is willing—and they will receive the blessing!

4. Finally, Esther fulfilled her destiny by *sacrificial obedience* (vv. 15–17).
   a. Esther responds, "if I perish, I perish."
   b. What she means is, "I have seen the enormous problem, I have tried out my excuses, I've considered the unacceptable second-rate alternative, and now I am ready to obey God."

Conclusion

The results of Esther's obedience to God were profound:

a. The Jewish people were rescued and revived (Est. 9:15–17).
b. Justice was served—Haman and his ten sons were hanged (Est. 7:10; 9:14).
c. Many Persians believed in the God of the Jews (Est. 8:17).
d. Mordecai was honored and left a lasting legacy (Est. 8:15; 9:4; 10:2–3).
e. The Feast of Purim was established (Est. 9:18–32).
f. Esther fulfilled her destiny.

CLOSE ENCOUNTERS

Found and Lost?

John 10:11–30

Dave Epstein

Introduction

Everyone and everything we love and value in life can be lost in a heartbeat! We lose our loved ones, friends, marriages, careers, health, and even our lives. But can we lose our salvation? Can we lose God's forgiveness? Can we lose God's love?

Our culture loves the hymn "Amazing Grace," even though it refers to us as wretches—because grace remains appealing:

> Amazing grace, how sweet the sound
> That saved a wretch like me
> I once was lost but now I'm found
> Was blind but now I see

Can I be lost, then found, then lost again? Can I be blind, then see, then be blind again? Many genuine and loving believers in Christ say yes—but what does Jesus say?

In John 10, Jesus teaches powerfully and unequivocally that God's love for His people is forever. Why?

Three Reasons God's Love Is Forever

1. The death of Jesus was not in vain (vv. 11, 27–28*a*).

   Jesus did not die for nothing! The death of Jesus accomplished atonement, reconciliation, redemption and salvation.

   a. If you believe that genuine Christians can lose their salvation, then you believe it is possible that *no one will be saved*, that all will be lost and that Jesus died in vain—for nothing!

b. But the Bible declares that Jesus' death was not in vain. It was effective in bringing salvation to His sheep (John 6:35–40, 51).

c. According to John 10 the death of Jesus was:

   I. Faithful (vv. 12–14)

   II. Selfless (v. 15)

   III. Inclusive (v. 16)

   IV. Voluntary (vv. 17–18)

d. His death continues to cause controversy (vv. 19–24).

e. But Jesus declares that His death was not in vain (vv. 25–30).

f. I say this reverently: Jesus did not die praying, "Father, I hope this works!" He declared, "It is finished" [mission accomplished] (John 19:30).

2. The promise of Jesus is not in doubt (v. 28*b*).

   a. "And they shall *never perish.*" How strong is this promise? In biblical Greek the strongest negative is called emphatic negation, which is used here. What Jesus means is that they shall by *no means, under any circumstances, ever perish.*

   b. If you believe that genuine Christians can lose their salvation and perish, then you believe that Jesus makes promises He does not keep. But His promise is not in doubt—they shall *never* perish (Rom. 8:1; Eph. 1:3–14; Phil. 1:6; Heb. 10:17–18; 1 John 5:13).

3. The power of Jesus is not in question (vv. 28*c*–30).

   a. "Neither shall anyone snatch them out of my hand."

   b. The Father has given the believers to the Son—we are the gift of the Father to the Son (John 6:37).

   c. The Son has purchased the believers for the Father—we are the gift of the Son to the Father (Rev. 5:9).

d. This is a two-fisted salvation!

e. Salvation is not just a gift that God gives to us, which is wonderful enough, but we are a gift exchanged between the Father and the Son. Salvation is not just something that belongs to us. But more importantly, we belong to Him. When will the Father take back the gift He gave to His Son? When will the Son take back the gift He gave to His Father? NEVER!

f. If you believe that genuine Christians can lose their salvation, then you believe that God's power is *limited.* But God's power is not in question (Rom. 8:28–39).

Conclusion

Jesus didn't die on Good Friday so the whole world *might* get saved —only to get lost again. Jesus died on Good Friday so the whole church *would* get saved—and stay saved forever. There is no *maybe*, or *hope so*, or *might be* in the death of Jesus—only *yes* and *know so* and *shall be.*

CLOSE ENCOUNTERS

The Untouchables

John 4:3–29

Dave Epstein

Introduction

God has a very eclectic taste in people. He is not prejudiced. He is not a respecter of persons. God loves all kinds of people.

Two people could not have been more different than Nicodemus and the Samaritan woman. In the world's eyes:

- He was a "somebody" (a Pharisee) and she was a "nobody."
- He was a man and she was a woman.
- He was orthodox (a Jew) and she was heterodox (a Samaritan).
- He was moral and she was immoral.
- He was a scholar and she was uneducated.
- He was a "churchman" and she was a woman of the world.

But in God's eyes, what they had in common was far more important than their differences:

- They both thought they were spiritually okay.
- But they were both spiritually dead and blind (lost).
- Therefore, they both needed the Savior of the world.
- And God loved them both.

And that's why after Jesus had spent some time with Nicodemus in Jerusalem and had told him, "God so loved the world that He gave His only begotten Son, that whoever believes in Him should not perish but have everlasting life. . . . He left Judea and departed again to Galilee. But He *needed to go* through Samaria" (John 3:16; 4:3–4, emphasis added).

Why? It was not a geographical necessity. Most Jews went east of the Jordan through Perea because they didn't want to have any contact with the Samaritans. It would make them ceremonially unclean. They also knew they would receive no hospitality from the Samaritans. Then why did Jesus need to go through Samaria? Because it was a moral necessity—a spiritual necessity. He wanted to love the *un-people* (vv. 5–7*a*).

The Samaritans were descendants of the intermarriage between the Assyrians and the Jews after the eighth-century BC Assyrian captivity. They were a mixed race, semi-orthodox plus cultic/pagan religious elements with their temple on Mount Gerizim. They were considered by the Jews to be racially, ethnically, culturally, and spiritually inferior—the *un-people*, uncool, unpopular, the *untouchables*.

How Did Jesus Reach the *Un-people*?

1. He did the *unthinkable* (vv. 7–15).
   a. Jesus loved her without prejudice (vv. 7–9).
   b. Jesus offered her the same gospel He offered Nicodemus (vv. 10–15).
2. He mentioned the *unmentionable* (vv. 16–18).
3. He touched the *untouchables* (vv. 19–29).

Some commentators believe the woman tried to change the subject because she was uncomfortable dealing with her sin—and they may be right; but I believe that in Jesus she had found a man she could trust to answer the questions about God that she had all her life. She was seeking God in her own way—but more importantly, God was seeking her.

Conclusion

You may have been treated like an un-person, an untouchable—you need to forgive. You may be treating others as an un-person, an untouchable—you need to repent and ask forgiveness. You may see yourself as an un-person, an untouchable, beyond the love and grace of God. Don't believe it! It's a lie. Receive His love.

CLOSE ENCOUNTERS

Even If . . .

Luke 16:19–31

Dave Epstein

Introduction

"For what profit is it to a man if he gains the whole world, and loses his own soul? Or what will a man give in exchange for his soul?" (Matt. 16:26).

Now let's listen to a story about two men: one who had nothing and found his soul and another who had everything and lost his soul.

Three Reasons Why Hell Is Hell (and Why You Don't Want to Go There)

In Luke 16:19, Jesus talks about a rich man. He doesn't name him, but it's possible he was one of the powerful religious leaders of that day. During the time of Jesus, wealth was often equated with righteousness. Wealth was a clear evidence of God's blessing upon you, God's favor. Clearly, if you were wealthy, you deserved heaven when you died, because God was with you. Can you imagine anyone believing that today? Wait a minute—that's exactly what we believe today. Not much has changed, and the worst offenders, the greatest Pharisees, are often the Christians! Turn on your TV (or not)! Welcome to the prosperity gospel. Welcome to the health-and-wealth gospel. Welcome to the name-it-and-claim-it gospel. Welcome to a Christianity where God is the cosmic bell hop and with the snap of my fingers will make me healthy, wealthy, and wise. (Well, two out of three ain't bad.)And Jesus was a man of sorrows and acquainted with grief with no place to lay His head.

In Luke 16:20–21, Jesus mentions a poor man, named Lazarus who was homeless, was hungry, and had lousy health care. Lazarus died and went to Abraham's side—he went to heaven, the place of the departed righteous (v. 22*a*).

The rich man also died and went to hell (Hades in Greek and Sheol in Hebrew). His body was buried and not yet raised for the final judgment (Rev. 20:11–15). In this experience of hell, his spirit/soul, which he had lost, which he had forfeited, was in agony (vv. 22*b*–24). This was the anguish of the soul. This was spiritual, mental, psychological, and emotional despair (the dark night of the soul).

What is the reason for such agony of soul? Because in hell:

1. You can never forget (v. 25).
    a. You *must remember* everything.
    b. You can never forget the bad choices, destructive words and actions, selfishness, lack of concern for others, greed and covetousness, lack of empathy, idolatry, and moral rebellion against a holy God.
2. You can never leave (v. 26).
    a. The gulf is fixed; it's unbridgeable. No crossing over. No one can go from heaven to hell—even on a rescue mission—and no one can escape from hell to heaven.
    b. There is no more freedom, no appeals, no second chances, no purgatory, no parole, no more hope, no more grace and mercy, just despair.
3. You can never make a difference again (vv. 27–28).
    a. Clearly the rich man loved his brothers but was now powerless to help them.
    b. In hell, you can never act on a good impulse again; you can never change your world; you can never matter.

Conclusion (vv. 29–31)

Abraham's answer is: let your brothers hear the word of God. And sadly, but unsurprisingly, the rich man's answer is: "No, father Abraham; but if someone goes to them from the dead, they will repent" (v. 30 NASB). Someone did, and we still don't!

"If they do not listen to Moses and the Prophets, they will not be persuaded even if someone rises from the dead" (v. 31 NASB).

CLOSE ENCOUNTERS

Burning Hearts

Luke 24:13–32

Dave Epstein

Introduction

These two disciples began their journey from Jerusalem to Emmaus with "sad hearts" in verse 17: "They walked and were sad." Why?

Because they were losing hope. They were believers in the God of Israel, they were followers of Jesus Christ, but because they had not yet experienced the reality and power of His resurrection, they had become discouraged, saddened, and fearful. They were in need of personal, spiritual revival.

The Emmaus road was a *revival meeting*, and it didn't happen by chance. Certain things had to happen for revival to break out. When Cleopas and his friend began their seven-mile, three-hour journey, they were at one end of a maze that said *despair.* When they emerged at the other end of the maze, they were men with *burning hearts.* What happened?

Five Steps to Revival

1. They had a *serious conversation* about Jesus Christ (vv. 13–16).
   a. Jesus was the focus of their discussion. They talked about His teaching, His ministry, His death, and His promised resurrection. It's possible that they saw Him crucified—but they hadn't seen Him raised.
   b. Why do you think Jesus restrained them from knowing it was Him? He could have revealed Himself and "presto"—instant revival. But Jesus was clearly interested in more than the *product of revival*; He wanted to teach them how to draw near to Him, the *process of revival.*

2. They declared some *serious convictions* about Jesus Christ (vv. 17–20).
   a. They didn't know everything, but they knew something. And what they knew about Jesus, they shared with this "stranger."
   b. The knowledge they had, they clung to for dear life.

3. They shared some *serious concerns* with Jesus Christ (vv. 21–24).
   a. They were *hoping* that Jesus would redeem Israel, but this was the third day and still no Jesus!
   b. They were *hoping* that the reports from their friends meant that He was risen—but still no Jesus.

4. They accepted some *serious criticism* from Jesus Christ (vv. 25–26).
   a. The Lord loves us so much that He tells us the hard truth: you're foolish sometimes, you're unbelieving sometimes, and your heart is very slow to respond.
   b. You're ignorant of my word. Don't you understand God's awesome purpose of glorifying Himself by His incredible plan of redemption—the *suffering* of Good Friday and the *glory* of Easter Sunday?
   c. I have some personal constructive criticism to make—will you receive it?

5. They received some *serious Bible teaching* from Jesus Christ (v. 27).
   a. The process of their revival continued with a serious study of the Word of God—"beginning at Moses . . . and all the prophets."
   b. Jesus, the greatest teacher of all time, taught them from the greatest book ever written about the greatest subject ever considered: Himself.

Conclusion

How will you know if you have had an Emmaus road experience and been revived?

1. You will be encouraged, comforted, and strengthened in the Lord and His word (vv. 28–32). "Did not our heart burn within us while He talked with us on the road, and while He opened the Scriptures to us."
2. You will have a greater passion and power in your witness (vv. 33–49).
3. You will have an increased joy and hunger to worship God in fellowship with other believers (vv. 50–53).

CLOSE ENCOUNTERS

Working 9 to 5

Colossians 3:22–25

Dave Epstein

Introduction

Does God really care about my work? And what does it take to please Him? To understand this passage we must appreciate the context, both general and specific.

The general context is that God never originally intended our work to be such an ordeal. Adam began his life as a landscaper in a beautiful untroubled setting (Gen. 2:8, 15). Then Adam and Eve sinned and the consequences were cataclysmic (Gen. 3:17–19). The general context is human sin and its ongoing consequences.

The specific, immediate context is the book of Colossians. The theme of this profound epistle is stated powerfully in Colossians 1:18: "And He [Jesus Christ] is the head of the body, the church, who is the beginning, the firstborn from the dead, that in all things He might have preeminence"—and that includes the way we work.

Two Essential Attitudes

Notice in this eye-opening passage of scripture *two essential attitudes* for the Christian worker:

1. A commitment to *sincere obedience* (v. 22).
    a. Paul is telling those of us who spend as much as half our waking lives working for someone else to obey our bosses in everything pertaining to the work we do (excluding of course sinful actions).
    b. Notice the motives for our obedience:

i. The wrong motive: "not with eye service, as men-pleasers."
That is, not as hypocrites who only obey while the boss is watching, to impress the boss and to curry the favor of the boss for personal gain and advantage.

ii. The right motive: "but in sincerity of heart, fearing God."
Christian employees are not to act deceitfully, hypocritically—rather we are to obey sincerely, honestly, with integrity, God pleasers, fearing God.

2. A commitment to *enthusiastic hard work* (vv. 23–24).
   a. Notice the two great truths the Lord uses to motivate us to diligence and enthusiasm in our work:
      i. My reward as a Christian is secure: "knowing that from the Lord you will receive the reward of the inheritance" (cf. 1 Peter 1:4).
      The greatest part of the inheritance is to fellowship with Jesus Christ face to face, to share His glory and to reflect His character (cf. 1 John 3:2).
      ii. Jesus Christ is Lord: "for you serve *the Lord Christ*." This is the only use of the phrase "the Lord Christ" in the Bible. It is Him whom we serve as we do our work day by day. Such knowledge of Christ can revolutionize our working lives!

Conclusion

In the modern history of Europe, 1848 was the "Year of Revolution." It was also the year that a man who had been greatly influenced by the gospel, but who had eventually rejected it, a man named Karl Marx, published the revolutionary classic *The Communist Manifesto*. His hero was the working man, the "have nots", and his dream was a "dictatorship of the proletariat," a "classless society"—a true workers revolution. He ended his manifesto with the words, "Working men of the world—UNITE!"

But Marx died. His vision was never realized—even today his concept of revolution is normally encouraged through the barrel of a gun! And much of communism is already collapsing under the weight of its own spiritual, philosophical, and moral bankruptcy.

But the Lord says a true revolution is still possible in the work place today, but it will not be a revolution founded on materialism, atheism, and a corrupt view of history—rather, it will be the revolutionary behavior of men and women motivated by the lordship of Christ—"for we serve *the Lord Christ*."

We differ in one insignificant way: we all work at different jobs. But we are united in one very significant common purpose as believers—to glorify Christ in our work and to be full-time workers by the commitments that we make and the attitudes we display. We will also stand one day, each of us, employees and employers, before the judgment seat of Christ and give a serious account of the life we lived since we trusted Christ—even our life at work. "But he who does wrong will be repaid for what he has done, and there is no partiality. Masters, give your bondservants what is just and fair, knowing that you also have a Master in heaven" (Col. 3:25–4:1).

God holds employers accountable for the way they treat their employees. Do they treat their workers justly? Do they evaluate them fairly? Are they motivated by power and greed and prejudice—or by God's love and concern for their fellow human beings? The only true boss is the Master in heaven!

So let's listen to our awesome Lord, the "head of the church," and let's give Him first place in everything—even in the workplace. "And whatever you do, do it heartily, as to the Lord and not to men."

CLOSE ENCOUNTERS

The Battleground of Christian Liberty

Romans 14:1–23

Dave Epstein

Introduction

There is a bitter civil war raging in the church of Jesus Christ. The issue here is not the freedom of Southern slaves and the unity of a nation, but rather the liberty of individual Christians and the unity of the church of Jesus Christ.

The context of Romans 14 is very important. Beginning in chapter 12, Paul gets very practical. He talks about how we owe God our lives and service because of the grace given to us in chapters 1–11. So he urges us to be transformed in our attitudes, relationships, and behavior through a renewed mind. He especially emphasizes the body life of the church and the way we treat one another as Christians. In chapter 14 Paul emphasizes *two major principles* of Christian liberty.

Two Major Principles of Christian Liberty

Stop Judging One Another—Let Freedom Ring (v. 1–13a).

Paul is concerned about the effects of a judgmental attitude on Christian freedom ("Therefore let us not judge one another anymore." [v. 13*a*]). Notice two major reasons for our judgmental attitude:

First, we are self-righteous by nature. "Receive one who is weak in the faith, but not to *dispute* over doubtful things" (v. 1). We dispute so quickly and we argue so readily! Our goal for younger Christians should be to see them grow in Christlikeness, not to see them conformed to our personal image. And yet, second, by nature we want to control and conform them to our personal attitudes, values and behaviors. There is always a *stronger and weaker brother*—this also encourages judgment.

"For one believes he may eat *all things*, but he who is weak eats only vegetables" (v. 2). (Some are more free than others.) So the situation is ripe for bad attitudes to develop: the believer with liberty despising his weaker brother—the weaker brother judging his stronger brother. Notice God's case against this judgmental attitude.

God is the *Savior* of every believer. "Let not him who eats despise him who does not eat, and let not him who does not eat judge him who eats; *for God has received him*" (v. 3, emphasis added). Thank God for mercy!

God is the *High Priest* of every believer. So the question becomes in verse 4: "Who are you to judge another's servant? To his own master he stands or falls. Indeed he will be made to stand, for *God is able to make him stand*" (emphasis added). Christians are going to disagree at times about everything except for salvation by faith in Christ alone. Paul said in verse 5, "One person esteems one day above another; another esteems every day alike." So what is the answer? "Let each be fully convinced in his own mind." God is the *Lord* of every believer. None of us lives to himself (v. 7*a*). There is only one Lord and we all belong to Him. Dead or alive—we are His (v. 8). That's why Jesus Christ died (and rose again) to become Lord of all (v. 9)! So the question becomes in verse 10: "But why do you judge your brother? Or why do you show contempt for your brother?"

God is the *judge* of every believer. "For we shall all stand before the judgment seat of Christ" (v. 10*b*). "So then each of us shall give account of himself to God" (v. 12). "Therefore let us not judge one another anymore" (v. 13*a*).

Stop Undermining One Another—Let Love Reign (vv. 13*b*–21).

It is not enough for a believer to exercise liberty; that liberty must be exercised responsibly in love. "Rather, resolve this, not to put a stumbling block or a cause to fall in our brother's way" (v. 13). Let's not be the cause of sin in a fellow believer's life. Notice two reasons for undermining behavior:

We are *selfish* by nature. Just as self-righteousness encourages a judgmental attitude, selfishness encourages unloving behavior towards our weaker brothers and sisters. It's as if we are saying, "We are free and we are going to enjoy our freedom, regardless of what anyone else thinks and regardless of who gets hurt."

We believers always seem to differ about what *is* and what *is not* acceptable (v. 14). The issue in Paul's time was *food*. Today the issues are more numerous and often more complicated, but the message is still the same: those activities not condemned by Scripture are areas of liberty, but there will always be differences of opinion. So we must look after one another. We are our brother's keeper. Notice God's case against undermining behavior: such behavior *hinders love* (v. 15); such behavior *hinders our testimony* (vv. 16–19); such behavior is *harmful to the work of God* (vv. 20–21).

Conclusion

The issue of Christian liberty is a war zone. We are self-righteous by nature—that's why we judge and despise one another. We are very willing to spoil everyone else's fun. We are also selfish by nature—that's why we hurt and undermine one another. We are very willing to have fun at everyone else's expense. The rule is: liberty must be allowed. The qualification is: liberty must be exercised in love.

Do you have faith to do what you are doing? Then go for it! Paul concludes in verse 22 that "happy is he who does not condemn himself in what he approves." Do you lack faith to do what you desire? Hold off! The spiritual warning light is on—don't do it! "Whatever is not faith is sin" (v. 23).

Let freedom ring—let love reign!

CLOSE ENCOUNTERS

Comfort One Another

1 Thessalonians 4:13–18

Dave Epstein

Introduction

Prophetic truth has a practical purpose: to convict the hearts of unbelievers; to encourage holiness in Christians; and to give hope and comfort to believers in the time of death. "Comfort one another with these words" (1 Thess. 4:18).

Paul wrote this letter to encourage Christians to live sanctified lives in light of the imminent return of Jesus Christ. Every chapter of this epistle ends with the promise of Jesus Christ's soon return. Then, in 4:13–18, the apostle Paul meets their very special need: he brings comfort to those believers whose Christian loved ones had died by informing them about the present circumstances and the future hope of departed Christians.

Hope and Comfort

1. Notice first, his *word of warning*—ignorance of death breeds hopelessness (v. 13).
   a. The one true God, who is infinite and eternal, who knows the end from the beginning, He wants to enlighten us about death! (We don't have to be ignorant anymore.)
   b. As believers, we do grieve and sorrow; and the more we love, the more it hurts. But we don't have to sorrow, to grieve, to be in pain, to be in distress as others with bad information and no relationship with God, who have no genuine hope.

2. Notice second, his *word of instruction*—the gospel legitimizes hope (vv. 14–17).
    a. The *reality* of the gospel: "if we believe that Jesus died and rose again." Of course we do! God says it and history confirms it. "Why do you seek the living among the dead? He is not here, but is risen" (Luke 24:5–6).
    b. The *return* of Jesus with the saints. "Even so God will bring with Him those who sleep in Jesus" (1 Thess. 4:14). The spirits of departed believers will return with Jesus.
    c. The *resurrection* of the bodies of departed saints. "The dead in Christ will rise first" (1 Thess. 4:16). Every Christian who has died since the time of Christ until the very moment He comes for His church will be resurrected. It doesn't matter what condition that body is in; it will be raised perfect and whole, from the dead.
    d. The *rapture* of living believers. "Then we who are alive and remain shall be caught up together with them in the clouds to meet the Lord in the air" (1 Thess. 4:17). When Jesus comes, the living believers will be raptured after the departed believers have been resurrected. The Lord is stressing the position of honor for those who have "died in Jesus." This order underscores the truth that "precious in the sight of the LORD is the death of His saints" (Ps. 116:15).
    e. The *reunion* of believers. "Together *with them* in the clouds to meet the Lord in the air. And thus *we* [all the saints] shall always be with the Lord" (1 Thess. 4:17, emphasis added). We will see our departed loved ones again; we will know them; we will be with Christ together and worship God together—forever! You can count on it.

3. Notice, finally, his *word of encouragement.* Future hope produces present comfort. "Therefore comfort one another with these words" (1 Thess. 4:18).

Conclusion

Christian hope has an immediate, practical benefit: it brings comfort to us *now*. But notice, this ministry of comfort is a ministry we have for *one another*, and it's based on sharing the truth (these words). There is no substitute for truth.

GROWING IN GRACE

Eight Principles for Sacrificial Giving

Exodus 35–36

J. D. Greear, Ph.D.

Introduction

Exodus 35–36 records one of the most generous offerings in history. This offering shows us eight principles of sacrificial giving.

1. The people gave in response to the initiative of God.

Clearly God was leading His people. The offering was not their idea. God was doing something through them and invited them to be a part of it.

God did not *need* their "stuff" either. He had done the hardest parts by Himself—the plagues, defeating the Egyptians, providing manna in the wilderness. But He invited them to be a part of the building of the tabernacle.

2. God used their "stuff" to build His tabernacle.

Even though God did not *need* their stuff, He *chose* to use it. The work God does on earth is always facilitated through the gifts of His people. Think about when Jesus fed the five thousand: He used a kid's lunch of five loaves and two fish. Clearly a God that could do that did not *need* the five loaves and two fish . . . as if He could not have pulled it off with one fish and a bread crust!

3. Everyone had something to contribute.

Exodus 35:20 says that "all the congregation of the children of Israel" was involved in this. Then the text begins listing all these different kinds of people. The *craftsmen* did this; some of the *women* did this; and the people who were good with *cloth* did this. *Everybody had a part because*

God was not after a few resources of a few wealthy people; He was after the hearts of all His people.

Sometimes people who do not have a lot of money say, "Well, why do *I* have to be involved. *That guy's* tithe would be more than my whole salary!" The answer—because God is after your heart. He does not need the money, but He wants the gift that represents the love of your heart. We do not always choose what God gives to us, but we can choose how we use what He has given us.

4. You cannot give what you do not have.

What you see throughout Exodus 35 (vv. 22–29) is that each person gave out of what God had given them. But you should not feel guilty about what you cannot give. God determines the seasons of your life. You are responsible to be faithful in the season He has you in. So do not feel bad that your gift is small—or if, at certain times, you have nothing to give.

Does that mean that you should never give until you are in a perfect place financially? No. Mortgage payments, credit card bills, and car payments are not excuses to keep you from being generous. Keep giving, even if it stretches you. But if you are *living* off of loans (students, for instance), you are living off of someone else's borrowed money. In that case, it may be wise to wait until you are making money to give it away.

5. They gave in response to grace.

The Israelites responded not only to God's deliverance from Egypt but also to the grace that God showed them in Exodus 34. There Israel had made a golden idol to worship, and God should have destroyed them. But instead He showed them mercy. They had a deep sense that every breath they took was one they did not deserve because of their rebellion.

Even the gifts they gave were a reminder of God's mercy. They gave "brooches and earrings and signet rings and armlets, all sorts of gold objects" (Ex. 35:22 ESV). Where did they get these? When God was leading them out of Egypt, God told them to ask the Egyptians for traveling supplies, and the Egyptians unloaded all of their jewelry, saying, "Just get out of here!" The text even says that they "plundered the Egyptians." In other words, *they are only giving to God out of what they had received from God.*

6. Giving was both free and Spirit-prompted.

Several times (Ex. 35:5, 21, 22, 29), the text talks about the people coming and giving whatever was in their heart to give. It was free giving, with no compulsion. "Whoever's heart moved him" gave to the tabernacle.

But then in other places (Ex. 35:30–34; 36:2), the Spirit is putting specific talents and gifts into the minds and hearts of His people. There is an interplay between the Holy Spirit and the hearts of the people throughout these chapters. Moses does not command anyone what to give. Instead he explains that the Holy Spirit will put in your heart specifically what to give.

Are you willing to listen to the voice of the Holy Spirit? This may not be a tingly moment when you feel like throwing all of your lunch money in the offering plate. Spirit giving can still be *planned.* But how many of you have actually sought the Lord's counsel on how much you should be giving?

7. They gave publicly.

The word translated in the ESV as "contribution" in Exodus 35:5 is *terumah*, which literally means "to raise up." In the King James Version they called this the "heave-offering." You would heave it up for all to see, showing them that you were "all-in."[1] There was a sense of solidarity as everyone saw the gifts being brought in.

I know this is a foreign idea for us. And yes, it can lead to people showing off their generosity in front of others. But public giving is also a way for God's people to encourage each other to give.

8. They had to hold a congregational meeting to tell them to stop giving.

This is my favorite one. Moses had to gather everyone together *to stop them from giving* because the gifts were *too plentiful* (Ex. 36:5–7)! Just one time, would you let me experience this? I promise I will do a really good job calling the congregational meeting.

Conclusion

Too often we see giving as a favor to a God who is short on cash. But truly sacrificial giving comes as a *response* to grace, not as a new task or spiritual discipline.

GROWING IN GRACE

Five Lessons about Prayer from an All-Night Wrestling Match with God

Genesis 32

J. D. Greear, Ph.D.

Introduction

Genesis 32 contains the fascinating story from the life of Jacob, where he wrestles all night with God. The whole wrestling match comes about in the midst of Jacob praying, and his physical struggle teaches us five lessons about prayer.

1. The blessings of God are released into our lives through prayer.

Before Jacob was even born, God had prophesied that the blessing would be his and not his brother's (Gen. 25:23). But it was not until Jacob *took it* in a prayer-wrestling match with God that it really became his. He laid hold of the promise of God through a night of prayer.

The Bible is a book full of promises—thousands of them! And while many of them apply to specific and unique situations, Paul calls *all* the promises of God yes in Jesus (2 Cor. 1:20). So in a Christ-centered way, every one of them is yes for me and for you.

So do not simply read through your Bible. *Pray through it!* The Bible is our primary prayer book, so read through it and lay hold of the promises of God!

2. Sometimes the blessings of God are released into our lives through persistent prayer.

In a sermon on Genesis 32, Martin Luther pointed out that the story of Jacob wrestling with God gives us a picture of wrestling with a *seemingly* hostile God in prayer. As another example of this, he mentions the story of the Syro-Phoenician woman who came to Jesus to get healing for her daughter (Mark 7). Jesus' response sounds rather harsh. He tells her that "it is not good to take the children's bread and throw it to the little dogs" (v. 27). Does Jesus actually want to send the woman away? No. *He is going to heal her, but at first He appears hostile and indifferent.*

What is going on here? God is not actually hostile and indifferent: the cross shows us how loving and engaged He is! But Jesus is showing us that praying often *feels* like that. Why? God often appears hostile to test the strength of our faith in His goodness: *"Like a child trying to push against the hand of a parent, the parent gives only enough resistance to test the resolve of the child. So God resists us in prayer, to see our resolve in his goodness."*[1]

3. The blessings of God are not obtained by our contriving.

At the end of this wrestling match, God asks Jacob for his name. He already knows the name, of course, but He wants Jacob to admit it. When Jacob had stolen the blessing, his daddy had asked for his name, and he lied: "My name is Esau." But now he tells the truth: "My name is *Jacob*. I'm a *deceiver*.[2] I've tried all my life to obtain these blessings for myself by my own manipulation. Now I am repenting."

So God gives him a new name, Israel, which speaks of *God* giving the blessing, not Jacob wresting it for himself. The blessing you are searching for is not going to come from more striving or deceiving. It comes by submitting. *Winning the blessing only comes by losing to God.*

4. God is Himself the blessing that we seek.

God does not end the encounter with Jacob by assuring him that everything will be fine. He simply says, "God to Esau. I am with you." There is no promise that he will live through the next day. In fact, God has made Jacob limp, so he cannot even try to run away.

But Jacob got a blessing that was greater than earthly blessing: the *restoration of relationship*. Whatever you are searching for, I can guarantee you that it cannot replace God. Sometimes God withholds blessing you are seeking in order to teach you just that, because a relationship with God is better than any of his blessings.

God may not promise you that you will get the job or the boyfriend or the healing you desire. *But He promises Himself.* God does not always change your situation; sometimes He changes your identity. He changes you from a "Jacob" to an "Israel." So you can say—even in the midst of the shadow of death—that God is with you, and that is enough.

The result of a night of prayer is not the resolution of all of your problems, but the restoration of your most desperately needed relationship.

5. We know that God hears us because He became weak for us.

Jacob's wrestling match was not an even fight. When you are in a wrestling match with someone beneath your weight class, you must hold yourself back. But what is *God's* weight class? How much does omnipotence weigh? Jacob should have been crushed, which means that God voluntarily held Himself back. God became voluntarily weak.

God feigned weakness to bring Jacob salvation, but centuries later, the full weight that Jacob deserved came down on Christ. As Tim Keller says, *"Jacob held on at the risk of his life to get the blessing for him; but Jesus held on at the cost of his life to get the blessing for us."*

So we can be sure that He hears us. It may seem like God is not listening. But He is. The cross assures us that He is. God cared enough to come down to Jacob and wrestle with him. God cared enough for us that He came down and took on our flesh, wrestling with our sin until it squeezed the life out of him. And now He has united Himself to us forever and said, *"I will never leave you nor forsake you."*

Conclusion

God is not distant, waiting for us to say the magic words or to fix our lives before He will hear us in our prayers. He stands ready and willing to hear us even now. So press into Him in prayer, and never, ever give up.

GROWING IN GRACE

Faith Is Action

Hebrews 11

J. D. Greear, Ph.D.

Introduction

Hebrews 11, the great "faith chapter," is full of actions. Abel *offered.* Noah *built.* Abraham *went out*. The word for "faith" in Hebrew, in fact, is only a verb. That is why all of the people in this chapter became famous: their faith manifested itself *in action.*

The author ends the chapter with a list of role models in two groups: the first group "conquered kingdoms, . . . quenched the power of fire, . . . were made strong." But those in the second group "suffered mocking and flogging, . . . were stoned, were sawn in two, were killed with the sword." What these two groups had in common was that they believed the word of God and risked everything upon it.

The first group received great deliverance and victory; the second group died with nothing on earth that validated their faith. What group would you want to be in? Of course, we want to be in the first group. But the life of faith requires a confidence in a God you cannot see and in promises you cannot always feel. Oftentimes you, like those in the second group, stand alone. *If you require earthly validation for your faith, you will not make it.*

Can you risk it all on what is invisible?

Like Abraham, will you obey what God commands?

Will you obey what God says about morality even if it makes no sense to you? People say, "Well, I believe the Bible and I love God, but I just don't agree with *this* or *that*." But if you are the kind of person who demands that you agree with God before you obey Him, I would submit that you still do not understand what it means for God to be God.

Can you, like Jacob and Joseph, have unwavering hope in the midst of darkness?

In the darkest hour of your soul, will you hope because the dawn is coming? When your cancer is not in remission, when your spouse is not coming back, when your prime age for getting married is passing you by—will you rejoice that God can turn tragedy into triumph? How you respond to disappointment or tragedy reveals whether (or how much) you actually believe God. *Your ability to be joyful in all things is the measure of your faith.*

So much of the Christian life is spent waiting. Read the Psalms: the word *wait* appears over and over again. Psalm 37:7 (ESV), "Be still before the LORD and *wait* patiently for Him"; Psalm 62:1a (ESV), "For God alone my souls *waits* in silence." Waiting patiently with hope is what we call faith.

Like the Israelites at the Red Sea, do you trust that God will provide for you in impossible situations?

I feel this as a parent. I look at the world and sometime I panic. *"God, how can I raise my children in this sort of world?"* Or I think of the next season for our church. There is just so much uncertainty, so many things that seem impossible.

But maybe our fear and panic reveal how little we actually believe that God will provide for us. As C. S. Lewis said, the depth of our faith is revealed only when it is a matter of life and death.[1] Most of us have never had to come to that point. But for those of you who have, will you trust God *in those times*?

Like Moses, will you leverage your earthly position because you believe in eternity?

God may be telling you to leave your lucrative career to carry the gospel to the ends of the earth. The crisis for you right now is, *do you believe in Him and His mission enough to do it?* Will you figure out how to re-engineer your career so that it can be used for the purposes of God's mission?

God might be telling you to take Him seriously in your giving. Do you believe Him enough to invest your pocketbook in Him? He might be pushing you to be bolder in your witness for Him. Do you believe in Him enough to overcome your fear and open your mouth? God is speaking to you: Will you listen?

Faith takes action. It is a bold dare on the promises of an unseen God. I am convinced that many in this church do not believe in the invisible. You are not willing to put it all on the line for eternity. You give a little money, a little time, and never take a bold dare on God. Faith gives till it hurts, because faith knows that eternity is real and that our earthly sacrifices are not true sacrifices at all.

Where our confidence comes from: Jesus' death and resurrection

Look at verses 39 and 40. God has provided *something better* for us. We have a reason to believe in God that none of the people in the Old Testament did—Jesus. We see the love and faithfulness of God demonstrated at the cross; we see the trustworthiness of God's provision demonstrated in the resurrection.

What the people in Hebrews 11 saw as a shadow, we see in completion. Jesus healed all those who came to Him and voluntarily died on the cross for us. So we know that if He does not heal our body or our broken situation *now*, it is not because He lacks the power or the compassion. God sought us when we were strangers and reconciled Himself to us while we were His enemies. Will He who gave His Son so freely not also freely give us all things?

Conclusion

Can you trust Jesus with your finances, with your kids, with your future? *Of course you can.* He has demonstrated how much He cares for you and how powerful He is to save. So as you look to Jesus, do not measure His compassion or His power by your current circumstances. Measure His compassion by the cross and His power by the resurrection.

GROWING IN GRACE

Five Lessons about Following God in Crisis Moments

Genesis 12:1–4

J. D. Greear, Ph.D.

Introduction

Genesis 12 depicts the call of Abraham, a special opportunity that changed Abraham's life. Abraham teaches us five lessons about following God in moments like these.

1. Following God means venturing into the unknown.

Abraham had to trust God with a completely unknown future. God told Abraham to "go" without telling him where he was headed. He told Abraham that he would have a son without explaining how. Later on, God would ask Abraham to sacrifice this son without explaining why. John Calvin summarized God's interaction with Abraham like this: *"Just close your eyes and take my hand."*[1]

If God is who He says He is, you have to be willing to trust Him. If not, you will never know Him or experience what He has for you.

2. God's calling to salvation and His commissioning into mission are one and the same.

There is a misconception among Christians that you get called to be God's child at one point and then later He puts you on mission. But in the Bible, the two calls are *always* one and the same. God called Abraham with a purpose—*to bless others*. He called Moses by sending him to Pharaoh (Ex. 3:7–12). He called Peter by telling him we would be a "[fisher] of men" (Matt. 4:19). *God is like a spiritual tornado. He never pulls you in without also hurling you out.*

3. You are blessed to be a blessing.

Are you more of a reservoir or a channel for the blessings in your life? If you are a channel, then because you have been loved by God, you will love others. If you have been given money, you share your money. If you have been given wisdom, you share it. You bless others because that is why God has blessed you.

4. To become the blessing, take your hands off of everything you have and make God your trust and His kingdom your delight.

God did not call Abraham to minor changes, but to a whole new basis of life. No longer would he find his security in how much he possessed or how able he was to provide for himself; he had to trust God. No longer would he spend his life building his own little kingdom; he left that to seek the building of God's.

Following God is not just "adding a little God to your lives." It means making God your trust for the future and His kingdom your delight.

5. To become the blessing, you have to believe the impossible.

Abraham had to believe what seemed impossible—and then act on it. For you to follow God you have to believe that He will use your life for blessing and that He will give you the resources to accomplish His will. It might seem like this is impossible. But God is calling you to *close your eyes and take his hand.*

Times like these are what the Bible calls *kairos* moments—special moments of opportunity that God can use to tear us away from the world. Wealth has a way, as C. S. Lewis said, of knitting a man's heart to this world.[2] That is a spiritually dangerous condition. But God can use *kairos* moments of sacrifice to transfer our allegiance from the kingdom of the world to another one.

Conclusion

Not every moment in your life is a once-in-a-lifetime opportunity, but everyone will have a moment like that sooner or later. Will you trust in God *now* so that He will carry you *then*?

GROWING IN GRACE

God Does Not Need Your Money

2 Samuel 7

J. D. Greear, Ph.D.

Introduction

Our God is not a weak, poor God who needs someone else's resources to accomplish His mission. He made everything with a word. He has a limitless supply of resources. He has no needs, and has never had one. If He did have one, He would not come to us with it. As He says in the Psalms, "If I were hungry, I would not tell you, *for the world and its fullness are mine*" (Ps. 50:12 ESV, emphasis added). What God wants from us, the psalm continues, is not our belongings, but a "sacrifice of thanksgiving" for what He has done for us (v. :14 ESV).

Reading 2 Samuel 7, we see that David starts by wanting to do something *for God*; but he ends by sitting in stunned awe of what God had done *for him*. This is not to say that God does not *use* our stuff in His mission. As this passage shows, David's generous response gives us three motivations for giving that are worthy of our emulation.

1. Eternal Investment

David wanted to leverage his money for God's eternal kingdom, and God said that this was a good thing, because David realized that what God was building on earth was more important than what David was building. David did not give to God because God was in need, but because he wanted to leverage his earthly resources for God's eternal kingdom.

2. Offerings of Gratefulness

David saw all that God had done for him and he *wanted* to give in response. When he went to set up the plot of land the temple would be built on, he insisted on buying it, even though the owner wanted to give it to David for free. David said, "I will not offer burnt offerings to the LORD my God that cost me nothing" (2 Sam. 24:24 ESV). David insisted on paying because he knew the issue was not providing a need (the field would be provided either way), but the statement the gift made about David's heart.

There are some gifts that are valuable for the good they can do in the world, and some gifts that are priceless for the statement they make about the heart of the giver and the value of the God they serve.

If David was grateful to God because of what he had seen God do, how much more should we be grateful to God? David was blessed with a temple, but we have been blessed with Jesus, the true temple, whose flesh was torn so that we could enter the presence of God.

3. Obedience to God's Spirit

David did with his money exactly what God instructed of him. This is often an overlooked element in giving—the involvement of the Holy Spirit. But a lot of the biblical stories about giving have statements like, "God stirred up so-and-so's heart to give" (Ex. 36; 2 Cor. 9). Giving is supposed to be a *Spirit-thing*, a *Spirit-driven thing*, in which the Spirit moves in your heart and you obey as He directs.

I sometimes think the reason a lot of us do not know what to give God is because we have simply never asked Him what He wants us to give.[1] Have you?

Conclusion

God did not need David's money, and He does not need yours, to accomplish His will here on earth. But He invites you to be a part of His plan in this world.

GROWING IN GRACE

To Love or Not to Love the World

1 John 2:15–17

J. D. Greear, Ph.D.

Introduction

What does John mean when he says, "Do not love the world" (1 John 2:15 ESV)? This is the same man who wrote John 3:16: "God so loved the world." So which part of the world should we love, and which part should we not love?

John is not saying that we should hate any of the following.

1. The Created Order

Some Christians hate earthly pleasures, like nice food or comfortable clothing. But God created the world and declared, *This is good!* When Jesus was here on earth, He was accused of being a "glutton" and a "wine-drinker" (Matt. 11:19, author's translation), which means that He knew how to enjoy a good meal.

So it glorifies God when you enjoy great music or a prime cut of steak. That is what these things were created for.

2. The Economic and Social Structures of Society

I have known a lot of Christians who thought that we should avoid secular professions completely. They usually try to start "Christian" versions of business and entertainment, which while commendable, is not the point of this passage.

3. Culture

When I grew up this verse was often interpreted to mean you should avoid rock music and contemporary clothing styles. Christians were supposed to—quite literally—*look and sound different.* But cultural style is not "worldly" in and of itself.

4. The People of the World

Sadly, I have known some "Christians" who felt they were being godly when they expressed their hatred or disgust toward non-Christians. They can point to this verse all day long, but that is clearly not an attitude that anyone who has experienced the gospel could harbor.

So What Is the World That We Are Not Supposed to Love?

When John says, "Do not love the world," he means *the world as it is arrayed in rebellion against God.* Look at the next verse: "for all that is in the world—the lust of the flesh, the lust of the eyes, and the pride of life—is not of the Father but is of the world" (2:16). The word translated "lust" is *epithumia*, which has the connotation of a desire that has taken on too much *weight* in your life. *Lusts are cravings that control you.*

So, for instance, "lust of the flesh" takes normally healthy desires for physical pleasures and wrenches them out of context. A desire for sex is raised to the level of absolute obsession.

"Lust of the eyes" happens when you see something good in the world that becomes so important to you that you sacrifice everything else for it. People do this with money all the time, putting themselves in bad financial situations and going into debt to obtain *stuff* that they think will satisfy.

The "pride of life" consists in raising some aspect of your life—which is not necessarily bad—up to the level that it defines you. But when something other than God is your confidence for the future, you are engaging in worldliness.

John says, "Do not be *consumed* with these things." Because if your life is consumed with things—even *good* things—then it shows that the love of the Father is not in your life. God has been displaced.

Conclusion

Too many Christians act as if "hating" the world means holing up in a Christian ghetto and avoiding everything that everyone else likes. But God wants us to *love* the people in this world, and the only way we can do that is by rejecting the idols that threaten to makes us slaves *to* the world.

GROWING IN GRACE

Two Ways to Know You Are Saved

1 John 5:13–18

J. D. Greear, Ph.D.

Introduction

In these verses, John identifies two ways that you can be sure of your salvation.

1. You Have Placed Your Hopes for Heaven Entirely on Jesus (1 John 5:13).

"These things I have written to you," John says, "who believe in the name of the Son of God" (1 John 5:13). It is so simple that you are liable to miss it, but assurance comes from believing in Jesus. This is the gospel: when you trust in his name, you cease striving to earn heaven by drawing upon your own moral bank account; instead, you withdraw on his righteous account in your place.

The gospel, by its very nature, produces assurance. Because the gospel proclaims "Jesus in my place," your assurance does not depend on how well or how much you have done. It depends on whether or not you rest in his finished work. So the question to ask is not, "Can I remember praying a prayer?" The important question is, "Am I currently resting on Jesus as the payment for my sin?"

A lot of Christians get caught up looking for assurance in a prayer they prayed two years, five years, or thirty years ago. But John does not say, "I write these things to you who prayed the sinner's prayer." He writes to those who believe. The point is not the prayer you prayed, but the present posture you are in. Those in a present posture of repentance and belief can have an assurance of salvation.

2. You Have a New Nature (1 John 5:16–18).

If you have been born of God, you have been given a new nature. And that comes with new desires. So you do not "keep on sinning" because you have new desires. For example, few of us require rules to keep us from Dumpster diving. Why? Because we find it disgusting. Now, a dog has a totally different nature, with different desires. Dogs find Dumpsters as appetizing as you find them disgusting.

God changes you, not by browbeating you with rules, but by giving you a new heart. You no longer love dishonesty, hatefulness and immorality. You do not avoid them because of threats from God, but because these things start to make you sick.

Of course, this does not mean that you no longer struggle with sin. But you stop engaging in sin willfully and defiantly. You cannot have a mouth that sings praise to Jesus with a life that openly crucifies him. It is not your mouth that best reflects your love for God; it is your life.

And when you do start to go back toward your sin—which we all do!—Jesus protects you and renews you (v. 18). In fact, one of the signs that your salvation is genuine is that even though you fall, you never permanently fall away. God brings you back, again and again: "The righteous falls seven times and rises again" (Prov. 24:16 ESV).

Conclusion

Your new nature is not demonstrated by never falling, but by what you do when you fall. Conversion does not means sinless perfection, but it does mean a new direction.

GROWING IN GRACE

Jesus' Sovereignty Does Not Keep Him from Weeping with Us

John 11

J. D. Greear, Ph.D.

1. Introduction: What Do We Do When God Disappoints Us?
2. Jesus' Two Existential Answers to Those in Pain
   a. The Theological Response—Martha
   b. The Response of a Friend—Mary
3. Jesus' Ultimate Answer
   a. The Defeat of Death at Calvary
4. Conclusion: Because God Loves Us, We Can Endure Present Pain

Vignette

John 11 shows us a pair of sisters who "cannot believe" because of pain and disappointment. Jesus responds in two very different ways to Martha and Mary—even though they ask the same question—because He knows that the disappointed need both responses. The response that He gives to Mary is *the response of a friend.*

I have always thought Jesus' tears (11:35) were a little odd. He knew that He was about to raise Lazarus from the dead and that in ten minutes everything would be made right. Why would Jesus weep with Mary? Why not just tell her to wait and watch?

Jesus weeps with Mary to give us a picture of how He goes through suffering with us. Even when Jesus knows the pain is temporary, He knows what it feels like *for you*, and He weeps with you. He weeps with you because He is your friend.

That is how you know a friend loves you: not that they can give you all the answers when you are hurting, but that they weep when you weep.

For Jesus, a period of ten minutes is not altogether different than ten thousand years. Jesus can already see the beautiful end to your story. He can see all of your suffering swallowed up in the glorious resurrection. But when you are hurting, as much as you tell yourself that Jesus sees the beautiful end, it is still painful *right now*. That is why sometimes what you need is not theological answers; *you need the presence of a Savior who feels your pain and weeps with you.*

Conclusion

What a friend we have in Jesus! "He took our sin and our sorrow, and He made it His very own. He bore our burden to Calvary, and suffered and died alone."[1] He feels, as His own, every broken-heart, every shattered dream, every sorrow.

There was another time in Jesus' life that He wept, but nobody was there to weep with Him. In the Garden of Gethsemane, Jesus would weep with such great anguish that the capillaries in His face would burst. But no one would respond. The Father turned His face away. Jesus would ask His disciples to stay awake with Him, but they would all fall asleep. He would die friendless, and Godless.

Because of that, you can know that He will never forsake you. He was forsaken so that you could never be. He died so that all that could have separated you from God would be removed. He died so that you would *never* have a season of suffering in which God would not weep with you in your pain. *Jesus cried alone and died alone so that when you cry and die, you would know that you are not alone.*

GROWING IN GRACE

For the Skeptic Who Can't Believe

John 20:24–28

J. D. Greear, Ph.D.

1. Introduction: Doubt Is a Common Part of the Christian Experience
2. The Reason for Thomas's Unbelief
3. The Limitations of Thomas's Revelation
4. The Willingness of Thomas's Surrender
5. What Finally Changed Thomas—And Can Change You
   a. The Fact of Christ's Resurrection
   b. Feeling Christ's Wounds

Vignette

I feel bad for the apostle Thomas. He gets a bad rap. One instance of doubt and he is forever known as "Doubting Thomas," as if he was just this hardened skeptic. Other apostles do not get named for their faults: Peter was known to be a coward at times, but no one calls him "Petrified Peter." What makes it even worse is that John puts Thomas's story where he does to act as an example of *faith*, not to beat up on Thomas. In fact, Thomas makes one of the clearest and boldest confessions of faith found anywhere in the Bible.

So what was it that overcame Thomas's doubts? It was not just the fact of Christ's resurrection that changed Thomas forever; it was *feeling* the wounds of Christ's resurrection.

Thomas would go on to give his life for Christ, to take wounds into his own body for Jesus' sake. He would give everything for Jesus because Jesus had given everything for him. And when he called out to God to deliver him from those trying to kill him—and Jesus did not answer—Thomas would not doubt Him again, because *he had seen the wounds of Jesus.*

Conclusion

Do you ever wonder why Jesus' resurrected body has wounds? The Father certainly could have healed them. But they remain because *Jesus' wounds are always supposed to be in front of us, reminding us of his steadfast loyalty and love.*

Jesus' wounds show you that while brothers and sisters, mothers and fathers, neighbors and friends may fail you, Jesus never will. They show you that even though your dreams may crumble, Jesus is the rock who will never falter. They show you that though you may not understand everything God is doing in the world, you can trust Him.

Have you seen and felt the wounds of Jesus *for you*? Thomas did not respond by saying, "Jesus is Lord!" He said instead, "*My* Lord and *My* God!" When Jesus' wounds become more than a historical fact, but a personal reality, then you will be able to trust Him through your doubts.

Others in your life may have let you down. You may have been used or abused by them. But Jesus will never do that. He was used and abused in your place. And if He was willing to endure torture for you to save you, you can be sure that He will never abandon you.

So when your days are dark, hold on to His nail-scarred hands. Press into His wounds. They are there to remind you that *sometimes the answer to questions beyond your comprehension is a love too wonderful for words.*

GROWING IN GRACE

Five Corrosives to Faith

Hebrews 12

J. D. Greear, Ph.D.

Introduction

Hebrews 12 offers five corrosives to faith, each of which seems rather mundane. But for most of us, the greatest danger to our faith is not a cataclysmic event, but the gradual dulling of our heart toward God.

1. Division (Heb. 12:14)

Division and strife have a way of making us forget all about how Christ is "our city." Someone offends us and our pride gets riled up; before long we are marshalling troops to protect our city. But the author of Hebrews encourages us to "seek peace," which means that we should be the first to offer forgiveness, even when wronged. It means that we take the towel and wash the feet of those in conflict with us, like Christ did. It means that we serve our "enemies" and seek their well-being. This takes the focus off of our city and refocuses it on Christ's.

2. Worldliness (Heb. 12:14)

The author of Hebrews tells us to pursue holiness, which is the opposite of worldliness. As long as our minds are saturated with worldly pursuits, we will never be able to "see" God.

The Greek word for "pursue" lets us know that this takes a lot of discipline. The word literally means "persecute" or "hunt." Think Jason Bourne. We are supposed to track it and hunt it down relentlessly.

3. Bitterness (Heb. 12:15)

Idolatry is like a poisonous weed, or as the author of Hebrews says, a "root of bitterness." It starts very subtly, but soon infiltrates the entire garden. Tragically, a lot of us will miss the grace of God because we are distracted by idolatry. We allow something to carry more weight in our heart than God.

Those of us who think idolatry is a non-issue should ask ourselves: What dominates our thoughts? What upsets us? What makes us jealous? Whatever that thing is, it is an idol to us, and if we are not vigilant, it will choke out any desire for God.

4. Sensual pleasures (Heb. 12:16)

For many of us, the addictiveness of immorality or bodily comforts is drugging us and keeping us from thinking about what really matters. Think about how much people arrange their lives just to "feel good." Many of us are slaves to "Esau's stomach," which the author compares to sex, and this keeps us from thinking about what is eternal.

5. Inattention (Heb. 12:25)

Many of us are familiar with the details of Jesus' brutal beating and death. A cat-o'-nine-tails with pieces of bone and metal shredded his flesh to the bone. Isaiah says that he was beaten so brutally that he no longer looked like a human. He was then nailed up on a cross, naked, in full view of the public, to suffer and die humiliated.

Conclusion

If God did all this to save us, and we make him a secondary thought, how can we hope to escape? *This is God speaking!* Our eternity depends on whether or not we listen—how can we take that so lightly?

GROWING IN GRACE

What Melchizedek Has to Do with You

Hebrews 7

J. D. Greear, Ph.D.

Introduction

Whether we are religious or not, all of us are seeking God in some way, looking for a "priest" to connect Him to us. That is probably why the author of Hebrews devotes an entire chapter to Melchizedek, the seemingly minor OT character. His story teaches us four important lessons about the one true priest, Jesus.

1. All of the Old Testament points to Jesus.

Other than this passage in Hebrews, Melchizedek is only mentioned twice. He shows up in Genesis 14 just long enough to receive a tithe from Abram, and then disappears until David mentions him in a prophetic psalm one thousand years later.

But the author of Hebrews sees Jesus even in this minor Old Testament character. This is what is so great about reading and rereading the Old Testament. You begin to see that the entire Bible is woven together to teach *one story, the story of the gospel.* As Jesus Himself said, *all* of the Old Testament stories—even the obscure ones—ultimately point to Him (Luke 24:27).

2. Jesus was both a King and a Priest.

One of the few details we know about Melchizedek is that he was both a king and a priest. This is true of no one else in the Old Testament. The kingly and priestly offices were ones you would not want combined. Just imagine combining the roles of pastor and police officer! Each one had a very specific function to fulfill. The king was the lawgiver; the priest was the counselor. *The king represented God to the people; the priest represented the people to God.*

In Jesus, however, the offices of king and priest converged. With His death on the cross, Jesus brought together absolute justice and the fullness of God's mercy. By taking our place, Jesus accomplished what justice required for our sin, but in a way that He could still approach us with the tenderness of a priest.

3. Jesus can save anyone, anywhere.

The problem with the OT priests is that they could only represent other Jews. Besides that, they had their own sins to deal with, and even the best of them died eventually. Melchizedek, though, has no genealogy, so he represents a new type of priest, not bound to the nation of Israel.

Jesus is the fulfillment of that new type of priest, not bound to the nation of Israel, nor bound by sin or death. He did not die for a certain type of person. He died for all people everywhere, so that anyone, anywhere could be saved. Or as Hebrews says, "He is also able to save to the uttermost" (7:25).

4. Jesus deserves our first and best.

When Abram met Melchizedek, he was *looking* for a way of giving thanks to God. So he tithed to Melchizedek, offering to this king and priest as to a shadow of the King and Priest to come, Jesus Christ. In the same way, we who have been saved by Jesus ought to offer to Him our first and our best. How can we say we have any concept of God's free grace if we persist in thinking of our money, time, and talents as things that *we* deserve because *we* earned them?

Conclusion

All of us bow down to *something*, because all of us are worshipers. But we can only know the one true God if someone stands in the gap for us. Praise God that Jesus has done that, and has done the work of priest and king as no other man could ever do!

GROWING IN GRACE

Your Strength Is in Your Rest

Hebrews 4

J. D. Greear, Ph.D.

Introduction

There is a certain irony about Hebrews 4. The author is concerned that his hearers have the strength to go "all the way" with Jesus, and so he tells them all about the absolute necessity of Sabbath rest. We might anticipate that our strength to finish strong comes from how hard we work. But the gospel is a message about resting in Christ before doing anything for Christ. The quality of our strength is proportional to the quality of our rest. *Without Christ, we will work even while we are resting. And with Christ, we will rest, even while we are working.*

The key to finding true inner rest is belief in Christ (Heb. 4:3). He alone is the true source of Sabbath rest. In Him, the strength *to do* comes from resting in what *has been done.*

Christ is our righteousness.

We are always trying to justify ourselves by diminishing our faults and exaggerating our virtues. But the gospel destroys this self-deceptive striving by telling us that God has given us *His* righteousness as a gift. *In Christ, there is nothing we can do to make God love us more, nothing we have done that makes Him love us less.*

Christ is our identity.

Many of us overwork because we find significance in our work. We believe that what we do gives us our identity, and so we work tirelessly, because if we slack off for a moment, our entire world is liable to fall. The gospel speaks differently. It gives us an identity that is founded on *Him,* not *our strivings.* It reminds us that we are held in highest regard by the highest Being.

Christ is our security.

One of the most practical reasons for the Sabbath is to remind us regularly that we are not in control, that we are not God. Many of us are so stressed out because we are carrying a burden of security that God never intended for us to carry. The gospel reminds us that our security is ultimately in God's hands, not our own. To paraphrase Paul, God did not spare His own Son—won't He also freely give us all that we need (Rom. 8:30)?

Christ is our priority.

There is *rest* in having Christ as our priority. If we honor Him above everything, He promises to provide everything we need (cf. Matt. 6:33). We no longer need to worry about money, about relationships, about work. With Christ as our priority, we need only to focus on faithfulness to God, and we will be *amazed* at how faithful God is to provide for us.

Conclusion

Christ offers inner rest: He will be our righteousness, identity, security, and priority, if we simply believe in His gospel. With this as our foundation, we will have the strength to go all the way with Him and give it all away for Him. Why? Because we can never give up all that we have until we know that Christ is all that we need.

GROWING IN GRACE

"The Five Core Gospel Truths from Jesus' Genealogy"

Matthew 1:1–17

J. D. Greear, Ph.D.

Introduction

Matthew begins his gospel with a genealogy, which most of us are tempted to skip. But all of the critical truths about the gospel are embedded within the contours of this one genealogy.

1. The gospel is not good advice, it is good news.[1]

Fairy tales and fantasy stories start out with phrases like "once upon a time." But Matthew begins with a genealogy, which is a way of saying, "What I'm about to tell you actually happened."

Many religions are built on teachings and principles that would be true whether their religious founder ever lived or not. Not Christianity. Christianity depends on a set of events that actually took place in history, because the core of Christianity is not what Jesus taught us to do, but what He would do for us.

2. Jesus is the center of history.

Matthew takes what the world considered an insignificant family line and organizes all of human history around it. It certainly did not *seem* like Jesus was the focal point of history at the time. Israel was an insignificant Roman province. But God had made a promise to Abraham to bring salvation to the world. And He did it in the face of the powerful nations that thought *they* were truly in control.

3. God is working in all things, good and bad, for His purposes.

Matthew concludes his genealogy (1:17) by commenting that the progression from Abraham to Jesus came in three sets of fourteen. Why does this matter?

Well, fourteen is two sevens, and seven is the biblical number of perfection.[2] *Matthew organizes the genealogy into fourteens to show that God has superimposed His seal of perfection on history.* When you consider the messy stuff in this genealogy (just look up Tamar's or David's stories), that is an astounding claim.

4. The gospel is for the outsider.

In Jesus' day, a genealogy was like a résumé, how a person showed the world their worth. And so back then—like today—résumés were fudged to include the best parts and to omit the nasty details.

Yet look who Jesus includes in His genealogy: *Tamar* and *David* (see point 3); *Ruth*, a Moabite, not even Jewish; *Rahab*, not only a foreigner, but a prostitute; *Manasseh*, one of the most wicked and godless kings in Israel's history. Jesus' line is filled with outsiders of every kind—moral, ethnic, gender.

5. Jesus is the ultimate rest.[3]

There is another detail about the sets of fourteen that Matthew mentions. Three sets of fourteen makes *six* sets of *seven*. This makes Jesus the seventh seven.

Remember, seven is a really significant number in the Bible. It points to perfection, but it also points to rest. God rested on the seventh day. Israel was supposed to let their land "rest" every seven years. And every *seventh seventh year* was the Year of Jubilee, in which all debts were forgiven and all slaves were freed.

Matthew shows us that Jesus is the seventh seven; Jesus is the Year of Jubilee. In Him all debts are truly forgiven; in Him all slaves are finally freed. Jesus is ultimate rest.

Conclusion

The genealogy that Matthew gives is not merely background information, but is the gospel in brief. God has opened a way for us—the outsiders—to be reconciled to Him by the work of His Son, Jesus. In Him is rest; in Him is hope; in Him is true life.

LIFE IN A HEALTHY CHURCH

Healthy Churches—Healthy Relationships

Philippians 1:1–2

Dr. Jeff Iorg

Introduction

Healthy churches are marked by healthy relationships—among the members and between the members and their leaders. A church is a relational network. We are sheep in a fold, branches on a vine, and members of a family. We must learn to live and work together. The quality of a church is greatly determined by the quality of its interpersonal relationships.

In Healthy Churches, the People Are Saints

The Philippians were called "saints." The word *saint* means set apart for a unique use. It can also mean holy—but this should be understood as "set apart" not "perfect, without sin." A holy building, for example, isn't a perfect building. It's a place set apart for special use—like worship. The Philippians were saints because they were "in Christ Jesus." Through their conversion, they had been set apart for Jesus. They were normal people, some of whom are introduced in the Bible—Lydia, a businesswoman (Acts 16:13–15); a demon-delivered slave girl (Acts 16:16–18); a jailer and his family (Acts 16:29–34).

You are a saint—set apart by Jesus to serve Jesus. You became a saint when you received Jesus as your Lord and Savior. You demonstrate your sainthood by serving Him.

In Healthy Churches, the Leaders Are Servants

Paul referred to himself and Timothy as "bondservants of Jesus Christ" (Phil. 1:1). Their perspective on leadership was dominated by this conviction. They provided leadership to others in the context of serving Jesus. They had been with the Philippians on multiple occasions (Acts 16:11–40; 19:21; 20:5–6; Phil. 2:22; 1 Thess. 2:2) and served them in many capacities.

Paul addressed the overseers and deacons—church leaders—immediately after describing himself as Jesus' servant. These leaders were expected to follow the model of Christian leadership they had observed in Paul and Timothy.

Church leaders are servant leaders. Servanthood describes both attitude and actions. Healthy church leaders make other people successful, sacrifice their interests for the church's best interest, and model humility in what they do. Authoritative influence is gained primarily through serving others (Mark 10:35–45).

In Healthy Churches, Grace and Peace Prevail in Relationships

Grace and peace originate "from God our Father and the Lord Jesus Christ" (Phil. 1:2). Grace and peace are extended person-to-person—"Paul and Timothy . . . to all the saints" (v. 1). Grace is God's spontaneous, intentional, loving acceptance. Peace is God's calm, trusting, restful atmosphere. God has extended grace and peace to us. He expects us to do the same for church members sharing community with us.

You extend grace when you initiate relationships with others, accept them as they are, and wait patiently for them to mature. Some church members are easier to relate to than others. Gracefully care for everyone, even people who are difficult or challenging. You extend peace when you recognize varying levels of spiritual and emotional maturity, tolerate mistakes and shortcomings, and give people room to grow.

Conclusion

Healthy churches are marked by healthy relationships demonstrating our shared life in Jesus Christ.

LIFE IN A HEALTHY CHURCH

Developing Spiritual Intimacy

Philippians 1:3–11

Dr. Jeff Iorg

Introduction

Intimacy is the elusive transparency, deep union, and unspoken acceptance we long for in our most significant relationships. We crave intimacy with our spouse, in a different sense with our children, and in a special way with a few dear friends.

How do you build intimacy in relationships—particularly with fellow church members? What must happen so you can join Paul in saying of fellow believers (v. 7), "I have you in my heart" (v. 7) and, "I long for you all with the affection of Jesus Christ" (v. 8)?

Intimate Relationships Rest on a Spiritual Foundation

Paul shared grace and peace (see previous message) with the Philippians. He reminded them "you are all partakers with me of grace" (v. 7). He also shared affection for them by writing, "I long for you all with the affection of Jesus Christ" (v. 8).

Grace and peace originate "from God our Father and the Lord Jesus Christ" (v. 2). Grace and peace are extended person-to-person like from "Paul and Timothy ... to all the saints" (v. 1). Affection originates with Jesus' "affection of Jesus Christ" (v. 8).

Grace, peace, and godly affection are the spiritual foundations for intimate relationships. Healthy churches are marked by relational grace and peace, expressed affectionately, among their members and between leaders and their followers.

Intimate Relationships Emerge from a Shared Purpose

Paul and the Philippians were partners in the gospel. Their partnership in the gospel started at the inauguration of the church in Philippi (v. 5, "fellowship in the gospel from the first day") and extended to the time of his writing to them (v. 5, "until now"). Paul considered them partners who supported him in his imprisonment (v. 7, "in my chains and in the defense . . . you all are partakers"). They were also partners in the "confirmation of the gospel" (v. 7).

Intimacy with other believers emerges from your shared commitment to the gospel. You are partners in gospel-sharing, even when it is difficult. You help one another defend the gospel. You work together to establish the gospel in new places (missions and church planting). Intimacy emerges from working together on the common purpose of communicating the gospel.

Intimate Relationships Deepen through Sustained Prayer

Paul thanked God for the Philippians (v. 3, "I thank my God"). Paul joyfully and continually prayed for them (v. 3, "always in every prayer of mine"). Paul even wrote a prayer for these special friends (vv. 9–11, "And this I pray"). He prayed, "love may abound" (v. 9), "you may approve the things that are excellent" (v. 10), "you may be sincere and without offense" (v. 10), and "filled with the fruits of righteousness" (v. 11).

You build intimate relationships by praying with and for other people. Praying together breaks down walls and brings people together humbly before God. Praying for each another changes attitudes and perspectives as we learn to bear each other's burdens.

Conclusion

Spiritual intimacy emerges from grace and peace shared through working and praying together toward the common goal of sharing the gospel.

LIFE IN A HEALTHY CHURCH

Focus on the Gospel

Philippians 1:12–18

Dr. Jeff Iorg

Introduction

Healthy churches keep their focus on the gospel. They don't chase fads or focus on lesser issues. Healthy churches maintain "mission discipline"—focus on the gospel as their core message and method. For churches to retain this focus, members must practice this same "mission discipline."

Make the Gospel the Center of Your Life

Paul understood his current circumstance—imprisonment—in the context of its purpose related to the gospel. He believed "the things which happened to me have actually turned out for the furtherance of the gospel" (v. 12). He believed his "chains" (v. 13) were for the gospel. He also interpreted his upcoming trial as an opportunity for the defense of the gospel.

Paul viewed his difficult circumstances as an opportunity to live out and communicate the gospel. He accepted what most perceived as negative events—imprisonment and trial for his faith—as positive opportunities for the gospel. He interpreted his life—all of it—in terms of the gospel.

Your life purpose is the gospel. God allows your circumstances to teach you the gospel, reveal how the gospel has changed you, and give you opportunities to demonstrate the power of the gospel. Rather than complain about your circumstances, ask God to use them for the gospel's advantage.

Share the Gospel with People You Know

Paul saw his imprisonment as an opportunity for "the furtherance of the gospel" (v. 12). This word is the same root word for tree cutters who opened a way for the Roman army. Paul saw his imprisonment as paving the way for sharing the gospel.

Paul shared the gospel where he was with the people he came in contact with—prisoners, guards, judges, and governmental leaders. His example prompted others to share the gospel more boldly.

You must share the gospel in your circle of influence. Your best opportunities to share the gospel are through relationships you already have—home, family, work, neighborhood, community, and so forth. Many people equate sharing the gospel with accosting strangers, street preaching, or going on a mission trip. Your best opportunities are in the current circumstances where God has placed you.

Communicate the Gospel as Clearly as Possible

Even among early Christians, some were preaching the gospel with poor motives like "envy," "strife," or "selfish ambition" (vv. 15–16). Some were using the gospel to their advantage, getting from it whatever they could rather than sharing it freely. But not even bad motives could stop the expansion of the gospel.

Your motives will not always be pure (no one is sinless). Your message, the pure gospel, can be accurate and powerful—even if your motives aren't perfect. Don't be intimidated from sharing the gospel because you fear having the wrong motives. Do your best and trust God to honor your message—despite your frailty as a messenger.

Conclusion

Your life—no matter your circumstances—is a conduit for the gospel. Share it right where you are.

LIFE IN A HEALTHY CHURCH

Thriving through Difficult Circumstances

Philippians 1:19–30

Dr. Jeff Iorg

Introduction

The only encouragement our culture offers people going through hard times are worn-out clichés like "every cloud has a silver lining," "when life gives you lemons make lemonade," or "the sun will come up tomorrow." The Bible reveals far better resources to help you thrive, not just survive, when facing difficult circumstances. When cancer invades, car accidents happen, children get sick, or careers collapse—God will see you through.

We Thrive by Drawing on Spiritual Resources

Paul trusted "prayer" by his friends and the sustaining work of the "Spirit of Jesus Christ" to keep him going (v. 19). He drew on two primary spiritual resources—the prayers of fellow believers and the support of the Holy Spirit to sustain him. Companionship with the Lord and with each other is essential for making it through dark times.

When you are going through tough times, turn to fellow church members and other Christian friends for support. Let them help carry your burdens. Ask them to pray for you and to pray with you. When you know someone going through a hard time, do the same for them. Tell them and show them you care for them. Pray for them. During tough times, depend on the Holy Spirit to help you. He is the Comforter, Counselor, and Companion (John 14:16). Ask Him to be all these things for you.

We Thrive by Confronting Our Problems Head-on

Paul was eager to face his troubles. The phrase "earnest expectation" can be translated "head erect" or "heads up" (v. 20). Paul was not cowering from his problems, but facing them directly. He claimed to have "all boldness" (v. 20) to deal with whatever might come his way. The phrase "all boldness" could more literally be translated "completely outspoken." He demonstrated that boldness on multiple occasions during his imprisonments (Acts 22–26).

Take action to confront the problems producing your tough times. If your problems are financial, get involved in a stewardship training program. If your problems are relational, find a counselor and work toward healing. If you are being victimized, lift your head and speak up! Reject being a victim of past choices, broken relationships, or abusive people.

We Thrive by Keeping Right Perspective on Our Problems

Paul's problems were serious—imprisonment, trial, and possible execution. He knew he might live. If so, he knew "to live is Christ" (v. 21), "fruit" would be borne (v. 22), and the Philippians would be blessed. He also knew he might die, which he concluded would also be "gain" (v. 21) and would mean he was with Christ. Whether he lived or died, Paul was convinced Christ would be exalted through him. He saw both positive and negative circumstances as conducive to glorifying God.

If you live through trying circumstances, you glorify God by experiencing Jesus' care, bearing spiritual fruit, and helping others know they can live through similar struggles. A friend lived for more than a decade with cancer. How she lived through cancer impacted hundreds of people. She ultimately died, but not before leaving a legacy demonstrating God's sustaining power. Even if you ultimately die from difficult circumstances, you can still bring glory to God. Your faithfulness to the end of life reveals the genuineness of your faith and its sufficiency for the darkest hour—death.

We Thrive When Our Character Reveals Jesus in Us

Paul challenged his followers to "let your conduct be worthy of the gospel of Christ" (v. 27). He wanted them to "stand fast in one spirit … striving together for the faith of the gospel" (v. 27) during their trials. He rejected fear as an option and told them to live like Christians no matter what they experienced. Paul was more concerned his followers reveal the character of Jesus through their trials than that they be delivered from their trials.

Choosing to live your faith means taking charge of your emotions. You choose your behavior based on the Word of God, not how you feel in the moment. You reject fear and cling to faith. No matter what comes, you determine to act like the Christian you truly are. You stand against the temptation to base your actions on fear, worldly advice, or ungodly counsel.

We Thrive by Sharing in Jesus' Sufferings

Christians are responsible to believe in Jesus and also "to suffer" for His name (v. 29). This suffering is real, a struggle that is agonizing and painful to endure. For Christians to share the sufferings of Jesus, we must go through hard times. We must feel pain—genuine pain—from broken health and bad relationships. We may also be persecuted or treated unfairly because of our faith.

When you suffer, remember how Jesus suffered for you. No one likes to suffer—but hard times are inevitable. Let them remind you of Jesus' death on the cross and your part in it. Keeping this in view gives meaning to your trials and helps you remember what Jesus went through on your behalf. No Christian is exempt from sharing pain similar to that endured by Jesus.

Conclusion

Thriving, not just surviving hard times is possible. When health fails, relationships struggle, or circumstances seem out of control—God is still at work. Trust Him and use the spiritual resources He provides to sustain you.

Reject the myth, "God will never let you experience more than you can handle." Yes He will! God will allow life to overwhelm you, not to punish or discourage you, but to draw you to Him. He will allow circumstances to take you to the end of your human resources so you learn to trust Him. Thriving, not just surviving is only possible when you face your problems with the spiritual resources God provides.

LIFE IN A HEALTHY CHURCH

Creating Unity in Your Church

Philippians 2:1–11

Dr. Jeff Iorg

Introduction

Church divisions, sometimes resulting in church splits, are ugly marks on the body of Christ. Unity within a church is important, but it doesn't just happen. It results from focused effort to build oneness with other believers.

Four Incentives for Unity in the Church

The four incentives for unity in the church are reconciliation in Christ ("consolation in Christ"), the love of Christ ("comfort of love"), fellowship with the Holy Spirit ("fellowship of the Spirit"), and the compassion of Christ ("affection and mercy," v. 1). These spiritual realities are foundational to unity.

Your unity with other believers rests on what Jesus has done for you and for them. Unity rests on your shared foundation of spiritual life in Jesus. Shared life in Jesus is the key.

Three Expressions of Unity in the Church

The three expressions of unity in the church are having the same worldview ("being like-minded"), sharing the same love ("having the same love"), and having the same purpose ("being of one accord, of one mind," v. 2). These expressions of unity bind us together to accomplish the core tasks Jesus had given the church.

You express your unity by sharing the same mind-set (Christian values), living from the same motive (love), and sharing the same message (the gospel). Unity doesn't mean lock-step agreement on everything—just the core issues that really matter.

Two Steps to Promote Unity in the Church

The first step to promoting unity is considering fellow members more important than you are. Paul advocated for "each [to] esteem others better than himself" (v. 3). The second step is to look out for the interests of others. Paul continued by challenging every Christian to "look out not only for his own interests, but also for the interests of others" (v. 4).

You build unity when you put the interests of others before your own. You facilitate unity by meeting the needs of others, not demanding service for yourself or your family. Unity comes from focusing on others, not on you.

One Supreme Example Who Models Unity

Jesus demonstrated the humility required for unity in the church. Christians must adopt Jesus' attitude and "let this mind be in you which was also in Christ Jesus" (v. 5). The sacrifice of Jesus—giving up heaven and becoming human—reveals the extent He humbled Himself to meet the needs of others. Christian unity can only be achieved when His example becomes our model.

Your attitude and actions, when modeled on Jesus, facilitate unity in our church. When you believe your church exists to meet your needs, you become a source of division. When you sacrifice yourself to meet the needs of others, you are a source of unity.

Conclusion

The countdown to unity is simple—four incentives, three expressions, two steps, one model. Working this simple process eliminates division, limits distractions, and facilitates unity. God does amazing work through a church unified around Him and His purposes.

LIFE IN A HEALTHY CHURCH

Jesus Is Lord

Philippians 2:5–11

Dr. Jeff Iorg

Introduction

Jesus is Lord—in the past, present, and future. His lordship was the theme of an early Christian hymn that Paul incorporated into his letter to the Philippians. The first part of the hymn (vv. 5–8) is about the Lord's humility. The second part (vv. 9–11) is about the Lord's exaltation. Healthy churches celebrate and submit to the Jesus as Lord.

Jesus Emptied Himself

Jesus existed for eternity-past as God, with God, and in the form of God. This is emphasized by the verb "being" (v. 6). It means to exist originally or to really exist.[1] The emphasis is on the actuality of being. Jesus really was "in the form of God" (v. 6), meaning in the nature of God. He was also "equal with God" (v. 6), meaning He was God in every way. Jesus did not regard His equality with God as something to grasp, cling to, or use to His advantage. Instead, He "made Himself of no reputation, taking the form of a bondservant, and coming in the likeness of men" (v. 7). Jesus came "in the likeness of men" (v. 7), meaning He was fully man. He did not don or cloak Himself with humanity. He became human. The contrast is stark—Jesus moved from eternal-existence as God to physical-existence as a man. His deity, while retained, was fully enmeshed with His humanity.

Jesus gave up so much for you. To become your Savior, He had to be fully God and fully human. He emptied Himself—leaving heaven and its privileges behind—to live among us. He became human, limiting Himself in every way and fully experienced humanity. Only a Person fully God and fully human could become the Perfect Sacrifice for your sins. Jesus modeled humility by sacrificing so much by becoming human. But that was just His first sacrifice.

Jesus Died on the Cross

Jesus did the unthinkable for a divine being: "He humbled Himself and became obedient to the point of death, even the death on a cross" (v. 8). Jesus humbled Himself in many ways—from being born in a stable to living as a commoner. His most humble act, however, was submitting to the most degrading death possible—crucifixion. Dying on a cross was forbidden for Romans and a curse for Jews (Gal. 3:13). The cross was a stumbling block for many (1 Cor. 1:23) and foolishness for others (1 Cor. 1:18). Crucifixion was more than a way to end a life. It was a horrific form of torture designed to slowly suffocate its victims. In addition, Jesus was brutally beaten prior to being crucified. He died the most degrading death possible.

Jesus gave up more than you can imagine identifying with you as human. He then allowed Himself to die in the most horrible fashion possible—by crucifixion. Fully God became fully human to fully die as only He could for the sins of the whole world. While He knew His resurrection and ascension would happen (Heb. 12:1–2), nothing mitigated the shame and suffering He endured. While He went through—not just to—the cross, Jesus still had to endure all its agony. His death commiserated with the sins of humankind for which it atoned.

Jesus Is Exalted

The cross was a means to an end for Jesus. God "has highly exalted Him and given Him the name which is above every name" (v. 9). Jesus was exalted by His resurrection. He was further exalted at this ascension. The phrase "highly exalted" (v. 9) speaks qualitatively in contrast to phrases like "He humbled Himself" (v. 8). More pointedly, God's exaltation (resurrection, ascension) stands in contrast to man's degradation (the cross). As part of His exaltation, Jesus was given a new title: Lord. A person's name speaks of their identity, character, and accomplishments. Everything about Jesus is summarized in His one-word title: Lord.

Jesus is now exalted. He is no longer the lowly Savior meek and mild. He is resurrected, ascended, and seated at God's right hand (Eph. 1:20–23). He is now the Lord Jesus Christ, Sovereign of the Universe and Ultimate Ruler of All (Col. 1:15–20). You can't make Jesus Lord; He is Lord. You can't define Him any longer as an infant, man, teacher, or servant. He was those things. Now He is Lord!

Jesus Will Be Worshipped

Jesus will be worshipped. Since God has seated Him in a place of honor with a new name commanding respect, "every knee should bow" (v. 10). Those who will worship Jesus include humans and spirit-beings, "those in heaven ... those on earth ... and ... those under the earth" (v. 10). Not only will every being in the universe bow down to Jesus, they will also speak submission to His name because "every tongue should confess that Jesus Christ is Lord" (v. 11). The life of Jesus—from birth, life, death, resurrection, ascension—points to one consummate conclusion. All Jesus accomplished was and is "to the glory of God the Father" (v. 11).

Jesus will be worshipped. Every created being—human and otherwise—will ultimately bow down before Jesus and confess His lordship. As a Christian, you have already submitted to Jesus and acknowledged He is Lord. If you are not yet a Christian, make this choice soon. Confess Jesus is Lord now. Live for Him in this life so you will be prepared to meet Him after death. Don't make the mistake of thinking you will be exempt from recognizing Jesus as Lord. No one—humans, angels, or demons—is exempt from His dominion. Jesus is Lord over all.

Conclusion

Jesus humbled Himself for you. He became fully man, while retaining His full divinity. Because of this miracle, He was the only person who could be your Savior. He died on the cross for you. God raised Him from the dead and established His eternal rule. He is Lord. Receive His gift of salvation and submit to His lordship today!

LIFE IN A HEALTHY CHURCH

Light Up the Night

Philippians 2:12–18

Dr. Jeff Iorg

Introduction

Fireworks are fun! They light up the night, drawing attention to spectacular displays celebrating national freedom or international holidays. This analogy—bright light against a dark background—is one picture of what happens when we live our faith openly and tell other people about Jesus.

Light Up the Night by Living Out Your Faith

Salvation is supposed to be lived out—practically, ethically, and visibly. Christians are charged to "work out your own salvation with fear and trembling" (v. 12). To "work out" means to carry to a goal or to its ultimate conclusion—like solving a math problem. Salvation is worked out by God's power since "it is God who works in you" (v. 13). This eliminates human effort as the source for spiritual growth.

Salvation is a personal spiritual experience with public visible results. When you work out your salvation to its logical conclusion, life change results. Your new life stands in stark contrast to the darkness of your old life. It also draws attention to Jesus as the Person who has made your new life possible.

Light Up the Night by Transforming Your Character

Christians are distinct in the character qualities they demonstrate. We have a unique attitude, meaning we live "without complaining and disputing" (v. 14). We have a unique morality, meaning we are "blameless and harmless" (or pure like a refined metal; v. 15). Our behavior stands in contrast to contemporary culture "without fault in the midst of a crooked and perverse generation" (not perverted, twisted, or distorted; v. 15).

When you meet Jesus, He changes you. Your attitude, morality, and public conduct are different than they used to be and also different than that of people around you. Your new life lights up the world around you when you credit Jesus as the Source of your life changes.

Light Up the Night by Telling Others about Jesus

Christians "shine as lights in the world" when we tell others about Jesus by "holding fast the word of life" (v. 16). To "hold fast" means to offer the good news like offering a guest a beverage. The "word of life" means the gospel. These word pictures indicate the gospel is offered like a refreshing drink. Paul then builds on and shifts the analogy to "being poured out as a drink offering" (v. 17). Offering the gospel, freely and undiluted, is the ultimate act of sacrificial service one person can offer another.

When you tell someone about Jesus, you light up their night with the good news of Jesus. When you take a risk to do this or sacrifice something of yourself in the process, your efforts are eternally significant. A sacrifice for eternal results is always worth making.

Conclusion

Our world is dark—and getting darker year by year. You can make a difference by living out your faith, shaping your character to reflect Jesus, and telling other people about the gospel.

LIFE IN A HEALTHY CHURCH

Make Yourself Useful

Philippians 2:19–30

Dr. Jeff Iorg

Introduction

My mother disapproved of anyone standing around watching other people work. She often said, "Find a way to make yourself useful." She felt it was our responsibility to discover what needed to be done and to find a way to get it done. God has a similar perspective on Christians. He wants us to find ways to get busy serving Him.

God Uses People Who Serve Others

Timothy served the Philippians by caring for them. He had provided a "[sincere] care for your state" (v. 20). His service to them was rooted in his devotion to Jesus. Epaphroditus also served the Philippians by delivering a message from them to Paul. After doing this, he also remained with Paul and served him as "the one who ministered to my need" (v. 25).

You are useful to God when you serve others as an expression of your service to him. Christian devotion to God is usually revealed in supportive service of others—meeting personal needs, caring in crisis, or otherwise easing human stress. Simple acts of service, when timely done, often have profound meaning to their recipients. Grand gestures are not required to make a real difference in the lives of others. Simple service will do it.

God Uses People Who Serve Consistently

Timothy was a man of "proven character." He served "as a son with his father" (v. 22). This description and the accompanying analogy speak of devotion, longevity, and loyalty. Epaphroditus also served consistently.

He is described as a "brother, fellow worker, and fellow soldier" (v. 25). These relationships also illustrate steadfast service over time.

You are useful to God when you serve consistently. Almost anyone can have a good day, occasionally serving others by doing good works. It's much harder to have a good decade. God desires consistency. The true measure of your service is your longevity—the ability to serve steadily over a long period of time. Be like a son, a brother, or a long-term employee—serve with staying power.

God Uses People Who Serve Sacrificially

Timothy served alongside Paul in difficult circumstances, yet faithfully despite the challenges (Acts 16:1–13; 17:14–15; 18:5; 19:22; 20:4). Paul reported "he served with me in the gospel" (v. 22). Epaphroditus also served sacrificially, even to the point of risking his health. Paul remind the Philippians Epaphroditus had been sick, "indeed he was sick almost unto death" (vv. 26–27).

Your service may require genuine sacrifice. You may work in difficult circumstances, face intense opposition, or even risk your health. While no one wants to suffer, spreading the gospel among hostile people may entail personal risk. Being useful to God sometimes means sacrificing your personal comforts, extending yourself beyond your perceived limitations, to meet the needs of others.

Conclusion

Make yourself useful! Find ways to serve others. Don't wait to be asked or have someone else tell you what needs to be done. See a need and meet it.

LIFE IN A HEALTHY CHURCH

Holding to the Gospel

Philippians 3:1–11

Dr. Jeff Iorg

Introduction

The gospel is central to the Christian faith. The good news about Jesus—His death, burial, resurrection—is our sustaining story. The gospel is always under attack from people trying to dilute it or define it in more palatable terms. Surprisingly, good people (even church attenders) can be among the gospel's detractors when they cite their morality as a means of relating to God. Christians must defend the gospel, since it is the only true source of salvation.

The Gospel Is Attacked Frequently

Attacks on the gospel happened so frequently, Paul had previously written the Philippians about the problem. He was now writing "the same things to you" (v. 1) to defend the gospel once again from its opponents. He felt his repeated warnings were a safeguard against error. While his warnings were repeated, they were "not tedious" (v. 1). Paul understood his role of continually shaping his followers' understanding of the true gospel.

You should not be surprised when people undermine the gospel. This has been happening since the first generation of Christians. The story of Jesus is so scandalous, and demands such a pointed response, people are motivated to mute its meaning. You learn to recognize counterfeit gospels by studying the true gospel intently. Any variance means you must reject the imposter, not adjust the true measuring rod. Be patient and steadfast. No matter how firmly and frequently you stand up for the gospel, another attack is soon to come.

The Gospel Is Attacked Perniciously

Paul warned against gospel-comprise with three analogies. He warned against "dogs," "evil workers," and "the mutilation" (v. 2). Dogs were disgusting street animals, not the pampered pets common today. Evil workers were malicious schemers, intent on concocting trouble in the church. "The mutilation" refers to Judaizers who demanded circumcision precede conversion. Paul felt quite strongly about that heresy (Gal. 5:12). He reminded the Philippians they were "the circumcision" (v. 3; meaning people truly in new covenant with God) who have "no confidence in the flesh" (or any fleshly act, like circumcision). He further underscored his personal pedigree that featured legalism, past trust in circumcision-covenants, and violent opposition to the gospel. If anyone had reason to trust these ways of attacking the gospel, it would have been Paul.

Heretics are aggressive. They require an aggressive response. Passive compliance and gentle negotiation doesn't work when one side is intent on undermining the core commitments of the other. While Christians strive for winsomeness in relationship with most unbelievers, these gospel-attackers are a different breed. They are so dangerous they must be confronted. It is hard to stand up for the gospel at work, in your family, and around your community. But stand up you must!

The Gospel Rejects Human Righteousness

Paul claimed personal righteousness based on his birth. He was "circumcised the eighth day, of the stock of Israel, of the tribe of Benjamin, a Hebrew of the Hebrews" (v. 5). He was purebred in every sense. Paul achieved some righteousness through religious service. He was "concerning the law, a Pharisee; concerning zeal, persecuting the church; concerning the righteousness which is in the law, blameless" (vv. 5–6). As a religious zealot, he had achieved status that earned him standing among the religious-elite. Paul "counted [as] loss" (v. 7) his human-received and human-achieved righteousness. He underscored that he counted "all things loss" and "as rubbish" (v. 8) when it came to knowing Jesus.

You may consider yourself a good person. You may have been born into a good family, have lived a moral life, and made mostly good choices in relating to others. None of this compares favorably, however, to the true standard of righteousness—Jesus Christ. You can't depend on your natural or spiritual legacy to gain righteousness before God. This temptation is powerful. Most people are defensive when their shortcomings are revealed. It's hard to admit you are a sinner and need a savior. The more respectable you are, the more difficult it may be to reject your false righteousness. Still, you must turn from all of it and receive the righteousness available in Jesus to have genuine salvation.

The Gospel Rests on Divine Righteousness

Salvation depends on God's righteousness, made possible through the atoning work of Jesus. Genuine righteousness comes from God—"from God by faith" (v. 9). Genuine righteousness is made possible by Jesus "through faith in Christ" (v. 9). Genuine righteousness is accessed by faith—"through faith . . . by faith" (v. 9). Paul was adamant about the divine priority in providing the possibility of human righteousness.

Righteousness before God comes only from God. Your sinfulness keeps you from generating righteousness (Rom. 6:23). Your situation is hopeless—no matter how well you mask the reality of the situation. You are a sinner. Jesus' crucifixion was God's means of extending righteousness to you. Because Jesus was fully God, His death on the cross satisfied the offense of your sin before God. Because Jesus was fully human, His sacrifice on the cross represented and included all humankind. Because of His perfect sacrifice, the broken relationship between God and humanity was "made right." Righteousness has been made possible. Your response must be to receive this gift of righteousness—being made right with God—by faith in Jesus. You can't generate it on your own. You can only receive it from God through Jesus.

Conclusion

The gospel is under attack in our generation. Even some religious leaders are at the forefront of undermining its foundations. You must discern any attack on the gospel and resist it. But winning apologetic battles isn't enough. You must also reject your own heresy about the gospel—that you are good enough to deserve it. You must turn from your sin and receive the righteousness offered to you as a gift from God. Only then will you have a right relationship with God and be equipped to help others have the same.

LIFE IN A HEALTHY CHURCH

Growing Up

Philippians 3:10–16

Dr. Jeff Iorg

Introduction

Sanctification is a high-sounding word. It means "to be made holy." Christians who pursue holiness are often lampooned as holy-rollers or having a holier-than-thou attitude. The challenge of true sanctification is growing in your faith without these negative connotations.

The Process of Christian Growth Is Relational

Paul described his pursuit of Christian growth in relational terms. He wanted to know Jesus and "the power of His resurrection, and the fellowship of His sufferings" (v. 10). Further, Paul wanted to share the power of Jesus' death and resurrection (vv. 10–11)—"conformed to His death . . . I may attain to the resurrection from the dead" (vv. 10–11). Paul wanted to know Jesus more intimately. He longed to experience the spiritual realities summarized in and through the life of Jesus.

Spiritual growth centers on knowing Jesus. It's focused on knowing a person, not completing a program. Your sanctification—being made more holy—is about becoming more and more like Jesus, not comparing yourself favorably against others.

The Challenge of Christian Growth Is Demanding

Paul didn't feel he had developed spiritual supremacy. He had not "already attained" nor been "already perfected" (v. 12). He didn't consider himself a fully mature Christian. Paul expressed the quest to continue growing in strong terms. He used phrases like "press on," "lay hold of" (v. 12) "reaching forward" (v. 13), and "press toward" (v. 14) to describe the intensity of the process. He continually reached "toward the goal for the prize of the upward call of God in Christ Jesus" (v. 14).

Spiritual growth is demanding. It requires focused effort. It's never fully accomplished. There is always something new to learn or do. When you think you "have arrived," it's a sure sign you haven't. Your sanctification means you will change, which is hard. You must change your attitudes and actions to reflect Jesus in your life. While that won't be easy, it's always worthwhile.

The Barriers to Christian Growth Are Deceiving

Paul warned the Philippians about pressuring each other to grow. He reminded them God would reveal how they needed to change. Paul also reminded them to live up to what they already knew they should be doing. The danger in both situations is creating legalistic pressure to grow for the wrong reasons and toward the wrong goals.

Spiritual growth will be stunted when it's motivated by exceeding others. Rather than focus on what others should be doing, focus on your growth. As part of this, work on what you already know you should be doing. Learning new things is important, but it's also vital to do what you have already learned. Don't be deceived—your growth is your responsibility.

Conclusion

God grows people at His pace and in His ways. God wants you to grow. Focus on becoming more like Jesus. Work hard at it! Don't try to keep up with the expectations of others. Do what you know you should be doing and trust God for the results.

LIFE IN A HEALTHY CHURCH

Standing Firm in Your Faith

Philippians 3:7–4:1

Dr. Jeff Iorg

Introduction

"A new broom always sweeps good," one wise friend cautioned me about trusting a new employee with too much responsibility. He advised me to let him prove himself, to see how he stood up over time, before promoting him. Making commitments is easy. Making a good start is not that hard. Standing firm and finishing well is much more difficult.

Stand Firm by Following the Example of Others

Paul challenged the Philippians to "join in following my example" as well as the example of other faithful Christians—"and note those who so walk, as you have us for a pattern" (v. 17). The Philippians had been blessed with leaders like Paul, Timothy, Epaphroditus, and others. They could draw strength from these examples of faithful, effective service. Since others had endured suffering for Jesus, they could do so as well.

Choose your role models carefully. Follow people you respect and admire who typify the kind of Christian you want to be. As you observe stalwart Christians, their modeling will motivate you to stand firm against illness, trials, temptations, and disappointments.

Stand Firm by Opposing the Enemies of the Gospel

Paul took opposition to the gospel seriously. He called gospel-detractors "enemies of the cross of Christ" (v. 18). He described them this way: their "end is destruction ... god is their belly ... glory is in their shame ... their mind [is] on earthly things" (v. 19). Paul was grieved by their efforts, weeping over the destruction they were causing. He characterized their opposition as persistent and consistent by describing their negative life-pattern as a "walk" (v. 18).

Stand against enemies of the gospel. Recognize the aggressive and progressive nature of their resistance. In contrast to the positive Christian examples mentioned previously, be on guard lest these negative influencers become your role models. Anyone who leads you away from Jesus and the lifestyle He mandates is dangerous to your steadfastness in the gospel.

Stand Firm by Anticipating Eternity in Heaven

Christians have current citizenship in heaven. This means we are eternally secure, right now, and can remain steadfast no matter our temporal challenges. It also means we have an eternal home, already secured forever. As we look to heaven, we also anticipate the return of Jesus who is there now and will return to take us to be with Him forever.

Reject temporal threats to your faith based on your eternal security in Jesus. He has already prepared a place for you in heaven. He is securing you now for His eternal companionship. You sustain your current commitment by anticipating your future in heaven. Since nothing can threaten your eternal security in the future, why should you allow it to threaten you now?

Conclusion

These are trying times to be a Christian. Threats abound. Standing firm in your faith is essential and possible. Use the spiritual resources outlined in this passage to endure—no matter what comes your way.

LIFE IN A HEALTHY CHURCH

Keeping the Peace

Philippians 4:2–9

Dr. Jeff Iorg

Introduction

Peace is more than declaring a truce. It's when sources or reasons for conflict are eliminated, not just ignored or set aside. Pursuing peace is an ever-present challenge. Finding peace, even in difficult or divisive situations, is possible.

Keep Peace in Your Relationships

Eudia and Syntyche were committed Christians whose "names are in the Book of Life" (v. 3). They were also dedicated workers who "labored … in the gospel" (v. 3). Some disagreement, significant enough to be singled out publicly in this letter, had marred their relationship. Paul pleaded with them to resolve their differences. He challenged the church's leaders to "help these women" (v. 3) heal their relationship.

Christians, even committed Christian workers, can have conflict. These broken relationships hurt the people involved and damage the fellowship of their church. When those conflicts become well known, church members or other Christian friends must facilitate healings. Peace in relationships is possible when both parties are "in the Lord" (v. 2).

Keep Peace in Your Circumstances

Anxiety can be produced by anything and everything. Prayer, focused on thanksgiving, is the primary strategy for overcoming worry and finding peace. Choosing joy in the Lord contributes to giving thanks in all circumstances. Peace is possible as you move through trying times. Through prayer, God's peace "will guard your hearts and minds" (v. 7). The word translated "guard" is a military term for standing guard duty. When you pray about your concerns, God takes up guard duty to protect you.

Everyone, including committed Christians in healthy churches, will eventually face daunting circumstances—illness, death, job loss, natural disasters, and so forth. When overwhelmed by fear, pray! When trouble comes, remember "the Lord is at hand" (v. 5) and choose to "rejoice in the Lord always" (v. 4). God draws near when others fall away. Like a first responder, God runs in when most people run away. Your most profound experiences with God will be during your darkest times, not when life is happy.

Keep Your Peace of Mind

Thoughts run amok during trying circumstances. Our minds race with all kinds of negative possibilities. When this happens, center your thoughts on what is true, noble, just, pure, lovely, of good report, leading to virtue, and worthy of God's praise. Determine to act on positive thoughts based on the example of how other Christians have responded to similar situations. Do what you have "learned and received and heard and saw" (v. 9) other Christians do to thrive through difficulty. Draw encouragement from the example of others.

The primary battlefield for most believers is in their mind. Controlling your thoughts is difficult, though not impossible (2 Cor. 10:3–5). Basing your behavior on sound thinking leads to peace. When random thoughts produce impulsive actions, chaos usually results.

Conclusion

Peace is possible in every situation—but it can be hard to find. Finding peace requires proactive steps like healing relationships, prayer, and wise thinking. Pursue peace.

LIFE IN A HEALTHY CHURCH

Getting to Give

Philippians 4:10–23

Dr. Jeff Iorg

Introduction

Giving is a special privilege for Christians. It's a means to several ends—learning to obey God, sharing in expanding the gospel's influence, and developing faith in God's provision. Give for all those good reasons.

Give to Send the Gospel to Others

The Philippians were early supporters of Paul's missionary efforts. He commended them that "in the beginning of the gospel … no church shared with me concerning giving and receiving but you only" (v. 15). They had also "sent aid once and again" (v. 16) when he was in Thessalonica. He now celebrated their help once again, rejoicing "in the Lord greatly that now at last your care for me has flourished again" (v. 10). Epaphroditus had delivered their most recent gift, which Paul received as a "sweet-smelling aroma, an acceptable sacrifice, well pleasing to God" (v. 18).

Christians send the gospel to new places by supporting people who take it there. Missionary work and pastoral leadership are done by people, not projects. Find some leaders who are extending the gospel to new places and support them financially. When you do this, you are part of the gospel's expansion.

Give to Care for Christian Leaders

Although the Philippians had supported Paul from the beginning, their gifts had lagged. Their most recent gift meant "at last your care for me has flourished again" (v. 10). He had been "in … distress" (v. 14) and had faced difficult trials. Paul viewed these difficulties as an opportunity to grow his faith. While his response is commendable, nevertheless, the difficulties were preventable—if financial resources had been more forthcoming and timely.

Christian leaders have practical needs and must have ample resources to meet them. When those resources aren't provided by their followers, both the leader and followers suffer. The leader must spend time solving his financial dilemma, taking time and energy away from service given to followers. The followers lose out because their leader isn't focused on serving them.

Give to Receive from God

Giving to get something in return is selfish. God, however, delights in giving to generous people. God blesses generous donors with spiritual "fruit that abounds to your account" (v. 17). God also blesses givers with more financial resources. Paul promised whatever need had been created by the support sent to him would be met because "God shall supply all your need according to His riches in glory by Christ Jesus" (v. 19).

Giving to get is a poor motive. But being replenished when you give is God's promise. When you give, He gives back—both spiritual and material blessings. Receiving back from God when you give in obedience to Him is an immutable spiritual law. Don't give to get—but you will get when you give.

Conclusion

Giving is a privilege. By your giving, you can expand the gospel, support worthy leaders, and assure yourself of God's ready supply to meet your needs and enable you to give even more to others.

PREACHING THE AUTHORITY OF THE WORD OF GOD

Gripped by the Holiness of God

Isaiah 6:1–7

Dr. James MacDonald

Introduction

Holiness. What image does that conjure up in your mind? Possibly you think of holiness as a list of rules to freeze freedom and crush your creativity. Maybe you have known some people who claimed to be fired up about holiness, but there's nothing appealing about their lifestyle or perspective on living a God-centered life.

That's not God's kind of holiness.

God does not present His holiness as a horizontal prescription for human activity. God displays holiness as the central and defining essence of His character.

To know God as He truly is requires dispelling our human notions of holiness and thinking about it in a fresh, new way. Let's start there—with a lofty view of exalted holiness from the God who said, "Be holy, for I am holy" (1 Peter 1:16). When we allow ourselves to be gripped by that reality, no human standard of goodness, no man-made regulation of righteousness, no plastic, legalistic creed will ever again substitute for such a fearful and wonderful encounter. That's what Isaiah discovered during the event recorded in Isaiah 6:1–7.

Gripped by the Holiness of God

a. Isaiah's vision is one we desperately need in the church today. Why? Because it blows away the comfortable, manageable God we've fashioned for ourselves. It reminds us how small we are and how great He is. So great, in fact, that He is unapproachable except in the ways He has prescribed.

b. When God instructed the children of Israel to build the tabernacle, He included a place for Himself called the Holy of Holies that was so sacred, so ominous that only one person once a year could enter, and only with an offering. This vision Isaiah had of entering God's throne room invites us, through Isaiah's eyes, into a place very few people have ever been. How many times have we said we want to know God? Well, here's our chance. Let's explore Isaiah's vision one piece at a time:

c. The date 740 BC marked the end of an era. King Uzziah had been a fixture in Israel, ruling the nation for fifty-two years. When Uzziah died, the nation's moral climate went into a tailspin. In the midst of this moral confusion, God called Isaiah to speak for Him.

> "I saw the Lord . . ."
> John 12:41 indicates that Isaiah actually saw the pre-incarnate Christ, the second person of the Trinity. It couldn't have been God the Father, as is commonly thought (John 1:18).
>
> "sitting on a throne, . . ."
> Sitting—not pacing back and forth. Sitting—not wringing His hands. Sitting—not struggling or searching. Not God. Where was He? He was seated. He was settled. He was secure. He was certain.
>
> "high and lifted up, . . ."
> I believe that the main reason the church has lost its moral vision is because it has lost its high and exalted view of God. We have embraced the comfort of His nearness at the expense of His transcendence.

"and the train of His robe filled the temple."
The train is the part of the robe that communicates honor. Isaiah cannot elevate his eyes beyond the hem of our Lord's garment.

d. Isaiah is so completely awestruck that he has to look away and says in effect with his next phrase, "Let me tell you about the angels."

"Above it stood seraphim; . . . (v. 2)
The seraphim are the angels that exist in the throne room who instantaneously do the bidding of almighty God—ever standing to serve the seated Sovereign. The Hebrew word *seraph* literally means "the burning ones."
And one cried to another . . . "Holy, holy, holy" (v. 3)
Imagine all the things they could say about God. But God, in a mystery we could guess at but never comprehend, chose that the words spoken continuously before His throne would be of His holiness. And this never stops. This emphatic praise never ceases.

e. "And the posts of the door were shaken by the voice of Him who cried out . . ." (v. 4).

It seems he thought just the doorway was shaking as if to say, "This far! No farther! You can go no closer to the holy presence of almighty God."

"and the house was filled with smoke."
Why smoke? I believe that it was God's protection of Isaiah, lest he be consumed in another moment by the utter terror, by the majestic purity and power, the unsearchable, unspeakable, infinite holiness of the triune God (Ex. 33:20).

Preferring the comforting truths of God's love and mercy, we have lost this awesome vision of His holiness. We desperately need to be gripped by this view of the highness and the holiness of God. Because we have failed to let it capture our hearts, we so seldom hear what comes next in verse 5.

Isaiah's Response

a. His only appropriate response to the impact of being gripped by God's holiness was "Woe is me, for I am undone!" (v. 5).

The word *woe* means literally the calamity has fallen or is about to fall (Mal. 3:2). The same is true today. You cannot gaze upon the holiness of God without being overcome (Ps. 130:3).

b. ". . . For my eyes have seen the King."

He discovered at a deeper level we are all immensely unclean before the holiness and righteousness of almighty God. In the purity of God's holiness, our sinfulness is exposed for public inspection.

Cleansed

a. "Then one of the seraphim flew to me" (v. 6).

Praise the Lord for the word *then*. We are only prepared to receive and comprehend the grace of God when we have understood His infinite holiness and our incredible sinfulness. Any presentation of the gospel that leaves that truth out is incomplete. It's the holiness of God that casts us upon His mercy.

God calls us to holiness. That's why that seraph went to the altar and got a coal to cleanse Isaiah. God wants us to be holy. That's a picture of our loving, forgiving, merciful God.

b. "And he touched my mouth" (v. 7).

In the fullest and most awe-producing vision in all of Scripture regarding God's holiness, there is this additional picture of His forgiveness.

What Isaiah experienced from the altar was symbolic of the sacrifice of Jesus once for all (1 Peter 3:18). And it can be yours in this moment if you embrace by faith the forgiveness God freely offers in Christ (Rom. 6:23).

Converted for Holiness

God does not offer to forgive us simply so we can come to a crisis of conversion and receive the eternal benefits of His forgiveness. God cleanses us because He wants to transform us, to make us holy just as He is (1 Peter 1:14–19).

Conclusion

Are you gripped by the awesome reality of this truth about God? Will you let the holiness of our awesome God take you and shake you so that you can never see temptation as tempting again? Begin by rejecting the kind of surface adjustments that substitute for holiness in so many corners of Christ's kingdom.

PREACHING THE AUTHORITY OF THE WORD OF GOD

Promise #1: God Is Always with Me (I Will Not Fear)

Deuteronomy 31:6; Hebrews 13:5–6

Dr. James MacDonald

Introduction

God's promises are great (2 Peter 1:4)

a. because they come from a great God (Ps. 145:3; Jer. 32:27).

b. because they address the great issues (Ps. 27:13). David was saying, "I'm not going to have to wait until heaven someday—I'm going to see God's goodness right here on earth."

God's promises are exceedingly great (2 Peter 1:4).

They are

a. greater than human wisdom (Prov. 18:2).

b. greater than white-knuckled obedience.

c. greater than wallowing in self-pity.

God's exceedingly great and precious promises are your best possession.

a. There's nothing remotely like them.

b. They will lead you through the darkest night.

c. They will carry you through the longest day.

d. They will accompany you through the deepest valley.

God's promises are . . . precious (2 Peter 1:4).

a. The older you get, the more you realize that *precious* takes time. *Precious* comes with a weight that conveys value.
b. Peter learned a lot about what is of greatest value in this world and in our faith (1 Peter 1:7, 19; 2:4, 6). The word he used was *precious*.

1. Promise #1: I will not fear . . .

The Bible recognizes that one of our greatest problems is fear.

a. We fear the *future*.
b. We're afraid of losing people.
c. We are terrified about emotional pain.
d. We fear failure.

Let us agree that fear is a universal problem. It hits us like a wave, threatening to swallow us in its undertow. Scripture identifies the overwhelming emotion of fear almost a thousand times. The word *fear* is used 438 times; *afraid*, 167 times; *tremble*, 101 times; and *terror* or *terrified*, 119 times.[1] The words *dread*, *frighten*, and *faint* are also used repeatedly throughout Scripture.

2. God is with me (Heb. 13:5*b*-6).

The antidote for fear is the promise of God's presence. *God is with you*; *God is with me wherever I go. How could I be afraid?*

a. Now "God is with me" includes more than the fact of God's omnipresence. Yes, God is everywhere; therefore He is where we are (Ps. 139:7–10; Jer. 23:23–24).
b. To the believer in Jesus Christ, this first promise is that God is with us *individually*. This is the sense in which *with* us also means *for* us, as in Romans 8:31.

c. Scripture assures us that Jesus Himself is praying for you. *This minute* (Heb. 7:25). With even more assurance, you can be certain that God listens when His Son is praying!

d. Hear the words Jesus prayed for you in John 17:13–19. After reading this scripture, you may think, "That is a great promise, James, but isn't God with everyone?" That's a good question. Scripture, as we will see, actually says "*No, He's not.*"

i. God is not "with" the proud (Ps. 138:6).
ii. God is not "with" the worldly (James 4:4).
iii. God is not "with" the rebellious (Isa. 1:5, 15).
iv. God is not "with" those who harbor sin (Ps. 66:18).

3. God is for us (Heb. 13:5*b*-6).

a. God is for us! Proof: He gave His Son (Rom. 8:31)
b. God is for us! Proof: He defends us (Rom. 8:33–34)
c. God is for us! Proof: He helps us (Heb. 13:5*b*–6)
d. The promise you can memorize: Deuteronomy 31:6

4. Best of all, God is with us (Ps. 23:4).

Illustrate with the story of John Wesley's final words: "Best of all; God is with us!"[2]

Conclusion

The God who knows the end from the beginning has made some promises. This is a great one: *God is with me. God is with you. We have nothing to fear.*

PREACHING THE AUTHORITY OF THE WORD OF GOD

Gripped by the Sovereignty of God

Isaiah 45:1–8

Dr. James MacDonald

Introduction

God's sovereignty has gotten a bad rap lately. Let's say tragedy strikes (for example, sudden bad news from a doctor that includes one or more of the following words: cancer, terminal, inoperable). Then, before the impact of the tragedy has gone from your head to your heart, some goody-two-shoes, wannabe theologian wraps his overly familiar arm around your shoulders and whispers words intended to comfort, but instead they cut like a knife. "God is sovereign; all that He allows is for a higher good."

If that's all I knew about God's sovereignty, then I would conclude, "God is good sometimes, but He's cruel other times. I guess you just can't trust Him."

That is not true, but it will take me some time to explain. Stick with me here:

1. Let's start with a foundational truth—God's display of His sovereignty is scary sometimes, but only because it's so not like us.
2. When it comes to how He directs the people and events of history, God doesn't need our permission.

God's Sovereignty Expounded

The term *sovereignty* means "independent." That means:

a. God is the ruler of all.
b. God answers to no one.

c. God can accomplish whatever He wants—in all things.
d. God sees history from beginning to the end. No obstacle or adversary can hinder His plan from happening.
e. God is afraid of nothing. Ignorant of nothing. Needing nothing.
f. God always knows what's best, and He never makes a mistake.
g. Sovereignty means God is in control of it all, both today and what was happening in Isaiah 45:1.
h. Nothing can ever stop or slow God's sovereign purposes.

    So 150 years before the events happened, God revealed to Isaiah the details surrounding Israel's return to the land (Isa. 45:2–6 and Ezra 1).

i. To sum up: God is the ruler of the universe, and He is the king of human history (Isa. 45:6–7).

The Sovereignty of God Explained (a Bit!)

a. God is not the author of sin, but He is the One who created a world in which we can choose. Much of the pain in our world is the direct consequence of individual sin, such as murder, greed, and hatred. But there is also the suffering we all must bear as members of a fallen race. In that sense it can accurately be said that God is the author of a world in which calamity does strike.
b. Two questions about God's sovereignty:
    I. Am I just a puppet? (See Deut. 30:15–20; Josh. 24:15; Matt. 11:28.)
    You absolutely have a choice. Christ calls and we choose if we are going to respond. Yes, Ephesians 1:11 says that God determines all things according to the counsel of His will. That's true too. Neither one of them can be diminished. God is absolutely sovereign in all things. We also have a

free will to make life choices for which we will give an account. (Deut. 29:29).

II. How can a loving God allow so much human suffering? God does not get up every day trying to figure how He can plant a bigger smile on your face. God is in the process of growing us and changing us. His love is a transforming love (Heb. 12:6).

God's Sovereignty Is Everywhere

a. God is sovereign in salvation (Deut. 7:8; Isa. 45:17; John 6:44).
b. God is sovereign in sanctification (Isa. 45:8–10).

The difference between people is not the circumstances we go through, but how we choose to deal with those circumstances.

God's Sovereignty Embraced

Three ways we can choose to embrace God's sovereignty:

a. I will be obedient when told. In your heart determine that "when God's Word says something, I will obey it."
b. I will be righteous when tempted (Isa. 45:8; 66:2).
c. I will be submissive when tried (Isa. 45:9).

Conclusion

Being gripped by God's sovereignty doesn't take away your questions … but it will take away your anxiety. Determine today to surrender your why? questions to God. From your will, release God to resolve or not resolve any issue that looms large in your life. Ask God to make this a turning point in your lifelong walk with Him. Live with the mystery of how He is working all things together for your good even when you cannot see it or even imagine how (Rom. 8:28; Eph. 1:11–12.)

PREACHING THE AUTHORITY OF THE WORD OF GOD

I'm Dead to That

Romans 6:8–11

Dr. James MacDonald

Introduction

Here's this whole sermon in a sentence: For life change to happen, we must apply the power of our identification to Christ at the specific point of temptation. Now let's explore what this means.

If we refuse to change personally, we'll be the only ones not changing—because everything around us is sure changing! It is unbelievable how fast things are changing. Consider just four areas:

1. Public media
2. Personal communication
3. Travel
4. Moral change

In spite of the dramatic, alarming rate at which our world is changing, most born-again, Bible-carrying followers of Jesus Christ are not changing. The "leavening" (Matt. 13:33), "salting" (Matt. 5:13), and "lighting" (Matt. 5:14–16) effects that Jesus said His true followers would have in society are spotty at best. Every study and every survey indicates the same thing: whether the statistics seem to be going up or down in any area like divorce, premarital sex, spousal abuse, the numbers don't differ much between church goers and non-churchgoers. How can we change the world when we ourselves are unchanged?

Forgiveness is just the beginning of life in Christ (v. 8). Know it.

a. Forgiveness is not the end of something; it's the beginning. Instead of saying after we come to Christ: "Man! I'm all set! It's done! It's settled! I'm on my way to heaven," we ought to be saying, "This is just the beginning." That's why Paul said here, "If we died with Christ [that's His death for my forgiveness], we believe that we shall also live with Him."

b. Not only must we live for Him now, but we must live by means of Him. All of our life is plugged into His life. We cannot live for Him without Him living out His strength in us. The grace of God demands that we be pursuing with our whole hearts the life change Christ died to bring us.

The power of sin is broken, once for all (v. 10*a*). Believe it.

a. Paul was using sin and death synonymously. When he spoke here of sin, he had death in mind; when he spoke of death, he had sin in mind also. All through the Bible, these two are connected (Rom. 5:12; 6:23).

b. Sin and death are synonymous in Scripture. Ezekiel wrote, "The soul who sins shall die" (18:20).

Living for God is day by day (vv. 10*b*, 12). Choose it.

a. Choose to live for God. You can choose it. Look at Romans 6:10. That biblical phrase belongs in a frame over every Christian life: "The life that He lives, He lives to God." God the Son lives toward the Father. He lives for the Father's pleasure. He lives for the Father's joy. He lives for the Father's glory.

b. Now as His followers, can we do any less? This is where living like Jesus begins, with our living to the Father.

Victory over sin is moment by moment (v. 11). Reckon it.

a. The phrase "consider yourselves to be dead to sin" (NASB) also has been translated "reckon yourselves to be dead indeed to sin" and "count yourselves dead to sin" (NIV). No matter the translation, Romans 6:11 is the absolute centerpiece of Christian victory in the entire New Testament.
b. The Greek word for "consider" or "reckon," *logizomai,* means assessing the facts, pressing your mind upon, calculating the importance of. It means considering myself dead to sin. Please believe me when I tell you that there is incredible power here.
c. Speak four little words: I'm dead to that!

Conclusion

If you want to be different at that point of temptation, exercise your faith. Believe in your heart that you are dead to sin and confess with your mouth—speak it out! There is great power in verbal confession. Almighty God honors faith expressed at the point of temptation. Believe in your heart and confess with your mouth those four words: "I'm dead to that." If you say those words—if you will speak them out—your behavior, your speech, your attitudes, whatever you are working on, will be changed!

PREACHING THE AUTHORITY OF THE WORD OF GOD

Replace a Complaining Attitude

Numbers 11:1–3

Dr. James MacDonald

Introduction

Here is the point of this sermon: complaining is an attitude choice that if left unchecked will wither my capacity to experience joy and genuine thankfulness. Let's take a hard look at the attitude of complaining.

When we express resentment over circumstances that are beyond our control and about which we are doing nothing, we are complaining. God hears it, hates it, and pushes everyone who persists in it toward the wilderness. Remember that those who choose complaining as their lifestyle will spend their lifetime in a wilderness.

We desperately need to learn how God judges our complaining with emotional fallout that makes our lives like "a dry and thirsty land where there is no water" (Ps. 63:1).

We Choose Our Attitudes (Num. 11:1–3)

It starts with us. Until we embrace as fact the idea that we choose our attitudes, we will never be able to choose differently, and life will always be a like a wilderness. Notice what Numbers 11:1 says: "the people"! They couldn't point the finger anywhere but at themselves.

What's an Attitude?

a. Attitudes are patterns of thinking. You develop a way of thinking about things—a way of approaching life. Every person, including you, has patterns of thinking; a way that you approach life. It goes back to the time when you were very young.

Imagine for a moment that you and I are observing a toddler who just dropped a large, red rubber ball. He has many attitudes to choose from:

i. "Dumb ball! Who made this cheap, lousy ball anyway? It's so slippery!"
ii. "Where's my parents? If they really loved me, they would help me pick up this ball!"
iii. "I always drop balls. What's wrong with me? I'm such a loser!"
iv. Or, he could choose to say: "It's my fault. I dropped the ball. People drop balls all the time. I'm going to have a positive attitude. I'm going to pick it up and go on."

The key to happiness is in the attitude we choose when we do "drop a ball." Attitudes are patterns of thinking. But here's the second part of the definition:

b. Attitudes are patterns of thinking *formed over a long period of time.* Trace the career of the children of Israel, and you will know they didn't suddenly become complainers in Numbers 11. Go back to the days when they were making bricks in Egypt. They were constantly whining and sniveling about everything.

You say, "Well, their lives were hard."

But some of them chose complaining and resentment toward God, and others in the exact same circumstances chose thankfulness instead. Attitudes are patterns of thinking formed over a long period of time.

Wrong attitudes are hard to change because they are habitual, harmful ways of thinking about life and circumstances. We get so used to reacting a certain way that our choices become automatic, and in time we cease to see them as actual choices. *Tragically, the consequences are also automatic,* and that is the cycle we must break. You can take the first step when you are willing to say, "I choose my attitudes."

The Truth about Complaining

a. Complaining Is a Sin

The word *sin* literally means "missing the mark"; "failing in regard to God's holy standard and just demands." So equating complaining with sin puts complaints in a dangerous category.

b. The Definition of Complaining

Complaining is expressing dissatisfaction with a circumstance that is not wrong and about which I'm doing nothing to correct.

First, complaining is about things that are not wrong. If the thing is wrong, and you express dissatisfaction, it's not complaining. It's not a sin to say to my spouse, "We need to spend more time with the children." That's not complaining. Complaining is grumbling about things that aren't wrong.

Second, complaining involves things that I'm doing nothing to correct. I'm choosing to whine about it, but I'm not doing anything to correct the situation. It is complaining to talk about your husband's lack of time with the children. It's not complaining when you talk with your husband and together try to reach a constructive solution.

Third, complaining involves circumstances. Please note that complaining doesn't involve people. Criticism involves people; complaining involves circumstances.

> **Finally, complaining involves expressing dissatisfaction.** This gets a little tricky. Some people pride themselves on verbal control. But introverts need to recognize that they're not simply living in victory because they have a piece of duct tape over their mouth (1 Sam. 16:7). Complaining is not just the outbursts of frustration; it's also what we think. In the short term, it separates us from God; in the long term, it becomes a lifestyle, and we spend our lifetime in the wilderness.

How Common Is the Problem?

Very! Think of the last time you were in a crowd that was disappointed for any reason—last ticket sold, movie showing has technical difficulties, power failure in the mall, carpeting or paint changed at church—what's the first response you hear? Complaining!

God Is Listening

God heard every word of every complaint of the children of Israel (Num. 11:1). The pillar of cloud by day and the pillar of fire by night should have been awesome and humbling evidences of God's nearness. Instead, the people took God for granted. This wasn't the only time they complained (Ex. 14:12; 15:24; 16:3; 17:3). God heard their complaints, and He hears *our* complaining

The Worst Kind of Complaining

Yes, God hears our complaining about the weather and whatever else we complain about. But one particular kind grates most on the ears of God. Look at Numbers 11:1 again: "Now the people became like those who complain of adversity in the hearing of the LORD" (NASB).

That's the worst: complaining about adversity. "Why do I have to go through that?"

Warning: "Do not regard lightly the discipline of the LORD. . . . For those whom the LORD loves He disciplines" (Heb. 12:5–6 NASB). God has entrusted to every person a measure of adversity.

Note: The very adversity that you so often complain about is the thing God wants to use to keep your heart close to His.

God Hates Our Complaining

Notice God's response to those who complained (Num. 11:1). This was not an isolated occurrence (see 11:10, 33; 12:9; 25:4; 32:14).

Today's thinking: *Well, that was then. This is now. God doesn't get angry anymore.*

But Psalm 7:11 says, "God is a righteous judge, and a God who has indignation every day" (NASB). Every day!

You say, "But God is a God of love."

Yes, He is. And in His infinite transcendence, God can both love us extravagantly and hate our sin passionately at the same time. This concept may be a bit confusing to us, but it is perfectly clear to the Lord. He loves us and hates sin. Both are true.

Watch Out! A Holy Judgment

In Numbers 11:1 the people's complaints not only kindled God's anger, but "The fire of the LORD burned among them." That phrase "the fire of the LORD" appears five times in Scripture. The phrase describes the all-too-common outpouring of God's wrath and judgment. His holiness creates a cleansing fire.

Let's Talk Solution

We need to ask ourselves some soul-searching questions:

1. *Am I a complainer?* Complaining is so hard to see in ourselves, especially when it's reached the habit stage. It's easy to see in others.

2. *Am I reaping the consequences of complaining in my relationship with God?* Imagine that God whispered into your heart right now, "I'm listening. I hear everything you say and think—all of it."
3. *Am I willing to repent?* Am I willing to turn from that attitude of complaining, acknowledge its wrongness, and ask God to change my attitude?

Conclusion

Review those three questions in a quiet time alone with God. Invite His Spirit to reveal His answers for you. If things aren't clear, ask someone you trust the first two questions. Deal seriously with question 3.

PREACHING THE AUTHORITY OF THE WORD OF GOD

. . . With a Thankful Attitude

Psalm 107; Luke 17:12–19

Dr. James MacDonald

Introduction

We are concluding the statement from the previous sermon by adding, ". . . With a Thankful Attitude." We're going to put off the old attitude of complaining, and put on the new one of thankfulness. Let's begin by summarizing the lesson in a sentence: *Thankfulness is the attitude that perfectly displaces my sinful tendency to complain and thereby releases joy and blessing into my life.*

If you ever thought thankfulness was not important to Christ, you were wrong.

Rare Gratitude

a. **Thanklessness is nothing new (Luke 17:12–13).** Since the beginning of time, humanity has called forth in an unbroken, mighty chorus: "God, do this for me! God, I need that!"
b. **God's faithfulness remains (Luke 17:14).** Jesus graciously healed.
c. **The thankful are unique (Luke 17:15–16).** Only one turned back. He was fired up with gratitude! Notice the humility. He not only fell down, but he did so as a Samaritan.
d. **Christ notices those who are ungrateful (Luke 17:17–19).** There is no doubt that Christ was aware of and disturbed by such a flagrant instance of ungratefulness.

God, Our Gracious Provider

a. Only when we acknowledge God as the gracious provider of general blessings, like life and breath, food and shelter, do we begin to comprehend our need for God in a personal way and begin to express faith in Him.

b. Paul made this same point on a cosmic scale in Romans 1. Apart from thankfulness, our awareness of God will always be *suppressed* (Rom. 1:19–20).

c. Only the most resolutely unbelieving person would ever stand and look at the universe and say, "There is no God." "The fool has said in his heart, 'There is no God'" (Ps. 14:1).

d. Note: Thankfulness is far more than saying the right words. The kind of life-changing heart attitude that God desires is much deeper than surface verbal gratitude.

The Power of Thankfulness (Ps. 107)

a. Thankfulness is a decision (Ps. 107:1, 8, 15, 21, 31). Thankfulness is a choice we make. It's just as real as any other decision.

b. Thankfulness is a decision based in reality (Ps. 107:8). Use your mind and ask, "Do I really have a lot to be thankful for?" The answer clearly is "Yes!" The classic book by Daniel Defoe, *Robinson Crusoe*, illustrates perfectly that thankfulness is a decision based in reality. (Reference his response to the shipwreck)

c. Thankfulness is a life-changing decision (Ps. 107:8). My favorite word is the first one, *Oh*. "Oh, that men would give thanks to the LORD ... for His wonderful works to the children of men!" That word *oh* tells us that something radical and life changing is coming.

Gratitude is the Attitude That Sets the Altitude for Living!

a. Unfortunately, there is a kind of low-altitude life that too many people live. It's a down-and-dirty, cloudy, damp, depressing, ungrateful, unthankful, complaining, negative, ugh! sort of living. We've all spent some days there. It's definitely a wilderness!

b. But there is another kind of living. It's a high-altitude attitude—up where the air is clean and the sun is shining and the future is as bright as the promises of God—gratitude!

Let's Talk Solution

Now it's your turn to look inside—to see if the attitude of gratitude resides in you. Here are three questions to ask:

a. *Am I a thankful person?* No doubt about it; thankfulness is a choice.

b. *Am I seeing the blessings of thankfulness in my life?* When thankfulness is part of the discipline of our lives, we will see increased joy and happiness.

c. *Am I choosing thankfulness over complaining moment by moment?* Gratitude is one moment at a time. Remember, attitudes are patterns of thinking formed over a long period of time. Choose to be thankful, moment by moment.

Conclusion

Here's a closing challenge. Can you commit to dedicating a notebook by your bed and recording each day, before you go to sleep, five things for which you are thankful to God from that day? If you will do this exercise regularly, it will transform your life—and sleep too.

PREACHING THE AUTHORITY OF THE WORD OF GOD

Self in the Dirt: A Picture of Repentance

2 Corinthians 7:8–11

Dr. James MacDonald

Introduction

Repentance is the funnel through which all personal revival flows. Repentance is the first, unavoidable step in a personal cleanup of the wreckage sin brings. Refusing repentance only takes us down and never takes us up. Repentance alone opens the way to a fresh outpouring of God's favor in our lives.

Repentance Is a Good Thing (vv. 8–9*a*)

Trust me on this one: you want more repentance in your life. The church at Corinth was the most problematic church in the New Testament. In the letter we call 2 Corinthians, Paul pleaded with them to halt their sinful behavior.

a. In verse 8 Paul refers to an earlier corrective letter that he had written them. Apparently the earlier letter was to the point, as in, "Hey, repent or else!"
b. Paul had some moments of doubt about his strong rebuke because he said, **"I did regret it"** (v. 8*b*).
c. Apparently they were wounded by the truth, but it was only temporary. Eventually they repented, and that was the cause of Paul's rejoicing (v. 9).
d. Paul rejoiced because he knew that only when the Corinthian Christians were wounded by the reality of their sinful choices

could they begin to experience the renewing power of His Spirit at work in their lives.

Jesus and Repentance

a. You say, "Well, preaching repentance is fine for the apostles, but that's not the tender heart of Jesus for me." In Revelation 2:5 Jesus says, **"Therefore remember from where you have fallen, and repent"** (NASB).

b. Repentance is the heart of Christ for the church even if it takes drastic measures (Rev. 2:16).

Five Marks of Genuine Repentance

a. Grief over sin (2 Cor. 7:9–10). The word *grief* is the Greek word *lupeo*, meaning "greatly distressed." This passage is the most concentrated statement in all Scripture about the feelings that accompany repentance (Gen. 18:27; Job 42:6; Isa. 6:5)

b. Repulsion over my sin (2 Cor. 7:11*a*). Repentance brings with it a new urgency about my relationship with God and strong negative feelings toward anything that would injure it.

c. Restitution toward others (2 Cor. 7:11*b*). When repentance is happening in your heart, you will have an immediate and urgent desire to get to the people whom your sin has wounded and fix the fall-out. Zacchaeus (Luke 19) is famous for this.

d. Revival toward God. Paul characterizes the Corinthians' renewed relationship with God in the words **"what fear"** (v. 11). Their genuine repentance had increased in them "the fear of the LORD" (Prov. 9:10; Eccl. 3:14).

e. Future focus (2 Cor. 7:11). As an outgrowth of repentance, the joy of the Lord has returned and you're excited about sharing your faith; you're looking forward to heaven. "What fear, what longing, what zeal," Paul says in verse 11 (NASB). Genuine repentance leads to moving forward and not looking back.

Conclusion

It's easy to spot people who haven't repented—they live in the past. They're stuck. I hope this doesn't describe you. Paul reminded the Corinthians (v. 9) that repentance was not a loss to them but actually a gain because it got them out of the rut of a self-condemning past and moved them forward into the freshness of a revived relationship with God. *Today is the first day of the rest of your life.* When you can say that and mean it from your heart, it's a fruit of repentance.

PREACHING THE AUTHORITY OF THE WORD OF GOD

Seven Habits of Highly Hypocritical People

Matthew 23:1–39

Dr. James MacDonald

Introduction

We can't start examining authenticity until we've confronted hypocrisy. All of us know people who wear masks; acting like they're something they're not. But if we're not careful, hypocrisy is an easy act to put on ourselves.

We can't read Matthew 23 attentively without feeling just a little uncomfortable, because Jesus didn't mince words when it came to hypocrisy. The first verses (1–7) are a backdrop. Jesus recognized that the current religious leaders had inherited Moses' authority. But they had no license to revise or rewrite what God said.

The Pharisees were famous for putting on a good show in public while they exempted themselves from their own rules in private. Jesus turned His attention toward them directly and used the strongest language of denunciation to address the subject of hypocrisy.

He will repeat that word *woe* seven times in the verses that follow. The Greek, *ouai*, is not so much a word but a heart cry of anger, pain, and denunciation. It expresses grief and profound dissatisfaction.

Making salvation as complicated as possible (v. 13)

a. The expression "the kingdom of heaven" is a reference to salvation; entrance into God's family.

b. Even a small child can receive Christ by faith. It's not easy (it wasn't easy for Jesus to provide our salvation and it's not easy to turn away from pride and sin to receive the gift with open hands), but it's simple. Hypocrites go out of their way to make it complicated.
c. Hypocrites leverage people into religion and out of personal relationship with Jesus Christ.

Getting what I need from people even if it hurts them (v. 15)

a. Hypocrites hurt people; they don't help them. They do damage in the name of God.
b. I am always amazed by Christians who can claim to love the Lord but leave a trail of hurting people in their wake.

Squirming my way out of any promise I don't want to keep (vv. 16–22)

a. This is probably the number one disappointment I've felt as a pastor; people who say they'll do things and then don't follow through.
b. The Pharisees had a "fingers-crossed-behind-your-back" clause in their commitments.

Making a big deal of little things and ignoring things of critical importance (vv. 23–24)

a. Inflating random issues out of size and importance is hypocrisy.
b. When Christ says justice, He's talking about doing what's right (Micah 6:8).

Exhibiting laziness in all matters of the heart (vv. 25–26)

a. In this judgment, Jesus pointed to *all* matters of the heart—anything having to do with my soul, my faith.
b. He exposed the laziness of hypocrisy in spiritual life—not willing to extend energy in loving God.

Looking good to others, no matter what the cost (vv. 27–28)

a. He was saying, "Crack your shell and, inside, all we'll find is a pattern of you saying one thing and doing the other. And your lack of concern about your spiritual condition will lead to lawlessness."
b. The hypocrite says, "I don't care what the Bible says. I'm going to do what I want to do."

Pretending to be better than others, no matter what the evidence (vv. 29–36)

a. Within days, these people will murder Jesus Christ. They are going to call for His unjust crucifixion. They are blind to their true condition.
b. A lifetime of unrepentant hypocrisy reveals that a person has never truly been born again.

Conclusion (vv. 37–39)

a. The offer from heaven flows in these words, alongside the sadness over the many who "will not!" They will hear the invitation and turn away. God will call; they won't answer. Stubbornness of the heart is a terminal sickness.
b. There is no solution for that condition apart from repentance and God's work of grace to break the heart.

PREACHING THE AUTHORITY OF THE WORD OF GOD

The Discipline of Personal Prayer

Matthew 6:5–13

Dr. James MacDonald

Introduction

As we develop the core disciplines of a sincere faith, we must include work on prayer. Even those of us who have grown up around praying people need instruction. And who better to talk to us about prayer than Jesus Christ. That's what we find Him doing in Matthew 6.

The twelve original disciples spent three years hanging out with Jesus. They watched Him, traveled with Him, and listened to Him. There is no record they ever asked Him, "Lord, teach us to teach," even though He was a Master Teacher. Not once did they say, "Lord, teach us how to do miracles," though we know He worked awesome wonders. As far as we know, the only request like this the disciples ever made to Jesus was, "Lord, teach us to pray" (Luke 11:1).

Jesus begins by acknowledging how much prayer is not authentic. He wants His disciples to practice prayer under certain directions we can discover with seven questions. Use them as you evaluate the current health of your prayer life.

Is my prayer real? (vv. 5–6)

a. By that phrasing, I don't mean, is it real prayer? I mean, is my prayer genuine, sincere—authentic? The hypocrites got an emotional rush out of displaying their holiness. If your public prayer exceeds your private prayer, and if you prefer it that way, well, you can see how Jesus goes on here (v. 5).

b. Solitary prayer is a mark of your sincerity, only seen by you. Who goes by themselves into a room with the door closed and gets on their knees to fake it? No one pretends in secret.

Get this: The secret to prayer is prayer in secret (v. 6).

Is my prayer simple? (vv. 7–8)

a. The Gentiles thought, "Well, this god is going to like it if I say it one more time. If I persist, God's going to hear me."
b. We can see this in the story in 1 Kings 18:17–40.
c. Prayers do not inform God. Prayers exercise faith in God.

Is my prayer worshipful? (vv. 9, 15*b*)

a. This short phrase is where people often make a mistake. Jesus wants us to pray, not pray *this* prayer.
b. I believe this prayer provides us with *categories* of praying. Each of the lines in the Lord's Prayer points to one of the categories. As follows:
c. The prayer expresses recognition. We are saying, "May You be recognized for who You are—absolutely holy." Now that's a category of praying.
d. The name of God has to do with God's person and reputation. (Review names of God, for example)

Yahweh-Tsikenu, "I Am your righteousness" (Jer. 23:5–6)
Yahweh-M'kaddesh, "I Am the One who is changing you" (Lev. 20:8)
Yahweh-Shammah, "I Am the Lord who is there" (Ezek. 48:35)
Yahweh-Shalom, "I Am the Lord, our peace" (Judg. 6:24)

Is my prayer submissive? (v. 10)

a. Whose kingdom, mine or God's? (God's.) Whose will, mine or God's? (God's.) That's one of the things going on in prayer—submitting our will and our territory to God.
b. Sometimes prayer changes things. And sometimes prayer changes me.

Is my prayer practical? (v. 11)

a. Our daily bread represents all the basics we require.
b. There are four essential needs covered by bread we can pray for: Income, physical health, emotional health, spiritual health.

Is my prayer repentant? (v. 12)

Authentic prayer includes repentance.

Is my prayer expectant? (v. 13)

The essence of the Lord's Prayer is an attitude of expectation that God does hear, He draws near, and He does answer.

Conclusion

Recognizing and using the categories Jesus included in His model prayer puts us on the right path for an authentic prayer life.

PREACHING THE AUTHORITY OF THE WORD OF GOD

The Power of Biblical Friendships

1 Samuel 23:16–18; 2 Samuel 12:1–15

Dr. James MacDonald

Introduction

Most Christians today are not living at the peak of their spiritual experience. They know how to fire it up, but they don't know how to keep it going. This message is about how to keep it going. The Christian life is not a solo thing. It requires teamwork. This is about how to download the incredible resource God has given us in our brothers and sisters in Christ. We desperately need each other so that when we want to quit we can't, because our friends "won't allow it!"

Lasting change requires biblical friendship.

a. The key word in this statement is *biblical*, because not all friendships are biblical. In fact, some are very unbiblical. Not only do they not help us; they impede our progress on the pathway toward transformation.
b. Instead we need biblical friendships. After twenty-five years as a pastor, I can tell you that people who change—people who develop a life pattern of change, becoming more and more mature as followers of Christ—are surrounded by biblical friendships. Without those kind of friendships, they cannot flourish spiritually. Neither can you.
c. Change does not happen in a silo. You may have the picture that transformation is just you and God. Maybe you have been seeing yourself with Bible open, eyes turned upward, and

the Spirit of God filling you—just you and God, and change happens. That is not a complete picture! We cannot flourish spiritually in the long-term without each other.

d. It's time to knock the silo down and begin to pay attention to the people God has placed around you as resources for change. That is why God has called together this thing called *the local church.*

A biblical friend holds you up when you stumble (David and Jonathan) (1 Sam. 23:16–18).

a. As you read God's Word, you cannot help noticing that great men and women of faith always had supportive friends around them. Always! (Illustrate: Paul had his team; Moses had Joshua; Mary had Elizabeth; Jeremiah had Baruch.)
b. The story of David and Jonathan is a picture of phenomenal, transforming, biblical friendship. If ever there was a friendship with the cards stacked against it, this was the one (1 Sam. 16:14–15; 18:10–11; 19:9–10).
c. Notice five ways that Jonathan supported David:
    1. *presence.* First, a biblical friend holds you up when you stumble because he is there for you (v. 16).
    2. *prayer.* Jonathan "strengthened his hand in God" (v. 16).
    3. *protection.* Jonathan gave his friend assurance (v. 17*a*).
    4. *personal loyalty* (v. 17*b*).
    5. *promise.* A biblical friend holds you up when you stumble by confirming the friendship with a covenant (v. 18).
d. The key ingredient is *love* (Prov. 17:17).

A biblical friend holds you down when you stray (David and Nathan) (2 Sam. 12:1–15).

a. A brutal story, told in love (vv. 1–6).

b. The key ingredient: truth (vv. 7–15). As I look back through my walk with Christ, at every point of change there have been these truth-telling friends.

Biblical friendship provides change that lasts.

a. Choose a friend committed to change. It's a two-way thing. Change flourishes when it's a partnership.
b. Review biblical pattern for change.
c. Commit to mutual accountability for change. Share your observations about how your friend is doing and hold each other accountable.

Conclusion

I believe a joyful life of transformation is possible, because the Bible says it is. I covet for you a personal relationship with Jesus Christ that leads not only to the forgiveness of sins, but, as a new creation in Him, to a life of victory and ongoing change in which you become more like Jesus. If you follow the process of change and access the power to change as taught in the pages of Scripture, you will experience the abundant life that Jesus promised: "I came that they may have life, and have it abundantly" (John 10:10 NASB).

PREACHING THE AUTHORITY OF THE WORD OF GOD

The Power Source

Romans 7:15–8:17

Dr. James MacDonald

Introduction

Before we unpack this message, let's hear the whole thing in a single sentence: for life change to happen, we must access the power of God for change, admitting that we do not have the strength within us.

Most of the Christians I meet are very tired. They don't have the passion for God they once had and feel a kind of vague guilt about it. The sequence is always the same: countless seasons of (1) renewed expectation, (2) energetic pursuit, (3) encroaching disappointment, and finally, (4) exhaustion. "What's wrong with me—why don't I learn? Why don't I change?

The Exhausting Christian Life (Rom. 7:15–19)

a. The victorious Christian life was eluding Paul, and amazingly, under the inspiration of the Holy Spirit, Paul admitted it.
b. I say to my own shame that I spent too many years trying to be a godly man in my own strength. The problem with approaching sanctification using the Bible as simply action steps is that the results are always temporary: be loving; be patient; be self-controlled; pray; study the Bible; and witness. All these things going in the air like some kind of professional juggler desperate to keep the "act" going, but knowing that very soon it is all going to come crashing down on top of us.

Make the choice to be done with all the silly posing and posturing and "look at me, how hard I'm trying to be a good Christian."

The Exchanged Life (Rom. 7:24–25)

a. Just as a person cannot come to Christ until he comes to the end of himself, so you cannot experience the power to change until you are done with your own efforts. That's what Paul did when he confessed (Rom. 7:24). Those are not easy words to say from your heart.
b. The answer is Christ (v. 25)! Our only hope is to get out of the way and let Him live His life through us.
c. The gospel can be summarized in four words: Jesus in my place.
d. God's plan for sanctification can also be summarized in four words: not I, but Christ.
e. Now how do you grow in Christ? The same way (Col. 2:6; 1 Thess. 5:16–24)!

The Empowered Life (Rom. 8:1–13)

Beginning in Romans 8:2, the apostle repeated a key word that indicates the source of a powerful life in Christ: *Spirit*. Until we let Jesus live His life in us by His Spirit, we are going to be exhausted.

a. Spirit filling defined. (Eph. 5:18)

   The filling of the Holy Spirit is very similar to being filled with pain or joy. It means to be overcome by a power greater than yourself, to be controlled by it.
b. Spirit filling analyzed.
   1. The filling is commanded. Nowhere in Scripture are we commanded to be indwelt, baptized, or sealed with the Spirit because those things happen to us at conversion, but we *are* commanded to "be filled."

2. The filling is passive. God does the filling when we ask Him. We cannot do it for ourselves.
3. The filling is for everyone—it's for you.
4. The filling is not permanent. Believers are never baptized by the Holy Spirit more than once. However, there were multiple fillings (Acts 2:4; 4:8; 9:17; 13:9).

Proof of the Holy Spirit Filling (Rom. 8:14–17)

This passage includes five indications of the Holy Spirit's filling and controlling presence:

a. Leading, v. 14
b. Confidence, v. 15*a*
c. Intimacy, v. 15*b*
d. Security, v. 16
e. Identity, v. 17

Hindrances to Spirit Filling

When our actions are not pleasing to the Holy Spirit, they greatly limit His work in our lives.

a. Grieving the Holy Spirit (Eph. 4:30). Doing things we should have left undone.
b. Quenching the Holy Spirit (1 Thess. 5:19). Refusing to do things He wants us to do.

Conclusion: How to Be Filled with the Spirit

a. Confess all known sin (1 John 1:9).
b. Ask the Holy Spirit to fill you (Luke 11:9–13).
c. Believe you have received the Spirit's filling (Mark 11:24).

PREACHING THE AUTHORITY OF THE WORD OF GOD

We Need a Downpour

Hosea 6:1–3

Dr. James MacDonald

Introduction

The Bible teaches in Isaiah 58:11 and in many other places that the human heart is like a garden. Your heart is the immaterial part of you that can know God; it's the part that will live forever. If you weed and water and tend your heart as Scripture instructs, you'll experience a bumper crop of God's grace in your life. Conversely, if you fail to garden your heart, first it will become overgrown with weeds, then it will become lifeless and dry, and eventually it will disappear in a dust storm. People who have lost heart are legion. Second Corinthians 4 twice exhorts us not to lose heart, because if we do, we've lost everything. No wonder the wisest man who ever lived exhorted, "Guard your heart!" (Pro. 4:23 NIV). You have to take care of your heart.

Read again this amazing assurance given by the prophet Hosea, found in 6:1–3.

Background: Hosea preached for about eighty years. Isaiah and Micah were his contemporaries. Hosea is the first, the largest, and the most theologically complete of the minor prophets. The question answered by Hosea is, *Does God love us even when our hearts are far from Him?* The answer: Yes, He does!

The Invitation to Revival

a. **Let us return to the Lord** (v. 1*a*). God invites you to come back to Him. No matter how far away you are right now or how long you've been gone, Hosea 6:1–3 opens the door. That passage is an invitation to revival. The Hebrew term translated "return" is used more than a thousand times in the Old Testament (Hosea 5:4; 7:10; 11:5; 14:4, 7). The entire book of Hosea proclaims the assurance that good things await those who *return* to the Lord.

Turning begins with the recognition that some things have to go.

Turning to the Lord is repenting.

Turning to the Lord is actually re-turning

b. **Let us press on to know the Lord** (v. 3*a*). There are four distinct aspects that fill out our understanding of how awesome this knowledge of the Lord really is:

Knowledge of the Lord consists of facts about God (Rom. 11:33).

Knowledge of the Lord is a heart understanding of those facts (Mark 12:30).

Knowledge of the Lord is an experience with God (Acts 17:28).

Knowledge of the Lord is a blessing from God (James 1:17).

c. **Are we pressing on?** It means waking up and giving that pursuit everything you have (Rom. 13:11).

The Pathway to Revival

a. Through pain to purpose (v. 1*b*). The word *torn* is severe and kind of unsettling to see it describing God's work in us. Why? God is drawing your heart back to His. God has a purpose for that pain.

b. Through death to life (vv. 1*b*–2). God's goal is always that the pain He brings would take us to a better place (Job 5:17–18). Sometimes God brings us to death or a state where death would be easier. God would rather see us in a world of hurt than not be the prize of our highest affections.

c. Will you let life's pain bring you to God's purposes?

The Experience of Personal Revival

a. It's available (v. 3*b*). Every day the sun comes up, and God continues His work all around you.

b. It's abundant (v. 3*b*). You can be on your way to a better place with God than you've been in a long time, if you will turn and return to God on His terms.

Conclusion

To make abundance abundantly clear, Hosea uses the analogy of rain in the nation of Israel: "He will come to us as the showers, as the spring rains that water the earth" (Hosea 6:3 ESV). When revival comes to the human heart, it's not some gentle, summer, sunshine rain. It's not a sprinkle here and there or a scattered shower. When revival comes to the human heart, it's a torrent, it's a cascade, it's a deluge. It's a downpour. That's what we're asking God to bring to us!

PREACHING THE AUTHORITY OF THE WORD OF GOD

Why Trials?

James 1:2–8

Dr. James MacDonald

Introduction

Why?

It's the question that hits the hardest.

It's the question that hurts the most.

It's the question that lingers the longest.

It's the question that every follower of Jesus Christ has asked. You've asked it and so have I. Why, God?

Does your heart pound a little faster reading that question? Is your secret exposed? Have you been quietly anguishing, even pleading with God for some answers: "Why this, why me, why now?"

Before we can go any further . . .

You've got to put this question to rest. The good news is that God does provide answers in James 1. But before those truths can take root in your life, you must ask yourself, *Am I willing not only to hear God's answers, but to embrace them?*

Consider Your Trials . . . *What*?

I'd like to nominate James 1:2 as one of the most outrageous scriptures in the Bible. That is what James wrote, through the inspiration of God's Spirit, but it doesn't add up from our perspective. Getting a more biblical definition of joy really helps us make sense of the encouragement to find joy when life is hard. Joy is something very different than what we commonly refer to as happiness. So when the Scripture says, "Count it all joy," the Lord is not saying, "Be happy about your trials."

So what is joy? Joy is a supernatural delight in the Person, purposes, and people of God.

a. **Joy comes only from God.** You can't make yourself joyful. Joy comes only from God. When James says, "Consider it all joy," he's telling you, "Reach out to God. Get God's heart in this matter."

b. **Joy is only for the family.** That's why James 1:2 says, "Count it all joy, my *brothers*" (ESV, emphasis added). Only Christians get to experience joy. Only a follower of Christ would ever consider a trial joy, because if life is only about here, now, and my happiness, trials really don't make any sense or give any good.

The Faith Test ... and the Faith Final Exam

"The testing of your faith" (v. 3). A trial is a test of your faith. Testing is God's good plan to get some good results. You have to take the faith final exam over and over in your life:

a. Do you believe that God is in control? (Please support your answer from Scripture.)

b. Do you believe that God is good no matter what you see, no matter what you face? (Trust me that I understand the gravity of the first two questions.)

c. Will you wait on Him by faith until the darkness becomes light? (See Ps. 27:13.)

Trials' Good Benefits

a. Trials produce staying power—understand the meaning of *hupomenō*.

Remain under the pressure by God's grace and in His strength and when you pass the test by persevering, a lot of great things are in your future. Will you remain under this trial and wait for God to accomplish His purpose in your life?

b. Trials produce life transformation

You can come to the place where the circumstance itself is less painful than the commitment not to give up. If staying put was easy, if submitting to what God allows and not giving up was simple . . . everyone would be doing it. The fact is, most Christians are going round and round with God about the very same things because they change scenery or marriage or job or church rather than remaining under the trial and letting God change them.

That's why God has you working in the place where you can do the most good: in the mirror. God is working on you and me from the inside. God is trying to change you and grow you on your own customized training program.

God's Wisdom Training Program

James 1:5 is one of the most abused verses in the New Testament. I'm guilty too. James 1:5 was not intended as a crib note to bypass study. The context of this promise is trials. God promises that if you will ask for wisdom in your trials, He will give it to you. Humble yourself before the Lord, and say, "I want to know why You've allowed this trial. What are You trying to teach me, Lord, and where can I begin to work on myself first?"

a. **Ask without doubting.** Tell God this, and He will answer you generously; He will not reproach you. But here's the key: Make sure you really want to know.

Notice what James 1:6 says. Ever watch a beach ball in the crowd at a sports arena? It floats here, then gets batted over there; then it drifts up or down. Now it's over there. A lot of us are like that in the middle of a trial.

You sort of want to know what God wants to teach you, but you've got these creeping doubts.

"For the one who doubts . . . must not suppose that he will receive anything from the Lord" (vv. 6–7).

You've got no more control over where your life's going than that beach ball. Instead, each of us must humble ourselves and say, "God, whatever You want to teach me—nothing is off limits. Take it all!" Only when I pray for wisdom with no strings attached, no limits of any kind on what God can talk to me about, can I expect the wisdom I need about the why of what's been so very hard.

You and I have got to ask in faith.

b. Refuse to be double-minded (1:8).

Someone who doubts is like a two-souled person—a person who's like, "I want what God wants, but I don't want what God wants. I want to learn, but I'm angry!"

I can think of a lot of times in my life where my focus in a trial was less on what God was teaching me and more on how hurt I felt by the actions of another. When my focus is on revenge, or making my point, or hurting you back, or getting the pressure off, I am very unstable—not just in the trial but in everything.

Conclusion

All right, ready to commit to *hupË˜omË˜en¯o*—to remaining under the trial? Ready to pray the real "why" prayer about the person in the mirror, the only one you can really change?

DETOURS, DEAD ENDS, AND DRY HOLES

Sermon Date: July 9, 2004

Exodus 13:17–22

Dr. Adrian Rogers

Outline

Introduction
I. The Discipline of Detours
II. The Dilemma of Dead Ends
- A. Fear Not
- B. Stand Still
- C. See the Salvation of the Lord
- D. God Shows Us the Way

III. The Disappointment of Dry Holes
Conclusion

Introduction

Take your Bibles and turn to Exodus 13. "And it came to pass, when Pharaoh had let the people go, that God led them" (v. 17 KJV). We'll just stop right there. And in a moment we're going to read a whole lot more. But just keep your Bibles open.

But notice the fact that God led them. "He leadeth me: O blessed thought!

O words with heavenly comfort fraught."[1]

He leadeth me. Aren't you glad that God does lead us? The Bible says, "As many as are led by the Spirit of God, they are the sons of God" (Rom. 8:14 KJV). "All the way my Savior leads me; What have I to ask beside? Can I doubt His tender mercy, Who through life has been my Guide?"[2] And we thank God for that, and we rejoice in that—that God leads us.

And yet, sometimes, friends, we find ourselves in the biggest messes. And we find ourselves on back roads. We find ourselves in dead-end alleys. We find ourselves in dry places. And we say, "Well, if God is leading us, then He doesn't know how to read a map. Or else, I don't know how to follow. Or, I must be out of His will, because, if God is leading me, how come I keep on ending up on detours and dead ends and desert roads?" Well, we're going to try to answer that today from the Word of God. We're going to find out that God does lead us. And we're on the King's highway. And we're on a journey to joy with Christ as our companion, and the Holy Spirit as our guide, and the Bible as our map. But yet many times it doesn't turn out just exactly like we expect. We find a lot of unexpected things along the road of life, and it's not, however, because we misread the map.

I. The Discipline of Detours

First of all, I want you to look here at the discipline of detours. "And it came to pass, when Pharaoh had let the people go, that God led them not through the way of the land of the Philistines, although that was near; for God said, Lest peradventure the people repent when they see war, and they return to Egypt: but God led the people about . . ."—now, look at that; just underscore that phrase: "God led the people about." That means that God led them in circles—"God led the people about, through the way of the wilderness of the Red sea: and the children of Israel went up harnessed out of the land of Egypt" (Ex. 13:17–18 KJV).

Now the Bible tells us very clearly that God did not lead them the short way—a direct route—but God led them on a detour. God led them 'round about. And it wasn't a mistake; it was a divine detour. And why did God lead them this way? Why didn't God just say, as God was taking the Israelites out of the land of Egypt, through the wilderness, and into the land that flowed with milk and honey—into the Promised Land—why didn't God just take the shortest route?

We say that a straight line is the shortest distance between two points. Well, it may be the shortest distance, but it's not always the best distance.

And God has a purpose, many times, in His detours. And He tells us, very quickly and very plainly, why He did not lead them directly, in verse 17: "And it came to pass, when Pharaoh had let the people go, that God led them not through the way of the land of the Philistines, although that was near; for God said, Lest peradventure the people repent when they see war, and they return to Egypt" (KJV). Now God knew that had He taken them the straight way they would have gone through Philistia. And if they had gone through Philistia, then they would have met the warlike Philistines. And when they saw the Philistines, they would have been frightened. And when they were frightened and their hearts were filled with fear, they would have turned around. They would have turned their heels, and they would have gone back to Egypt. They would have become dismayed. They would have become discouraged. And they would have become defeated. And so God didn't lead them that way.

Now God knew that they weren't ready. They were to battle. There was a war. And God has called us to a war—a holy war. "For we wrestle not against flesh and blood, but against principalities, against powers . . . against spiritual wickedness in high places" (Eph. 6:12 KJV). But I'm so glad that God knows what I'm ready for. And I'm so glad that God knows what you are ready for.

Now God has a land of blessing for you. And God has a place of fulfillment for you. And God has a job for you to do. And God has blessing upon blessing that He wants to give to you. And yet He may have you right now out in the wilderness, going 'round and 'round in circles. And you may think that you are out of the will of God. But you're not out of the will of God. God is leading you 'round about, because God knows that you're not quite ready for some of the things that He has in store for you. And so that winding road, that rocky road, that desert road, and that wilderness road that sometimes we find ourselves on does not mean that we're out of the will of God. God led them. This is the whole point: that God led them on a detour. God did not lead them on the straightest route.

Sometimes, folks, you can get there too quickly. I've seen these ninety-day wonders. They go up like a rocket and come down like a rock. They get out there, and they want it, and they want it now. But, you see, the reason that God led them in the wilderness was because it was God's boot camp. It was out there that He was going to toughen them. Notice where God led them. The Bible says, "But God led the people about, through the way of the wilderness of the Red sea" (Ex. 13:18 KJV). Now, what was that like? It was a place of hardness; it was a place of drought; and it was a place of discipline. What was God doing with them out there? Well, God was just simply toughening them up. It was God's boot camp. It was God's training camp. And God was getting them ready.

Now, doubtless, they didn't understand it. They didn't know what was going on at that time. They didn't know all that God had in store for them. But they didn't have to know: it's enough that God knew. They had never seen the Philistines. Doubtless, they had never heard about the Philistines. They didn't know what was out there. God knew that they weren't quite ready. Maybe you've been asking God to give you a certain job, and you don't have it. Maybe you've been praying and asking God to give you a home. Maybe you've been praying about your date life, or the person you're going to marry. Maybe some of you are wanting to go to school. Maybe some of you are wanting to get into a ministry. Maybe some of you are wondering why you seem to be going around in circles. You're just not ready. God is never in a hurry. God called Moses, and to get Moses ready he spent forty years in the backside of the desert. God called Paul, and Paul wasn't ready. Paul went down to Arabia. And God was just simply getting them ready.

You know, that's a blessing to me, sometimes, because we all think we have to be achieving, and we have to be going in straight lines, or we are out of the will of God. Not necessarily so. The important thing is not that you know; the important thing is that God knows, and that you follow Him. Notice the Bible says, "And the LORD went before them by day in a pillar of a cloud, to lead them the way; and by night in a pillar of fire, to give them light; to go by day and night: He took not away the pillar of cloud by day, nor the pillar of cloud by night, from before the people" (Ex 13:21–22 KJV). That pillar of fire and that pillar of cloud represent the Holy Spirit. As they came out of Egypt, the Passover lamb represents the Lord Jesus Christ. And the pillar of fire and cloud represents the Holy Spirit to lead them. You see, after God redeems us, God sends His Holy Spirit to lead us. And Jesus said, "He, the Spirit of truth ... will guide you" (John 16:13 KJV). And just as that pillar of cloud was their guidance in that wilderness, the Holy Spirit of God is my guidance in this wilderness. And the important thing, ladies and gentlemen, is not that I see where I'm going; the important thing is that, day by day, I have my eyes on the pillar of cloud, and, night by night, on the pillar of fire. Moment by moment, I need to walk in the Spirit.

Now it may be that you're out of the will of God. And it may be that you're going around in circles because you haven't read the map right and because you haven't listened to your guide. It may be that you're completely out of the will of God, and you're stumbling; and you're stumbling around out in some wilderness waste, and you've got no business being there. That may be. But I'm going to tell you something else. It may also be that you are perfectly in the will of God, and God knows exactly what He's doing with you, and you're still going around in circles. So, you see, it is your job just to make sure that you have your eyes on the Lord Jesus Christ—that, moment by moment, there is that inner witness of that pillar of cloud and that pillar of fire.

And that's all you need to know. You don't need to know the rest, and you don't need to understand why it is that things don't seem to work out for you right now. God knows some things that you don't know. God sees some Philistines you don't see. God sees some weaknesses you don't see. And God knows some things that you may not know. So you just keep your eyes on Him and remember the discipline of divine detours. God had them in the wilderness for a purpose and in His boot camp to tighten them up and to strengthen them up. "All the way my Savior leads me, cheers each winding path I tread; gives me grace for every trial, feeds me with the living Bread."[3]

II. The Dilemma of Dead Ends

Now the second thing I want you to notice is not only the discipline of detours. He led them on a detour to discipline them, to help them to grow, and to toughen them up. But I want you to notice also the dilemma of dead ends. "And the LORD hardened the heart of Pharaoh king of Egypt, and he pursued after the children of Israel: and the children of Israel went out with an high hand. But the Egyptians pursued after them, all the horses and chariots of Pharaoh, and his horsemen, and his army, and overtook them encamping by the sea, beside Pihahiroth, before Baalzephon. And when Pharaoh drew nigh, the children of Israel lifted up their eyes, and, behold, the Egyptians marched after them; and they were sore afraid: and the children of Israel cried out unto the LORD. And they said unto Moses, Because there were no graves in Egypt, hast thou taken us away to die in the wilderness? wherefore hast thou dealt thus with us, to carry us forth out of Egypt? Is not this the word that we did tell thee in Egypt, saying, Let us alone, that we may serve the Egyptians? For it had been better for us to serve the Egyptians, than that we should die in the wilderness" (Ex. 14:8–12 KJV).

Now, remember they are still being led of the Lord, and this time they come to something more aggravating than a detour. Now detours are aggravating. Nobody likes to get on a detour, a back road. But there is something worse than a detour: it's after you've been on a detour for a long time, and you come to a dead end. Now that's where these Israelites had come to now. And God is still leading them. There—on one side the mountains, and on the other side are the mountains, and in front is the Red Sea, and behind them comes Pharaoh with his sword glittering in the sun, and blood in his eye, and all of his armies, and all of his chariots—they were between the sword and the sea. They were boxed in; they were hemmed in. There was no way out that they could see.

And now they begin to blame Moses. And their aggravation with their detour turns from aggravation to desperation. "Moses, can't you read a map?" He read it, all right. He was following the Lord. They were not there by happenstance. It is very clear that God led them there. Look in Exodus 14, if you will: "And the LORD spake unto Moses, saying, Speak unto the children of Israel, that they turn and encamp before Pihahiroth, between Migdol and the sea" (vv. 1–2 KJV). That's exactly where God wanted them. God put them there. God led them there. And God did it for a purpose. God had a wonderful purpose. And what was the purpose? Look at verse 3: "For Pharaoh will say of the children of Israel, They are entangled in the land"—now, you see, God entangled them there. God put them in that dead end, because He was baiting His hook. He was going to bring judgment on old Pharaoh, and He was using the Israelites to bait His hook. And—"Pharaoh will say . . . They are entangled in the land, the wilderness hath shut them in." *That is, they are at a dead end, and God says,* "And I will harden Pharaoh's heart, that he shall follow after them; and I will be honoured upon Pharaoh, and upon all his host; that the Egyptians may know that I am the LORD. And they did so" (Ex. 14:3–4 KJV). God had a purpose.

Now, let me tell you something else. In life you're going to come to some situations that are not just aggravating; you're going to come right up against it. And if you have not been right up against it, then you're going to come there. There is no home without its hush. And when God leads, God is going to lead you to a place of desperation time after time again. And you won't see any way out. I mean, there's no preacher who can give you a sermon that will tell you a way out. There is no book that is going to help you. You are just there, and there is no human way out. It is not a discipline; it is a dilemma: the dilemma of dead ends. That's where they were.

I want to tell you something, friend. When you come to that place, there is still no panic in heaven: only plans. There has never been any panic in heaven—never! God knew exactly what He was doing. Now the Jews didn't know what God was doing. And the point I want to make is they weren't out of the will of God when they came to this dead end. They were right in the will of God. It was God that led them there.

And why did God lead them there? So that the place of desperation would become the place of dependence; that we come to the place so that we see absolutely no way out, and then we have to cast ourselves completely, totally, upon the Lord. Look in 14:13, and notice what God said to the children of Israel to do: "And Moses said unto the people, Fear ye not, stand still, and see the salvation of the LORD, which he will shew to you to day: for the Egyptians whom ye have seen to day, ye shall see them again no more for ever. The LORD shall fight for you, and ye shall hold your peace. And the LORD said unto Moses, Wherefore criest thou unto me? speak unto the children of Israel, that they go forward: but lift thou up thy rod, and stretch out thine hand over the sea, and divide it: and the children of Israel shall go on dry ground through the midst of the sea" (Ex. 14:13–16 KJV). Now God brought them to the place of desperation that He might bring them to the place of dependence.

What is the purpose of the dead end in your life? When you come to the place—I mean, by the hand of God that God brings you there—what is the purpose of it? Well, there are four things that God told the Israelites that are true of you today. What does God want you to do?

A. Fear Not

Number one: Fear not. Look in verse 13—look at it: "And Moses said unto the people, Fear ye not" (KJV). You see, God will allow you to come to a place where there seems to be all kinds of things to fear, and then He says, "Fear not."

A man I'll call Steve has blessed my heart many times, but I think he never blessed my heart more than when I talked to him one night in a hotel room after one his sons committed suicide. Steve is a preacher. His son had some mental problems. And mental health professionals worked with him and worked with him. But over the Thanksgiving holidays this boy died by his own hand. And I talked with Steve after that. Steve had been preaching victory in Jesus, and he'd been preaching how the Lord was sufficient. That is the message that Steve preaches. If he had just one message, then I would say it is that Christ is sufficient. And I talked with Steve in the late hours in a motel room, and he said, "Adrian, I've learned one thing: There is nothing to fear." He said, "The reason I know that is I believe I've met the worst the devil can do, and, Adrian, Jesus is still sufficient. Jesus is still sufficient. Now," he said, "had it been less, I would have said, 'Yes, Jesus is sufficient for this, but I don't know if He'll be sufficient for the ultimate.'" But, friend, I want to tell you that Jesus Christ is sufficient for the ultimate.

I don't know where you may come to, but you're going to come to the place. And God has to bring you to that place of desperation that you may learn that there is nothing to fear. Three hundred and sixty-five times in the Bible—one time for every day of the year—the Bible has said, "Fear not," or its equivalent. "The Lord is my helper, and I will not fear what man shall do unto me" (Heb. 13:6 KJV). And so God brings you to this place of desperation, that He might bring you to this place of dependence, that He may say to you, "Fear not."

B. Stand Still

And then He says to you, "Stand still." Look in verse 13: "And Moses said unto the people, Fear ye not, stand still ..." (KJV). That is, it is out of your hands. Finally, there is nothing you can do. The Bible says, in Psalm 46:10, "Be still, and know that I am God" (KJV). And, oh, we hurry around. We're so busy manipulating, trying, conniving, scheming; but finally we come to a place where God hems us in: the sea here, the mountain here, the mountain there, and the devil behind. And there is no way out but up. Just stand still. "Be still, and know that I am *God*." We always think that we have to do something even if it's wrong, don't we?

Somebody talked about those hogs. You remember those two thousand hogs, those demons that were driven out of that demon-possessed man and they went into a herd of swine? And the Bible says that the swine went into the sea and drowned (Mark 5:13). Do you remember that story in Mark 5? Someone imagined one of those hogs saying to the other hog, "Look, we're in a mess. But whatever we do, let's stay together and keep moving."

Now I think that's really the way human beings think today. We've got to do something—just do something. Sometimes God places us in a place where there is nothing we can do. There is no counsel we can go to. There is no banker to help. There is no doctor to help. There is no one to help us. God just says, "Fear . . . not; stand still"; "Be still, and know that I am God." And the place, the dead end that He brings us to—I mean, just the dead end, a dilemma—and then we just fear not and stand still.

C. See the Salvation of the Lord

And then, notice next: "and see the salvation of the LORD" (Ex. 14:13 KJV). Now that doesn't mean to see it after it takes place. It hasn't taken place when He told them to see it. In other words, you, by the eye of faith, see what God is going to do. It means, stand still and watch God do it, because God didn't do it until they started moving again. It meant, stand still long enough for you to see what God is going to do before He does it. You see, we see things that are not, as though they are, that it might be so. There is just this time of faith where we just simply say, "I refuse to fear. I stop. I place myself, dear God, in Your hands. And, God, if You don't do it, then it won't be done. And now, by faith, I see my way out, even when I don't see it."

D. God Shows Us the Way

All right. And then God shows us the way—the way that we've never seen before. Look in verse 15: "And the LORD said unto Moses, Wherefore criest thou unto me? speak unto the children of Israel, that they go forward" (KJV). There is no contradiction here, where it says, on the one hand, "Stand still," and then, on the other hand, where it says, "Go forward." We have to come to that place of rest and confidence, where, by faith, we see God in action, and then, again, we move in a way that we've never seen before.

And notice what God did when God said to them, "Go forward," in verse 16: "But lift thou up thy rod, and stretch out thine hand over the sea, and divide it: and the children of Israel shall go on dry ground through the midst of the sea" (KJV). Do you know what God did to that dead end? He turned it into an eight-lane superhighway, and, dry-shod, they went through the Red Sea. God knows the way through the wilderness.

> Got any rivers you think are uncrossable?
> Got any mountains you can't tunnel through?
> God specializes in things thought impossible
> And does the things that others cannot do.
>
> —Oscar C. Eliason[4]

"I am the LORD, the God of all flesh: is there any thing too hard for me?" (Jer. 32:27 KJV). And that so-called impossibility is God's opportunity to display His glory and His might, if you are living in the Spirit, and if you have your eye on that pillar of cloud and that pillar of fire.

III. The Disappointment of Dry Holes

Now I want us to move on and think not only of the discipline of detours, and I want us not only to think about the dilemma of dead ends, but I want us also to think about the disappointment of dry holes. Continue to read in 15:22: "So Moses brought Israel from the Red sea." Now notice that Moses, God's man, is still leading. The Israelites still haven't got lost. They still haven't misread the map. God is still leading, but notice now the strange way that He leads them now: "Moses brought Israel from the Rea sea, and they went out into the wilderness of Shur; and they went three days in the wilderness, and found no water" (KJV).

Detours, dead ends, and dry holes. You think, "Brother, better throw this map away and get another one. All night long, we thought, at least we had a motel. Now we find a motel, and the one we found hasn't got running water." Here it is. They come to the end of the road now—at least, they are on the road—and they are bone-weary, and they come to this place. God hasn't sent them here because they've done wrong. This is not punishment when they come to this place of bitterness and barrenness. They are here by divine providence. God brought them here for a purpose.

You want to see what that purpose was? Well, continue to read: "And when they came to Marah, they could not drink of the waters of Marah, for they were bitter: therefore the name of it was called Marah." The word *marah* means "bitter." "And the people murmured against Moses, saying, What shall we drink? And he cried unto the LORD; and the LORD shewed him a tree, which when he had cast into the waters, the waters were made sweet: there he made for them a statute and an ordinance, and there he proved them" (Ex. 15:23–25 KJV). "There he proved them" literally means, "Therefore, he tested them."

You know, they make a new automobile, and they take the model of that automobile out to the test track—the proving ground—and they put it through rigors and the bumps. You've seen advertisements of them going around skids, and through water, and over bumps, and all of that—they call that the proving ground. That's exactly what this was for God's people: there, God was proving them. The reason why it was arid there was that God was testing them. God gave them a test, and they failed it miserably.

Incidentally, turn to Deuteronomy 8:2, right there in the neighborhood, and you'll see, again, what God's plan was for them: "And thou shalt remember all the way which the LORD thy God led thee these forty years in the wilderness, to humble thee, and to prove thee, to know what was in thine heart, whether thou wouldest keep His commandments, or no" (KJV). Now, you see, God knew exactly what He was doing. And when they came to this place in the wilderness where there was no water, it wasn't because God was mad at them. And it wasn't because they had sinned. And it wasn't because Moses was a bad leader. The devil didn't do it to them. It was perfectly normal and natural.

You are going to come to the same place, friend. If you follow the Lord, then you're going to find that your life is going to be one of detours, and dead ends, and dry holes, because you're walking in the Spirit. Now that's quite a revelation, because so many times we say, "Well, what went wrong?" Nothing went wrong; not a thing in the world went wrong. God is on the throne, and He's leading you. And in this particular instance, when you come to the disappointment of a dry hole, God is giving you a test. And I pray to God that you won't fail it.

Now, how did Israel do when they came to their test? They failed it, and they failed it miserably. Now, look, in verse 24, and see how they failed the test. The Bible says, in Exodus 15:24, "And the people murmured against Moses, saying, What shall we drink?" (KJV). And they started to murmur against Moses. Now that's a remarkable thing, because the fifteenth chapter of Exodus is what we call "the Song of Moses." They'd just come through the Red Sea on that superhighway that we were talking about, and they were dancing, ecstatic with joy, and they were praising the Lord. And now, just three days later, they are murmuring, and they were complaining. I just declare, I believe that was the very first Baptist church, out there in the wilderness. There they were: just three days ago they had been singing the Moses Song, and now they are murmuring against Moses. Moses has gone, in three days, from hero to zero.

And I want you to learn this if you are a murmurer. When you come to a disappointment in life, when you come to a dry hole along the road, when there is no motel anywhere with hot and cold running water, and it just seems like life has done you dirty, I want you to notice, when you complain, what you're really doing. Moses says, in the last part of 16:8, "Your murmurings are not against us, but against the LORD"—one of the greatest lessons you can ever learn. You teenagers who are murmuring about your parents, God gave you those parents. People murmuring about their teacher, their pastor, or murmuring about their boss. You see, God gave them Moses, and they murmured against Moses. And so, if God gave them Moses, and they murmured against Moses, what they were really doing was murmuring against God. God leads you into a circumstance. And when God, somehow, in His wisdom, leads you to one of life's dry holes and to some of life's bitter waters, and you murmur and you complain, you are really murmuring against God.

Murmuring is no little sin. Murmuring is a great sin. And God lists murmuring with idolatry and fornication. Just turn to 1 Corinthians 10 for just a moment. "Now these things were our examples, to the intent we should not lust after evil things, as they also lusted. Neither be ye idolaters, as were some of them; as it is written, The people sat down to eat and drink, and rose up to play. Neither let us commit fornication, as some of them committed, and fell in one day three and twenty thousand. Neither let us tempt Christ, as some of them also tempted, and were destroyed of serpents" (vv. 6–9 KJV). And now, notice verse 10: "Neither murmur ye, as some of them also murmured, and were destroyed of the destroyer."

Notice God lists murmuring with tempting Christ. God lists murmuring with fornication. God lists murmuring with idolatry. God listed murmuring with lusting. You see, why did they murmur when they came to this place? God was leading them. The pillar of cloud was there. The pillar of fire was there. They were being led of the Lord. Moses was there. The Word of God was there. Why did they murmur when they came to a place like this? It was a lack of faith, and it was also a lack of reason. God had just brought them through the Red Sea.

Now, folks, be reasonable. Would God have brought them through the Red Sea so wonderfully just to bring them to a place to let them die without water? I mean, would God do that? Had God so marvelously delivered them in order to destroy them? That doesn't make sense. Now I want to ask you a question. If Jesus Christ died for you on that cross and has saved you, do you think He saved you to abandon you? Do you? When you come to some place like that, do you think God brought you so far, that God did so much, that God had so much invested in you, that He did all of that for you, and after having brought you that far and having died for you, that now He's going to abandon you? Can't you understand that their murmuring was rooted in unbelief, and it was a terrible, horrible sin against God?

Well, there was no need for them to murmur. They couldn't see it. There was no water. The water that was there was bitter—you couldn't drink it. And as far as they were concerned, it was terrible. But I want you to notice what God did, again. Look in Exodus 15:24: "And the people murmured against Moses, saying, What shall we drink? And he cried unto the LORD"—and there are always those two classes of people in the church: those who bellyache at the pastor, and those who know how to pray. And the people murmured against Moses. But Moses went to the Lord—"And he cried unto the LORD; and the LORD shewed him a tree, which when he had cast into the waters, the waters were made sweet: there he made for them a statute and an ordinance, and there he proved them" (Ex. 15:24–25 KJV).

God showed Moses a tree, and the thing I want you to see is, the whole time they were murmuring. The whole time they were complaining that tree was there—the whole time, the whole time. God had already made provision. God already knew what He was going to do. There is no panic in heaven, only plans. God didn't create the tree; He showed the tree. It was already here. And that tree, of course, speaks of the Lord Jesus Christ that Jeremiah called the "righteous Branch" (Jer. 23:5 KJV). It speaks, of course, of Calvary, for the Bible says, in Peter, that Jesus died upon a tree (1 Peter 2:24). And there, God brought them to this place of dryness and this place of desperation that He might display to them by type, by picture, and by symbol, the sufficiency of Calvary and of the Lord Jesus Christ.

Conclusion

Even in the barren places and even in the bitter places, Jesus is enough. Oh, He wants us to learn it. So many times, we come to the test where God wants to take us and He wants to prove us, and we come to some dry hole along the road of life—some place of barrenness, some place of bitterness. Oh, I pray to God that you won't fail the test.

You see, the amazing thing about this bunch of murmurers is this: that right over the hill—they couldn't see it, but they were following God's map—and right over the hill, not very far away, was a gorgeous, beautiful oasis. Look, if you will, please, in verse 27: "And they came to

Elim, where were twelve wells of water, and threescore and ten palm trees: and they encamped there by the waters" (KJV). I mean, one of the most beautiful oases that you could even imagine—and it was right over the hill. They couldn't see it.

Now there's somebody right here, you're camped right now by a dry hole, and the water that you can find is absolutely bitter. You're saying, "God has forsaken me." God hasn't forsaken you. God is proving you. You're not out of the will of God. God brought you there. It is right on the map. That's the route. That's exactly where God wants to bring you. Don't complain. Don't murmur. Calvary is sufficient for you. Right over the hill, God has an oasis. You can't see it, but God can see it.

Now, look. The important thing in life is not for you to know what God knows—you'll never know that. His ways are not your ways, and His thoughts are not your thoughts (Isa. 55:8). The important thing for you in life is this: that you keep your eye on that pillar of cloud and that pillar of fire, which, translated out in New Testament times, is that you walk in the Spirit and that you keep your heart right with God. And if you go on a detour, praise God. If you come to a dead end, praise God. If you come to a dry hole, praise God. My Lord knows the way through the wilderness. All you have to do is follow. Will you follow Him, and let Him have His way, and not complain, and not murmur?

"Lord, I would clasp Thy hand in mine, nor ever murmur nor repine; content, whatever lot I see, since 'tis my God that leadeth me."[5]

FOUR PRINCIPLES OF VICTORY

Sermon Date: July 11, 1999

Exodus 17:8–13

Dr. Adrian Rogers

Outline

Introduction
I. Receive a Gracious Provision: Salvation
II. Realize a Grand Purpose: The Spirit-Filled Life
III. Respect a Grievous Problem: The Flesh
IV. Remember a Glorious Principle: The Victory Is God-Given
Conclusion

Introduction

I want to tell you something about a church member that I had difficulty with. As a matter of fact, I've had difficulty with this church member for a number of years. Really, he's given me a lot of trouble, and he has disappointed me many, many times. And I have had to just expend a lot of energy with this particular church member who really—frankly, we are a wonderful congregation—but this member has given me much, much sorrow and heartache at times. Maybe I ought to tell you his name. I think I will: Adrian Rogers. You're looking at the guy who has given me a lot of trouble. You know, my biggest enemy is my own self.

Have you found that true? We have an enemy inside the fort called *self*. Sometimes the Bible calls that *the old man*. Sometimes the Bible calls that *the flesh*, but we're all in a battle. You see, we have three enemies: the world, the flesh, and the devil. Now we're going to be talking about that center enemy, the flesh; and when I'm talking about the flesh, I'm not talking about your material body—not talking about your skin and bones. Your body is the temple of the Holy Spirit of God. It is crafted of God, and it is to be wholly dedicated to Him. But when I'm talking about the flesh, I'm talking about the lower part of our nature that we inherited from our parents, who got it from Adam. It is a disposition against the things of God. The Bible tells us, in Galatians 5:17, that "the flesh lusts against the Spirit, and the Spirit against the flesh; and these are contrary to one another, so that you do not do the things that you wish" (KJV).

Now, what does that have to do with the seventeenth chapter of Exodus? Well, let me tell you a secret to understanding the Bible. Now, while the Old Testament is history, it is more than history. Are you listening? It is devotional literature. I'm talking about the Old Testament, and I'm talking about the history of the Old Testament; and I'm talking particularly of the coming of the Jewish nation out of Egypt through the wilderness and into Canaan. The Bible tells us, in 1 Corinthians 10, that "all these things happened unto them for examples" to us (1 Cor. 10:11 KJV).

Now you're going to learn a lesson today about the life of conquest. Remember that at one time the Jewish people were in Egypt and they were slaves. Now Egypt represents the world, therefore, that we've been called out of. But God called them out of Egypt. Pharaoh was the king of Egypt. Pharaoh represents the devil. Then they were headed toward Canaan, a land of oil and wine; and corn and figs and pomegranates; and milk and honey; and rivers and trees; and valleys and hills; brass and iron. They were called into Canaan. What does Canaan represent? Not heaven someday. Canaan, in the Bible, represents victory. Canaan represents the Spirit-filled life—not in the sweet by-and-by, but in the nasty now-and-now, for we can have victory day by day.

So, as Christians, we have come out of Egypt. We're coming through a wilderness, but we're headed toward Canaan; and we ought to already be there. So Canaan represents the Spirit-filled life; Egypt: the world; Pharaoh: the devil; Canaan: the victorious life. But we're going to meet somebody now in just a moment who represents the flesh: that member

I've been having such difficulty with. And I know that, if you're saved, you've been having the same difficulty.

Now, with that in mind, begin in verse 8: "Then came Amalek"—Amalek represents the flesh—"and fought with Israel in Rephidim. And Moses said unto Joshua, Choose us out men, and go out, fight with Amalek: tomorrow I will stand on the top of the hill with the rod of God in mine hand. So Joshua did as Moses had said to him, and fought with Amalek: and Moses, Aaron, and Hur went up to the top of the hill. And it came to pass, when Moses held up his hand, that Israel prevailed: and when he let down his hand, Amalek prevailed" (Ex. 17:8–11 KJV). I can imagine a television news reporter being there saying, "There's a battle. Our man on the field is reporting something. Let me get it here in my . . . Oh, yes, yes," he says, "there's an old man, some man who has a rod in his hand. And as the old man holds up his hand, something is happening down here in the valley, ladies and gentlemen. It seems that, when the old man holds up his hands, Joshua's army is victorious; but when the old man's hands go down, the armies of Amalek are victorious. It's a strange thing that we report today." All right now, notice verse 12: "But Moses hands were heavy; and they took a stone, and put it under him, and he sat thereon; and Aaron and Hur stayed up his hands,"—that is, "held up his hands"—"the one on the one side, and the other on the other side; and his hands were steady until the going down of the sun. And Joshua discomfited Amalek . . ."—that's just a fancy way of saying, "He whooped him"—"Joshua discomfited Amalek and his people with the edge of the sword" (Ex. 17:12–13 KJV).

Now I want to talk to you about four principles of victory, and I want to talk about some Canaan conquest. Now you might right now say, "Well, I've come out of Egypt, but I surely haven't gone into Canaan. I have been dunked in the desert." Well, let me tell you how you can change your life sincerely now—sincerely—from the monotonous to the momentous, from failure to victory; and before you get to heaven, you can bring heaven to earth. I'm talking to you about absolute truth: truth that the Bible teaches, and that I have experienced in my own life.

There are four things I want to lay on your heart. And I've got to do it very quickly; and so you listen in a hurry.

I. Receive a Gracious Provision: Salvation

Number one: You need to receive a gracious provision and that provision is salvation. Now, go back to the first verse of this chapter: "And all the congregation of the children of Israel journeyed from the wilderness of Sin, after their journeys, according to the commandment of the LORD, and pitched"—that is, they "set up their tents"—"in Rephidim: and there was no water for the people to drink. Wherefore the people did chide with Moses,"—they scolded him—"and said, Give us water that we may drink. And Moses said unto them, Why chide ye with me? wherefore do you tempt the LORD? And the people thirsted there for water; and the people murmured against Moses, and said, Wherefore is this that thou hast brought us up out of Egypt, to kill us and our children and our cattle with thirst?" Friend, I've been there, to this place. You talk about a barren, desolate place: it is indeed a barren and a desolate and a dry place. "And Moses cried unto the LORD, saying, What shall I do unto this people? they be almost ready to stone me. And the LORD said unto Moses, Go on before the people, and take with thee of the elders of Israel; and thy rod, wherewith thou smotest the river, take in thine hand, and go." *Now Moses had a rod that was a miraculous rod; we're going to say more about it later on.* "Behold, I will stand before thee there upon the rock in Horeb; and thou shalt smite the rock, and there shall come water out of it, that the people may drink. And Moses did so in the sight of the elders of Israel" (Ex. 17:1–6 KJV).

Now I want you to get the picture. They're out there in the barren land. They're dying of thirst. And then Moses says, "God, what shall I do?" God says, "You take the elders of Israel, and you take a rock; you take a rod, and you go to this rock, and you with that rod smite that rock; and when you do, water will come from the rock." Did you ever try to get water from a rock? "Water will come from that rock."

Now, what is all of this about? Well, I'm not being fanciful when I tell you this is a glorious illustration; though it literally happened, it's a glorious illustration of our salvation. Now, remember, I told you, "All these things happened for examples." *Remember?* "All these things happened ... for examples" (1 Cor. 10:11 KJV). First Corinthians 10:4—the Bible says, "And [they] did all drink the same spiritual drink: for they drank of that spiritual Rock that followed them: and that Rock was Christ" (KJV). That rock pictures the Lord Jesus Christ: the Rock of ages, smitten for us. Isaiah 53:4, says, "We did esteem him stricken, smitten of God" (KJV). You see, Jesus, the Rock of ages, was smitten for us; and because Jesus was smitten for us, out of His riven side, came forth water. And that water represents the Holy Spirit, which is the water of life. And because the rock was smitten so long ago, when Jesus hung in agony and blood upon that cross, and He died—out of His side has come that refreshment, that Holy Spirit that is in me right now—in you right now. Thank God for the blessed, precious Holy Spirit.

I want to ask you a question, my friend. If you're here today, and you've never received Jesus, are you thirsty? Do you know—do you know—that there's something missing in your life? If not something, it is someone. What you're thirsting for is Jesus: I can tell you that. You'll never be satisfied, you'll never feel contentment, until you know the Lord Jesus Christ.

I have an evangelist friend of mine who was on an airplane one time. And this flight attendant came to my friend and said, "Sir, would you like a drink?" He said, "No ma'am." He said, "I had a drink about twenty years ago that satisfied me completely." She said, "You did? Must have been some kind of drink!" He said, "It was." She said, "Tell me about it." He said, "You serve everybody else, come, and I'll tell you about it." The flight attendant served everybody their drinks, then came and sat down beside my friend and said, "Tell me about it." And, friend, he did. He told her about that drink, that Rock of ages, that out of His side has come forth that water of life, and Jesus said, "If you're thirsty—if you're thirsty—come to Me and drink" (see John 7:37).

I wonder, are you thirsty today? Are you thirsty? You say, "God knows I'm empty." I didn't ask you that. My car's been empty many times. It's never once been thirsty. Are you thirsty? Do you want more? Thank God for the smitten Rock.

II. Realize a Grand Purpose: The Spirit-Filled Life

So, the first thing, if you want to live a life of victory—number one—you must receive a gracious provision, which is salvation. Number two: You must realize a grand purpose, because being saved is wonderful, but God has more—much more—for you. You see, God's plan for His people was not merely that they come out of Egypt and go into the wilderness of Sinai; God's plan for His people was that they go into the land of Canaan. I'm not talking about pie in the sky; I'm talking about victory right now. God brought them out, that He might bring them in.

Just go to Exodus 13:3: "And Moses said unto the people, Remember this day, in which ye came out from Egypt, out of the house of bondage; for by strength of hand the LORD brought you out from this place: there shall no leavened bread be eaten. This day came ye out in the month Abib. And it shall be when the LORD shall bring thee into bring thee into"—Notice He brought you out, that He might bring you in—"bring thee into the land of the Canaanites, and the Hittites, and the Amorites, and the Hivites, and the Jebusites, which He sware unto thy fathers to give thee, a land flowing with milk and honey, that thou shalt keep this service in this month. Seven days thou shalt eat unleavened bread, and in the seventh day shall be a feast to the LORD. Unleavened bread shall be eaten seven days; and there shall no leavened bread be seen with thee, neither shall there be leaven seen with thee in all thy quarters. And thou shalt shew thy son in that day in that day, saying, This is done because of that which the LORD did unto me when I came forth out of Egypt" (Ex. 13:3–8 KJV).

Now, what's all this saying? God says, "Look, I brought you out, that I might bring you in." Now God says, "When you get into the land"—notice, the land flowing with milk and honey—"then I want you to celebrate; then I want you to keep the feast of the Passover. I want you to keep the feast of unleavened bread. I want you to celebrate. And when you celebrate the feast, your son's going to come to you, and your son's going to say, 'Dad, what does all this mean?' And you can tell your son, 'Son, we are celebrating what God did for us when God brought us out of Egypt and God brought us into this land.'"

I want to ask you a question. Why is it that the devil is getting the kids of the best families in our churches today? I'm talking about people who are faithful, my friend on the plane: people who sing in the choir, people who take up the offering, people who teach Sunday school, people who love God, people who are saved, people who are tithing, people who live clean lives; and yet their kids, many times, are into drugs, won't come to church, are running with the wrong crowd—maybe sleeping around. How does that happen? Well, I think it's a complicated thing, and we can't put everybody in one category. But I'll tell you, one reason that a lot of it happens is this—and you listen to me: There are people who have come out of Egypt, but they've never gone into Canaan.

Now you know what they had in the wilderness to eat? Do you know what they ate in the wilderness? Manna. Do you know how long they ate it? Forty years. Now manna was not meant to satisfy them; it was only meant to sustain them until they got into the land that flowed with milk and honey, oil and corn, and figs and pomegranates. It was only meant as a temporary food. They were only to spend a little time in the wilderness. They were to come out of Egypt, and they were to go to Canaan. But because of their unbelief, they're going around and around and around in the desert, not believing God. They've come out of Egypt, but they've never gone into Canaan; but they're in the wilderness.

Now in that time—forty years—there were children born in that time. Let's imagine a kid: he's fourteen years of age; he's born in the wilderness; his parents have come out of Egypt, but he's a wilderness boy. He never says, "Mama, what's for breakfast?" He knows what's for breakfast: manna. He never says, "Mama, what's for lunch?" He knows what's for lunch: manna. He never says, "Mama, what's for supper?" He knows what's for supper: manna. He doesn't say, "Mama, what are we going to have tomorrow?" He knows what we're going to have tomorrow: manna, manna, manna, manna, manna! Manna in the morning! Manna in the evening! Manna at suppertime! Manna all the time! Just manna, manna, manna: that's all the kid gets. Now, suppose they've decided they're going to celebrate there in the wilderness. Now, remember, God says, in this passage, "You celebrate; you celebrate in the land, not in the wilderness. You don't have a lot to celebrate in the wilderness."

Now, suppose, there they are: the father sitting on a hot rock, the son sitting on a cactus, and the father says, "We're going to have the feast of Passover." The son says, "Well, Dad, what are we doing?" He says, "We're celebrating, son." Now, remember, this kid has heard sermons about Canaan. That's all he's heard: just sermons about Canaan. He's never seen Canaan. He might have heard Pastor Rogers preach about Canaan, but he's not seen Canaan. His parents are not living in Canaan; his parents are not living the victorious Spirit-filled life; they're not living in victory. All his parents are saying—they've come out of Egypt, but they've never come into Canaan—and they say, "Now, son, we're celebrating." He looks around. He says, "We're what?" A rattlesnake goes by. "What?" Sun is broiling. The tumbleweed is coming along. "What are we doing, Dad?" "Oh, son, we're celebrating what God has done for us." He said, "Dad, don't you think it's about time we got back to Egypt; I mean, where there was fish, and garlic, and leeks, and melons, and fun? All we're doing out here is being dumped in the desert."

I'm going to tell you, that's why the devil's getting a lot of our kids of good people. They have come out, but they've never gone in. They have never learned how to live in victory before their children. And their children know that their parents somehow are sincere, but they feel like they have just simply missed it.

Now, friend, God brought us out that God might bring us in; and if you have been one of those simply dumped in the desert, you have to understand, not only must you receive a gracious provision—salvation—but you must realize a grand purpose, which is victory that God has for you.

III. Respect a Grievous Problem: The Flesh

Now, here's the third thing: You must respect a grievous problem. There is a grievous problem. And what is that problem? Go back to our text now in Exodus 17:8: "Then came Amalek, and fought with Israel" (KJV). What is Amalek? Who is Amalek? Amalek was a king, but he was the grandson of Esau. And who was Esau? Well, Esau, you remember, was the man who sold his birthright for a mess of pottage. I don't have time to get into it, but Esau was a profane man. Esau sold his spiritual things for a bowl of stew; and then he was more interested in the present than in the future, the material than the eternal, the things of the flesh, not the things of the Spirit. And, therefore, the Bible calls Esau, in Hebrews 12, "a profane person … who for one morsel of meat sold his birthright" (v. 16 KJV).

And the Bible teaches, in Malachi, that God has a perpetual warfare declared upon Esau. Listen to this scripture: "The burden of the word of the LORD to Israel by Malachi. I have loved you, saith the LORD. Yet ye say, Wherein hast thou loved us? Was not Esau Jacob's brother? saith the LORD: yet I loved Jacob, And I hated Esau, and laid his mountains and his heritage waste for the dragons of the wilderness. Whereas Edom saith, We are impoverished, but we will return and build the desolate places; thus saith the LORD of hosts, They shall build, but I will throw down; and they shall call them, The border of wickedness, and, The people against whom the LORD hath indignation for ever" (Mal. 1:1–4 KJV).

Now, what's God talking about? God, here, is not talking about little baby Esau when He says, "I hate Esau." He's talking about a whole nation. He's talking about the Edomites. And He's not just talking about people of the flesh, and people in physical bodies. He's talking about a principle—and that principle is the flesh. Now it gets a little complicated here, so pay attention. Amalek is the grandson of Esau. He is a part of that category of persons that God says, "I have a perpetual war with." What does Amalek represent? Amalek represents what all of us have in us—and it is the flesh. Say that word *flesh*—"flesh." Say, "my flesh": that's your enemy.

Remember I said I had a church member I have a lot of difficulty with? Friend, there's an Amalek in you: he's the grandson of Esau, and you have this. "To be carnally minded"—that word *carnally* means, "fleshly minded"—"is death; but to be spiritually minded is life and peace. Because the carnal mind is enmity against God: for it is not subject to the law of God, neither indeed can be" (Rom. 8:6–7 KJV). And then Galatians 5:17: "The flesh lusteth against the Spirit, and the Spirit against the flesh" (KJV). There is that principle that will come against you: the flesh. You say, "Well, I'm over here in Egypt. I'm going to give my heart to Jesus Christ today. I'm going to get saved. I believe on Christ." And you give your heart to Jesus; and, as soon as you drink of that water, as soon as that Rock is smitten for you, as soon as that water comes to refresh you, then the Bible says, "Then came Amalek" (Ex. 17:8 KJV). Immediately, when you come out of Egypt, the flesh comes—Amalek comes—to say, "You are going no further. You are not going to get into Canaan." "Then came Amalek." Deuteronomy says, "he … smote the hindmost of thee, … when thou wast faint and weary" (Deut. 25:17–18 KJV). God will test us in our strongest point. The flesh will attack us in our weakest point to keep us from entering into Canaan.

IV. Remember a Glorious Principle: The Victory Is God-Given

Now, how are we going to have victory, not over the world, not over the devil, but that internal enemy, the flesh? We all have that enemy with us day by day. All right, I've got to fast-forward here. Here's the next thing I want you to notice; and, very quickly, if you would, you must remember a glorious—a glorious—principle. What is the principle? "And Moses said unto Joshua, Choose us out men, and go out, fight with Amalek: to morrow I will stand on the top of the hill with the rod of

God in mine hand. So Joshua did as Moses had said to him, and fought with Amalek: and Moses, Aaron, and Hur went up to the top of the hill. And it came to pass, when Moses held up his hand, that Israel prevailed: and when he let down his hand, Amalek prevailed. But Moses hands were heavy; and they took a stone, and put it under him, and he sat thereon; and Aaron and Hur stayed up his hands, the one on the one side, and the other on the other side; and his hands were steady until the going down of the sun" (Ex. 17:9–12 KJV).

What is the glorious principle? Here's the glorious principle: the victory is God-given. How am I going to overcome the old Adrian, that church member that I have the most difficulty with—how am I going to overcome him? By rededicating my life? By struggling? No! There is a perpetual warfare. That flesh is in me, in you; and when you get saved, the flesh is not eradicated. But, thank God, you can have victory, and the victory is God-given.

God said, "Moses, you take that rod." Now, remember, it was the rod of God; it represents the power of God. It was that rod that opened up the Red Sea. It was that rod that smote the rock and sent forth water, and the rod that led them out of bondage. The rod that led them out of barrenness now is the rod that is going to lead them in battle. He says, "Take that rod; go up to the mountaintop; hold that rod up; and when you hold that rod up, Amalek will be defeated."

Listen. The victory—the victory over Amalek, over your flesh—is a God-given victory. The Bible says, "Walk in the Spirit, and ye shall not fulfil the lust of the flesh" (Gal. 5:16 KJV). If I've learned one thing in all of my Christian life, it is this, precious friend: that holiness is not the way to Christ; Christ is the way to holiness. Now I'm not just playing with words. Listen. He does not say, "If you will not walk in the flesh, then you can walk in the Spirit." He doesn't say that. He says, "Walk in the Spirit, and you will not fulfill the lusts of the flesh."

I'm telling you that the victory over your flesh is a God-given victory: that's the only way that you're going to come out of Egypt, through the wilderness, into Canaan, because there's an Amalek within you that stands against you to try to keep you from living in victory. But, thank God! Hallelujah! Praise God there is a victory when you take the rod of God, which is the Word of God, the power of God, the Spirit of God, and you hold that high. Now that's the reason we need to pray one for another and help one another.

Now I come back to what the whole morning is about. Friend, we need to hold up one another's hands, because the victory is God-given. The victory is won on the mountain, is realized in the valley. Oh, there's a battle! You can't just roll over and not get in the battle. But the battle is the Lord's.

Having said all that, I want to say this. I thank God for this dear man right here, Bob Sorrell, who has helped me to hold my hands up high. The victories that we've had at Bellevue Baptist Church: Do you think we strut, when I tell you what's happened since 1979? Do you think we say, "Look what we did"? I tell you, we'd be sheer fools—any of us, all of us. That's God! That's God: the God who has given us the victories individually. It is a God thing. He is the One who's had His hand upon Bellevue Baptist Church. And may we ever hold high the rod of God, the power of God, and understand that this church will continue to move on as we hold it high.

You know what Aaron was? He was a priest. He represents prayer. Hur, who held up the hands of Moses, his name means "whiteness" or "purity." Purity and prayer—that's it: holding up the hands of a people of God. The victory is God-given.

Conclusion

You know what we're going to do next Sunday? Well, tonight, we're going to celebrate this man who's been holding my hands for twenty years. We're going to do that. I'll tell you what we're going to do next Sunday. Next Sunday night, God willing, we're going to break ground on our Fellowship Building. Do you know why? Because when we came out here, we called this our Canaan: "claiming our Canaan." Well, we had a lot of work to do, but when you get into Canaan, friend, that's the time for the fellowship. That's the time—not that you lay down the sword and pick up a fork, oh no! Some of the sweetest times that Jesus ever had with His disciples were times when they fellowshipped together. And we're going to enjoy the victory that God has given us; we're going to break ground on the Fellowship Building. This building we call the Praise Building. The other building behind us, the activities building, is the Grace Building. The building we put our little children in over here is the Love Building. And we're going to build, starting next Sunday, the Fellowship Building. Won't that be wonderful? Amen! Glory to God! Amen! Glory to God!

Friend, you receive that provision, that salvation. You remember God's purpose: that is Canaan. You recognize a problem: that's the flesh. But then, you believe a principle: and that is, if we walk in the Spirit, we'll not fulfill the lusts of the flesh.

GENUINE CONFESSION

Sermon Date: March 7, 1976

Exodus 9:27

Dr. Adrian Rogers

Outline

Introduction
I. The Horrified Confession
II. The Hypocritical Confession
III. The Half-Hearted Confession
IV. The Hedged-In Confession
V. The Haunted Confession
VI. The Healing Confession
Conclusion

Introduction

Friend, there is only one thing that can take the peace out of your heart. Not two, not three, not four, just one. Sin, that's all. If you don't have peace tonight, it's because of sin. Sin robs you from peace. Now, let me say, furthermore, there's only one kind of sin that can cause you not to have peace. It's your sin: not what your husband did, not what your wife did, not what your teacher did, not what your mother, your father did, not what your pastor did, and not what your boss did to you. Someone can slap you in the face, and you'll still have perfect peace, if you're right with God. But when you get an attitude toward their slapping you in the face that's wrong, at that moment, you'll lose your peace. Only one thing can take away peace: sin. Only one kind of sin: yours. Only one thing that will restore peace: confession. Oh, but not every confession. Some confession does not bring peace, and some confessions don't bring pardon.

Now, what kind of confessions don't bring peace? We're going to do a Bible study through the Bible tonight, and I want you to notice where different Bible characters will use precisely the same words, and yet they'll not have their sins forgiven. The words that these Bible characters will use are these: "I have sinned." They will confess their sin, but they won't find peace.

I. The Horrified Confession

First of all, we find these words on the lips of Pharaoh in Exodus 9:27: "And Pharaoh sent, and called for Moses and Aaron, and said unto them I have sinned" (KJV). Well, that sounds like a mighty orthodox confession. And the Bible says, "If we confess our sins, He is faithful and just to forgive us our sins, and to cleanse us from all unrighteousness" (1 John 1:9 KJV). But there's something wrong about this confession. There was something wrong about Pharaoh's confession. The confession of Pharaoh we will call the horrified confession. And you can judge the value of his confession when you see the circumstances that surrounded his confession.

So back up to 9:22–27: "And the LORD said unto Moses, Stretch forth thine hand toward heaven, that there may be hail in all the land of Egypt, upon man, and upon beast, and upon every herb of the field, throughout the land of Egypt. And Moses stretched forth his rod toward heaven: and the LORD sent thunder and hail, and the fire ran along upon the ground; and the LORD rained hail upon the land of Egypt. So there was hail, and fire mingled with the hail, very grievous, such as there was none like it in all the land of Egypt since it became a nation. And the hail smote throughout all the land of Egypt all that was in the field, both man and beast; and the hail smote every herb of the field, and brake every tree of the field. Only in the land of Goshen, where the children of Israel were, was there no hail. And Pharaoh sent, and called for Moses and Aaron, and said unto them, I have sinned" (KJV).

When the hail fell from heaven, when the lightning flashed, when the thunder roared, when the fire ran along the ground, when Pharaoh was horrified, when he was frightened out of his wits, when he trembled, when his heart palpitated, he said, "I have sinned." But I want you to notice something. The repentance that was born in the storm died in the calm. I want you to notice, if you will, another verse. And here's the key. Here's why Pharaoh found no peace with God. Here's why Pharaoh found no pardon with God. Notice in verse 34: "And when Pharaoh saw that the rain and the hail and the thunders were ceased, he sinned yet more, and hardened his heart, he and his servants" (KJV).

Do you know anybody like that? I know lots of them. And I'm preaching to some of them: people who, when they get in a bad circumstance, when they get into a tight, when they have a problem, when the wife is about to leave and walk out, or when the doctor's given a bad prognosis, or when they're about to see the doctor, when there's about to be a cancer smear, or when the child lies sick in the hospital, or when the job is about to collapse, or when life is closing in, and when, so to speak, there's thunder and hail and lightning and fire and calamity, they come to God, face white, lips trembling—"God, I've sinned. God, have mercy"—and they make holy vows to God, sacred promises. The crisis passes, the storm clouds blow away, the thunder quiets, the lightning sheaths its fearful sword, and they're right back in the same business—and sometimes worse.

Some of you men who were overseas made holy, sacred promises to God in a foxhole. "O God, O God, if You'll just get me back home safe; O God, if You'll just deliver me, here's what I'll do, God. Here's what I'll do." I wonder if it wouldn't do us all good to think back on those times when we made some holy sacred vows to God and we've broken those vows.

May I tell you what a broken vow will do to you? Here's the danger of a broken vow. It will harden your heart. Promises unkept harden your heart. Notice in verse 34: "And when Pharaoh saw that the rain and the hail and the thunders were ceased, he sinned yet more, and hardened his heart, he and his servants." You may have forgotten those holy vows that you made to God, but God has not forgotten them. There's the horrified confession. But it didn't bring peace, and it didn't bring pardon.

II. The Hypocritical Confession

Now I want you to notice these same words on the lips of another Bible character. I call this confession the hypocritical confession. In Numbers 22:34, we find these words on the lips of a strange character whose name is Balaam: "And Balaam said unto the angel of the LORD, I have sinned"—sounds good, sounds orthodox, sounds all right, sounds like it ought to bring peace, sounds like it ought to bring pardon, but it won't do it—*"I have sinned; for I knew not that thou stoodest in the way against me: now therefore, if it displease thee, I will [return] again"* (KJV).

What's the background of all of this? Without trying to tell the entire story, because time would not permit it, let me just give you the meat of the coconut, as we would say in Florida. Balaam was a prophet, of sorts. He was a strange man. He uttered some of the most eloquent prophecies in all of the Bible, and yet he offered some of the most diabolical and treacherous advice that ever fell from the lips of a man. He had, in a sense, the lips of an angel and the heart of the devil. Balaam was a prophet of God, who knew some things about God. But there was a king whose name was Balak. He was the king of Moab. And the king of Moab was fearful of the children of Israel. And so he tried to bribe Balaam to put a curse upon the children of Israel, thinking that, since he was a prophet and a man of God, he could pronounce a solemn, holy curse upon the Israelites and they would not prevail.

Balaam was too smart for that, because he knew that God had said, "Those that curse Israel, I'll curse" (see Gen. 12:3). He said, "I can't do that. I can't put a curse upon them." But then he thought of the reward that he was going to get. And his palms got itching for that money, and greed took over. He said, "I'll tell you what I will do, however. I'll tell you how you can get God to curse them. You just get them to sin." And then he said, "You get some of the women of Moab to take up with some of the men of Israel, and so forth. And I know the lustful hearts of these men. I know what they'll do. They'll mix and intermingle, and they'll commit fornication. They'll commit adultery. Then I won't have to curse them. God will curse them."

Can you imagine such a thing coming out of the heart of a man who knew the ways of God so much that he himself refused to curse the people of God? I'm saying, here was a man with a mixed heart. Here was a man who was an A-number-one garden-variety hypocrite. Here was a man who wanted to run with the hare and hunt with the hounds at the same time. He wanted to play both sides of the fence. And God had forbidden him to follow after the king of Moab for gain. And, finally, when God almost kills him—and you remember the story: the angel had stood there with a drawn sword ready to take Balaam's life if he'd have come a step further, and the poor donkey had fallen out beneath him. You remember the story of Balaam's donkey that talked and rebuked him (Num. 22). That all took place here—and then Balaam has the audacity and the nerve and the gall to say, "Oh well, I've sinned; if it displease thee, I'll go the other way"—"if it displease thee." That hypocrite! It was a hypocritical confession. It was a confession from a man who really did not mean business.

Now, my dear friend, let me tell you something. Admitting your sin and confessing your sin are really two different things. Some of you will come to church on Sunday and confess your sins, and go out on Monday and live like the devil. And you'll be just like Balaam. You'll not find any peace, because there's been no genuine repentance in your heart; there's been no change of life. Someone described the average Sunday churchgoer this way: "They are praising God on Sunday. But they'll be all right on Monday. It's just a little habit they've acquired." The hypocritical confession: it doesn't bring peace, doesn't bring pardon. And, mister, I want to tell you I don't care how much you confess your sins: unless there's a change of heart about that sin, unless you're willing to repudiate that sin, unless you're willing to take sides against that sin, you'll never find peace, and you'll never find pardon.

III. The Half-Hearted Confession

The third confession I want you to notice. Look, if you will, in 1 Samuel 15. These words are on the lips of a man named Saul who was the king of Israel. First Samuel 15:24: "And Saul said unto Samuel, I have sinned." There it is: sounds orthodox, sounds good, sounds like it ought to bring peace, sounds like it ought to bring pardon. "And Saul said unto Samuel, I have sinned: for I have transgressed the commandment of the LORD, and thy words: because I feared the people, and obeyed their voice" (KJV).

Now, what was wrong with this confession? I call this confession a half-hearted confession. Here was a confession, not necessarily from a man who was a hypocrite like Balaam, but from a man who never really felt guilty. It was a confession that was accompanied with an alibi. It was a confession that had, along with it, an excuse. There's one thing that God will never accept for sin—and that's an alibi. There's one thing that God will never accept for sin—and that is an excuse. You see, he had a wonderful little excuse. God had told Saul to do a certain thing. Saul, as God's commander-in-chief, was commanded to destroy the Amalekites, who were demonic demon-worshipers, and who were a cancer to the human race, and who were the sworn enemies of God. And God said the Amalekites were to be destroyed, all of them, and God also said to destroy all of their cattle—the sheep, the oxen, and all of their cattle.

Samuel came to Saul, and he said, "Saul, did you do what I told you to do?" Saul said, "Yes, I've done just what the Lord told me to do. Blessed be the name of the Lord." Samuel said, "What's this I hear? The bleating of the sheep, the lowing of the oxen—what's this?" "Oh, those. Well, oh, Sammy, I'll tell you. I saved those out. They were the very best. And it seemed such a shame to put them to death. I'll tell you what I'm going to do with them. I'm going to sacrifice them to the Lord. You see, I am going to make an offering to God out of these." Now God said, "Put them to death." But Saul had a better idea.

Now, if you had said to Saul, "Saul, you're being disobedient," Saul would have said, "No, not really. This is such a shame to put all these oxen and all these sheep to death. And, besides that," he said, "the people were pressuring me. I feared the people. I mean, after all, I'm just a king, and there are all these people out here." And, as you read this whole story, you get the idea that Samuel didn't accept this confession. As a matter of fact, God said to Samuel, "You tell Saul that he's rejected from being king. I'm not having anything to do with this phony confession." It was a confession with an alibi (1 Sam. 15).

And that's the oldest indoor sport known to man: alibiing our sins. It started in the Garden of Eden. God said to Adam, "Adam, did you sin?" Do you know what Adam did? He alibied. He said, "Well, the woman You gave me, she caused me to eat." Now Adam was saying, in effect, "Whoever's fault it was, it wasn't mine. It was Yours, or hers. You gave her to me, and she made me do it."

You'll find the same thing when God spoke to Eve: "Eve, did you do thus-and-such?" "The devil made me do it." That's what she said: "The serpent beguiled me" (Gen. 3:13 KJV)—a confession with an alibi.

You'll find the same thing with Aaron, who was Moses' brother, as the Israelites were there encamped in the wilderness, and Moses went up on Mount Sinai to get the Ten Commandments, and down in the valley Aaron had made a golden calf, fashioned after the gods of Egypt, and the children of Israel were lewdly, lasciviously dancing nakedly around a golden calf, worshiping the golden calf. And when Moses came down from the mountain, and he said, "Aaron, what on earth is going on?" Aaron said, "You know, it's the strangest thing. I put a lot of gold in the fire, and out came this calf." That's really what he said. You read it: "I put in the gold, and out came the calf" (see Ex. 32:24). That hypocrite! That alibier! "Oh," he said, "the people's hearts, they were just set on it." I'll tell you, Moses didn't buy it. And God didn't buy it. And God brought judgment.

You talk to people today about sin: they'll call sin anything but sin. "Take your keys out of your car. Don't help a good boy go wrong." My soul! Let me tell you something, my friend. You take the keys out of your car so a bad kid won't swipe it. The way they make you think is that you're the criminal if you leave your keys in the car. "Look what you did to that kid! You ought to be arrested!" You see, we don't want to call sin *sin* today; we want to call it anything but sin: a glandular malfunction, a stumble upward, a mistake, a chemical imbalance, psychological maladjustment.

You know here's a kid who thinks that, because his mother wouldn't let him push his mush off the high chair when he was a little kid, now he's got a blank check to rob banks—because he was frustrated. Listen. That's being taught all over—that there is no such thing as real genuine moral responsibility and culpability—but it won't wash. And any time you come before God with an alibi—an excuse for wrongdoing—you'll not find peace, you'll not find pardon. A half-hearted confession.

IV. The Hedged-In Confession

All right, I want you to notice another confession. Turn to Joshua 7:20. These are the words that fall from the lips of a man named Achan. And I want you to notice what he says: "And Achan answered Joshua, and said, Indeed"—now, underscore these three words—"I have sinned against the LORD God of Israel, and thus and thus have I done" (KJV). Sounds orthodox; sounds good; certainly sounds like Achan ought to have forgiveness; sounds like he ought to have peace; sounds like he ought to have pardon—but he doesn't. His confession gets no higher than the ceiling. The ears of God are stopped up against this confession. Why? Because this confession is what I call a hedged-in confession.

Who was this fellow Achan? Achan was one of the Israelite soldiers who had gone into the city of Jericho after Jericho had fallen, and had taken some of the booty and some of the treasure from the fallen city of Jericho, and had taken it home and hidden it in his tent. He actually dug a hole in his tent, the floor of his tent, buried the treasure—a wedge of gold, shekels of silver, a Babylonian garment—and then he covered the hole, hid the deed. And because of what he had done, and because there was sin in the camp, Israel was tragically, ignominiously defeated when they went against another little city: the city of Ai. And Joshua knew that there was something wrong. And Joshua stretched himself out before the Lord in prayer, and said, "God, what happened? Lord, why are we failing? Lord, why can't we go forward?" And God said to Joshua, "Why are you lying there upon your face? Get up. Israel has sinned."

Joshua knew there was sin in the camp, and he knew that sin had to be ferreted out, and he knew that sin had to be judged, and so finally lots were cast. And the omniscient God enabled His commander-in-chief to put the finger right on the sore spot. And Achan, not willingly, but unwillingly, had the finger put on him. And he's faced with the man of God, who is representing the judgment of God. And Joshua says, "Confess it; tell it." And Achan confesses. But do you think that Achan is forgiven? Do you think he is pardoned? No. You see, there was nothing else he could do. The Bible says he was stoned, and a heap of stones was left upon him as a solemn reminder of how God hates sin.

You say, "Well, surely God would have had mercy on him." Yes, God would have had mercy on him, had he confessed at the right time. Suppose Achan, who had done this terrible heinous thing, had lain down in his tent. And suppose that he couldn't sleep. Suppose his conscience is thundering in his heart, reverberating through his soul. Suppose his lips quiver, his hands tremble. He says, "My God! What have I done? What a fool I am! Do I think that I can sin against the thrice-holy, omniscient God of Israel and get away with it?" Suppose he wakes up, unrolls his bedroll, claws into the dirt, and takes these things that he stole and goes over to Joshua's tent, and says, "Joshua, wake up! Oh, Joshua, what a fool I have been! Joshua, I have sinned. Here, Joshua, I give it back. Joshua, get the high priest. Let's go to the tabernacle. Let's offer a lamb, a blood atonement. I'm so sorry! I want God to forgive me." Do you think he would have been forgiven? Of course he would have! "He that covereth his sins shall not prosper: but whoso confesseth and forsaketh them shall have mercy" (Prov. 28:13 KJV).

Oh, listen! Had he come at the right time, in the right motive, God would have fully, completely, freely forgiven. Why was not this man forgiven? Because he waited until he was hedged in and hemmed up, and then he confessed. Did you know that every sinner will confess his sin at some point? It's only a matter of time. Did you know that? It's only a matter of time. Do you know what God has said in His Word? "As I live, saith the Lord, every knee shall bow to me, and every tongue shall confess to God" (Rom. 14:11 KJV). So then, every one of us shall give an account of himself unto God—every one of us. And God swears by Himself. He can swear by no higher. "As I live, saith the Lord, every knee shall bow to me, and every tongue shall confess to God." But do you think those people who bow in that last day will be forgiven? They will not. They'll confess and then be cast into hell. Every demon will confess that Jesus is Lord.

There are some of you here tonight—you're not saved. I don't even know why some folks are here. Some folks come to church, and when I preach, they make smart remarks. Some kids come to church, swap stories, write notes. Some people come and they just kind of argue back and forth mentally when the preacher's preaching, and they make wisecracks about religion, and they curse the name of Jesus. I want to see if, when you come to that day, you make a wisecrack before Jesus Christ. You joked about it behind His back. I wonder if you're going to joke about it to His face. You cursed Him behind His back. I wonder, when you stand face to face with Him, if you're going to curse Him. No, you won't. You won't curse Him then. "As I live, saith the Lord, every knee shall bow to me, and every tongue shall confess to God." You'll be hedged up then. You'll be hemmed in then and it will be too late. "And I saw the dead, small and great, stand before God; and the books were opened: and another book was opened, which is the book of life: and the dead were judged out of those things which were written in the books, according to their works. And the sea gave up the dead which were in it; and death and hell delivered up the dead which were in them: and they were judged every man according to their works" (Rev. 20:12–13 KJV).

It's what the spiritual talks about when it says, "I went to the rock to hide my face, and the rock cried out, 'No hiding place!'" Hedged up, condemned—"I've sinned"; and you'll bow, and you'll confess it; but you'll not find pardon, and you'll not find peace, because you waited too late. You waited until the stroke of judgment fell. Some of you think, "Well, I'll wait till Jesus comes, and then I'll get right." Too late. You say, "I'll wait till I die. Then I'll get right." Too late. "I'll plead for mercy at the bar of God." Too late. If you want mercy, you may have it. If you want forgiveness, you may have it. If you want grace, you may have it. But, "Now is the accepted time; ... now is the day of salvation" (2 Cor. 6:2 KJV). "To day if ye will hear His voice, harden not your hearts" (Heb. 3:15 KJV).

V. The Haunted Confession

All right, I want you to notice another confession. Look in Matthew 27:4. These words we find on the lips of Judas Iscariot, the one who betrayed the Lord Jesus Christ for thirty pieces of silver: "Then Judas, which had betrayed Him, when he saw that he was condemned, repented"—*"repented"*—do you think he was forgiven? Let's go on and read—"and brought again the thirty pieces of silver to the chief priests and elders, saying, I have sinned"—the same three words: underscore them—"I have sinned in that I have betrayed the innocent blood. And they said, What is that to us? see thou to that. And he cast down the pieces of silver in the temple, and departed, and went and hanged himself" (Matt. 27:3–5 KJV).

Do you think that Judas's confession brought peace? Do you think it brought pardon? No. This is what I call the haunted confession. Here Judas is haunted by the ghost of guilt. He repents, but it is not repentance towards God and faith in the Lord Jesus Christ. It is the confession of remorse. It is the confession of despair. It is the confession of a damned soul who has committed the unpardonable sin and crossed God's deadline. Judas died and went to hell. Some people think that Judas was saved, and lost his salvation. No, he never had his salvation. The Bible says He "knew from the beginning who they were that believed not"

(John 6:64 KJV). Jesus said, "Have not I chosen you twelve, and one of you is a devil?" (John 6:70 KJV).

Judas sinned with his eyes wide open. He sinned against light. He lived in the very presence of the Son of God. The Holy Spirit of God had convicted Judas of his sin. But Judas betrayed Jesus for thirty pieces of silver. And Jesus said of Judas, *"It had been good for that man if he had not been born"* (Matt. 26:24 KJV). The Bible says he died and he went to *"his own place"* (Acts 1:25 KJV). This Bible calls him "the son of perdition" (John 17:12 KJV). The only other time a person has been ever called by that terminology in the Bible, to my knowledge, is the Antichrist: *"the son of perdition"* (2 Thess. 2:3 KJV). Judas sinned. But his confession was a haunted confession. He was haunted by the ghost of guilt. He was crushed by remorse. But he never did repent toward God and put his faith in the Lord Jesus Christ.

VI. The Healing Confession

One last confession. And I want to call this one the healing confession, or the heartfelt confession, or the happy confession. Call it what you want. But I want you to see what kind of a confession God hears. Look in Luke 15:18. And one more time you're going to read these words, but this time I want you to see how God expects us to say them and what He wants us to mean. In Luke 15:18, you read the words of a prodigal son who had forsaken his father's house and gone into a far country, and wasted his substance with unrighteous living. And notice, as we begin to read here in verse 18, the prodigal son said to himself, "I will arise and go to my father, and will say unto him, Father, I have sinned . . ."—same three words: underscore them. But what a difference they made!—"I have sinned against heaven, and before thee"—oh, get the difference! See where the direction of this confession is, and notice the humility of this confession—"and am no more worthy to be called thy son: make me as one of thy hired servants. And he arose, and came to his father. But when he was yet a great way off, his father saw him, and had compassion, and ran, and fell on his neck, and kissed him. And the son said unto him,

Father, I have sinned against heaven, and in thy sight, and am no more worthy to be called thy son. But the father said to his servants, Bring forth the best robe, and put it on him; and put a ring on his hand, and shoes on his feet: and bring hither the fatted calf, and kill it; and let us eat, and be merry: for this my son was dead, and is alive again; he was lost, and is found. And they began to be merry" (Luke 15:18–24 KJV).

What made this confession a real confession? What caused it to bring peace and pardon? May I tell you that it was marked by genuine sorrow. May I tell you that it was delineated by his turning from his sin. The Bible says he left the hog pen. He was not only broken over his sin; he was broken from his sin. He forsook his sin. "He that covereth his sins shall not prosper: but whoso confesseth and forsaketh them shall have mercy" (Prov. 28:13 KJV). Genuine sorrow, genuine repentance, and coming to the true source of forgiveness: "Father, I have sinned against heaven, and before thee" (Luke 15:18 KJV). And I tell you, when you come to God that way, I will guarantee you, on the authority of this book, "If we confess our sins, He is faithful and just to forgive us our sins, and to cleanse us from all unrighteousness" (1 John 1:9 KJV).

Conclusion

There's only one thing that can take away your peace—and it's sin; and only one kind of sin: it's your sin. There's only one thing that can take away your sin—and it's confession; but only one kind of confession: genuine confession.

GOD'S REMEDY FOR WORN-OUT PREACHERS

Sermon Date: August 9, 1982

Exodus 18:13–26

Dr. Adrian Rogers

Outline

Introduction
I. The Limits That Must Be Sensed
  A. The Limit of Time
    1. He Was Neglecting His Family
    2. He Was Neglecting His Quiet Time
  B. The Limit of Physical Strength
  C. The Limit of Emotional Strength
II. The Loads That Must Be Shared
  A. The Size of the Task
  B. The Sharing of the Task
III. The Lives That Might Be Saved
  A. Moses' Ministry Would Be Saved
  B. The Lives of Many Others Would Be Saved
Conclusion

Introduction

I want you tonight to turn to Exodus 18. And the title of my message is a long one: "God's Remedy for Worn-Out Preachers." That's really what I'm going to be preaching about tonight, but it's going to apply to you. And I'm trying to preach a message that will really touch about three areas. I hope that you're going to learn something that will keep you from being a worn-out person, whether you're a preacher, a pastor, or whatever you might be, but also that you'll keep from wearing me out, and we'll find what God's plan is for us to get His work done here.

So I want to begin reading here in Exodus 18:13: "And it came to pass on the morrow, that Moses sat to judge the people: and the people stood by Moses from the morning unto the evening. And when Moses' father in law saw all that he did to the people, he said, What is this thing that thou doest to the people?"—notice he doesn't say, "what you do for them," but "what you do to them"—"why sittest thou thyself alone, and all the people stand by thee from morning unto even? And Moses said unto his father in law, Because the people come unto me to enquire of God: when they have a matter, they come unto me; and I judge between one and another, and I do make them know the statutes of God, and His laws. And Moses' father in law said unto him, The thing that thou doest is not good. Thou wilt surely wear away . . ."—now you see where I got my topic, "How Not to Wear Out the Preacher"—"Thou wilt surely wear away, both thou, and this people that is with thee: for this thing is too heavy for thee; thou art not able to perform it thyself alone. Hearken now unto my voice, I will give thee counsel, and God shall be with thee: Be thou for the people to God-ward, that thou mayest bring the causes unto God: and thou shalt teach them ordinances and laws, and shalt shew them the way wherein they must walk, and the work that they must do. Moreover thou shalt provide out of all the people able men, such as fear God, men of truth, hating covetousness; and place such over them, to be rulers of thousands, and rulers of hundreds, rulers of fifties, and rulers of tens: and let them judge the people at all seasons: and it shall be, that every great matter they shall bring unto thee, but every small matter they shall judge: so shall it be easier for thyself, and they shall bear the burden with thee. If thou shalt do this thing, and God command thee so, then thou shalt be able to endure"—that is, "you won't be worn out"—"and all this people shall also go to their place in peace. So Moses hearkened to the voice of his father in law, and did all that he had said. And Moses chose able men out of Israel, and made them heads over the people, rulers of thousands, rulers of hundreds, rulers of fifties, and rulers of tens. And they judged the people at all seasons: the hard causes they brought unto Moses, but every small matter they judged themselves" (Ex. 18:13–26 KJV).

Now, let me say, at the outset of this message, that I'm not feeling sorry for myself. And let me say that, lest some of the dear little ladies who love me—and I'm so grateful for their love—feel that I am run down, I am not. I feel terrific. And I want to set this in proper context. I just want to stay feeling terrific. And let me tell you that God has a wonderful, wonderful plan for Bellevue Church. He doesn't want our church to stop being blessed. He doesn't want our church to stop growing. And so we need to learn how we can continue to grow without somehow wearing away the pastor and without discouraging the staff.

Now what happened here was that God was blessing His people in a tremendous way. And with the blessings came some problems. Now blessings sometimes bring problems. Look at the blessing that they had. Look in 18:1. The Bible says, "When Jethro, the priest of Midian, Moses' father in law, heard of all that God had done for Moses, and for Israel His people, and that the LORD had brought Israel out of Egypt" (KJV). "All that God had done for His people"—that's a beautiful, beautiful verse.

And I just think of all that God has done for us. I tell you, folks, God just keeps on pouring it on, doesn't He? I mean, blessing after blessing. You'd think that after a while He's going to run out of blessings.

I've been to see Niagara Falls, as some of you have, and you see that water coming over the falls, and you say, "Well, it's going to run out after a while. I mean, it just can't keep pouring over the falls like that." But it just keeps coming, and it just keeps coming, and just keeps coming. That's the way the grace of God is. Out of His infinite riches in Jesus, He giveth and giveth and giveth again. And so God just keeps pouring it on.

And then, look, if you will, in verse 9: "And Jethro rejoiced for all the goodness which the LORD had done to Israel, whom He had delivered out of the hand of the Egyptians" (KJV). How good God had been! And then, look in verse 10: "And Jethro said, Blessed be the LORD, who hath delivered you out of the hand of the Egyptians, and out of the hand of Pharaoh, who hath delivered the people from under the hand of the Egyptians. Now I know that the LORD is greater than all gods: for in the thing wherein they dealt proudly He was above them" (Ex. 18:10–11 KJV).

Indeed, God was blessing His people. However, in the midst of this blessing, Moses—that I'm going to liken unto the pastor and compare with the pastor—had taken more responsibility upon his shoulders than he really ought to have taken. And Moses had started to counsel the people. And he was dealing with the people from sunrise to sunset, from *can* to *can't*.

Look in verses 13–17 (KJV), and you'll get that thought again: "And it came to pass on the morrow, that Moses sat to judge the people: and the people stood by Moses from the morning unto the evening." Now he just had a list of people outside his office. They were coming to see him. "And when Moses' father in law saw all that he did to the people, he said, What is this thing that thou doest to the people?" I always laugh at that a little bit. He doesn't say, "What is this you're doing for the people?" Moses, if you'd have asked him, he would have said, "Oh, I'm doing something wonderful for them." Jethro said, "It looks to me like you're doing something to them." And he said, "What is this thing that thou doest to the people? Why sittest thou thyself alone, and all the people stand by thee from morning unto even?" "You're just making them wait here. They're trying to see you, and you're trying to settle this thing all by yourself." And then verse 17: "And Moses' father in law said unto him, The thing that thou doest is not good."

And there are a lot of preachers sometimes, I suppose, who have an exaggerated sense of their importance. They think, if they suddenly cease to try and do it all, that somehow it will all cave in right on their heads. And so Jethro, who was Moses' father-in-law, was used of God to give this man some great wisdom and some great advice so that the work of God could continue.

And so, with that in mind, I want you to notice several things.

I. The Limits That Must Be Sensed

First of all, I want you to notice the limits that must be sensed—the limits that must be sensed. Look in verse 18. Jethro said to Moses, "Thou wilt surely wear away, both thou, and this people that is with thee." "It's not just you, Moses, that's going to decay. It's not just you that's going to wear out. You're going to find that, the people that you're trying to lead, you're not going to be able to lead them. You are going to wear out, and you're going to wear your people out." You see, what Jethro was wise enough to know is there's a limit to what any one man can do, even if he's a Moses.

Now, really, it doesn't take much sense to understand that the man who does the work of ten men is not nearly as good a man and great a man and wise a man as the man who can get ten men to work. That man is a better man and a wiser man and a smarter man—not the man who can do the work of ten men, but the man who can get ten men to work.

A. The Limit of Time

You see, first of all, there's a limit of time. Look in verse 13: "And it came to pass on the morrow, that Moses sat to judge the people: and the people stood by Moses from the morning unto the evening." There was the limit of time. And because Moses was getting up early in the morning, going to the office, sitting down, and starting with the first one, and then the second, and then the third, then the fourth, all day long he went from sunrise to sunset, sunrise to sunset. Well, what was so bad about that?

1. He Was Neglecting His Family

Well, number one: He started neglecting his family. You say, "How do you know he was neglecting his family?" Go back to verses 5 and 6 and look at it: "And Jethro, Moses' father in law, came with his sons and his wife unto Moses into the wilderness, where he encamped at the mount of God: and he said unto Moses, I thy father in law Jethro am come unto thee, and thy wife, and her two sons with her" (KJV). "Hey, buddy, you recognize these kids? You know who they are? Have you ever seen them before? And, this lady, you happen to be married to her, Moses." And so here comes Jethro bringing the preacher's family out to him.

I remember when our church was growing so fast down at Merritt Island, I think Joyce said to me one time she was going to come forward in a service and make a decision so she could talk with me for a few moments, you know: "Honey, the kids need some new shoes." And here was this situation. Here was a man who had been neglecting his family. And any man, any preacher, any businessman, anybody else who neglects his family is too busy. They're your first responsibility.

We often talk about the problem of preacher's kids who don't love God, and preacher's kids who are hellions, and preacher's kids out of fellowship with God. Why is it? Here is a modern-day Moses who's going down from sunrise to sunset taking care of everybody else's problems and not taking care of his own family. The Bible says, "If a man know not how to [take care of] his own house, how shall he take care of the church of God?" (1 Tim. 3:5 KJV).

2. He Was Neglecting His Quiet Time

And so there are the limits of time. He didn't have enough time with his children, with his family. But not only had he been neglecting his family, I'll tell you something else he'd been neglecting. He'd been neglecting his quiet time. He'd not been alone with the Lord. You say, "How do you know that?" Well, look at verse 19. Here's what Jethro said. He said, "Hearken now unto my voice, I will give thee counsel, and God shall be with thee: Be thou for the people to God-ward, that thou mayest bring the causes unto God" (KJV).

He said, "Now, Moses, you've been speaking to the people about God, but you've been failing to speak to God about the people." That's exactly what he's saying. Look at it: "Hearken now unto my voice, I will give thee counsel, and God shall be with thee: Be thou for the people to God-ward." Now he says, "Moses, you really want to help your people? Then you need to get alone. You need to be quiet before God."

I want to tell you something, friend, and I mean this with all of my heart. The greatest service that a man of God will ever perform for his people is not when he is standing before them speaking to them about God, but when he is before God speaking to God about them. And, oh, we need more ministers and people of God and men of God who will know how to get alone with God. You see, there is the limit of time. And every man of God needs time to be alone with God.

Now, don't just apply that to Adrian Rogers, friend. If you're too busy for your family, you're too busy. Mr. Businessman, if you're too busy with your business, you're too busy. If you're too busy, madam, with your affairs to spend time with God, and time with your husband, and time with your children, you, too, are too busy. And you are going to wear out rather than last out. And so there is a limit of time. The man, the preacher, who is always available isn't worth a whole lot when he is available. He needs some time somehow to be alone with God, and so do you.

B. The Limit of Physical Strength

But not only is there the limit of time, verses 13 and 14, there's also the limit of physical strength. Look in verses 17 and 18: "And Moses' father in law said unto him, The thing that thou doest is not good. Thou wilt surely wear away, both thou, and this people that is with thee: for this thing is too heavy for thee; thou art not able to perform it thyself alone" (KJV).

You know, I'm getting to the age now—well, I guess it pains me to use this phrase—but middle age. As a matter of fact, I might be past middle age. I don't think I'll last to be a hundred. But anyway, I'm in that period of time known as middle age. And I have a lot of my buddies, my preacher friends, guys I went to college with, and guys I went to seminary with, who are already wearing away. I mean, they are already getting on the scrap heap, and the junk pile, and so forth. I see many of my compatriots and many of my peers who at the tender age that I'm at are already burned out in the ministry. You see, dear friend, it's not a sin, it's a crime, to not take care of yourself physically.

And it was Jesus Christ Himself who said to His disciples, "Come ye ... apart ... and rest a while" (Mark 6:31 KJV). And you know Dr. Vance Havner's classic statement on that passage. Vance Havner said, "We'd better come apart, or we will come apart." And that's good. "Come ye apart and rest a while." That's what the Lord Jesus said. And I want to tell you something, friend. If you do not understand that God put you in a physical frame, and God gave you a body which is the temple of His Holy Spirit, and if you do not recognize the limits of your time, and the limits of your strength, if you're running around knocking things over, and calling it serving God, you're not really serving God; you're dissipating your body. You can move too fast. You can do too much. And it's a lot of wasted motion.

I was reading. I actually read this. It sounds humorous, and it sounds like it didn't happen, but it literally happened. A fighter plane was moving so fast that it fired its cannon, overtook the shell, and shot itself down. And I thought, "You know, I've known some people who've done that same thing. I've known some preachers who've shot themselves down just moving too fast. I've known some Christian businessmen who have not known what it is to come apart and rest."

And somebody has described a football game, a football stadium, as something like this: Twenty-two men on the field desperately in need of rest; 50,000 people in the stands desperately in need of exercise. And that's what the average church is like. I mean, you've got the people who are trying to do it all. And then there are people who are sitting there not doing anything.

And so Jethro says, "Moses, you're not wise. The thing that you're doing is not good. You have not recognized the limits of time. You've not recognized the limits of strength. You're neglecting your family. You're neglecting your quiet time. You are neglecting your physical health."

C. The Limit of Emotional Strength

But not only was there the limit of time, and not only was there the limit of physical strength; there was also the limit of emotional strength.

Now every one of these people that Moses talked to were taking a little out of him, if he was a good counselor. Nobody can counsel, and nobody can minister, without giving. It costs. It costs to preach. Do you know what preaching is? It's standing up here and dying a little bit. That's what it is. It is giving of yourself. Do you know what counseling is? If you don't give of yourself, mister, you don't counsel. I just came out of a counseling session before I came up here, where I got on my knees and wept. You cannot counsel, you cannot serve, without paying a price.

It was said of John the Baptist, he was a burning and a shining light. And, friend, there will be no shining without burning. And when you burn, you're consumed—you're consumed. John the Baptist was a burning and a shining light. And emotional strength goes out of you when you serve. Jesus said, when that woman touched Him, "Virtue has gone out of me." He meant by that, strength was gone out of Him.

And these people had been coming to Moses. And I'll tell you, it cost Moses. Go back to 17:2–3. "Wherefore the people did chide with Moses, and said, Give us water that we may drink. And Moses said unto them, Why chide ye with me? wherefore do ye tempt the LORD? And the people thirsted there for water; and the people murmured against Moses."

Do you like that word *murmur*? *Mur-mur, mur-mur, mur-mur, mur-mur*: it's an ugly word, isn't it? The people murmured. Now, you know, a murmuring is the worst kind of thing. You know, if you have just a red-hot argument, maybe you can deal with that—if you have an intellectual confrontation. But it's the murmurers, you know. The people, they were just picking at Moses.

I think you heard about the man who said he didn't mind being swallowed by a whale; he just hated to be nibbled to death by minnows. And that's what they were doing to Moses. They were nibbling at him and nibbling at him and nibbling at him. And it's like being stoned to death with popcorn. No one gets hurt, but it all just keeps coming and coming and coming.

And here was Moses, from morning to evening, morning to evening, morning to evening, morning to evening, the same thing. And it was taking a toll on him, not only physically, but emotionally. And I'm not just talking about being in the ministry. It can be the same thing if you're a physician, if you're a lawyer, if you're a mechanic, if you're a secretary. It doesn't matter what you are.

II. The Loads That Must Be Shared

You see, there's only so much time that you have. There's only so much physical strength that you have. There's only so much emotional strength that you can give. And, dear friend, there are some limits that must be sensed. Secondly, there are some loads that must be shared because of the limits that must be sensed. Look, if you will, in verses 18–20. Here's what Jethro said. Here was the God-given advice that Jethro gave to his son-in-law: "Thou wilt surely wear away, both thou, and this people that is with thee: for this thing is too heavy for thee; thou art not able to perform it thyself alone. Hearken now unto my voice, I will give thee counsel, and God shall be with thee: Be thou for the people to God-ward, that thou mayest bring the causes unto God: and thou shalt teach them ordinances and laws" (KJV).

A. The Size of the Task

Now, listen. There was the size of the task. It was an immense task. Moses had a congregation of three million Old Testament Baptists, and he was trying to lead them in a big program. And it was something that one man was not able to do.

Now, very frankly, pastoring a big church like this is easier than pastoring a small church, because I have some helpers. I don't think a church ever had a better staff than we have. And I'm not saying that because it sounds good. I thank God for our staff. I believe that God has brought our staff together. I wish you could sit in some of our staff meetings and sense the camaraderie, the love, the fellowship, and the spiritual ingenuity that these people have. You would have a greater appreciation for our staff. I'll tell you what. We've got a staff that skunked the deacons playing volleyball Friday night. That's the kind of staff we've got. Those deacons, however, are not much. And we have a tremendous staff—a tremendous staff. And so, therefore, my work is a little easier, perhaps, than the work of a pastor of a smaller church that does not have the staff that I have.

But let me tell you what a modern minister has to do. He has to win the lost. He has to deal with the despondent. He has to instruct children. He has to guide you. He has to strengthen the old people. He has to visit the sick. He has to comfort the bereaved. He has to plan programs. He has to conduct services. He has to prepare sermons. He has to perform weddings. He has to conduct funerals. He has to administrate the business. He has to watch for the lonely and the widowed. He has to handle correspondence. He has to do denominational work and duties. He has to administrate his staff. It's no wonder that many of them go under. It's no wonder that many of them come apart.

They remind me of a stevedore who was unloading a ship down in New Orleans, and as he was walking off the ship, the gangplank broke, and he sank into the Mississippi. He went down once, and came up and yelled for help. He went down the second time, and came up and yelled for help. He went down the third time, and came up, and he said, "If somebody doesn't come help me, I'm going to have to drop one of these anvils that I'm carrying."

Now there are pastors who are carrying such a load that they're about to go under for the third time and sink. And I'm preaching to some of you seminarians now. You need to listen. You see, dear friend, the size of the task means that no one person can do it alone. Now there are some people who say, "Well then, what we need to do is just stop growing, and what we need to do is stop being blessed, and what we need to do is stop the work of God." No! We just need to get more people working. I mean, anytime we stop growing, we start dying. We'll grow and glow, or we'll dry and die. We will evangelize or we'll fossilize. But, dear friend, we won't just stand still, I'll guarantee you that.

B. The Sharing of the Task

But, you see, there's a task, and that task needs a sharing. So the size of the task speaks of the sharing of the task. And what is the sharing of the task? Look in verse 21: "Moreover thou shalt provide out of all the people"—that's you, folks. Now, listen—"able men, such as fear God, men of truth, hating covetousness" (Ex. 18:21 KJV). Now, let me just pause right here. You know, sometimes it's said of a church, "Well, you know, you just can't break into the inner circle in that church. I mean, there's a little clique, a little group of people who run everything, do everything. I'm on the outside, and they're on the inside, and they make all the decisions." Hey, how would you like to get on the inside? All right, here it is. Listen to it again: "Thou shalt provide out of all the people able men,"—are you able?—"such as fear God, men of truth, hating covetousness." By the way, that means you'd be a tither, doesn't it? Say *amen*. Be honest. It's okay. I don't care. All right: "hating covetousness." What I'm trying to say is, you show me a man, a woman, a person that is right with God; I mean, able people who want to serve God, and they'll be in the inner circle quicker than you can say *supercalifragilisticexpialidocious*. They will be in that inner circle, dear friend. There's no little clique of people around here.

God knows that we need a sharing of the task. And here's what Jethro said. "Thou shalt provide out of all the people able men, such as fear God, men of truth, hating covetousness." Now, notice what he says. And he says here that we are to place them over the people.

Now there's an old saying in the country, but it's a good saying: "Many hands make light work." You know that's true. If only a couple of us were to try and move that piano, it would be a job. If we were to take this choir, and all of us get around it, we'd move it fairly easy, because all of us could make a hard task an easy task. It's amazing what can be done when people work together.

I told our Sunday school workers something that I discovered in a little thing I was reading about Canadian geese. The naturalists tried to understand and figure out why the geese, as they go south, or go north, always fly in a V-formation. You see them going overhead in a V-formation. And one lead goose gets out there, and he flaps for a while and leads. And then, after a while, he wears out, and he falls back to the end of the line, and another one comes up. And that's the way they fly. And then they found out—the men, the specialists in aerodynamics, understood it. Two engineers calibrated in a wind tunnel what happens in a V-formation. And they found out that each goose, when he flaps his wings, creates an inward and an upward lift for the goose that follows. And all of the geese, when they do their part, they increase their range by 71 percent over what they could achieve if one goose were flying by itself. Isn't that amazing?

And God knows that same thing would be true about our church. "Behold, how good and how pleasant it is for brethren to dwell together" (Ps. 133:1 KJV). That's something to honk about, even if you're not a goose—as we work together.

Now, look. There were some things that only Moses could do. I believe, dear friend, that if I were a layman, knowing what I know about the pastors, I would say to my pastor, "Pastor, I don't want you to do anything that we can do, so that you can do everything we can't do." That's what I'd do. I'd just try to figure it out that way. "Pastor, don't you do anything we can do, so that you can do those things." You see, there were some things that Moses was supposed to do, and those were the things that God wanted him to do.

Look again in verses 19 and 20. Here's what Moses was to do: "Hearken now unto my voice, I will give thee counsel, and God shall be with thee: Be thou for the people to God-ward, that thou mayest bring the causes unto God: and thou shalt teach them ordinances and laws, and shalt shew them the way wherein they must walk, and the work that they must do" (KJV). Now what Jethro said: "Moses, you get in that study, and you get on your face before God, and you pray to God and intercede for these people. And then you get a message burning in your heart, and you stand before those people, and you tell them what God said. You tell them of God's laws. And you tell them of God's statutes.

And you tell them of God's ordinances. What they need is a word from God. What they need is a man of God coming from his study with brimming eyes and bursting lips and burning hearts to preach the Word of God."

I don't believe there's much wrong in America that could not be cured if we had a generation of preachers who'd stand on their feet every Sunday morning and preach a message freshly baked in heaven's oven, and let the people feast on it and feed on it: the Word of God. And so there are certain things that only Moses could do. And Jethro knew that Moses had that responsibility.

And the apostles knew the same thing. You remember that time when the early church was growing, and it was growing at a great rate. And, again, anything that moves makes friction. And there came a friction in the church, and some of the Hellenistic widows, some of the Greek widows, felt that they were being neglected. And perhaps they felt that those who were administrating the church, who were primarily Jewish at that time, were a little prejudicial toward these Hellenistic widows. And, again, the murmuring started. And so, what did the apostles do? They said, "Choose ye out seven men full of the Holy Ghost and of good report whom we may set over this business, and we'll . . ."—do what?—"we will give ourselves continually to the ministry of the Word and to prayer" (see Acts 6:3–4 KJV). And the Bible says, "And the word of God increased" (v. 7 KJV). The church grew mightily as those men of God were getting alone by themselves. And God said to that early church the same kind of advice that God gave to Moses through Jethro: "Get you some godly laymen. Get you some men, some women, some people, and put them to work, so that you can do those things that only you can do."

Now I was interested, as I looked at this passage of Scripture, to find something of the ratio that God worked out. Now, notice again in verse 21 the ratio that is here: "Moreover thou shalt provide out of all of the people able men, such as fear God, men of truth, hating covetousness and place such over them, to be rulers of thousands, and rulers of hundreds, rulers of fifties, and rulers of tens" (KJV).

Now, let's take our church. Let's suppose that we've got 12,000 members, round figures. All right, so, if we had a ruler of thousands, that means that we'd have to have about twelve of these. And, friend, that's what we have on the executive staff: this kind of men. Now, let's go on. If we had rulers of hundreds, and we had 12,000, that means that we'd have to have 120. And that's just about what we've got: 120 deacons. Isn't that interesting? And if we had rulers of fifties, that means that we'd have to have about 240. And that's what we've got: about 240 Sunday school teachers. And then, if we had to have rulers of ten, that means we'd have to have about 1,200. And that's about how many we have in our total work and committee system, and so forth, at Bellevue. That's pretty neat, isn't it? That's wonderful what God is doing here. And I just kind of backed into that. And I'm not trying to make it fit, and I'm not trying to prove anything, but it just made me kind of feel pretty smart. No, really, it didn't, because that's of God. I just praise the Lord for it, and bless the Lord.

But what I'm saying is, dear folks, look. There is a limit that must be sensed. And then, there's a load that must be shared. And what I want to say to you is, I believe that our church can continue to grow and continue to be blessed as each one of you say, "Dear God, what do You want me to do? What do You want me to do? Where is my place in this body called Bellevue Baptist Church?" The Bible says God has set every member in the body "as it hath pleased him" (1 Cor. 12:18 KJV). And, friend, there is family love to share, and there's a family load to bear—and don't you forget it. We're all in the family. And there's plenty of love in the family. And there's plenty of work in the family. And, oh, if you would just say, "Dear God, I want my church to continue to grow," only God knows what can be done through this church, if we don't wear out the pastor, and if we don't wear out the staff, and if we don't wear out certain people, but if we would just simply use the common sense. We don't need, on the one hand, to say, "Pastor, you do it all, or we're not going to grow," or, on the other hand, say, "Pastor, you can't do it all, so we'll stop growing." We need to say, "Pastor, together we'll work together, and we'll never stop growing till Jesus comes." That's what we need to do—and just see to it that every need is met and that we're reaching people for Jesus Christ.

III. The Lives That Might Be Saved

Now the third thing I want you to see—and time is running out—but, not only the limits that must be sensed, and not only the load that must be shared, but I want you to notice the lives that might be saved. Look, if you will, in verse 23. Here's what Jethro said to Moses: "If thou shalt do this thing, and God command thee so ..."—wasn't that neat? Wasn't he a good counselor? He said, "This is what I think, but you'd better check with God." Isn't that wonderful?—"If thou shalt do this thing, and God command thee so, then thou shalt be able to endure, and all this people shall also go to their place in peace" (KJV).

A. Moses' Ministry Would Be Saved

Now, first of all, Moses' ministry would be saved. Moses would endure. It's too bad when many preachers are worn out rather than worked out. I hear preachers say sometimes, "Well, I'd rather burn out than rust out." Well, friend, you don't have to burn out or rust out. You can last out. Do what God would have you to do. And so many times what we call being burned out is just simply not resting in the Lord and abiding in His wisdom that He's given us.

B. The Lives of Many Others Would Be Saved

And not only could Moses' ministry be saved, but the lives of many others would be saved. Notice that Jethro said to Moses, "Moses, thou wilt surely wear away, both thou, and this people that is with thee." It's not just, "Moses, I'm trying to take care of you." "I'm not just trying to save you for the people. I'm also trying to save the people themselves."

Conclusion

And, you see, if everybody gets involved, the work is going to be done, and nobody is going to be overlooked, and everybody is going to have something to do. You know what you need in order to be happy? Someone to love, something to believe in, and a cause to serve. That's a recipe for happiness: someone to love, something to believe in, and a cause to serve. Jesus is all of those. And you need, dear friend, to say, "Dear Lord, show me the place." Some of you could be nursery workers. We need them. We need some extended service workers. I tell you, you cannot believe the task that these people go through every week—every week—just to see to it that that nursery is clean, sanitary, safe, and happy—and it is. You can thank God for our nursery—finest in the land. But it is work! And I don't want Mary, our preschool director, to wear out. I want her to last out. And some of you dear ladies need to call Mary this week, because God the Holy Spirit is telling you to, and say, "Mary, if I'm qualified—check me out and see if I'm qualified—but if I am qualified, put me to work for Jesus."

We're trying to start two Sunday schools. And, folks, listen. I mean, we're starting a whole brand-new Sunday school. And in staff meeting they sit around and say, "Pastor, we've still got this many classes, and we don't have workers, and the time is coming." We're going to make do. We're going to do it. But I believe God the Holy Spirit is speaking to some of you. You need to be calling our children's director and saying, "I want to make myself available. If I need to be trained, train me. If I'm qualified, check me out and see if I'm qualified. If I'm not qualified, then I don't want to force myself on you. But if there's something I can do, put me to work." I don't want you to wear out. I want you to last out. I want the work to go on.

You say, "Well, I can't teach." Have you ever thought about coming down here and pulling weeds? Don't you think this ought to be the most beautiful place in the midtown? I do. It ought to sparkle like a diamond. Come down here and tell our house and grounds crew, "Put me to work.

I can cut grass. I can pull weeds. I can do something." Friend, God is blessing our church. And we sit here, and we soak in this love. But you know that when there's the family love to share, there's the family load to bear. We're in it together, folks. Let's don't let up, back up, or shut up, until we're taken up. Let's make this, under God, the church that He wants it to be.

HOW TO ENJOY THE PRESENCE OF GOD

Sermon Date: January 19, 1997

Exodus 33:1–4

Dr. Adrian Rogers

Outline

Introduction
I. Direct Disobedience
II. Divided Devotion
III. Displaced Dependence
IV. Determined Defiance
Conclusion

Introduction

If you were to give a definition of worship, what would it be? Is worship enjoying God? I believe it is. I think that worship is enjoying the presence of God. Just put it in a sentence: Worship is enjoying the presence of God. And that's what I want to talk to you about today: "How to Enjoy the Presence of God."

Now, folks, the longer I live, the more I study, the more I experience, the more I realize that that is the bottom line, the highest good, the most wonderful fulfillment: to know God intimately and to enjoy Him personally—enjoying the presence of God. Now, let me ask you a question. Do you know God personally? I'm not asking if you know about Him. You might know about George Washington. I'm asking, "Do you know God personally?" Is He today, this moment, in your heart, in your life, a bright, living, vital reality? If so, you know the deepest pleasure. You have fulfilled the deepest need. You have attained that for which you were created: to know God personally, because, you see, worship is enjoying the presence of God. You need nothing more; you should settle for nothing less. You need nothing more; you should settle for nothing less.

Now there are many Christians today who do not have the conscious presence of God in their lives. They show up at church. They sing the songs. They may muster an *amen*, but there is a deadness, a blindness, and a void in their life. Now, let me tell you some of the most frightening words in all of the Bible. They're found here in Exodus 33:1–3: "And the LORD said unto Moses, Depart, and go up hence, thou and the people which thou hast brought up out of the land of Egypt, . . . Unto thy seed will I give it: and I will send an angel before thee; and I will drive out the Canaanite, the Amorite, and the Hittite, and the Perizzite, the Hivite, and the Jebusite: unto a land flowing with milk and honey: for I will not go up in the midst of thee; for thou art a stiffnecked people: lest I consume thee in the way" (Ex. 33:1–3 KJV). What are the frightening words? God says, "I'm not going with you. I will not go up in the midst of you."

Now, what is the situation? The Jewish people, the sons of Abraham, were out there in the wilderness. God has given them a covenant, and God has given them a promise. And they're headed toward the Promised Land, and in the middle of that journey they sin terribly against God. And God said, "All right, I promised that I'm going to give you the land, a land that flows with milk and honey. I will give you an angel escort into the land. And when you get there, the land will flow with milk and honey. But," God says, "I am not going with you."

Now that's frightening: to have success, to have possessions, to have protection, but not to have the presence of the Lord. "I'm going to give you an angel to take care of you," He says. "I'll get you into the land, but I am not going with you." That would be like people getting married, and the husband taking care of the wife, but they're living in separate bedrooms. Don't settle for success without the Lord. What happened? Our seeming success without the Lord. As a matter of fact, it has well been said that, whatever a man does without God, he will either fail miserably or succeed even more miserably.

Now, let's get a little of the background. Moses had gone upon Mount Sinai to get the Ten Commandments and instructions for the tabernacle. While Moses was gone, Aaron, his brother, led the people into a revolt against Almighty God. What Aaron said is, "We don't know what's happened to Moses. He's been up there a long time. Maybe he's never coming back. We need some guidance. We need some help. We need some leadership. You people give me your bracelets and your earrings, and we will make a golden calf, and we will worship that golden calf." And that's what the people did.

Just go back to 32:4, and you'll pick it up: "And he received them at their hand, and fashioned it with a graving tool, after he had made it a molten calf: and they said, These be thy gods, O Israel, which brought thee up out of the land of Egypt" (KJV). Now the people there are having a Bacchanalian feast, an orgy: "And they rose up early on the morrow, and offered burnt offerings, and brought peace offerings; and the people sat down to eat and to drink, and rose up to play. And the LORD said unto Moses, Go, get thee down; for thy people, which thou broughtest out of the land of Egypt, have corrupted themselves: they have turned aside quickly out of the way which I commanded them: they have made them a molten calf, and have worshipped it, and have sacrificed thereunto, and said, These be thy gods, O Israel, which have brought thee up out of the land of Egypt. And the LORD said unto Moses, I have seen this people, and, behold, it is a stiffnecked people: now therefore let me alone, that my wrath may wax hot against them, and that I may consume them: and I will make of thee a great nation" (Ex. 32:6–10 KJV).

Now what happens is this: When Moses comes down off the mountain, he sees this charade, this orgy, this feast. They made themselves naked. They are committing immorality. They're doing terrible, horrible things—dancing around the golden calf. Moses is so grieved that he takes the Ten Commandments and casts them to the ground, and breaks those tablets of stone. Then he takes that golden calf and has it ground into powder, and mixes that powder with water and makes the people to drink it. And their greatest delight now has become their greatest displeasure. And then 3,000 of the chief rebels are slain and put to death. Moses knows that this is a crisis, so Moses goes to God to intercede.

And look in verses 30–32: "And it came to pass on the morrow, that Moses said unto the people, Ye have sinned a great sin: and now I will go up unto the LORD; peradventure I shall make an atonement for your sin." Moses goes up to stand up between God and judgment; he goes up to intercede. "And Moses returned unto the LORD, and said, Oh, this people have sinned a great sin, and have made them gods of gold. Yet now, if thou wilt forgive their sin . . ."—it's sort of an unfinished sentence; his heart is just broken—"Yet now, if thou wilt forgive their sin—; and if not, blot me, I pray thee, out of thy book which thou hast written" (KJV). And Moses is praying, and interceding, and putting himself in the place of these people.

Now after this intercession is the text that I've just read to you in Exodus 33:1–3. God says, "All right, I won't destroy them. All right, I'll not destroy them. Moses, for your sake, I will bring them into the land. I will give them an angel escort. I will give them protection. I will give them provision. I will fulfill my promise, but I will not go with them into the land." Now, look up here, and let me tell you something, folks. If you're a brother and sister in Christ, do not settle for a deal like that. Do not settle for protection; do not settle for provision; do not settle for Promised Land, without the presence of God. Just don't do it. Now I'm telling you—I'm telling you—when you have the presence of God, you need nothing more, but you should settle for nothing less.

You say, "How does that apply to me this morning, pastor?" Well, there are a lot of you today who are saying, "I have salvation. I have eternal security. I'm not walking in joy. I'm not walking in victory. God is not real to me, but I honestly expect to go to heaven." And when the pastor asked, "How many of you know, if you were to die today, you'd go to heaven?" you'd lift your hand. But if you would be honest with me, you would say, "Pastor, God is not real in my life. I do not have the manifest presence of God in my life. I have His protection. I have His provision. I have His promise. But I do not have that presence of God in my life."

Now, don't think that, just because you have provision and protection, you're right with God. Don't think that for even one moment. Oh, you may be on your way to heaven, but I'm going to tell you one thing. You're certainly traveling there second-class. I remind you that even a nonbeliever has certain provisions: food, and air, and clothes, and houses. And, you know, we can be so preoccupied with getting that provision, and that protection, and claiming that promise, that we fail to have His presence.

Israel, however, knew better than that. And thank God that they did. Look in Exodus 33:4: "And when the people heard these evil tidings, they mourned" (KJV). And I want to say to you today that it is an evil thing to have gifts without the Giver, to have blessings without the Blesser, to have the promise without the Provider and the manifest presence of God.

Again, I want to ask you this question: Is God real to you? Is the presence of God, the Shekinah glory of God, this moment very real to you? Or, are you just fulfilling your duty, sitting in church Sunday morning, listening to some pastor preach away, and, really, very frankly, you're not very interested, and when the group stood and sang "Our God Reigns," your heart was not thrilled and filled with the presence of God? This message is for you, because worship is enjoying the presence of God. We're going to show you, in a moment, you need nothing more; you should settle for nothing less.

What made Israel different from the other nations? It was the manifested presence of God in the midst of them. It was the Shekinah glory. I wonder, are there some of you who once knew the glory of God, and now that glory has departed, and that glory has faded, and the glory of God is gone, and your life is dry?

What caused God to withdraw His manifested presence from His people? I want to mention four things. Those four things are the same four things that will rob you, denude you, of the manifested presence of God in your life, and will be the archenemy of worship. Worship is enjoying the presence of God. Now, what were these four things? What happened to Israel, where God said, "Well, I'll not destroy them; I'll send an angel, but I will not be in their midst"?

I. Direct Disobedience

Number one: They disobeyed God. Look, if you will, at Exodus 32:7 again. "And the LORD said unto Moses, Go, get thee down; for thy people, which thou broughtest out of the land of Egypt, have corrupted themselves" (KJV). Notice God calls them, to Moses, "your people," now. And, because they disobeyed God, the manifested presence of God was withdrawn from them.

Do you know what the problem with a lot of people, and some in this auditorium, is? You walk down this aisle; you've confessed faith in the Lord Jesus Christ; you have subscribed to the authentic doctrines of the church; you've followed the Lord in believer's baptism; but you do not have the presence of God. You don't even have the assurance of your salvation. And I have people come to me and say, "Pastor, could you help me? I don't know whether I'm saved or not." Well, let me tell you, I can't tell you whether you're saved or not. That's not my job; that's not my responsibility. Do you know whose responsibility it is to tell you that you're saved? It's the Holy Spirit's. It's the Holy Spirit of God that gives you the assurance that you belong to Him. That is the work of the Holy Spirit.

Listen to these verses, and put them down—1 John 4:13: "Hereby know we that we dwell in Him, and He in us, because He hath given to us of His spirit" (KJV). How do we know that we belong to Him? The Holy Spirit. Let me give you a companion verse—Romans 8:16: "The Spirit itself beareth witness with our spirit, that we are the children of God" (KJV). Now those two verses make it crystal clear that it is the work of the Holy Spirit to give us that assurance that we belong to the Lord Jesus Christ. John says, and Paul says, because of the Holy Spirit, we have the assurance of our salvation.

"Pastor," you say, "what does that have to do with a manifested presence of God? And what does that have to do with disobedience that you just read about?" Simply this: When you knowingly, willingly, with eyes wide open, disobey God, do you know what you do to the Holy Spirit? You grieve the Holy Spirit of God. That's the reason the Bible says that you're not to give place to the devil and grieve the Holy Spirit of God: "Do not grieve the Holy Spirit of God" (Eph. 4:30).

Did you know that you can only grieve somebody who loves you? Let me illustrate this, and you'll understand what I'm talking about. The neighbors' kids may vex you. Your own children grieve you. What's the difference? *Grieve* is a love word. The Holy Spirit of God loves you, but you can so grieve Him, when you disobey the commandments of God, that the Holy Spirit just closes up. Again, the Bible says, "Quench not the Spirit" (1 Thess. 5:19 KJV). Do you know what the word *quench* means? It means, "to pour cold water on a fire." The Holy Spirit is like a gentle dove. The Holy Spirit is like a glowing ember. You can frighten away that dove. You can pour water on that ember. The Bible says, "Be filled with the Spirit" (Eph. 5:18 KJV). Then the Bible says, "Grieve not"; "quench not." "Be filled." "Grieve not." "Quench not."

Now, listen again. I want to ask you this question: Who gives you the assurance of your salvation? The Holy Spirit of God. Who is it that manifests the life of God in you? The Holy Spirit of God is to you, in this age, what that pillar of cloud was to those people in that day. He is the Shekinah glory of God. He is the manifested presence of God. The Holy Spirit of God is the manifested presence of God in your life. The Holy Spirit of God is the manifested presence of God in your life. Now, listen to me. If you willfully, knowingly, deliberately disobey God, you grieve the Spirit; you quench the Spirit; and when you do, God ceases to be real to you. You can even wonder, "Am I saved?" I've met many people who doubt their salvation, that, I believe, were truly saved, but they're living in direct disobedience to God; and, as a result of that, they do not have the manifested presence of God.

Now, put this verse in your Bible—John 14:21. It's one of the key verses in enjoying the presence of God. Now, listen to it. Jesus said, "He that hath my commandments, and keepeth them, he it is that loveth me ..."—now, folks, when people truly love God, you don't see it just when they stand in the congregation and sing "Oh, How I Love Jesus," but they obey Him—"He that hath my commandments, and keepeth them, he it is that loveth me: and he that loveth me shall be loved of my Father,"—and watch this—"and I will love him, and will manifest myself to him" (KJV).

Aren't we talking about the manifest presence of God? Do you see how the Bible links the manifest presence of God with keeping the commandments of God? Because, when we disobey God, we grieve the Holy Spirit; we quench the Holy Spirit. The Holy Spirit of God is in us to make God real to us, and when we do that, we might have eternal security; we might go to heaven; God may send an angel escort to bring us to heaven when we die; but would you settle for that rather than the manifest presence of God? Many Christians are.

A man came and talked to his pastor, and he said, "Pastor, I don't know what's wrong with me, but God is not real to me anymore. I don't have any joy. The presence of God is not real in my heart, in my life, like He used to be." This wise pastor asked him a direct question. He said, "Is there any known sin in your life—any unconfessed, unrepented of sin in your life?" That moment, that man, in a moment of honesty, said, "Well, pastor, let me tell you something." He said, "I used to bring a tithe of my income to God. I believed the Word of God when the Bible teaches that we're to bring all the tithe into the storehouse. But," he said, "some time ago, I got the idea that perhaps God didn't need that as much as I needed it; and," he said, "yes, pastor, I have ceased to be honest with God."

And you know what this pastor told him? The pastor said, "Do you know what you've done? You've begun to steal from God." He said, "Sir, you wouldn't put your hand in the offering plate, would you, when the offering is passed—put your hand in the offering plate, and take some money out that other people have given to God? Would you steal from the offering plate?" And then he said, "Malachi says, 'When a man is not faithful in stewardship, he's robbing God'" (see Mal. 3:8).

Now he said, "What do you think God does when His child does that—when God sees His child willingly disobeying Him? Will God say this: "My child has chosen to disobey Me; number one, He's stealing from Me; number two, He cannot trust Me to take care of his needs, He cannot trust Me with his resources; number three, He will not obey Me; now this week I think I will bless him with even more financial resources, and I will make My presence very real to him"? Do you think God would do that? And God says, "I'm going to display Myself. I'm going to give him a deeper sense of My presence and My approval"? No, no. Why? Because here was a man in willing disobedience to Almighty God.

Now I want to say something else. Do you know who it was that encouraged these people to disobey God and lose the manifest presence of God? It was Aaron. You know who Aaron was? Aaron was a priest, a religious leader. And I'm going to tell you something else. There will always be plenty of people who will give you a reason, an excuse, to disobey God. It may even be a religious leader. They'll lead you into unscriptural marriage, some immorality, some transgression of the commandments of God, and they'll say, "That's all right; times have changed, and things are different." But I remind you one more time that Jesus says, "He that hath my commandments, and keepeth them, he it is that loveth me: and he that loveth me shall be loved of my Father, and I will love him, and will manifest myself to him" (John 14:21 KJV).

Now if you want an angel escort, and if you want to go to heaven without having the presence of God in your life, that's your business. But I don't. I want the manifested presence of God in my life. I need nothing more. I will settle for nothing less.

So ask yourself this question; if God is not real to you, ask this question in your heart this morning: Have I rejected a direct command of God? Am I living—am I right now living in disobedience to a known command of God? If you are, there's no reason that I can think of in all of the Bible where you ought to have a sense of the manifest presence of God. God loves you too much to manifest Himself to you in glory and joy, and yet have you to live in disobedience, because I cannot think of a worse lesson that He would teach you.

II. Divided Devotion

So, question number one: Can I discern any direct disobedience to God? Let me ask you the next question, if God is not real to you: Can I discover any divided devotion to God? Not only direct disobedience, but divided devotion. Look again in 32:4: "And he received them at their hand, and fashioned it"—*that is, the golden calf*—"with a graving tool, after he had made it a molten calf: and they said, These be thy gods, O Israel" (KJV). Now, what had these people done? They had divided devotion. They claimed to be Israel. The word *Israel* means, "people of God." And yet they made a golden calf. They made for themselves a god that was no bigger than their own imaginations. And then, rather than trusting Almighty God, they began to trust the work of their hands. This was idolatry.

As I've told you before, the Bible says, "When people make an idol, they become like the idol." First, the man molds the idol; and then, the idol molds the man. What is an idol? An idol is just a magnified sinner. A man just takes his own ideas and puts them into the work of his hands, and then he begins to worship it. And what he's really worshiping, ultimately, therefore, is himself.

You say, "Well, Adrian, I'm not guilty of idolatry." Well, let's check up and find out whether you are or not. Maybe there might be a golden calf in your life. What is an idol? Anything that you love more than God is an idol. What is an idol? Anything that you fear more than God is an idol. What is an idol? Anything that you serve more than God is an idol. Anything that you trust more than God is an idol. G. K. Chesterton said it well. He said, "When we cease to worship a true God, it is not that we worship nothing; it is that we'll worship anything." Is there any direct disobedience? Is there any divided devotion? Is there something that you love more, fear more, serve more, or trust more than Almighty

God? If there is, no wonder God's presence is not real in your heart and in your life—divided devotion.

Now, answer this before God. Don't answer to me out loud, but answer it. If the glory of God is gone in your life, if God is not real to you, ask this question: Is there anyone or anything that takes precedence over God in your life? You say, "Well, I give God a place in my life." God doesn't want a place in your life. You say, "Well, I give God prominence in your life." God despises prominence in your life. God demands preeminence in your life. He will take nothing less. God's throne is not a duplex. Is there anything that is a greater controlling factor of your behavior? Is there a relationship that means more to you? Is there treasure that means more to you? Is there anything that gets more of your attention than Almighty God? Then, friend, it should not come as a surprise to you that, because of that golden calf in your life, God says, "I'm not going with you; I'll not be in the midst of you; I just won't do it"—any direct disobedience; any divided devotion.

My wife knows that I love her with all of my heart, but she knows she's second place, not first place in my life. And she doesn't mind being second place, because she knows that, when God is first place, I will love her with a love I could never love her with if she were first place. Now, friend, there are certain relationships in your life that are wonderful relationships, but none can take the place of an undivided relationship to Almighty God. Idolatry is the mother sin, the father sin, the sin of all other sins.

III. Displaced Dependence

Now, here's the third question that you might ask yourself, if God is not real in your life, if you do not have that manifested presence of God—and worship is enjoying the presence of God: Do you, thirdly, detect any displaced dependence? Direct disobedience. Divided devotion. Displaced dependence. Look, if you will again, in verses 7–8: "And the LORD said unto Moses, Go, get thee down; for thy people, which thou broughtest out of the land of Egypt, have corrupted themselves:

they have turned aside quickly out of the way which I commanded them: they have made them a molten calf,"—all right, there you have direct disobedience and divided devotion. Now, what's this?—"and have worshipped it, and sacrificed thereunto, and said, These be thy gods, O Israel, which have brought thee up out of the land of Egypt" (KJV).

Now they begin to put their dependence in the work of their hands, their ugly god that they've made with their own hands. And now no longer is there dependence upon Almighty God that brought them through the Red Sea. Do you know what happens when you do that: when God gives you a victory, and you give the glory to something else or someone else, and then depend upon that rather than the God who gave you the victory? You're going to lose the presence of God.

I was thinking about that this morning. These buildings that we worship in today: I love this land; I love these buildings. I'll tell you, these walls are saturated with prayer, and these carpets are saturated with the tears of God's people. I want to tell you about this place. This place is the place that prayer, faith, and obedience built. Somebody said to me the other day on an airplane, "Oh, Rogers, you've done a good job out there; you've really built a great thing out there." I thought, "Dear God, it's a lie; and, dear God, help me never to believe that kind of a lie." God has done this. God has done this. But suppose, after God has done it, then we get to saying, "You know, we have a pretty good building committee. You know, we really did give our money. You know, we're pretty smart folks. Look what we have done." And that moment God says, "All right now, you've got it. I'm out of here," when we begin to depend upon our ingenuity, our wit, our wisdom, and say, "Look what we have done."

You see, they took those earrings off their own ears. They took those bracelets off their own hands. And with a graving tool they made a god, and then they said, "That's our god, and that's what is delivering us." And God says, "All right, I'm not going with you anymore." I can remember how we used to get in those building committee meetings, and cry and weep before God, and say, "God, we don't know what to do. There's no way we can do it." And yet God did it. God did it.

Not long ago, when George H. W. Bush was the president of the United States, our nation came up against what we thought was an implacable foe: Saddam Hussein. And the word *Hussein* sounds a lot like *insane*. And that man, I really believe, is demonic—I really do. And there's a malevolent force. And, you know, they basically say, "In any kind of a war, you cannot defend your life against the man who's not afraid to lose his." And these fanatical Iraqi Republican Guards were marshaling for war. I can remember staying up at night and watching CNN, and watching those missiles fly in the air—those Patriot missiles. I can remember this church after that happened. I can tell you, my dear friend, that Sunday morning our attendance, it seems to me, was up twenty-five percent. People across the land filled the churches of the land. And they cried out to God, and there were prayer meetings—fasting and prayer—saying, "Oh, God, we don't want to get bogged down in the Middle East in some desert war. And, God, you know, what could be germ warfare, could be atomic warfare, could break up in the Middle East, where they're shooting those missiles over—the Scud missiles—into Israel. And Israel may retaliate with atomic bombs. Who knows but what? It's all about to blow up right in our face." Do you remember those times? Or have you forgotten? And our boys were going off, and we were praying, "Oh, God, help us; oh, God, deliver us."

And I want to tell you something, friend. God answered prayer. And do you know what happened as soon as Desert Storm was over? Rather than giving God the glory, do you know what we did? We began to say, "Boy, Schwarzkopf: what a general! Colin Powell: what a strategist! What about those Patriot missiles! Boy, we showed him, didn't we? We kicked some *you know what*." I heard all that kind of talk. Isn't that true? I want to tell you we failed to give God the glory. We failed to have national revival. We failed to continue to follow God, and love God, and serve God. And since that time our nation has gone down into a cesspool of rottenness and filth. Never since I've been preaching have I seen a nation take a nosedive like this nation has taken since Desert Storm. Never did we have a more glorious victory, I don't believe. Never did God protect the people, and, in mercy, move into us, and let us get out of a mess like we got out of, with such blessings. But then we made a golden calf, and said, "Look what brought us out of Desert Storm"—just like they made a golden calf, and they said, "These are our gods that brought us through the Red Sea," and they failed to give God the glory.

I'm going to tell you something, precious, sweet friends. You listen to me. God has said, "I will not share My glory with another." And when God gives you a blessing, and when God is good to you, and God brings you through the storm—whether it be Desert Storm, or any other kind of a storm—and then you have that displaced dependence—you begin to give credit where credit is not due, and fail to give God the glory—is it any wonder that His presence is not real in your life?

IV. Determined Defiance

Is there any direct disobedience? Is there any divided devotion? Is there any displaced dependence? One last question, quickly, and I'll close this message this morning: Is there any determined defiance? Listen. Look, if you will, in Exodus 32:9: "And the LORD said unto Moses, I have seen this people, and, behold, it is a stiffnecked people" (KJV). What does that mean? *Stiffnecked* is the opposite of being meek and pliable. God was wanting to lead them, but they were like a horse with a stiff neck, who rears up, who will not yield.

You want God to be real to you? Don't be stiffnecked. If God gives you a specific revelation—God speaks to you about what He wants you to do—then obey Him. Has God told you there's somebody He wants you to witness to? Has God been laying somebody on your heart and you're not witnessing to that person? No wonder God's not real to you! Has God been putting some impulse in your heart to serve in this church—perhaps to work in the preschool, the nursery; perhaps to be a youth worker; perhaps to work on the parking lots; perhaps to serve in the kitchen; but you say, "I don't want to do that"? Has God been laying something on your heart that He wants you to give, some sacrificial gift—not even to a need, but for the glory of God? Has God been laying on your heart somebody that you need to go to and apologize to and reconcile with and make things right? Has God been telling you there's a relationship that you're in that you need to break off, young lady or young man, and get out of it—that it's a wrong relationship? Has God been speaking to your heart and calling you into missions or into full-time Christian service? Has God been telling you to do something, go somewhere, be something, give something, and you have said *no*? You've had a stiff neck? And then you say, "I wonder why God is not real to me. I wonder why God says, 'Oh, all right, I'm going to take you on to heaven. I'm going to give you an angel escort all of the way, but I'm not going in the midst of you.'" Thank God, Moses had enough sense to say, "No deal." He said, "God, if You don't go with me, I ain't going. I am not going without You, the manifest presence of God, in my life."

Conclusion

What is worship? Singing songs? No. Saying prayer? No. Coming to church? No. Giving money? No. Worship is enjoying the presence of God. Is God real to you? He wants to be real. Again, Jesus said, "He who has My commandments, and keeps them, it is he who loves me. And he who loves Me will be loved of My Father, and I will love him, and will manifest Myself to him" (John 14:21). Lord Jesus, manifest Yourself to us. Be real to us.

A WALK THROUGH THE PSALMS

A Righteous Relationship

Psalm 23:1

K. Marshall Williams, Sr.

Introduction

The Twenty-third Psalm is perhaps the most popular and frequently quoted passage in the Scriptures. It is the pearl of the Psalms. And I am convinced that its popularity has to do with its depiction of the Lord as a loving and all-sufficient caretaker, a loving shepherd who meets every need of those in under his watch. The relationship is such that the sheep rely totally upon the shepherd and cannot travel safely without him.

In Psalm 22, the Lord God is depicted as the Suffering Savior, and in Psalm 24, He is the Supreme Sovereign, but in the Twenty-third Psalm, He is the Good Shepherd who relates to those in His care. Because He is our Shepherd, David says there will be no lack when it comes to whatever we need (Ps. 23:1; Phil. 4:19). Mutually loving, caring relationships is a universal phenomenon. All of us long for and seek relationship through spouses, parents, siblings, neighbors, colleagues, acquaintances, and even passersby.

All relationships should offer some measure of reward and fulfillment, but nothing is as fulfilling and rewarding as being in relationship with the Good Shepherd (Ps. 73: 26; John 15:13; Rom. 5:6–8). Especially since we, like sheep, are defenseless and vulnerable, easily enticed and mislead, inclined to wander off and get lost and therefore in need of protection (Prov. 14:12; Rom. 7:18).

Reciprocity

The Shepherd-sheep relationship is one of reciprocity. We can claim Him as our own (my Shepherd), and He claims us as well (Ps. 100:3; Jer. 23:4). For He is our God; and we are the people of His pasture, and the sheep of His hand (Ps. 95:7). Righteous relationships are never one-sided!

1. The Shepherd won't run off (John 10:11–12)
2. The sheep won't chance after any other (John 10:4–5)

Companionship

The Shepherd-sheep relationship is one of companionship. The Good Shepherd never abandons His sheep; rather He provides a sense of family for them. Righteous relationships generate unity!

1. A walk in the park (Ps. 23:4)
2. A family reunion (John 10:18)

Dialogue

The Shepherd-sheep relationship is rooted in dialogue. Not only do they walk with each other, they talk to each other. Righteous relationships are based on mutual understanding.

1. The Shepherd knows our names (Matt. 10:3; John 10:3)
2. The sheep know His voice (John 10:4)

Conclusion

The biggest threat to healthy relationships is deception, and sheep are so very easily deceived. It's important that we not confuse the shyster with the Shepherd. The shyster comes to rob, steal, and destroy (John 10:10) but the Shepherd comes to give us life. Neither should we confuse the hireling with the Shepherd. The hireling is just there for monetary gain and is no help to us. The hireling does not love the sheep (v. 13) and he will abandon us at the first sign of hardship or danger. The Good Shepherd on the other hand will give His life for the sheep. Righteous relationships are sacrificial!

A WALK THROUGH THE PSALMS

A Good Night's Rest

Psalm 23:2*a*

K. Marshall Williams, Sr.

Introduction

Rest is one of the most important elements in the cycle of life. Approximately one-third of our lives is spent in periods of rest. In most cultures around the world, rest is built into the workday. Caregivers for the young and old alike establish rest times for those in their care. And of course the Sabbath ritual is founded on the principle of rest, for even God Himself rested so as to solidify for all mankind that rest is essential to life (Gen. 2:2–3).

Sound bodies, souls, and spirits are predicated upon rest. God commanded us to rest: "six days you shall do your work, and on the seventh day you shall rest" (Ex. 23:12). Still there are times when rest eludes us. Sometimes we are too anxious. Or perhaps there is too much commotion. Sometimes we are in pain or distress or burdened by the cares of the world. Sometimes we cannot identify the source of our restlessness other than to say we are sheep.

Sheep are very restless animals. They don't hold up well under pressure, they are easily led astray, and almost anything will have them up on their feet running to and fro even to the point of passing out from exhaustion. Often the shepherd literally has to force them to lie down and rest. Likewise, the Good Shepherd forces us to lie down in quietness and stillness that we may rise up to newness of life.

The Quietness

It's difficult to find rest in the midst of noise. In a sickroom or street brawl associated with struggle and distress. Quiet, on the other hand, is associated with peace and contentment. The Good Shepherd provides quiet places for His sheep to rest.

1. Blessed quietness (1 Chron. 22:9)
2. Holy quietness (Josh. 6:10)
3. Quiet assurance (Job 34:29)

The Stillness

In the clamor and chaos of life, we are fatigued and suffer loss. Prolonged fatigue can lead to hopelessness and despair and can distort our sense of possibility. To counteract the confusion that arises in the midst of chaos, the Good Shepherd offers stillness:

1. Be still so that you can hear (Num. 9:8)
2. Be still so that you can see (Ex. 14:13)
3. Be still so that you will know what's really going on (Num. 13:30)

The Newness

Often after a good night's rest the things that seemed so daunting and insurmountable late in our midnight hours are manageable in the light of day. The Good Shepherd ensures renewal for His sheep.

1. Destruction at noonday (Ps. 91:6)
2. Sorrow at nighttime (Pss. 30:5*c*; 91:5)
3. Joy in the morning (Ps. 30:5*d*)

Conclusion

Rational perspective hinges on rest. Endurance through difficulty hinges on rest. And our ability to trust God in every situation hinges on rest. So the next time you find yourself being irrational, distrustful, or overcome by routine living ask, the Lord to give you rest. He'll make you lie down.

A WALK THROUGH THE PSALMS

Spiritual Refreshment

Psalm 23:2*b*

K. Marshall Williams, Sr.

Introduction

The very air we breathe, the water we drink, and the food we eat—all serve to refresh us. Clean air, clear water, and healthy foods are life sustaining. Prolonged periods of time without any one of the three will seriously compromise our health, and prolonged periods of time without all three is certain death. In an effort to be our best selves, most of us commit to sound nutrition, hydration, and exercise at some point in our lives. Many of us commit and recommit time and time again. Still we find ourselves unable to honor those commitments as we juggle the day-to-day demands of life—home life and work life and even church life. Somehow our good intentions are usurped by our bad habits, and we miss the mark (Rom. 7:19, 21).

In the hustle and bustle of life, we eat and drink the things that are most readily available, and we never make time to engage in the kinds of activities that might expand our lung capacity. And as time goes on, our bodies begin to crave junk-foods and sugary drinks and loathe and resist exercise. It all happens so gradually that we're convinced that we never liked healthy foods: never liked water, never liked to walk, and so the story goes. And just like our bodies devolve into unhealthy specimens as a result of care, so too do our souls (Ps. 1:2–3; Matt. 4:4; 1 Cor. 6:19–20).

In order to maintain proper spiritual health, we have to nourish, hydrate, and exercise our souls (Ps. 63:1; Phil. 3:10; 2 Tim. 2:15). And God, in His infinite wisdom, has provided all that we need to be spiritually healthy, including a trainer in the person of the Good Shepherd who gives us that which pertains to spiritual life (Ps. 23:2*b*; 2 Tim. 3:16; 2 Peter 1:3–4).

The Breath of Life

1. The breath of life (Gen. 2:7; Job 33:4)
2. Godly exercise (1 Cor. 8:8; 1 Tim. 4:7–8)
3. Walk in the Spirit (Gal. 5:16–17, 25)

Bread of Life

1. Bread of heaven (Ex. 16:4, 15; Ps. 78:24)
2. The bread of life (John 6:33–35, 48)
3. Our daily bread (Matt. 6:11; Luke 11:3)

Living Water

1. Broken cisterns (Jer. 2:13; 17:13)
2. Spiritual drink (1 Cor. 10:3–4)
3. Living water (John 4:10–11; 7:38)

Conclusion

A fully paid spiritual health plan is included in the benefits package of those who enlist in the army of the Lord (Rom. 8:16–17, 32, 35–39). If we daily allow the eternal to perform divine surgery on the internal, His Spirit will manifest Himself through us in the external (1 Cor. 11:1; Phil. 4:9; Heb. 5:8). This regimented plan of God will ensure optimal spiritual health (Rom. 12:1–2). The Good Shepherd will regularly refresh us with life-giving water, food, and air, but we must commit ourselves to a healthy spiritual lifestyle in order for His provision to be of use (Acts 20:32; 3 John 2).

A WALK THROUGH THE PSALMS

Restoration

Psalm 23:3*a*

K. Marshall Williams, Sr.

Introduction

Picture, if you will, a flock of sheep grazing in green pastures. Everything is going along just fine when one or more of them begin to wander. Sheep have a staying nature. They often wander and find themselves separated from the flock and the shepherd. The shepherd must then go off in search of the missing sheep because they cannot survive apart from the flock and they do not have the wherewithal to make their way back on their own. Sheep are dense and defenseless!

And such is the case with the Good Shepherd and us (His sheep). Our sin nature (Ps. 51:5; Rom. 5:12) causes us to wander and go astray: Isaiah 53:6 says that all we like sheep have gone astray; everyone hath turned his own way and the Lord hath laid on them the iniquity of us all. We have a natural propensity to stray from our Shepherd (Rom. 14:12). Lost in the darkness of the world, we are unable to make our way back to the fold. We are subject to blind attacks and can fall victim to any aggressive force (Luke 22:31; 1 Peter 5:8).

When the Good Shepherd finds wandering sheep He restores them to the fold. (Ps. 23:3*a*; Isa. 55:7). The Good Shepherd understands that sheep are prone to wandering and He does not hold that against them. The Good Shepherd restores favor, restores wealth, restores life. The first act of restoration is remission.

Remission

1. Remission (Matt. 26:28; Heb. 10:18)
2. Restored favor (Pss. 50:12; 90:17)

Redemption

With remission comes redemption—the Bible says we have blood-bought, borrowed bodies (1 Cor. 6:20). We were bought with a price (1 Cor. 7:23; 1 Peter 1:18–19). We serve a God who paid enough to purchase our salvation and restore all that the enemy has stolen (Gal. 2:20)!

1. Redemption (Luke 1:68; Gal. 3:13)
2. Restored wealth (2 Sam. 2:7; Ps. 37:25; 1 Tim. 6:17)

Reconciliation

And with redemption comes reconciliation. No longer do our lives hang in the balance. The finished work of the cross fully reconciled us with God (Rom. 5:1). Whereas we once had a life that was subject to sin and death, we now have eternal life through Jesus Christ our Lord (John 3:16; 5:24; Rom. 5:8; 6:23; 10:9–10).

1. Reconciliation (Rom. 5:10–11; 2 Cor. 5:18–19)
2. Restored life (2 Kings 8:5; John 11:25–26)

Conclusion

Christians or those of us who have been accepted into the beloved, the world over, regularly worship and celebrate the redemptive work of our Lord Jesus Christ on the cross and restoration it brings (1 Sam. 12:24; 1 Cor. 15:50–56). Only through the power of the cross can we cease from our wandering (Acts 1:8; 1 Cor. 1:18). The finished work of the cross affords our weary souls the opportunity to come home, reestablishes our place among the flock, and ever connects us to the Shepherd (Luke 15:17–24; John 10:28–30; James 5:19–20).

A WALK THROUGH THE PSALMS

Refuge

Psalm 23:4

K. Marshall Williams, Sr.

Introduction

Let's blow the dust off some very familiar landscape, and with microscopic precision, let us descend on this timeless truth seeing what another shepherd said about the Chief Shepherd. The Twenty-third Psalm is the pearl of the Psalms because everybody knows it. When I was playing football in college we recited this psalm before the game. This psalm has a particular placement and providential position in Scripture. When you accept the Suffering Savior in Psalm 22, you can receive the promise of a sufficient Shepherd in the Twenty-third Psalm and then you will be able to lift up your heads to the Supreme Sovereign in Psalm 24! He is a Savior on a cross, who is a Shepherd who cares and a Sovereign King who sits on the throne. David explains that it is of paramount importance that we know who it is that is the Shepherd. So he gives us an ocular demonstration and a pictorial illustration of what our Shepherd does to meet the needs of His dense and defenseless sheep.

Refuge

"Yea, though I walk thru the valley of the shadow of death, I will fear no evil, for thou art with me; thy rod and thy staff they comfort me" (Ps. 23:4).

Shadow of Death

When sheep get lost, trapped between two mountains, and if it's the right time of day, the sun casts a shadow and the sheep think night is coming and get afraid. David says when the shadows of life come over us, don't be afraid (2 Tim. 1:7). Going into the valley will document, authenticate, and validate what and who we are and who we really depend on. The valley is a place where we will definitely find out who He is. The Christian life is not like a rose garden, tiptoeing through the tulips; we're going through the valley (John 16:33). We're going to have some problems in life, but He will write a prescription that will guarantee His presence and His power to overcome all of our problems (1 John 5:4–5). The psalmist says, "Yea, though I walk through the valley of the shadow of death." It's the picture of sheep led by the Shepherd walking down a steep hill fearful because of the possibility of death. Death-like shadows can't hurt us. Nobody's afraid of a shadow, but a shadow appearing down a dark street, reflected off the street light, can stop you in your tracks and have you afraid, thinking someone's following you. A shadow is like a knife that won't cut or a bee that don't sting or a dog that can't bite. Walking through this is like the shadow of death.

His Comfort

Then the psalmist says, "I will fear no evil; for You are with me" (Ps. 23:4*a*). David is saying that when you are going through something that makes you feel like you're going to die, don't worry because the Lord is with you! You see, the Shepherd whipped the shadow (John 11:25–26). What the valley will do is show you who you can really depend on. Most of us will try to flesh it out with our own mental muscle, but God has a way of showing us that life doesn't consist of the abundance of the things a man possesses (Luke 12:15). You'll find out Swiss bank accounts can't purchase healing. Brass bed, Sealy mattresses with new and improved springs, and you still can't sleep at night. House alarmed, insurances in place, but you still can't purchase security. Even your familiar friend will turn his heals up against you in the valley (Ps. 41:9).

But God's greatness—that He is, always was, and always will be—shows up in the valley (Ps. 90:20). He validates who He is and what He can do, by allowing us to deplete what it is that we are in the flesh, to show us that He is more than enough even without us (Gen. 22:14; Zech. 4:6).

He'll put us in the valleys that are beyond us to show us it's really not about us but it's all about Him! He leads us through the valley of the shadow of death so we won't fear any evil. Why? Because He's the one who is with us (Ps. 46:1).

His Rod and Staff

And even if we slip, He has a rod and a staff to comfort us. The rod was a club the shepherd used to beat away enemies that tried to prey on the sheep. The staff was a long stick with a hook. The shepherd could reach into the bushes and lift sheep out when they were caught in the thicket. Aren't you glad we have somebody watching over us in the valley (1 Cor. 10:13)? As you go through the valley, don't pitch a tent there. You're in the university of adversity for kingdom advancement (James 1:2–5)! David got tangled up in the thickets of life because of his immorality and murder (2 Sam. 12:9–17). The shadow of death was all over him, but when he dealt with his sin (Ps. 51:4) and returned to God, God's rod protected him and His staff pulled him back in and God's grace covered him (Ps. 51:12).

Conclusion

When the Lord is your Shepherd, He'll be a constant companion, watching over us with His rod and His staff (Ps. 121:7–8). David was saying, the Lord is my Shepherd who is acquainted with my past, and can deliver me in the present, and He's the one who overseas my future. What consideration that the infinite Lord of Glory assumes toward us in the character of a Shepherd (1 John 3:1). It's mighty nice to be under the pastoral care of Jehovah!

When the Lord is your Shepherd, He'll soothe your doubts and calm all your fears (Ps. 55:22; 1 Peter 5:7). If you're lonely, He'll be your company keeper in the midnight hour (Acts 16:25–26)! That's what a shepherd does for his sheep! We have security in our Shepherd.[1]

A WALK THROUGH THE PSALMS

Rescue

Psalm 23:5

K. Marshall Williams, Sr.

Introduction

Life is filled with trouble. "Man who is born of woman is of few days and full of trouble" (Job 14:1). Either I am in trouble, just got out of trouble, or am about to be in trouble! If you haven't had any trouble yet, just keep on living. Jesus put it this way in John 16:33: "In the world you will have tribulation; but be of good cheer, I have overcome the world." If you're a blood-bought believer who has been born into the body of Christ, you've got double trouble! Paul said in 2 Timothy 3:12 that all who desire to live godly in Christ Jesus will suffer persecution. The world will hate you because of who you are and whose you are (John 15:18–21). The flesh will rage war with you underneath the skin in the unseen realities of life, because you are now a partaker of a divine nature (2 Peter 1:4) and the devil will try to wreck your witness and rob you of enjoying life to the fullest measure (Luke 22:31; John 10:10). But David, a shepherd, knew what it took, using his rod and his staff, to protect and meet the needs of sheep. Therefore he knew that the Lord who is the Chief Shepherd (1 Peter 5:4) knew how to take care and *rescue* him from the *enemy*, as his *emancipator*.

Rescue

When the Lord is your Shepherd, the psalmist says, "You prepare a table before me in the presence of my enemies; You anoint my head with oil; My cup runs over" (Ps. 23:5).

The Enemy

A shepherd will locate and prepare a pasture, taking out all poisonous plants and rocks because sheep have trouble discerning good food from bad food. Then he brings the sheep to the pasture he prepared for them to be nourished. But in the bushes and the cliffs are predators waiting, salivating at the mouth because they want to kill the sheep, but they won't dare come out and attack they sheep because the shepherd is there with his rod and staff. Inside the shepherd's belt is a pouch, filled with fodder and grains, so whenever David found a lost sheep, he would spread a little cloth on the ground and put grain from his little pouch on it. That was the table for the sheep. Foxes, hyenas, and other predators would hang around, but again all they could do was look because of the shepherd's presence. What does all of this mean? We all have enemies. Doesn't matter how good a Christian you are; you have some enemies. They hated Jesus without a cause (Matt. 10:22; John 15:25). But God will bless you and prosper you right in front of your enemies or haters, if you please. They'll get mad at you and want to hurt you, but they can't touch you (Ps. 32:31–32; Isa. 54:17). They'll get upset about the blessings of God in your life, but they can't hurt you because you have a Shepherd that keeps anybody from messing with you (Ps. 121:5, 8). But the Lord allows enemies for three reasons (Job 1:8). First, enemies show us how not to act (Rom. 12:21). Then, enemies need to see what a real Christian looks like (Phil. 4:9).

And lastly, enemies are necessary because we'll need a place to rest our feet on; because Scripture says that one day all of our enemies are going to be made our footstool (Ps. 110:1; Acts 2:35).

So thank God for enemies. For the God we serve will not withhold one good thing from those who walk uprightly (Ps. 84:11*b*). What God has for you, it is for you (Jer. 29:11)! He'll bless you right in front of your haters and they'll sit and scratch their heads and wonder how you received what you have. Then they'll talk about you and say you think you're somebody. The truth is, you're a nobody whom God took and made somebody (1 Cor. 6:9–11). An heir of God, joint heir with Christ

(Rom. 8:16–17), the apple of His eye, held in His hand, sheltered by His wings, a son of the Most High God (John 1:12).

The Emancipator

Then the text says, "You anoint my head with oil; my cup runs over" (Ps. 23:5*b*). In the east oil was used as a means of refreshment to weary travelers, and healing oils were sometimes rubbed into the fleece of the sheep to refresh them. The shepherd would also take a cup that he carried in his belt, dip it in water, and as he walked over to the sheep the water would splash out the top of the cup. The cup would be running over, letting the sheep know that there was going to be more than enough water to satisfy his thirst. That's the way God is with us. No matter what the economy does, my cup is still running over. It doesn't matter who is laying off or who's hiring, because the king's heart is in the hands of the Lord (Prov. 21:1)! He anoints my head; He refuels and refreshes me (Matt. 11:28–30).

Conclusion

When the Lord is your Shepherd, there will be no lack. He'll meet all emotional, physical, social, intellectual, and spiritual needs. He'll give you rest. He'll give you refreshment. He'll give you restoration. He'll give you righteousness. He'll give you refuge. And He'll rescue you from your enemies (Ps. 23:1–5)! For that's why we have a Good Shepherd, because He gave His life for His sheep and moment by moment watches over them (John 10:15–16).

I'm talking about Jesus, the I AM in the book of Exodus. The Ancient of Days of whom Daniel spoke. The fountain of hope on whom Zacharias prophesied. Ezekiel said, He's my wheel in the middle of a wheel. My sweet rose of Sharon. The lily of the valley and the bright and morning star! He's the one who'll be handling all of your troubles for today![1]

A WALK THROUGH THE PSALMS

Revival

Psalm 23:6

K. Marshall Williams, Sr.

Introduction

This psalm of David is special because everybody knows the Twenty-third Psalm. From toddlers to teenagers, singles, spouses to seniors, everybody knows this one. It's a unique and precious hymn of confidence because David explains that it is of paramount importance that we know who it is that is the Shepherd whose been faithful to him (Ps. 37:25). He's the Lord, and because He is who He is, there shall be no lack (Ps. 34:9–10).

Rest

"He makes me to lie down" (Ps. 23:2*a*). He gives rest from heavy burdens (Heb. 4:15–16). Sheep, like us, can't handle pressure. The shepherd has to literally make them lie down and rest so he can nourish them with his healing.

Refreshment

"He leads me beside the still waters" (Ps. 23:2*b*). The shepherd will allow some water to flow into a trench, which will cause it to be still so that the sheep lay down beside and drink from the still waters. We are sometimes stressed out by the rough waters of life, so He'll slow us down so that we can be refreshed and cleansed.

Restoration

"He restores my soul" (Ps. 23:3). Sheep wander off and get separated from the shepherd. We like sheep find ourselves wandering from the Shepherd, and we need to be restored. It's in us to wander (Ps. 51:5; Rom.

5:12). We have a natural propensity to stray away from the Shepherd (Isa. 53:6*a*). But it's nice to know that we have a caring Shepherd who will restore our souls (2 Cor. 5:17–20).

Righteousness

"He leads me in the paths of righteousness for His name's sake" (Ps. 23:3*b*). He guides us in right living (2 Tim. 3:16–17) because His name is on the line. We represent the Good Shepherd, and we are supposed to be different (2 Cor. 5:20).

Refuge

"Yea, though I walk through the valley of the shadow of death, I will fear no evil: for thou art with me; thy rod and thy staff they comfort me" (Ps. 23:4). David says when the shadows of life come over us, don't be afraid (2 Tim. 1:7). David is saying that when you are going through something that makes you feel like you're going to die, don't worry because the Lord is with you (Ps. 46:1). His rod will beat away the enemy. His staff, a long stick with a hook on it, will pull stuck sheep out. The Lord always watches over us (Ps. 21:7–8).

Rescue

Look at what else He does when the Lord is your Shepherd. "You prepare a table before me in the presence of my enemies; You anoint my head with oil; My cup runs over" (Ps. 23:5). The shepherd spreads a little cloth on the ground and puts grain on it. That was the table when predators were looking but the shepherd was present. All of us have enemies, but God will prosper you in their presence (Ps. 121:5, 8).

Revival

When the Lord is your Shepherd, there will be no lack. He'll give you rest, refreshment, restoration, righteousness, refuge, and, lastly, revival!

The psalmist closes by saying, "Surely, goodness and mercy shall follow me all the days of my life; and I will dwell in the house of the LORD forever" (Ps. 23:6).

a. *God's Goodness and Mercy.* The psalmist does something for our future. Only goodness and mercy or loving-kindness will follow us. God is good not only for time but also for eternity. That's good because sometimes sheep have a tendency to look back and lag back (Matt. 9:62; Phil 3:14). So sometimes the shepherd uses sheepdogs to keep sheep moving forward and to protect them from anybody or anything behind them. The sheepdog will come behind the sheep and nip at their heels to keep them in the flock. The sheepdogs also cover the tracks of the sheep, sprinkling droppings to throw off the scent for the sheep from the predators that are trying to catch one of the sheep lagging behind.

   Well, beloved, every now and then you might think about going back. You thought you left something in the world, wondering if there is something that you missed or that you didn't try, but you find yourself not able to go back. Peter said it's like a dog returning to his vomit (2 Peter 2:22). You know why you can't go back. It's a sheepdog called goodness and mercy. They start nipping your heels saying you can't go back now. Every now and then we get predators in our lives. People who don't like us, who try to reach back in our past and dig up some sin. They try to be the Jerusalem Federal Bureau of Investigation but can't come up with a thing because those sheepdogs covered our tracks (Ps. 103:12; Mic. 7:18). Nobody can come back and dig up our sin from our past (2 Cor. 5:17).
b. *God's Dwelling Place.* Because goodness and mercy, they follow us all the days of our lives and we will dwell in the house of the Lord forever. Aren't you glad? We are already

seated in heavenly places, citizens of heaven. Aren't you glad about it (Eph. 2:6; Phil. 3:20)? Praise His Holy Name!

Conclusion

Thank You, the Lord, for being our Shepherd. You're a sure foundation that never shakes. A faithful friend that never forsakes. A High Priest that never fails. An eternal fountain that never ceases to flow. An ark that never leaks, an anchor that never lets go. A rock that never moves, truth that never lies. A bridge that never collapses. A judge that never misguides. A promise that never defaults. A true vine that never whithers. A companion who never departs. A counselor who never betrays. But most of all He's King of kings and Lord of lords![1]

A WALK THROUGH THE PSALMS

A Refuge for My Soul

Psalm 46:1

K. Marshall Williams, Sr.

Introduction

Today there is growing satanic antagonism toward Christians (Eph. 6:10–12; 2 Tim. 3:1–5). Weariness in the battle can leave one wondering if there is a refuge for my soul. No matter what we are going through, God wants us to know that He is for us, and nobody or no weapon formed against us can stand or succeed (Isa. 17; 54; Rom. 8:31)! He's the source of hope in the face of trouble. "Therefore we will not fear" (Ps:46:2*a*). Even in the worst conditions, God has unlimited, inexplicable, and unimaginable ways of working things out in our lives, because He is for us (Ps. 62:11; Eph 3:20)! This text shows us three ways God is for us (Ps. 46:1).

He's a Refuge

He's a safe place of protection to which we can run to. The God of the universe says, "I'll be your refuge when you're defeated, depressed, and in despair! You can come to Me and I'll wrap My arms around you and won't let any harm come to you, for I am your refuge!" In hyperbolic language He says even if the earth gives way and the mountains fall into the sea and floods come and the earth quakes, I'll still be your safe place. If all the pillars of your life leave you, it really doesn't matter, because I am the God of transcendent stability (Heb. 13:8). Nothing can erode His protective fortification. The psalmist says God, and God alone, is our only source and security (Ps. 62:5).

He Is Our Strength

He is our internal provision of power for enduring conditions, curses, and crosses (Acts 1:8). He promises to give us moment-by-moment infusion of His substance (Luke 11:3; Phil. 4:13). He'll be our strength in weakness (2 Cor. 12:9)

He's a Present Help

He's a helper who is always there who is attentive to our needs. He's there when we're sick! He's there when we're well! He's there when we're rich! He's there when we're broke, busted, and disgusted! He's there when we're happy, He's there when we're sad, so I will bless Him at all times and His praise shall continually be in my mouth (Ps. 34:1).

Conclusion

The Lord God Almighty and all the forces that operate at His command are with us! And the God of Jacob is our refuge. God of Jacob? He is letting us know that God will also be present for those who are liars and schemers jockeying for position like Jacob. He's the God of people who haven't arrived yet, those whose lives aren't altogether. So don't wait until you feel you're good enough to come to Jesus (Rom. 3:10). Come now (Isa. 1:18*b*; John 6:37)! Let Him rule in your life (Matt. 6:33). He's our safe place standing with tip-toe anticipation for us to experience His person, His presence, and His power in the midst of our predicaments.

A WALK THROUGH THE PSALMS

Paths of Righteousness

Psalm 23:3*b*

K. Marshall Williams, Sr.

Introduction

One road, many pathways! "Wide is the gate and broad is the way that leads to destruction" (Matt. 7:13). This is perhaps the most frequently rehearsed biblical caution. The passage goes on to say "narrow is the gate and difficult is the way which leads to life, and there are a few who find it" (v. 14).

Can you imagine trying to trek across town by foot while being confined to a narrow path? Neither can I. It's virtually impossible to keep your footing on a narrow path. In addition to the narrow path, the gate is strait. That's strait or extremely difficult (as in dire straits), not as in straight (without bend). So the path that leads to life is extremely difficult to navigate, narrow, and potentially winding. And if all that's not bad enough, it's also hard to find (and few there be that find it).

And here we are lost sheep, aimlessly wandering on the very tedious, long, narrow, winding, obscure road of life. Talk about a dire strait! Were it not for the Good Shepherd we would never, ever, ever find our way. But thanks be to God the Shepherd who leads us. Not only does the Shepherd know the way; He is the way (John 14:6; Acts 4:12)!

Sometimes our wandering lands us in enemy entrapments. Sometimes our wandering allows the enemy to follow us so closely that He knows where we live and how to gain access to what should be our safety zones (Eph. 4:27). But that's where the Good Shepherd comes in. The Shepherd will lead His sheep away from paths of destruction on which the enemy hides and guide them in paths of righteousness where we can find rest, and water, and safety (Ps. 23:3*b*; 2 Tim. 3:16–17). And although the ultimate destination (green-pastured reunification with the flock) is the same for us all, the paths that safely lead to the destination can vary based upon the scope of our wandering (2 Chron. 7:14; Isa. 55:6).

His Paths

1. From the north, south, east, and west (Ps.; 107:3; Isa. 43:5–6)
2. From the secret place (Pss. 27:5; 31:20; 91:1)
3. From the unknown path (Job 28:7)

His Leading

1. Lamp unto my feet (Pss. 105; 119:9,11; 139:24*b*)
2. Green pasture (Ps. 65:11–13; Ezek. 34:11–12)
3. Still waters (John 10:14; Rev. 7:17)

His Reputation

1. The Lord is a strong tower (Ps. 91:2; Prov. 18:10)
2. The Lord is my defense (Pss. 46:1; 71:7)
3. The Lord is my light and salvation (Ps. 27:1)

Conclusion

We can't make this journey by ourselves! The road is too rough, the night is too dark, and the enemy is too fierce. But our Shepherd is more than able to keep us from faltering (John 15:5; Eph. 3:20; Jude 25), and He will do so because we are ambassadors for Him (2 Cor. 5:20), and His reputation and glory are at stake. And He deserves all the glory due His name (Ps 29:2).

A WALK THROUGH THE PSALMS

Blessed by the Best

Psalm 103:1–5

K. Marshall Williams, Sr.

Introduction

God is awesome! In His essence. He's holy, omnipotent, omnipresent, omniscient, and immutable. His longsuffering and loving-kindness are better than life (Ps. 63:3)! His goodness and mercies are new every morning (Lam. 3:23). He's faithful and just (1 John. 1:9). He's our creator, reconciler, and keeper! As the assembly of the called, we're innumerably blessed (Eph. 1:4)!

Blessing

We kneel honoring Him. We speak well of the God of our salvation. That's why David said, "Bless the LORD, O my soul; and all that is within me, bless His holy name" (Ps. 103:1). In light of that, from the rising of the sun to the going down of the same, His name is worthy to be praised.

Preeminence of Praise

Praise must be preeminent! Worship Him for who He is! Praise Him for what He's done! Ascribing worth to Him by obedience brings unobligatory acts of kindness (James 1:22–25). David twice encourage himself (1 Sam. 30:6), thinking out loud about rendering God, enthusiastic praise with his all! Public or private, dependent disciples, instantaneously with every inclination and body faculty give affirmation and acclamation to the Almighty (Ps. 105:1–3)! We ought to praise Him for His unforgettable acts done for our wellbeing (Ps. 103:2–5).

Benefits

Forgiveness of Sin

The prosecutor (Satan) demanded death. The Judge (God) examined the evidence, ready to pronounce us guilty, when a Mediator of Mercy (Jesus) came in and said, "I'll pay the penalty and satisfy justice. I'll be disgraced so they may receive My amazing grace" (Isa. 53). The Judge (God) said case dismissed, saved by grace (Titus 3:5–6)! His benefits, in verse 3: He forgives *all* my sins.

Redemption from Destruction

The psalmist says that He redeems my life from destruction (Ps. 103:4*a*). He gifted us with redemption from the slave market of sin and death by His perfect sacrifice (Rom. 6:23). A new creature in Christ with no condemnation (Rom. 8:1)!

Loyal Love

The psalmist says that He crowns us with His love, which is unconditional and sacrificial (1 John 3:14–18). If you ever doubt God's love, just look at Calvary where they hung Him high, stretched Him wide, and dropped Him low; but early Sunday morning, He got up from the grave with all power in His hands (1 Cor. 15:3–4)!

Soul Satisfaction

"Who satisfies your mouth with good things" (Ps. 103:5*a*). "Blessed are those who hunger and thirst for righteousness, for they shall be satisfied" (Matt. 5:6 NASB). We will be renewed and have the speed and strength of an eagle (Isa. 40:31). When you're blessed by God you won't wear out, for the Lord preserves the faithful (Ps. 31:23*b*).

Conclusion

God promised Israel with comprehensive blessings of respect, prosperity, purity, and dominance if they would but follow Him (Deut. 28:3–5, 12). So follow Him so you can be in a place to add value to others. You have already been blessed with the greatest blessing in the person and presence of God, so be a blessing to a blessing to someone today (2 Cor. 9:6–8)![1]

A WALK THROUGH THE PSALMS

Thank You, Lord!

Psalm 100:1–5

K. Marshall Williams, Sr.

Introduction

We live in a day where ingratitude is the norm and thanksgiving is limited to a holiday with parades, football games, and turkey with all the trimmings. We are presumptuous! So much so, that without regard for price or provider, we persistently pursue perishable products (Luke 12:15; James 4:13–15). And it is this presumptuous spirit of ingratitude, that robs us of the spirit of thanksgiving God requires. But this psalm of thanksgiving is written to restore unto us a spirit of gratitude to the Lord, and with it a sense of generosity and humility.

We see right away that ingratitude is a universal problem because the psalm is addressed to all races of people the world over, across all ages and in all stages of life (v. 1). Psalm 100 lets us know that God expects us to recognize who we are relative to who He is, respond to His works with enthusiasm, and offer a reply of thanksgiving.

Recognize

"Know that the LORD, He is God; It is He who has made us, and not we ourselves" (v. 3). How many times have you heard someone say, "I'm a self-made man"? Although it is only a figure of speech, referring to ourselves as self-made contributes to our ingratitude. Self-aggrandizement and ingratitude go hand in hand. Our sinful flesh, the world, and Satan would have us arrogantly believe that we really are self-made with no need to give thanks to anyone else.

Yes, beloved, we are wondrously and marvelously made, but we are certainly not self-made. Even our professional accomplishments are gifts and blessings born of God (Josh. 1:8; 1 Tim. 6:17; 1 Peter 4:10). It is God who hath made us. "We are His people, and the sheep of His pasture" (Ps. 100:3). God made us just a little lower than the angels and crowned us with glory and honor (Ps. 8:5). We are uniquely unique, fearfully and wonderfully made—in His image and in His likeness (Ps. 139:14–15), and we must always acknowledge that! It's not enough to acknowledge Him as Savior; we must recognize that He is our Lord (Matt. 16:24–25; Rom. 14:7–9) who is conforming us to His image (Rom. 8:29). Isn't it nice to know that we are God's sheep under God's care (Ps. 55:22; John 10:27–29)? Recognizing the deity, sovereignty, and creatorship of God will give us cause for thanksgiving!

Respond

"Make a joyful shout to the LORD. … Serve the LORD with gladness; come before His presence with singing" (vv. 1–2). Has anyone ever walked up on you while you were singing, but you didn't know you were singing until they pointed it out? That's how we ought to respond to God. We ought to sing as if He is our only audience (Col. 3:23–24). Over the corridors of time, God has done some things for us that we just shouldn't keep quiet about. Merely thinking of God's goodness should invoke involuntary singing, not just a quiet hum but loud, boisterous singing such that the noise of our praise can be heard by anyone within earshot, especially when we come to the house of worship.

Worship is not a spectator sport. It's a participatory event! So come into His presence (Ps. 116:12) with thanksgiving in your heart and enthusiastic praise on your lips, because He is worthy of all our praise (Ps. 50:23; 116:12)! Sing with the joy of the Lord in your heart, for He is your strength (Neh. 8:10). Serve the Lord and others with a smile on your face (Prov. 17:22; Matt. 20:26–28)! God is looking for cheerful and thankful saints, who willingly serve and encourage others (2 Cor. 9:6–7) by bearing each other's burdens, reconciling sinners and restoring saints to the Lord, which He has commanded us to do (Matt. 28:19–20; Rom. 15:1; Gal. 6:1–4; James 5:19–20).

Reply

"Enter into His gates with thanksgiving, and into His courts with praise. Be thankful to Him, and bless His name" (v. 4). Have you ever given something to someone and waited for a reply but none was forthcoming? I imagine that God is often left expecting a reply from us but none is forthcoming. Unlike singing, which can be an involuntary response to the gladness within our hearts, thanksgiving should be a deliberate act of appreciation for God's goodness (v. 5a). We should hasten to the place where the saints gather to intentionally worship Him in spirit and in truth (1 Kings 8:10–11; John 4:24; Heb. 10:25). This imperative to publically thank God is so important that it is stated twice in this brief psalm. God should never be left waiting for our thankful replies. Whenever we come before Him, it is important to say. "Thank You, Lord, for all that You have done!"

Conclusion

Gratitude, and the ability to appropriately express it, is not only important in our relationship with God, but gratitude is essential to healthy human interactions as well. We can be assured that at some point in our pilgrimage, our parents, our spouses, our children, our neighbors, and our colleagues will all expect us to express appreciation for their contributions to our lives. For many of us, the feeling of gratitude for benefits bestowed upon us tends to be instinctive. In contrast the expression of gratitude is a learned behavior. Its perfection requires practice, and failure to practice and express gratitude can easily destroy our most meaningful relationships. But God, in His love for us, has laid out this formula for the expression of thanksgiving that addresses the who, what, where, when, why, and how of being appreciative.

Without question the safest place to rehearse expressions of gratitude and appreciation is before the presence of the Lord. No one in our lives is more deserving of gratitude than the Lord, and we can be assured that He will receive our gratitude as a sweet-smelling sacrifice of praise. And when we have persistently practiced gratitude toward God, it will be manifested toward others in humility and generosity. Amen!

A WALK THROUGH THE PSALMS

Singing in the House of God

Psalm 138:1

K. Marshall Williams, Sr.

Introduction

Singing in the house of God today is often like auditioning and/or performing for popular television shows like *American Idol* or *The Voice*! Singing in the house of God is an opportunity for the saints of God to worship, adore, give thanks to, and praise the Lord of Glory! "I will praise thee with my whole heart: before the gods will I sing praise unto thee" (Ps. 138:1). We were created to worship or ascribe worth to Him (Rev. 4:11)! Consecrated personal praise leads to authentic and energetic corporate praise; and one way it's manifested is through singing. Many don't sing in worship. Perhaps they are uninformed about how we are to sing, what we are to sing, why we are to sing, or to whom and for what causes we are to sing!

How Should We Sing?

There's nothing worse than lethargic, half-hearted, sad-sack sorry singing! The psalmist says, "Sing praise to the LORD, you saints of His" (Ps. 30:4a). "Sing to the LORD as long as I live" (Ps. 104:33). "Sing aloud to God our strength" (Ps. 81:1) We sing to glorify God or to advertise Him, put Him on display, and show Him off! (1 Cor. 10:31). Sing with expression to the Lord even when we don't particularly care for the song (Col. 3:23–24). Joyful singing lifts the worship to a new level.

What Should We Sing?

Foremost, sing songs that are biblically accurate (1 Cor. 14:15*c*). Controlled by the Spirit, we are to encourage one another with psalms (James 5:13*b*). We are to also sing hymns focusing on the lordship of God the Son (Matt. 26:30). And sing spiritual songs that testify of deliverance from spiritual bondage (Eph. 5:18–19). Like the children of Israel, they remind us how far the Lord has brought us!

Why Should We Sing?

We sing to magnify, extol and praise the Lord! The psalmist said, "Praise the LORD! Sing to the LORD a new song . . . in the assembly of the saints" (Ps. 149:1). As saints of the Most High God, we are to sing songs exalting our God for His gift of salvation! Being filled with the Spirit enables us to teach the Word of God through songs (Col. 3:16). We are making melody in our hearts to the Lord (Eph. 5:19*b*)!

Conclusion

Singing prepares the way for deliverance. In 2 Chronicles 20, King Jehoshaphat was afraid, surrounded by enemies, but he worshipped God, appointed a praise team, and the moment they started worshipping and singing, the Lord sent an ambush and their enemies destroyed each other! Sing unto the Lord, saints, for the battle is not yours but the Lord's! I don't know why you sing, but I sing because I'm happy! I sing because I'm free. His eye is on the sparrow and I know He watches over me! Sing unto the Lord for the battle is not ours but the Lord's!

A WALK THROUGH THE PSALMS

His Way

Psalm 27:11*a*

K. Marshall Williams, Sr.

Introduction

The world offers a plethora of ways to get to God. The psalmist pleaded with God to be taught His way because of his problems with his enemies. We need to know the way to God because of the enemies of our Christ today (2 Tim. 3:1–9). Two ways—broad-death and narrow way-life (Matt. 7:13–14). Many hear the word but few respond (Matt. 20:16). Jesus is the way to, the truth of, and the life in God (John 14:6). The psalmist cries, "Teach me Your way, O LORD, and lead me in a smooth path, because of my enemies" (Ps. 27:11). Three ways to discover His way: reverence His will, receive His Word, and rejoice in His way!

Reverence His Will (Prov. 3:5–6)

Many want Him to teach them His way but won't submit to His will (1 Peter 5:6). Jesus was all about His Master's will (John 5:30*b*).

- IN HIS WILL—REMISSION OF SINS (Eph. 1:7)
- IN HIS WILL—REDIRECTION OF SERVICE (Rom. 6:13)
- IN HIS WILL—RESURRECTION OF SPIRIT (John 11:25–26)

THE REVELATION OF HIS WILL IS FOUND IN HIS WORD!

Receive His Word (James 1:19)

Saved by the Savior—Be born again (Rom. 10:9–10; 1 Cor. 2:14–15).
Serve the Sovereign—Witness by your life (Matt. 5:16).
Study the Scriptures—Study the Word (2 Tim. 2:15).
Submit to the Shepherd—Matt. 16:24–25; He gave His life for the sheep (John 15:13).

His Word Is . . .

1. PLAIN—(Ps. 119:105)
2. PRACTICAL—(Prov. 22:7)
3. PROFITABLE—(2 Tim. 3:16)
4. POWERFUL—(Heb. 4:11–12)

Rejoice in His Way (Ps. 37:34; Phil. 4:4)

David prayed to the Lord, "Restore to me the joy of Your salvation (Ps. 51:12*a*). Jesus dispenses abundant living (John 10:10*b*). "Commit your way to the LORD, Trust also in Him, and He shall bring it to pass" (Ps. 37:5).

"WAIT ON THE LORD, and keep His way and He shall exalt you to inherit the land; when the wicked are cut off, you shall see it" (Ps. 37:34).

Conclusion

For if it wasn't for His way, MY PREACHING is EMPTY and MY FAITH is also EMPTY.

- I'd be still yet in my sins.
- My faith would be null and void.
- The dead in Christ would stay dead.
- Death would still have its sting and the grave its victory (1 Cor. 15:13–19:55).

THANK GOD FOR HIS WAY! He who keeps His way preserves his own soul (Prov. 16:17*b*). For He is a waymaker! He preserves the way of the saints (Prov. 2:8). He establishes the way of the upright (Prov. 21:29*b*). He delivers us from the way of evil, from the man who speaks perverse things (Prov. 2:12). He makes ways out of no way even when it looks like there is no way! For His way is the foundation of our faith, the cornerstone of our confession, the basis of our belief, the surety of our salvation, and the capstone of our conversion. Joshua says, "But as for me and my house, we will serve the LORD" (Josh 24:15). Choose HIS WAY today!

A WALK THROUGH THE PSALMS

Protection That Can't Beat

Psalm 121:5*a*

K. Marshall Williams, Sr.

Introduction

In life, we are concerned about protecting ourselves. We visit doctors to protect our bodies. We secure home owner's, auto, life, health and disability insurances, retirement plans, and wills, as wise stewards to protect ourselves, but I want to recommend somebody whose protection you can't beat! Our text says the Lord is your keeper. He is the one who watches over you (Ps. 139:16).

Who Is the Lord? What Is He Like?

The psalmist knew Him in a very personal way. He said, "The LORD is my light and my salvation" (Ps. 27:1), "my strength and my shield" (Ps. 28:7), my shepherd (Ps. 23), my refuge (Ps. 46:1), and my song (Ps. 118:14). He upholds all who fall and raises up all who are bowed down (Ps. 145:14). And then he said the Lord is your guardian (Ps. 121:5).

He is the Sovereign Savior who constantly surrounds and actively observes.

He Keeps Us From

He keeps us from being pressed into this world's mold (Rom. 12:1–2). He keeps us in the battle with our flesh (Gal. 5:16–17). He keeps us from the power of Satan (Heb. 2:14).

He Keeps Us For

Ultimately the Creator created the creature for His glory (Rev. 4:11). Glory is what the media does when they make something look so appetizing, that you say, "I got to have it." Well, our lives are to look so appetizing that others look and see Jesus in us and say, "I want it!" That's glory (Matt 5:16)! Our sole purpose for living is to bring glory to His name through every situation in our lives (Ps. 29:2)!

He Keeps Us Through

Nowhere in Scripture does it tell you to take care of yourself (1 Cor. 10:13). He keeps you through the shadow of death, in sickness and in health (Pss. 23:4; 147:3). He kept Daniel by giving a lion lockjaw (Dan. 6:4–28). He kept the Hebrew boys by air-conditioning a fiery furnace (Dan. 3:8–30). He kept Paul and Silas by sending an earthquake while they were in a Philippian jail (Acts 16:16–31). He will keep you through life's difficulties. He is a shield to all who trust in Him (Ps. 18:30*d*).

Conclusion

The Lord not only keeps us from, for, and through some things, but He also keeps something special for us: an inheritance, incorruptible, undefiled that cannot fade away, that is reserved for every believer (1 Peter 5:4). It's reserved in eternity for you and me who are kept by the power of God. It's nice to know also that our Lord keeps us for eternity (Ps. 121:8). When you trusted Him as your Savior and Lord, He wrote your name down in the Lamb's book of life (John 5:24; Rev. 21:27). He's the dispenser of all that you need (Pss. 34:10; 121:1–2) and your defender when you're in trouble (Pss. 121:3–6; 124:8); and lastly He'll be your deliverer when you're tempted, your keeper forever (Ps. 121:7–8; 1 Cor. 10:31). He is protection that can't be beat!

THE FUNERAL

Dr. O. S. Hawkins

Across the years I have observed that there is nothing, outside of the pastor leading his people to Christ, which binds the pastor's and the people's hearts together like funerals. As years of pastoral ministry turn into decades, there are funerals that most of us in ministry do not remember. But, I guarantee you, people never forget who officiated the funerals of their loved ones and brought comfort to them in times of need. When performed in love and in the spirit of a servant's heart, the pastor's pastoral ministry endears him to his people forever and provides his best opportunity of being Christ's hand extended to the people under his pastoral care.

Weddings and funerals are like bookends of emotion for the pastor. Many a pastor has had to go from the hurt and sorrow of ministering to one family at the time of a loved one's death straight to the church to perform a wedding where he is immediately thrust into the joy and celebration of another family's festivities. Perhaps this is why our Lord's first miracle was at a wedding in Cana where he was the life of the party (John 2:1–11), and His last miracle was at a funeral in Bethany where he "wept" (John 11:35) at the grave of Lazarus. Any pastor who senses a call from God to a particular place and who genuinely loves his people will live with this range of emotions. There are times of great joy and rejoicing and times of great sorrow and heartbreak.

The pastoral ministry which the pastor performs with his people is one of the things which legitimizes his ministry and binds his heart to the hearts of the people God has given him. The pastor is the one who stands with his people and walks with them on the mountaintops and also in the valleys. He weeps when they weep and laughs when they laugh. He provides help and hope to those who hurt.

There are few times that afford the pastor to be looked upon as Christ's hand extended to his people more than those times of sorrow which surround the death of a loved one. His mere presence with the people is often more important than anything he might say. He represents the Lord in such a holy moment.

There are several practical matters related to the funeral experience. I call these "Be-Attitudes." First, BE PROMPT. Get to the bereaved one's side as quickly as possible. You do not have to stay long, but your simple prompt presence will speak volumes and offer comfort in time of need. Also, BE PERSONAL. This is not a time for formality but an opportunity to "touch" your people in a very personal sort of way. Weep with your people when they are weeping. Don't shy away from speaking of how much the departed one meant to you personally, and remind the loved ones that they cannot really lose someone when they know where they are. By all means, BE PRAYERFUL. It should go without saying that the pastor should pray with the family on such sorrowful occasions. And, he should leave them with the comfort of a passage of scripture. On such occasions, I often remind them of the words of the Psalmist in Psalm 57:1, "Be merciful to me, O God, be merciful to me! For my soul trusts in You; and in the shadow of Your wings I will make my refuge, until these calamities have passed by."

There will be occasions when the pastor preaches the funeral of one who may not have been a believer. I have often found it helpful to preach a message on the adequacy of God at such times with the following outline: (1) God is adequate for our feelings. He is adequate to comfort us. At this point I use passages such as John 11:35; 14:1–6; and Psalm 23 to illustrate that He is a God of comfort in time of need; (2) God is adequate for our friends in the Lord who go on before us. I am careful here to speak in third-person terms if I do not know the deceased well or have confidence of his or her salvation. Here I speak of heaven and the hope it holds for all those who have put their faith in the Lord Jesus Christ; (3) God is adequate for our future. We may be saying, "What will I do? I have lost my wife, husband, dad, mom, friend or whomever." Here I seek to direct people to the hope that God is adequate for tomorrow. Often I will use 1 Corinthians 15:58 at this point: "Therefore, my beloved brethren, be steadfast, immovable, always abounding in the work of the Lord, knowing that your labor is not in vain in the Lord." God is adequate for our feelings, our friends and our future. Great is His faithfulness.

The pastor may also feel pressure at the point of "preaching the deceased into heaven." If the pastor is uncertain of the person's salvation, he should avoid at all costs the temptation to "preach a lost man into heaven." There will be many people at the funeral who knew the man and knew his ways. If the preacher places the departed one in heaven, then it gives a false hope of eternal life for all the listeners, many of whom, most likely, need to be converted themselves. The pastor should be caring but honest and present the gospel in some form at the funeral service. I have often felt the pressure of loved ones who feared their lost loved one was unsaved and wanted some kind of assurance from me that God would receive him or her into heaven. I would often quote to them the passage from Genesis 18:25, "Shall not the Judge of all the earth do right?" We must leave all judgment to God who alone searches our hearts and knows our inmost thoughts. Ultimately, we can rest in the truth that God will do what is right.

There are many other practical ways to go about the funeral service. If at all possible, the pastor should make the funeral service personal. I have often used an outline which speaks of the person's faith, faithfulness, family, friends and future. With this simple outline the pastor can address saving faith, faithfulness in life, the love of family, the importance of friends and the future and hope of heaven to all who know Christ.

Once the funeral proceeds to the graveside, there are some practical matters of which the pastor should be aware. Above all, the pastor should be as brief as possible. I usually seek to remind the people that we do not leave their loved one there; we leave simply the house the Lord gave him or her to live in while on earth. I remind them of this truth for the believer, "to be absent from the body and to be present with the Lord" (2 Cor. 5:8). I also state something to the effect that, "yesterday, we read in the newspaper that _______________ was dead. But don't you believe it. He is more alive today than he ever was because Jesus said, 'I am the resurrection and the life. He who believes in Me, though he may die, he shall live. And whoever lives and believes in Me shall never die. Do you believe this?'" (John 11:25–26). End the committal service with a prayer, a word of hope, as you dismiss the people back to their cars and to their homes and back to the business of living their own lives, reminded that heaven has been made sweeter for walking this way today.

There is one final word regarding the funeral. Pastor, do not fail to follow up with the family after the funeral. Within the next immediate days, at least one more visit should be made to the home. I cannot express how important this simple act of kindness and concern will mean to the bereaved family. Your presence and prayers will help seal the experience in their hearts and will ensure their love and commitment to you and the church. I also found it helpful to write a personal Christmas letter to every family who lost a loved one during the year. The first Christmas without their loved one is often a very emotional one to say the least. In the letter I reminded them I was thinking of them and praying for them.

Funerals are a vital and important part of pastoral ministry; and are an incredible way of legitimizing your care and concern and binding your heart to the people's hearts.

FUNERAL SERVICE FOR BETTE SIBLEY

Dr. O. S. Hawkins

"You have done a beautiful thing to me."
—Mark 14:6, author's paraphrase

I'm thinking today of the first funeral I ever preached as a young preacher so many decades ago. My home church had been requested by a funeral home to say a few words at a funeral of someone who had no pastor. On a hot Texas day I arrived at a windswept cemetery to find two funeral directors, a single casket, and no one else in attendance. I stumbled through a few words about a lady I had never known and who had no one attending her service. I thought about what a contrast today as we gather to remember the sweet life of Bette Sibley who loved her Lord, loved her family, loved her church, and this large gathering today attests to the fragrance of Christ which she shared with so many.

When I received word of her death, the first verse that came into mind was the verse found in Mark 14:6 when Jesus looked into the face of Mary of Bethany who had anointed His feet with precious ointment and said, "You have done a beautiful thing to Me." Anyone and everyone who knew Bette knew that her life and legacy were witness to the fact that she was beautiful in every aspect of her being. This beauty is laced throughout Proverbs 31 and the story of a woman of whom Bette epitomizes.

She Lived a Beautiful Life

When I think of Bette Sibley I think of her FAITH. It is said of the Proverbs 31 woman that "A woman who fears the LORD, she shall be praised" (v. 30). Betty's faith was firmly fixed in the Lord Jesus Christ. Many years ago as a child she placed her faith in Christ and loved Him and lived for Him throughout the days of her journey.

It was an occasion similar to this one though not exactly a funeral, when Jesus gathered the disciples in an upper room. In fact, it was the night before He Himself was crucified. And there, in that setting, He spoke these words. "Let not your hearts be troubled neither let them be afraid. In My Father's house are many mansions. If it were not so, I would have told you. I go and prepare a place for you and if I go and prepare a place for you, I'll come again and receive you unto Myself that where I am there you may be also. And where I go you know and the way you know" (see John 14:1–6). I have no doubt that if our Lord were here physically today and speaking audibly (we know He is here in spirit as He promised wherever two or three of us would gather in His name, there He would be in our midst), He would speak these same words to you sweet family members. "Let not your hearts be troubled. Neither let them be afraid . . . ." Yes, Bette was beautiful in her life because of her faith.

I not only think about her faith today but her FAITHFULNESS. Of the Proverbs 31 woman the writer says, "strength and dignity are her clothing" (v. 25 NASB). It says of her husband that "she does him good and not evil all the days of her life" (v. 12). Betty Sibley was faithful. She was faithful to her Lord. She was faithful to her husband, George, throughout the decades. She was faithful to her family. She was faithful to her friends. If it could ever be said of anyone, it could be said of her, "Strength and dignity are her clothing."

Bette Sibley was beautiful in her life. Because of her faith and her faithfulness, I am sure our Lord looks at her today and says, "You have done a beautiful thing to Me."

She Left a Beautiful Legacy

When I think of Bette Sibley, I not only think of her faith and her faithfulness but I think of her FRIENDS. It is said of a Proverbs 31 woman that "she extends her hand to the poor, yes, she reaches out her hand to the needy" (see v. 20). The many of Bette's friends who are gathered here today can testify of the numerous times in each of our own experiences that she "extended her hand to us and reached out." She encouraged us all and left us a legacy of beauty which should challenge us all throughout our remaining days on this earth.

She not only left a legacy to her friends, she left a legacy to her FAMILY. The Bible says of the Proverbs 31 woman that "her children rise up and call her blessed; her husband also, and he praises her" (v. 28). Yes, George, she did you good and not evil all the days of her life and today you and your children rise up to call her blessed. She was devoted to her family and loved them with an uncompromising and unconditional love. Bette Sibley taught us how to live, but she also taught us how to die in those last days and weeks. She's left us all a legacy that is beautiful, and it is no wonder that our Lord must be looking at her today to say, "You have done a beautiful thing to Me."

She Loved a Beautiful Lord

When I think of Bette Sibley, I not only think of her faith, her faithfulness, her friends, and her family, but I think of her FUTURE. "She smiles at the future" (see Prov. 31:25). As a pastor I've seen a lot of people live and a lot of people die, but I'm not certain I've ever seen anyone die like Bette Sibley. When the days were drawing to an obvious end, someone came by to tell her that they were praying for her to be healed, upon which she said, "Stop it!" Bette Sibley smiled at the future and was confident she was about to begin the great adventure for which Christ had created her.

Heaven is a wonderful place. It is beautiful. God loves beauty or He would not have made things on our earth that is so cursed with sin so beautiful. John got a glimpse of it one day when from his lonely island called Patmos; he wrote down a few simple symbols that our poor finite minds could understand and said, "The walls are of jasper, the foundation is garnished with precious stones, the gates are pearl and the city is of pure gold." No wonder that earlier the inspired apostle Paul had said, "Eye hath not seen, nor ear heard, neither have entered into the heart of man, the things which God hath prepared for them that love him"

(1 Cor. 2:9 KJV). What a future is before those of us who know and love the Lord Jesus Christ!

Bette loved the hymns of Fanny Crosby, the old blind hymn writer who never saw the beauty of a sunrise or the glory of a sunset. Yet she saw so many things that some of us never see. In one of her last hymns she put it like this: "Someday the silver cord will break and I no more as now shall sing, but oh the joy when I shall wake within the palace of the King and I shall see Him face to face and tell the story saved by grace."[1] Let us imagine some of the joy that must be Bette's having already looked upon the face of Christ in glory where God shall wipe away all tears from our eyes and where we'll never grow old.

Yes, Bette, you have done a beautiful thing to Christ … and to us! You left us a legacy, and the sweet fragrance of your life will linger with us forever. You've given us added reason to also "smile at the future." You lived a beautiful life, you left a beautiful legacy, and all because you loved a beautiful Lord. We'll see you in the morning.

FUNERAL SERVICE FOR GENE SMYERS

Dr. O. S Hawkins

> When he came and had seen the grace of God, he was glad, and encouraged them all that with purpose of heart they should continue with the Lord. For he was a good man, full of the Holy Spirit and of faith. And a great many people were added to the Lord.
>
> —Acts 11:23–24

My own life was radically transformed when as a seventeen-year-old young man I responded to the gospel and received Christ as my personal Savior. At that time in my life I could count on one hand the number of times I'd been in a church and did not even know that Matthew, Mark, Luke, and John were books of the New Testament. However, instantaneously, "old things passed away and all became new." There was a young businessman in the church that morning who instantly befriended me and became a mentor in the faith and in life. Gene Smyers became closer than a brother throughout the decades of our friendship. For forty-five years I never made a major decision in life without consulting with the Lord . . . and with Gene. He was there when I was feeling called to ministry. He was there to meet Susie who would become my wife. He was there in every transition of ministry from church to church I made as we talked and prayed about it. So many firsts in my life came because I knew Gene. His winsome way and faithful friendship opened so many doors for me.

When I received word that he had slipped into heaven, immediately these words about Barnabas came to my mind and I was captured by that phrase, "He was a good man." That was Gene Smyers. Like Barnabas, "he saw the grace of God. He was glad and he encouraged us all."

Gene Lived a Life of Gladness

In Acts 11 Barnabas had been sent up to Antioch from the church fathers in Jerusalem to check out what was happening in the new church plant there. Gentiles were coming to Christ and were not doing things exactly like "old First Church" in Jerusalem thought they should. Consequently, they sent Barnabas up to check it out. Barnabas rejoiced in what he saw God doing in others and he was "glad."

Gene Smyers was like that. "He saw the grace of God and was glad." He was happy in the Lord that he loved and served so well. Family and/or friends could never think of Gene without a smile coming to their face. He lived a life of gladness. He saw the grace of God and was glad.

In my last moments with him while he was barely lucid, a smile came upon his face as I read to him the promises of Psalm 23. There was a real joy in being in Gene's presence. Anyone who had been with him always felt better when they left. He lived a life of gladness and like Barnabas "he saw the grace of God and was glad."

Gene Lived a Life of Goodness

Barnabas was not the real name of the man in Acts 11. It was a name that had been given to him by those in the church. It literally means "son of encouragement." Every time Barnabas has center stage in the Bible he is lifting people up and encouraging them. In Acts 4 when he is first mentioned, he sells a parcel of land he had on Cyprus and laid it at the apostles' feet. In Acts 9 he encourages Paul and journeys with him to Jerusalem. In Acts 11 he goes to Antioch and sees the grace of God and encourages them there. In Acts 15 when Paul is about to leave on his second missionary journey and dismisses John Mark, it is Barnabas who takes him up and encourages the young minister.

All of these events point to the Gene Smyers that I knew and loved. He found his greatest joy in encouraging others. He lived a life of goodness. One of my first jobs in ministry was to lead a bunch of rag-tag boys from a government housing project in a Sunday school at a mission church. I put together a baseball team of those little kids who had nothing and one day received a call from the leading sporting goods store in Fort Worth and they asked me to stop by. I went by and there was a huge bag with twenty baseball gloves, bats, balls, jerseys, and everything else that goes into a team. I found out later that it was Gene Smyers who provided that as he did so many other things in so many anonymous ways. Once when he was traveling in Israel worshiping in the Baptist church at Nazareth, people were packed in with coats and frost coming from their lips as they sang the carols. Not long after Gene returned to Texas a gift was sent to the church to provide heat for the building. All of us who are here today could testify about his life of goodness in our behalf. Like Barnabas, "he was a good man" and "encouraged us all."

My mother used to have an old book on the coffee table called *Leaves of Gold*. I remember memorizing a poem that was found in that book by a man by the name of Edgar Guest. Surely he had Gene Smyers in mind when he said:

> I'd rather see a sermon than to hear one any day
> I'd rather one should walk with me than merely show the way
> The eye's a better pupil and more willing than the ear
> Fine counsel is confusing but examples always clear
> And the best of all the preachers are the ones who live their creed
> For to see the good in action is what everybody needs
> Oh, I can soon learn how to do it if you'll let me see it done
> I can watch your hands in action but tongue too fast may run
> And the lectures you deliver may be very wise and true
> But I'd rather get my lesson by observing what you do.
> For I may misunderstand you and the high advice you give
> But there's no misunderstanding how you act and how you live.

Gene Lived a Life of Grace

Like Barnabas, while others often sat in judgment Gene sat in grace. He saw the grace of God. How? He received it while a young man in his thirties and knew the Lord Jesus as his own personal Savior.

Last Saturday that grace got Gene into heaven. He left us a legacy of grace and he would have me to tell all of you that once you reach this place along your journey it is ultimately not going to matter who you know, nor how high you climbed in worldly circles, nor how many worldly goods you've accumulated. All that will ultimately matter is what you do with the Lord Jesus Christ.

Yes, Gene lived a life of gladness, a life of goodness, and a life of grace. "He saw the grace of God and was glad and he encouraged us all for he was a good man." Yesterday in the obituary section, the newspaper said that Gene Smyers was dead. But don't you believe it! He's more alive today than he's ever been because Jesus said, "I am the resurrection and the life and he that believeth in me though he were dead, yet shall he live."

So it is with the peace of Christ in our hearts that we bid an earthly farewell to Gene with the rock-solid assurance that those of us who know the Lord will meet again one day at His feet where He will wipe away all tears from our eyes and where we will never grow old. Thank you, Gene, for seeing the grace of God . . . being glad . . . and encouraging us all. Like Barnabas, "you're a good man!"

PREPARING TO PREACH

Dr. O. S. Hawkins

King Zedekiah once asked the prophet and preacher Jeremiah, "Is there is any word from the LORD?" (Jer. 37:17). This question should resonate in our hearts and minds as we prepare to study and bring the Word of God Sunday by Sunday. The preacher of the gospel is challenged to "devote himself to prayer and the ministry of the Word" (see Acts 6:4). We often see in the life of Christ that He would "arise a great while before day." For me there has been no better time to devote myself to "prayer and the ministry of the Word" than the early morning hours. "Keep your mornings for God." A thousand times I heard those words ring from the lips of my pastoral predecessor and mentor, Dr. W. A. Criswell. In the morning hours our minds are fresh and uncluttered from the busyness and bustle of phone calls, letters, e-mails, visits, appointments, and so many other distractions that keep us from the study desk.

As we prepare in the study, there should be three important questions permeating our thinking processes. First, will what we are preparing to preach exalt the Lord Jesus Christ? It is amazing how many modern sermons never mention the name of Jesus, much less His atonement or the gospel message. Second, we should ask ourselves if what we are preparing to preach will explain the text. It is equally amazing how little the text is explained and exegeted in modern preaching even by those who consider themselves to be expository preachers. Finally, we should be asking ourselves if what we are preparing in our message will extend the gospel. We call ourselves preachers of the gospel and yet the gospel, that is, the death, burial, and resurrection of our Lord, is absent in so many sermons. If we enter into our preparation with a concern to exalt the Lord, explain the text, and extend the gospel in every message, it will pilot us throughout the hours of our preparation.

In a very practical sense, as I reflect across the decades of my own preaching experience, my preparation to preach has involved three key areas: the hand, the heart, and the head. In other words there is a very practical dimension that is often overlooked. There is a spiritual dimension that should always fuel our preparation. Finally, there is an intellectual dimension that should always accompany such a serious assignment as delivering God's Word to God's people.

To begin with, there is the element of the hand in sermon preparation. This is the work ethic within the body of Christ. I always considered my Monday evening and Saturday morning visitation times as an essential part of my sermon preparation and not just a part of the pastoral ministry I had received from the Lord.

I was fortunate to have a wonderful mentor in ministry. A man who was a pastor at a Texas church for forty years led me to Christ when I was seventeen years of age. When the Lord called me to preach, this man instilled within me the passion to never stand and preach on Sunday without personally sharing the gospel with someone through the week. This not only brings credibility to the pulpit, but makes a tremendous difference in the preaching event itself. During my days of ministry at the First Baptist Church in Fort Lauderdale, Florida, I led evangelism training and outreach on Monday evening. Hundreds of our people were involved in this outreach effort, and numbers of people would open their hearts to Christ every Monday evening upon hearing the gospel. Then on Saturday, our staff would go into the homes of those converted on Monday evenings and confirm those decisions and explain the necessity of baptism and church membership. On Sunday mornings, our staff would meet before each service and spread out over the auditorium as people gathered for worship. It was common that one of the staff members would come to me and say, "That man in the blue coat sitting in the middle section on the aisle made a decision for Christ this past Monday evening when Bill visited his home. I was there yesterday and explained baptism and church membership to him." After hearing this and getting his name, I would walk around to the gentleman, call him by name (he would be amazed the pastor knew his name), tell him I had heard of his decision, and give him an opportunity to confirm it to me. Then I would explain briefly to him that at the end of my message that morning, I was going to ask men and women who had made that decision this week to come forward and make a public pledge to Christ and that I would look for him to be the first one down the aisle. Each Sunday, by the time I stood in the pulpit to preach, it was not uncommon to know of several new converts who were already going to respond. This brings a new dynamic to your pulpit preaching.

The hand, this practical element in preparation, plays a vital part in preparing to preach. It brings integrity to your message and a sense of credibility to your pulpit.

There is also the element of the heart in sermon preparation. The preacher's heart is an important part of his preparing to preach. As our church in Fort Lauderdale grew, I realized I needed a way to stay in touch with our people and somehow, someway, be able to feel their hearts as I prepared to preach to them week by week. I adapted a prayer ministry whereby I prayed for five families in our church each day. Two weeks before their appointed day, they would each receive a card from my office letting them know I would be praying specifically for them and their family on the given date and encouraging them if they had a prayer request to confidentially return it to me. While the primary purpose of this endeavor was to pray for my people, it also served to burn into my heart the needs, struggles, burdens, and challenges of my people as I was preparing my weekly messages.

On Saturday mornings, I would gather in our worship center with those involved in our various prayer ministries to pray for the services on Sunday. We would scatter over the auditorium, kneeling at every seat to pray for the one sitting there the next day. Then, on Sunday mornings in worship, those in the prayer ministry were challenged to pick out someone in the building and pray for him or her during the message. They would often pray for the pulling down of such strongholds as pride, procrastination, and presumption. These various prayer efforts had an amazing effect on my own sermon preparation as I better understood my people and knew that those to whom I would be preaching would be saturated in prayer before and during the message.

In order to be effective, the sermon must emerge from a burning heart. Many great communicators produce little abiding fruit and deliver their messages with little or no anointing. To me, it was always as important what I was when I preached, as it was what I preached. The only way to keep a burning heart is to be like those disciples on the Emmaus Road whose "hearts burned" within them "as He spoke to us along the way." The pastor without a consistent and effective personal prayer and devotional life will not be effective in the pulpit for an extended period of time. The hand and the heart are vital elements in the pastor's preparation.

Of course, the head is essential in sermon preparation. That is the actual work of study. This is the intellectual aspect, the preparation stage of the sermon itself. The calling and vocation of the pastor is one in which study never stops. He should be constantly about the business of reading and studying. It was always my practice to reread two books each and every summer. One was *Preaching and Preachers* by David Martyn Lloyd-Jones, and the other was *The Preacher's Portrait* by John Stott. They helped to keep me focused on my preaching task and served to remind me of the serious and high calling of being a steward of the gospel message.

For many, determining the text or what subject to preach is one of the most time-consuming and difficult tasks of preparation. For me, this has always been the easiest because I preach through books of the Bible and seek to do so in a culturally relevant way while being true to the text and applying it to present-day issues. Thus, my text, usually a paragraph or more of Scripture, is ever before me.

I begin by looking at the passage, living with it for a while, reading and rereading it sometimes scores of times. If it is short enough, I write it down on a note card and put it in my pocket for a couple of days. During the day, several times while waiting on a phone call, sitting in a traffic jam or in a doctor's waiting room or wherever, I will read it over and over.

One of my common practices is to put an inflection on a different word each time I read it. I have found it helpful to read it and ask the following questions: Who? What? When? Where? How? When inflecting a different word and asking these questions, it is amazing how an analytical outline often begins to emerge.

Next, I do the exegesis of the text. So many sources are available today through Internet sites that even the preacher without a working knowledge of the biblical languages can do a proper exegesis including word study, parsing of verbs, and the like. It makes no sense to me that if we have the Greek language in which the New Testament was given us, that the one assigned to deliver the Word to the people of God would not want to know it and use it.

After the above steps, an outline will generally emerge in my mind issuing out of what I have construed to be the specific object of the text and sermon. I go to all the commentaries at my disposal, all the information I may have in decades of filing in my filing system, and other resources I find through searching the Internet. I then take my computer and place an introduction, various points of the sermon, and a conclusion on my screen. Next, I take all the notes I have made and the resources I have read and begin to type them in at the appropriate points in the outline, usually in the order of explanation, illustration, and application under each point. Before the days of the computer, I would do this on legal pads. Once this process is completed, I begin to arrange the various notes I have under each point in an analytical manner. Now the sermon is complete and ready. Since my earliest days in my first pastorate, I have prepared each sermon with the intention that it might someday be in print. Now, I knew full well most of them would not, but this discipline forced me to be original, to footnote sources, and to prepare a complete manuscript. My sermon files today contain thousands of such messages that make for easy and readily supplied resources.

Once the sermon is completed, I will live with it the final two days or so before it is to be delivered. While I do not memorize it word for word, I am so familiar with it that I only take a brief outline of it into the pulpit. This is most often written in the margin of my Bible. Preaching without full notes has an extremely liberating effect upon me.

Before preaching the message, I go back to my original three questions and ask myself again: Have I exalted the Lord Jesus in this exposition? Have I explained the text adequately? Have I extended the gospel? That is, is the gospel in the message at some point? Then I preach it, hopefully for God's glory and the people's good.

One of the biggest pressures the pastor faces with his preparation is his limitation of time. There are so many time constraints upon the pastor. It seems that everyone must see him, that he must be at every meeting, every event. The pastor must guard with all diligence his time for study. Schedule it. Block it out. Let nothing interfere with it. Give it priority. Plan your time, I always sought to have my outline by Tuesday, if possible, to begin to hang the meat and muscle on it by Wednesday, and to have it finished by Thursday in order to have Friday and Saturday for living with it in its completed form.

Perhaps the biggest pressure we face might be in going to seed on one of the three areas of preparation mentioned above: the hand, the heart, and the head. Some are tempted to spend all their preparation time on the hand and little on the heart or head. By that I mean they spend so much time touching people's lives, they have no time for spiritual preparation or study. Others spend all their time on the heart and sometimes little on the heart or head. In other words, they are devoted to the spiritual life but removed from people's needs and their own study. Then there are those who go to seed on the head. For these, all they want to do is study. They seldom touch their people. They may call themselves pastors, but they only want to be preachers. Those who get overbalanced with the hand lack authority because they are not in the Word. Those who become overbalanced with the heart lack authenticity if they do not know their people. And those overbalanced with the head often lack anointing by discounting the spiritual aspects of the heart. We have all seen preachers who were theoretically and homiletically astute but who lacked power and anointing in preaching.

In our day, with the media infiltration and all the high-profiled preaching therein, there comes pressure for some preachers to produce in such a way that is beyond their calling and gifts. The pastor must resist this and avoid that pressure at all costs. Be yourself. You are unique. God has called you and gifted you for the task to which He placed you. Be honest in everything you do and do not hesitate to give credit where credit is due.

Finally, as you prepare to preach, make sure you follow the apostolic method. This is clearly delineated for us in Peter's Pentecostal Proclamation found in Acts 2:14–47. This apostolic method involves our being prophetic. Peter took a text from Joel, illustrated it with two psalms, and established a biblical basis for what was transpiring at Pentecost. His message was plain and not difficult to understand. "Let this be known to you" (Acts 2:14). Peter's method, as Paul's in his first recorded sermon at the city of Antioch in Acts 13, made great emphasis on the resurrection. Hear Peter as he says, "This Jesus God has raised up" (Acts 2:32). Another important factor in apostolic preaching was that it was personal. So much preaching today is in first- and third-person plural, but the apostles preached in second-person singular and plural. Peter put it like this: "You have taken [Jesus] by lawless hands" (Acts 2:23). Our preaching predecessors were also pointed in their approach. They called for repentance on the part of their hearers. Peter pulled no punches, and as we prepare to preach, we should be asking ourselves if this element is found in our own messages (Acts 2:38). They were also passionate and persistent and "with many other words he [Peter] testified and exhorted them" (Acts 2:40). Peter pled for souls with many other words on that day of Pentecost.

And the result of this type of apostolic preaching? They were "praising God and having favor with all the people. And the Lord added to the church daily those who were being saved" (Acts 2:47). May God grant us as we take seriously our high calling in the preparation of our sermons the same favor with God and man.

PREACHING THE GREAT DAYS OF THE CHRISTIAN CALENDAR

New Year's Day

Deuteronomy 11:10–24
Dr. O. S. Hawkins

New Year's Day always brings an opportunity for a new beginning. For the children of Israel it had been a long journey. Moses had led them all the way from Egypt, through the Red Sea, to Kadesh Barnea, through the wilderness, and now they were encamped on the eastern bank of Jordan overlooking the promised land. The book of Deuteronomy in the Old Testament records the sermons Moses preached to his people before he went up on Mount Nebo, viewed the promised land, and died. In the aftermath of his death the children of Israel went on into the promised land and possessed it. Along the wilderness route there were often times when there were those who wrung their hands and doubted that they could go on and wished they were back in Egypt. Moses continued to remind them that God "brought us out from there that He might bring us in, to give us the land of which He had swore to our fathers" (Deut. 6:23).

Thus, before the blessing of the promised land becomes a reality for his faithful followers, Moses challenges them with these words from Deuteronomy 11:10–24. He reminds them as they cross over to their promised possession that they do so with God's provision, God's presence, God's promise, and God's protection.

As we stand at the brink of a new year, our hearts are filled with anticipation and challenge. Only God knows what the future holds, but the possibilities are limitless. As we cross over into a new year, we do so with the same challenges Moses gave his people so long ago. As we cross over into a new year, we're reminded of:

God's Provision

But the land you cross over to possess is a land of hills and valleys, which drinks water from the rain of heaven. (Deut. 11:11)

What is Moses saying to Israel here? Better yet, what is God saying to us through their experience? He will meet our needs! He is our source. Like the land of Israel, our land will "drink water from the rain of heaven." How many times have we seen this across the years...when it looked like hope was almost gone? In those times when we began to feel our source was running out, "God would rain from heaven the blessing upon us." We cross over into a new year reminded that He is our source.

Moses reminded the people that the land that they were about to possess was a land of "hills and valleys." God never promised us the way would always be easy. It is not a mountaintop experience all the time. Sometimes we, too, like the Israelites, walk through the valley. And then, there are those times when we come face to face with a mountain along the journey that humanly speaking looks impossible to climb.

Yes, it is a land of "hills and valleys." Anyone who's ever traveled in the promised land knows the reality of this visual expression. There are deep valleys. I've walked through the Kidron Valley and through Wadi Kelt. There are high mountains like Mount Hermon and Masada. There are desert places in the Judean wilderness and then there's the beautiful oasis of Jericho. It did not take the children of Israel long to discover that it was indeed a land of hills and valleys. They began their conquest of the promised land with the great victory at Jericho only to descend into the valley of defeat at Ai in the days that came afterward.

The same is true for us along our own journeys. Ours, too, is a journey through "hills and valleys." Thank God for the hills, the mountains. Often in the valleys we forget about the mountains. And, unfortunately, often when we're on the mountain we forget about the valleys. Both are important! If there were no valleys there would be no mountaintops. We never learn spiritual lessons on the mountain. They are always learned in the valley where we're trusting, depending on the living God to get us through. Mountains are there to enlarge our vision, to let us see our potential, to give us a spirit of conquest. But in the valleys, that's where we become more like our Lord. We would not choose the valleys. But His ways are not our ways. He is in fact the God of the mountains. He is also the God of the valleys. Do you remember what Elijah said to Ahab when Ben-Hadad, the cruelest general to ever march an army, besieged the city of Samaria? Elijah said, "'Because the Syrians have said, the Lord is God of the hills but He is not God of the valleys,' therefore, I will deliver all this great multitude into your hand, and you shall know that I am the Lord" (1 Kings 20:28). Yes, it is a land of hills and valleys.

But look closely at Deuteronomy 11:11. Note that we take with us into a new year the promise of God's provision. "It is a land that drinks rain from heaven." That is, He provides for us supernaturally.

For the children of Israel, the land of Israel was quite a contrast from the past years of Egypt. Moses reminds them that the land they were about to possess was "not like the land of Egypt . . . where you sowed your seed and watered it by foot" (Deut. 11:10). What was the difference? The land of Egypt depended on human resources. There was not much rain. The Nile was their source and it overflowed once a year. Therefore hard work was involved. By hand and by foot they dug trenches, canals to irrigate the land. In Egypt it was all done by human effort. Work, work, work was the motto. In Egypt there was no need for God. Water was stored by artificial means, and fields were irrigated by human sweat and toil. Egypt did not depend on God like Canaan did.

There are a lot of churches today that operate like the children of Israel in Egypt. That is, they have it all calculated with human ingenuity. They dig their own trenches. There's no real need for God. They go right on operating without Him, with their own initiatives, plans, and promotions. They do not do anything that cannot be explained by human means. Most everything happens by human effort and ingenuity.

But note the contrast of the promised land. It "drinks water from the rain of heaven." Canaan was and is totally dependent on God. Rain was His gift. In fact, this land has always been solely dependent upon His provisions. Perhaps that's why He chose this land and those people to train His church. First Corinthians 10:6 reminds us that everything that happened to the children of Israel did so as an example to us in this dispensation of grace. How beautiful to know that He proves this with both autumn and spring rains (Deut. 11:14). He sends the early rain for seed time and the latter rain at harvest. Both are important for growing a good crop.

As we cross over into a new year, we do so with the assurance that the same God who sends us the autumn rains of the past will send us the spring rains in the future. It may be a land of hills and valleys, but it is a land that "drinks rain from heaven." As we cross over we're dependent on the supernatural provision of God. God is our source and He has a way of using us to accomplish His purpose. As we cross over into a new year, we do so with God's provision. We also cross over with:

God's Presence

> *A land which the Lord your God cares; the eyes of the Lord your God are always on it, from the beginning of the year to the very end of the year. (Deut. 11:12)*

Remember, the apostle Paul reminds us that everything that happened to the children of Israel happened as examples for us (1 Cor. 10:6). There were some who said to Moses that they doubted they could accomplish the task of taking the promised land. After all, the land was filled with giants and walled cities. But they had forgotten that they crossed over with God's provision and God's presence. It was "a land which the Lord your God cares; the eyes of the Lord your God are always on it, from the beginning of the year to the very end of the year" (Deut. 11:12). The year upon which we embark is a year that God cares for. He purposed it. He planned it. He knows the way through the wilderness, and all we have to do is follow.

Some of the sweetest words in Deuteronomy 11:12 are often overlooked. Moses refers to the God of Israel as "your" God. He is a personal Lord and Savior. We are in covenant with Him. We are His and He is ours. Moses reminds his people that this is true "from the beginning of the year to the very end of the year." As we cross over into a new year, we're reminded that God is watching us, that His eyes are upon us.

New Year's Day brings a fresh vision of new opportunities. What a blessing to cross over into a new year with the very presence of God Himself. The eyes of the Lord are upon us! He is watching the dear mother who faces the year raising children without a husband. He is watching the dad who's under tremendous pressure to provide. He's watching the teenager with all the pressures of adolescence. He's watching each of us. Yes, "For the eyes of the Lord run to and fro throughout the whole earth, to show Himself strong on behalf of those whose heart is loyal to Him" (2 Chronicles 16:8–10). Like the children of Israel, He did not bring us out except to take us in. We go into a new year with God's provision and God's presence. We also go with:

God's Promise

> *And it shall be that if you earnestly obey My commandments which I command you today, to love the Lord your God and serve Him with all your heart and with all your soul, Then I will give you the rain for your land in its season, the early rain and the latter rain, that you may gather in your grain, your new wine, and your oil. And I will send grass in your fields for your livestock, that you may eat and be filled. (Deut. 11:13–15)*

What was Moses saying to Israel? Better yet, what is God saying to us? Remember that all these things happened to the children of Israel who are examples to us in this dispensation of grace. The single most important thing we can do as we cross over into a new year is to love the Lord our God and to serve Him with all our hearts.

Note that this promise is conditional. Verse 13 begins with "if" and verse 14 begins with "then." Thus, this promise is not for everyone. It is for whom? Those who love the Lord their God and serve Him with all their heart and soul. Think about it. What could be more simple? Israel only had to walk in obedience to God's word and to love Him. All that kept them from the blessing of God was disobedience. It is the same with us. I often wonder what would happen to the church of Jesus Christ if all of the members began to truly love the Lord with all their heart and serve Him with all their soul.

Here we find the Israelites' primary purpose. It was to love God! Everything in life has a primary purpose. The primary purpose of a pen is to write. I would rather have a cheap plastic pen that worked than an expensive one that didn't. The primary purpose of an automobile is to transport us from place to place. I would rather have a ten-year-old automobile that always started than a shiny new one that did not work. When something ceases to fulfill its primary purpose, it becomes useless. We've all seen wrecking yards with hundreds of cars lined up side by side that once were valuable. Could it be that so many Christians are defeated because so few are fulfilling their primary purpose? All of God's commandments are pure, but the Lord Jesus said one was the greatest. It was to love God with all of our hearts (Matt. 22:37). I might add that the reason we break most of the other commandments is because we do not obey this great commandment. Men and women would not defile their bodies in adultery or fornication if they loved God with all their hearts. No wonder Moses spoke this stern warning related to God's promise in Deuteronomy 11:13–14.

Moses reminded the children of Israel, and us, what is of utmost importance—loving God. We're to love God first and love man second. This is the fallacy of humanism that infiltrates so much of our culture. It says that the way to love God is to love man first. The Bible says the only way I can truly love others on the highest level of love is to love God supremely.

As we enter a new year, we do so with God's promise. What is our primary purpose? It is to love Him. It is to love God and serve Him with all of our hearts and souls.

Thus, we cross over into a new year with God's provision. We are reminded that He is our source. We cross over with God's presence. We are reminded that His eyes are upon us from the beginning of the year to the end of the year. We cross over with God's promise. If we love Him and serve Him with all of our hearts, then His blessing will be upon us. Finally, we cross over to a new year.

God's Protection

> *Take heed to yourselves, lest your heart be deceived, and you turn aside and serve other gods and worship them, Lest the Lord's anger be aroused against you, and He shut up the heavens so that there be no rain, and the land yield no produce, and you perish quickly from the good land which the Lord is giving you.*
>
> *Therefore you shall lay up these words of mine in your heart and in your soul, and bind them as a sign on your hand, and they shall be as frontlets between your eyes. You shall teach them to your children, speaking of them when you sit in your house, when you walk by the way, when you lie down, and when you rise up. And you shall write them on the doorposts of your house and on your gates, That your days and the days of your children may be multiplied in the land of which the Lord swore to your fathers to give them, like the days of the heavens above the earth.*
>
> *For if you carefully keep all these commandments which I command you to do — to love the Lord your God, to walk in all His ways, and to hold fast to Him —Then the Lord will drive out all these nations from before you, and you will dispossess greater and mightier nations than yourselves. Every place on which the sole of your foot treads shall be yours: from the wilderness and Lebanon,*

from the river, the River Euphrates, even to the Western Sea, shall be your territory. (Deut. 11:16–24)

What is Moses saying to Israel? Better yet, what is God saying to us since what happened to them was simply an example for us? He is reminding us that the Lord will go before us and drive out our enemies. His protection carries with it a warning. "Take heed to yourselves, lest your heart be deceived, and you turn aside and serve other gods and worship them, lest the Lord's anger be aroused against you, and He shut up the heavens so that there be no rain, and the land yield no produce, and you perish quickly from the good land which the Lord is giving you" (Deut. 11:16–17). Again, note the repetition of the importance of loving our God. "For if you carefully keep all these commandments which I command you to do—to love the Lord your God, to walk in all His ways and to hold fast to Him" (Deut. 11:22). For any of us who wonder why we may be living outside the provision and protection of God, the reason might be found in this verse.

Moses is tying his people to the word of God. Hear him as he challenges his people: "You shall lay up these words of mine in your heart and in your soul, and bind them as a sign on your hand, and they shall be frontlets between your eyes. You shall teach them to your children, speaking of them when you sit in your house, when you walk by the way, when you lie down and when you rise up" (Deut. 11:18–19). Moses knew the only way his people could love the Lord with all their heart was to saturate themselves with a conscious awareness of His word. As we cross over into a new year, we do so with God's protection. Moses goes on to tell them that "Then the Lord will drive out all these nations from before you, and you will dispossess greater and mightier nations than yourselves. Every place on which the sole of your foot treads shall be yours: from the wilderness and Lebanon, from the river, the River Euphrates, even to the Western Sea, shall be your territory. No man shall be able to stand against you" (Deut. 11:23–25).

Yes, it was a long, continuous journey for the children of Israel through the decades of wilderness wanderings. Moses led them all the way. And thus he comes to the end of his own life and says, "The land which you cross over to possess is a land of hills and valleys, which drinks water from the rain of heaven, a land which the Lord your God cares; the eyes of the Lord your God are always on it, from the beginning of the year to the very end of the year" (Deut. 11:11–12). As we cross over to this new year, Moses stands to remind us that as we go, we too will need God's provision. To depend on human effort is sheer folly. We will need God's presence. There will be times when we, like the children of Israel, wonder where God is. But His eyes are upon us. We cross over with God's promise. There may be times that this is all we have to hold. And, we go with His protection. There may be times when we'll be without help or hope unless God supernaturally intervenes.

We, too, have been on a journey. Now we are crossover people ourselves. We are crossing over into a new year with new opportunities and new beginnings. Yes, He brought us out from there that He might bring us into a land of blessing. As we enter a new year, let us, like those who've gone before, love God...walk in His ways . . . and hold fast to Him.

PREACHING THE GREAT DAYS OF THE CHRISTIAN CALENDAR

Palm Sunday

Luke 19:28–44

Dr. O. S. Hawkins

In our hearts we are all dreamers. Most all of us know what it is to dream dreams and see visions of what we might hope to become or what we think would bring happiness and contentment to our lives.

Who of us in our childhood days did not dream of the future? Even as I type these words my mind races back in time to an old vacant lot on Crenshaw Street in east Fort Worth. A thousand times I played ball on that old makeshift diamond and dreamed it was the bottom of the ninth in Yankee Stadium. That old tattered ball with its red threads unraveling was tossed to the plate. The crack of the bat...home run...I could hear the roar of the crowd as I trotted around those bases. As children we were all dreamers at heart. We dreamed of being astronauts, firemen, doctors, ballplayers, and even presidents.

We started college with big dreams of what we were going to do and what we were going to become. We began our careers with dreams of how we were going to advance and where we hoped to be by the time we reached forty (which seemed so long away back then). We started our marriages with dreams of being the all-American family who would live happily ever after with no heartaches and no problems.

But as the days have extended into weeks, the weeks into months, and the months into years, many of us have spent much of our time picking up the pieces of broken dreams. Often things do not work out just as we had hoped. Careers don't always develop. Unplanned recessions appear and steal jobs away. Downsizing can knock on our door at the peak of our earning potential. A husband dies ... or leaves. Kids make wrong decisions and bring heartbreak. Yes, broken dreams are no stranger to most of us.

Are there any broken dreams on this Palm Sunday? There were a lot of big dreamers on that first Palm Sunday in Jerusalem. Great crowds had lined the parade route down Palm Sunday Road from the summit of the Mount of Olives down the western slope, through the Kidron Valley, up the eastern slope of Mount Moriah and into the gate of the city. There was dancing in the street. The crowds were singing at the top of their lungs as they waved their palm branches. A festive mood permeated the atmosphere. After all, everyone loves a parade.

But, in the midst of all the palm branches there were broken dreams. Most of the emphasis on Palm Sunday today is centered on the pep rally, the parade, and the palm branches. But all that was really a sham. Our Lord knew this. In a few days they would all be gone and their cheers for Him would turn to jeers at Him.

Can you picture the Lord Jesus in this Palm Sunday scene? He is the center of attention. He must have had a smile on His face as He came riding down the hill on the back of that donkey as though He were in a convertible in a parade. The people were waving their palm branches, shouting and singing. The party was on. And then we read these words—"As He drew near, He saw the city and wept over it" (Luke 19:41). Do you see Him? He is weeping! In the very midst of all the hoopla, He is weeping. Yes, there was a broken dream amid the palm branches.

His kingdom was not of this world. Over eighty times in the Gospels He had spoken about "the Kingdom of God." But they didn't get it. They continued to raise their voices, shouting, "Blessed is the King who comes in the name of the Lord" (Luke 19:38). They were not really celebrating because of Him but because of what they thought they could get from Him. They had missed it...and He knew it. Somehow they had read right past Isaiah's prophetic words of a coming suffering servant who would be wounded for our own transgressions.

Yes, they were cheering, all right. But He knew their hearts and thus the Bible records, "Now when He drew near, He saw the city and wept over it, saying, 'If you had known, even you, especially in this your day, the things that make for your peace! But now they are hidden from your eyes. For days will come upon you when your enemies will build an embankment around you, surround you and close you in on every side. And level you and your children within you, to the ground; and they will not leave in you one stone upon another, because you did not know the time of your visitation' " (Luke 19:41–44). And so our Lord wept. He cried.

The crowds? They thought they were getting what they wanted. They thought they were welcoming a king who would deliver them from the oppression of Rome. They thought they were getting a liberator in the form of a "Stormin" Norman Schwarzkopf, or better yet, a Jewish George Washington who would liberate them against seemingly insurmountable odds. They only had eyes that day for their physical and temporal needs; not those needs that were spiritual and eternal.

When they realized they were not getting what they wanted a few days later, those Jerusalem crowds faded away and what was left were no longer cheering but jeering. Oh, we made Him a king, all right. We platted a crown of thorns and pressed it upon His brow and then mockingly bowed down with our sarcastic hails to the king. And we laughed. We beat Him. We spit on Him. We stripped Him naked and then we put a robe on Him, stuffed a reed for a scepter in His hand, and mocked Him, asking, "Are You the King of the Jews?" What a joke, we thought. And we laughed some more. He was a King, all right, but His kingdom was not of this world; it was a kingdom of the heart.

As our Lord rode down Palm Sunday Road that day, He knew how fickle the crowd really was and, thus, He wept. He had come to really liberate them forever, but they wanted no part of that. So in the midst of all the cheers . . . He cried. He knew. And so on Palm Sunday Road we find a broken dream in the midst of all the palm branches.

What do we do when our own dreams fall apart? How can we pick up the pieces of our broken dreams and begin to dream again? Our Lord is teaching us three things on this Palm Sunday. Broken dreams can hurt.

He felt the pain of a broken dream and He wants us to know that when everyone else is waving their palms and shouting their hosannas that it is okay to cry. Broken dreams can hurt. He also wants to remind us that broken dreams can heal. He went from Palm Sunday to the Garden of Gethsemane where He prayed, "Not my will, but thine, be done" (Luke 22:42 KJV). Broken dreams can heal when God is in control. Finally, our Lord reminds us that broken dreams can help. He kept on doing right. He kept on moving forward on His journey to the cross with a renewed sense of dependence upon the Father. Let's look and learn as our Lord teaches us on this Palm Sunday about broken dreams and palm branches.

Broken Dreams Can Hurt

"Now as He drew near, He saw the city and wept over it." (Luke 19:41)

Look at our Lord. Can you picture the scene? He is seated on the back of a donkey and as He comes in view of the Holy City He begins to weep. This was not the first time we find Him shedding tears in Scripture. Earlier, and ironically, on the same mountain although on the opposite slope, in the little village of Bethany, we read, "Jesus wept" (John 11:35). He was standing at the tomb of His friend Lazarus, and John records that He began to weep. Interestingly, John uses the Greek word δακρύω to describe this weeping. The word means to shed tears but in more of a silent vein. Thus, when He stood on the eastern slope of the Mount of Olives at Bethany, He did not weep with loud sobs, but more quietly. The word indicates that most likely a lump came in His throat; tears welled up in His eyes and spilled silently down His bronze cheeks.

But when we find Him weeping here on the western slope on Palm Sunday, that particular word is not used to describe what was taking place. Here the word is indicating pain or deep grief that leads one to cry with deep and loud sobs. On that day you could have heard our Lord weeping two blocks away.

I have heard men and women who wept this way in pain. I have heard children weep this way when they are really hurt. A parent knows the difference in his or her child's cry when they are truly in pain. I have been with men and women who wept like this in grief as they stood at the open grave of a loved one. As a pastor I have heard the deep sobs of a mother whose only child met a tragic and sudden death. Incidentally, this same Greek word is used in Luke 22:62, when Simon Peter, upon hearing the rooster crow, went out and "wept bitterly."

Look once more at the Lord Jesus. He is seated on the donkey. The people are cheering. The palm branches are waving. He tops the hill, sees the city, and begins to weep. Luke in writing this account is inspired to use this word that means to cry with loud and deep sobs. On Palm Sunday Road Jesus did not simply get a lump in His throat and brush a tear away before anyone saw it. No! He broke down and cried with loud sobs from a deeply grieved heart. Yes, broken dreams can hurt.

He had healed their sick. He had cleansed their lepers. He had fed their hungry. He had given hope to their depressed. But, He had failed to win their hearts. They wanted Him, all right, but primarily for what they could get from Him. So, the Lord Jesus, seated on a lowly donkey, broke into tears. This very One who had spoken the world into existence, flung the stars in place and put the planets in their orbits met the closed doors of the human hearts He had come to save. And it hurt.

Yes, broken dreams can hurt. Do you hear that...you with a broken dream? Look at Him. He cares. He says to any and all of us with broken dreams, "I understand. I have been there. I know." One of the lessons of Palm Sunday is that it is okay to cry. Broken dreams can hurt and it is no shame to acknowledge this fact.

When we see Him on this original Palm Sunday Road, what does it say to us today? It reminds us that it is okay to cry. If we do not feel the hurt and grief of a broken dream, it was not much of a dream in the first place. God gives us the gift of tears in days of broken dreams and tears have a way of being therapeutic. The world tells us to be strong. The world tells us that others see our tears as a sign of weakness. But that is not the message of our Lord. He reminds us through Paul that we do not have to be strong. We can be weak because strength comes through weakness (2 Cor. 12:9–10).

Some live with broken dreams on this Palm Sunday and they are too proud to admit it. So they ride down their own Palm Sunday Road with their shoulders tilted back, their heads held high, and their jaws set like stone. And many of them live a lifetime without real healing. In fact, those who insist on "staying strong" in the midst of broken dreams most usually become weak in the process. But the truth is . . . it is okay to cry. Jesus did.

What can be done about it? Be honest and stop trying to push your broken dreams into some imaginary closet. Admit it. Broken dreams can hurt. It is okay to cry. Some never learn to dream again for the simple fact that they allow their broken dreams to embitter them instead of allowing them to enable them to move on and dream again.

Broken dreams can hurt. But, only for a season. The Lord Jesus didn't cry forever. He went on from Palm Sunday to show us that broken dreams can also heal.

Broken Dreams Can Heal

> *"'Father, if it is Your will, take this cup away from Me; nevertheless, not My will, but Yours, be done.' Then an angel appeared to Him from heaven, strengthening Him." (Luke 22:42–43)*

Look at our Lord now. He went from Palm Sunday to the Gethsemane Garden a few days later. He admitted His grief, saying, "My soul is overwhelmed with sorrow" (Matt. 26:38 NIV). But He left Gethsemane a victor. No more tears. No tears even in the face of His accusers, tormentors, persecutors, and executioners. He was in charge! He had won the victory of Calvary in the garden the evening before. Hear Him—"Not My will but Yours be done." He found His comfort in the fact that the Father was in control of the situation. And the broken dreams of Palm Sunday found healing in the Garden of Gethsemane.

What does this say to us on our own Palm Sunday Roads this morning? Broken dreams can hurt. But, they can also heal when we come to the place of surrendering our will to His. One of the tragedies of modern Christianity is that we seem to have lost that word, "surrender." Perhaps in our Western mind-set we are just too macho. We would rather talk of conquest and commitment than to speak of surrender. But in the Christian life our Lord teaches us that surrender to His will is the only thing that brings true healing.

We all have our own share of broken dreams. The real issue becomes what we do with them. Some allow broken dreams to so embitter them that they live the rest of their lives with hurt. Others go on to a personal Gethsemane and allow them to heal. But the Lord Jesus teaches us there is more. Broken dreams can hurt. They can heal. And, broken dreams can also help.

Broken Dreams Can Help

> *"... and He said, 'Peace to you.' ... and He opened their understanding that they might comprehend the scriptures ... and He led them out as far as Bethany, and He lifted up His hands and blessed them ... and they worshipped Him, and returned to Jerusalem with great joy and were continually in the temple praising and blessing God." (Luke 24:36–53)*

Yes, we can dream again! Our Lord kept doing what was right. Broken dreams that once hurt and then were healed now actually helped others along the way. The disciples had their own broken dreams. On the Emmaus Road they lamented, "We had hoped He had been the one." Peter said he was going back to the fishing business. Scripture simply records, "They all forsook Him and fled." But, what a difference when they had been with Him. They "returned to Jerusalem with great joy." Broken dreams can help us face the future with courage.

Once the Lord left Gethsemane, the crowd's cheers on Palm Sunday turned to loud jeers before Pilate. But Jesus? He kept on walking toward the cross. He knew His best friends would desert Him, and that He would be humiliated, beaten, and finally nailed to a cross, but He never missed a step. He kept walking to Calvary. He faced it with courage. He died with dignity, and a Roman soldier even exclaimed, "Surely, this was the Son of God."

What does all this say to us on this Palm Sunday? Be faithful where you are. God has a plan for you. Just because you have a broken dream, don't quit. Don't give up. Broken dreams can actually help you and bless others.

Many of those who have been most used of God seem to be those who have had their fair share of broken dreams and learned to dream again. They were those who got knocked down and then got back up. Simon Peter comes to mind. He followed from afar off after the arrest and found himself warming by a fire when Jesus was led by and simply "looked" at him. Peter learned that broken dreams can hurt. He went out and "wept bitterly" (Luke 22:62). He also learned that broken dreams can heal. We find him a few days later seated at breakfast on the shore with the resurrected Christ affirming his love repeatedly. And, in Peter, we see that broken dreams can help. He went on from there to become the undisputed leader of the Jerusalem church and the great preacher at Pentecost. Yes, broken dreams can end up helping.

We all start out with dreams. Many of them get broken along the way. Some of us are shouting our hosannas today, outwardly putting on a good front. But inwardly, we are filled with broken dreams. As we wave our palm branches today, does this story tell us anything about ourselves? Do we, like they, shout and support as long as we think we are going to get what we want? Do we shout our own hosannas because of who He is or because of what we want from Him? Even in the midst of our own Palm Sunday, He may still be weeping. The good news on this Palm Sunday is that we can dream again.

After the Palm Sunday Parade, whoever thought that in just a few days there would be a crucifixion? What a shock! But that is not the biggest shock. Whoever thought that after the crucifixion there would be a resurrection!

Where do we begin to dream again? We begin in the same place our Lord did. We begin in the same place Simon Peter did or anyone else who ever found healing. That is, at the feet of the Father in our own Gethsemane praying, "Not my will, but Yours be done." Broken dreams can heal. And broken dreams can help.

PREACHING THE GREAT DAYS OF THE CHRISTIAN CALENDAR

Easter Sunday

John 11:25–26

Dr. O. S. Hawkins

There are many questions that fill our minds during the easter season. What shall I wear? Did you order the lilies? Where will we hide the Easter eggs? Where will we eat Easter brunch and who should we invite? Should we attend the early worship service or the late? But there is one question that is truly Easter's bottom-line question. It is the question Jesus asked at Bethany when, after proclaiming that He, Himself, was the resurrection and the life and that those who believed and put their trust in Him would have eternal life, He asked, "Do you believe this?" (John 11:26).

The preacher's task on Easter morning is not to convince his hearers of the resurrection. After Jesus' resurrection He appeared to His disciples. They saw Him. They spoke with Him. But Thomas was absent and when told the good news he doubted and demanded proof for his own eyes. Quite frankly, if Simon Peter, James, John, and the others could not convince Thomas, the preacher should be under no illusion that in a few minutes he is going to convince his own hearers. But, what he can do is confront each and every one of them with Easter's bottom-line question—"Do you believe this?"

The resurrection is what separates our Lord from a thousand other gurus and prophets who have come down the pike. Easter's bottom-line question drives any responsible hearer to either accept or reject the Christian faith. Almost yearly now there comes another book or movie, in the ilk of *The DaVinci Code*, that is nothing more than a blasphemous frontal attack on the claims of our Lord. This is nothing new. It is the same type Gnosticism the early church faced and the apostle Paul confronted when he said, "Beware lest anyone cheat you through philosophy and empty deceit, according to the tradition of men, according to the basic principles of the world, and not according to Christ" (Col. 2:8).

Our Easter text finds us this morning in Bethany. The Lord is standing at the tomb of His friend Lazarus and makes an astonishing claim, "I am the resurrection and the life. He who believes in Me, though he may die, he shall live. And whoever lives and believes in Me shall never die" (John 11:25–26). Then He looks into their faces, and into our hearts this morning, and asks Easter's bottom-line question—"Do you believe this?" (John 11:26). Some try to avoid this question throughout life. Let it sink in a moment. "Do you believe this?"

In reading this text I have often wondered how our Lord inflected this question. Did He ask, "Do YOU believe this?" After all, it is personal. Did He ask, "Do you BELIEVE this?" It is, after all, pointed. Or, did he ask, "Do you believe THIS?" It is precise. May we on this Easter morning answer it in the fashion that it was answered in Bethany, "Yes, Lord, I believe that You are the Christ, the Son of God, who is to come into the world" (John 11:27). Let's search Easter's bottom-line question for ourselves.

It Is Personal

"Do YOU believe this?" (John 11:26)

Perhaps the Lord put the inflection on the "you" in the question in order to drive home to our hearts that it is personal. After all, when it comes to saving faith in the finished work of Christ, this is what matters most . . . not what my mother or my wife or anyone else believes. This is a personal matter. I have known people who have virtually lived their lives on what someone else believed as though they would eventually benefit by some sort of spiritual osmosis. Ultimately, Easter's bottom-line question is, "Do YOU believe this?"

An increasing number in our twenty-first-century Gnostic culture are captivated by documentaries, movies, and books that question the veracity of the gospel account. Is that what you really want to believe? That is, that Christ was really not the Son of God as He said He was? Do you want to believe that His death was an unnecessary event and not a voluntary, vicarious death for you? Or, that the account of the resurrection should be relegated to some ancient shelf of obscurity along with other myths and fables?

Easter's bottom-line question is personal. Jesus claimed to be "the resurrection and the life." Jesus is still asking today, "Do YOU believe this?"

It Is Pointed

"Do you BELIEVE this?"

Perhaps when our Lord asked this question in Bethany He put added inflection and emphasis on the word "believe." After all, faith is the acceptable response to the Christian gospel. He was not inquiring of His hearers as to whether they were giving intellectual assent to His claims. But, He wanted to know if they would trust in Him and take Him at His word by faith. "Do you BELIEVE this?"

It is one thing to know about the gospel story intellectually. It is one thing to hear about it through one avenue or another. It is one thing to try to conform ourselves to it and to a new set of moral standards that accompany these truths. It is even one thing to argue for it apologetically and reason about it. It is, in fact, possible to conform to the truth of the gospel without ever being transformed from within by grace through faith.

The real issue on this Easter morning is, "Do you BELIEVE this?" Have you transferred your trust from yourself and your own good efforts over to Jesus Christ alone? Has this saving faith, this resurrected life, this "Christ in me" experience, made a difference in your life? Paul reminds us that it is "by grace you have been saved through faith, and that not of yourselves; it is the gift of God, not of works, lest anyone should boast. For we are His workmanship, created in Christ Jesus for good works, which God prepared beforehand that we should walk in them" (Eph. 2:8–10). Do you BELIEVE this?

It Is Precise

"Do you believe THIS?"

Now we come to the heart of the issue, for true faith must rest on objective truth. It may be that the Lord Jesus inflected Easter's bottom-line question with His emphasis placed on the last word—"Do you believe THIS?"

"Do you believe THIS?" What we ask? THIS! What? Note the context. "I am the resurrection and the life. He who believes in Me, though he may die, he shall live. And whoever lives and believes in Me shall never die" (John 11:25–26). Immediately on the heels of this incredible attestation comes Easter's bottom-line question. "Do you believe THIS?"

His Claim About Diety

"Do you believe THIS?"

"I am the resurrection and the life" (John 11:25). When He used that phrase, "I am," it captured the attention of those around him. Seven times this "I am" affirmation is recorded in John's gospel. In John 6 Jesus said, "I am the bread of life." In John 8 He said, "I am the light of the world." In John 10 He said, "I am the door." In John 10 He also said, "I am the chief shepherd." In John 14 He proclaimed, "I am the way, the truth and the life." In John 15 we hear Him say, "I am the true vine." And here in our Easter text He states, "I am the resurrection and the life." He is the great "I am" and not the great "I was." We first hear God use this "I am" way back in Exodus 3:13–14. When Moses encountered the living God in the burning bush, he asked Him to reveal His name so that when he returned to Egypt with the message of emancipation, he might reveal who had sent him. God simply replied, "Tell him 'I AM' has sent you."

When our Lord made this statement at the tomb of Lazarus, all those around recognized it as an affirmation of deity. Modern-day Gnostics tell us that Constantine muscled this truth of Christ's deity through the Nicene council in AD 325 and into the Nicene Creed and that the church never believed it until then. If so, then why did John begin his gospel saying, "In the beginning was the Word and the Word was with God and the Word was God . . . and the Word became flesh and dwelt among us" (John 1:1, 14)?

The most fundamental belief of the Christian faith is that Jesus Christ is God Himself. This is why the apostle Paul said, "He is the image of the invisible God...all things were created by Him and for Him" (Col. 1:15–16 KJV). It was this faith in the deity of Christ that led all the apostles except John to their own martyr's deaths. It was the insistence upon this Christological truth that had Ignatius of Antioch thrown to the wild animals at the end of the first century and Polycarp of Smyrna burned at the stake a few decades later. Easter's bottom-line question is precise—"Do you believe THIS?"

Martha answered this question immediately, "Yes, Lord, I believe that You are the Christ, the Son of God, who is to come into the world" (John 11:27). Martha was a devout Jew. When she used the word "Christ," Χρίστος, it had a deep meaning to all those who heard this confession. Their minds went immediately to the Temple and the Passover season when the sacrificial lambs were slain and when the high priest on the Day of Atonement, Yom Kippur, entered the Holy of Holies to sprinkle the blood over the Mercy Seat above the ark of the covenant. Yom Kippur means "day of covering." It was then that the sins of the people were "covered" by the blood. Like most people today I use a credit card. When I go to make a purchase, I give them my card and they accept it as cash. Now, that plastic card has no real intrinsic value in or of itself. But it is accepted. Why? It is a forerunner of the true cash payment that soon will come when I receive my monthly bill. Until then the credit card "covers" my purchase. As such the old covenant "covered" the sins of the people who looked for Christos, the Anointed One, the Christ who was to come to make final payment for the sins of the world. And He did and it is no wonder there have not been sacrifices made on Temple Mount in two thousand years now. All that was in Martha's reply. "Yes, Lord, I believe that You are the Christ."

Who is He to you this Easter season? Merely some figure out of history? Or, the subject of some sentimental story out of childhood? Or, can you say with Martha, "Yes, Lord, I believe that You are the Christ." Easter's bottom-line question is precise. "Do you believe THIS?" That is, His claim about deity?

His Claim About Death

"Do you believe THIS?"—"though he may die" (John 11:25).

Many live their lives in total denial of their coming appointment with death. Jesus says that one of the facts of life is that we are going to die. Do you believe THIS?

Recently I was going through a stack of pictures that were made a decade ago. I was stunned. My hair was darker then. I certainly looked younger in the face. It dawned on me that this body of mine has death in it. I am decaying before my eyes. Certain parts of me are seeing some deterioration. Oh, some opt for plastic surgery. Others for liposuction. Others eat vitamin-enriched foods and do all they can to keep their cholesterol down. But none of us can stop the fact that we are marching toward the grave. Death is our final enemy.

Death is the real common denominator of all men. If you do not believe it, just pick up the obituary section in any city newspaper. On the society page you will read about only one class of people. In the business section you will read about those who are excelling in various professions. In the sports section you will read about those who are athletically gifted. But on the obituary page everyone is listed side by side and usually in a cold alphabetical order. The rich and the poor side by side. The talented and the not so gifted side by side. The famous and the not so famous side by side. Death knocks on the door of the wealthiest billionaire and the poorest peasant and sends them both to stand before the Judge of all the earth. Yes, death is man's common denominator.

There are a lot of books on the best-seller lists that tell us how to live today. But there is only one Book that tells us how to die. Easter's bottom-line question is not just personal and pointed, it is precise—"Do you believe THIS?" Do you believe our Lord's claim about death?

Long centuries ago the prophet Amos thundered down his warning, "Prepare to meet your God" (Amos 4:12). We prepare for everything in life. Your medical doctor didn't just hang out a shingle that announced his or her medical practice. Years of study, preparation, and planning went into that. We prepare for everything in life. We prepare for our children's college education. We even prepare for those we will leave behind through various insurance policies and the like. But too few of us "prepare to meet our God." The Bible says, "And as it is appointed for men to die once, but after this the judgment" (Heb. 9:27). Isn't it foolish to spend all our time and energies on this life alone when there is another life that is more than a million times a million times longer than this one? Every one of us has an appointment with death. "Do you believe THIS?" That is His claim about death.

His Claim About Destiny

"Do you believe THIS?"—"he shall live" (John 11:25).

It is strange how so many today live their lives as if this were all there is. Jesus indicates here that even though death is sure, we are going to live again. The body may indeed die, but not the Spirit, not that part of you that will live as long as God lives and then one day be reunited with a glorified body for the endless ages of eternity. Do you believe His claim that even though we may die we will, in fact, live again?

I once heard of a hypothetical conversation between a mother and her unborn child. "In just a few days you are going to be born," excitedly declares the mom. "But I don't want to be born. I don't want to leave this womb. I like it here. It is comfortable and warm. I feel so secure and cozy here. I like it like this," argues the soon-to-be-born baby. The mom continues, "But, you don't realize what you are missing. There is laughter and sunshine and there are brothers and sisters with whom to play. And, there is music and picnics and toys." And the debate continues with the baby arguing against the very idea of birth because she cannot begin to relate experientially to the concept. The baby does not understand that to remain in the womb too long could result in tragic consequences.

Some of us today struggle against the thought of death in the same way and with the same ignorance. Why? Because we do not understand Easter's bottom-line question with its accompanying fact that, "though we shall die, we shall live again."

The real question for many of us on this Easter morning is, "What are we doing about that part of us that is going to live forever?" Many do not want to think about this on an Easter morning. After all, we have new dresses and shoes and a big family lunch on the day's agenda. And sadly, fewer churches in the Western world ever confront their hearers with Easter's bottom-line question anymore due to this "feel good" culture that permeates most every part of our being. But Easter confronts us with a question for eternity—"Do you believe THIS?" What? His claim about deity, "I am the Resurrection and the Life." His claim about death, "he who believes in Me though he dies." His claim about destiny, "he shall live."

His Claim About Deliverance

> *"Do you believe THIS?"—"whoever lives and believes in Me shall never die" (John 11:26).*

The Lord is making it very plain here. Eternal salvation is through faith in Him alone and not through human effort or good works. And note, "whoever LIVES and believes in Me shall never die." Faith is only possible this side of the grave. In the Sermon on the Mount, Jesus spoke of those who would make their appeal after this life to whom he will reply, "I never knew you" (Matt. 7:23). Eternal life can be ours in this life now and through faith in Him alone. It is no wonder Paul said, "In Him we have redemption through His blood, the forgiveness of sins, according to the riches of His grace" (Eph. 1:7).

Easter is a day of decision when we are confronted with its bottom-line question. In fact, there are only three possible responses to His Easter claims. One, He was divine. And thus, He did in fact rise from the dead. His body was gone. His friends surely did not take it. They had already fled in fear and cowardice. His foes did not have the body. They would have loved to present His dead body before those who were later heralding His resurrection. Another possibility is that He was deceptive. That is, that Jesus was a sort of con artist as portrayed in some modern movies and blasphemous books. Was He simply deceiving people by claiming to be "the Resurrection and the Life"? The only other possibility was that He was demented, some kind of a first-century David Koresh.

On this Easter morning, if you do not believe He was demented or deceived, then you must believe He was divine, who He said He was! The Lord! If so, then what do you intend to do about it? Will you simply continue to tip your hat to Him at Christmas and Easter, or will you face Easter's bottom-line question? "Do you believe this?" Do you believe that He is Lord, that you will one day die, that you will live again, and that if you put your trust and faith in Him alone you will inherit eternal life?

There are a lot of big questions in life. Where will I attend college? What vocation shall I pursue? Whom shall I marry? But there is only one big question in death. "Do you believe this?" That's it. "Do you believe this?" It is personal. "Do YOU believe this?" You cannot live your life on what someone else believes. It is pointed. "Do you BELIEVE this?" Faith is the key. It is precise. "Do you believe THIS?" Jesus Christ is Lord and if you put your faith in Him alone to save you, you will never die.

Look at Lazarus in the context of our question. He is a picture of all of us. He is dead. There is nothing he can do for himself to bring life. But then Christ calls for him and brings him out of death and into life (John 11:43–44). This same Jesus calls us out of spiritual death and darkness into a brand-new life with Him.

Finally, note Martha's own reply to Easter's bottom-line question—"Yes, Lord, I believe that You are the Christ, the Son of God, who is to come into the world" (John 11:27). Would you join her on this Easter morning by simply saying, "Yes, Lord, I believe"?

PREACHING THE GREAT DAYS OF THE CHRISTIAN CALENDAR

Mother's Day

Matthew 1:5

Dr. O. S. Hawkins

It is Mother's Day and all over the Christian world preachers are pointing this morning to the mother we have come to call the "Proverbs 31 woman."

What a lady. This wonder woman gets up before dawn and stays busy until the early hours of the next morning. We have developed a mental image of her. She has the looks of a movie star, the domestic abilities of a master chef, the stamina of a world-class athlete, the intellect of a professor with a PhD, the tenacity of a political operative, the wisdom of a godly missionary, the sensitivity of a Mother Teresa, the business sense of a Fortune 500 executive, the grace of an etiquette expert and the spirituality of the Virgin Mary. Wow. No wonder so many mothers leave church feeling down on Mother's Day!

Can any of us measure up to this standard of perfection? She is certainly a worthy goal for which to aim, but we are all in a process here. If it is the church's intent to reach her city for Christ, then she must begin to deal with men and women where they are and not simply where each of us should be.

In preparation for this Mother's Day message, I asked myself a question, "If the Lord Jesus was in my pulpit Sunday and preaching audibly, what would He say?" I am convinced He wouldn't simply speak trite platitudes or read a sweet poem or two. I believe He would do exactly what He did in Scripture. He would leave the ninety and nine and go after that one who is hurting and lost. Perhaps, it is the woman today who has never borne children. Or, the one who aborted her child in the past. Or, the mother who birthed a child and loved him so much that she entrusted him to someone else to raise and wonders, today, what he looks like and where he lives. On this Mother's Day let's allow our Lord to speak to each of us at the very point of our need.

While the woman in Proverbs 31 is a worthy example to emulate, she is not among those listed in the lineage of our Lord. But two women in Matthew 1:5 are listed there for all posterity to see. Who are these two mothers? They must be paragons of faithfulness to be in this righteous list. Not really. One is Rahab, the prostitute of Jericho. She was the madam who ran the house of ill repute in that ancient town in the Jordan valley. The other mother listed is Ruth, the godless Moabite. She was raised in a heathen environment worshipping pagan idols and gods. But something wonderful happened to each of these two mothers. Their experience with the living God caused them to be converted into two of the godliest mothers in the Bible and they live on in history and in heaven today.

Rahab and Ruth were mothers who overcame their circumstances. Like many modern moms they were torn between work and childcare. Many moms are divorced today; others may be remarried and they are dealing with incredible adjustments and the struggle of divided loyalties. Others live with all sorts of unspoken heartaches in the home and are making the best of very difficult situations. Still others have husbands who cannot be trusted.

Rahab is listed here in the genealogy of Jesus to show us that there is hope for those who have been engaged in sinful pleasures. Ruth joins her in this list to show us that there is hope for those who have been engaged with societal pressures. Both of these women are remembered forever as virtuous women. Let's look at them and learn from them on this Mother's Day.

Rahab Shows Us How We Can Overcome Sinful Pleasures

Who is this mother named Rahab listed here in Matthew 1 in the genealogy of Jesus? Her story is told in the second and sixth chapters of the book of Joshua. Here we find a lady with a reputation that was far from spotless. She was quite popular with the men who stopped in their caravans while journeying through the oasis city of Jericho. Everyone knew where her house was located. The local kids would point to it as they passed by. Five of the six times she is mentioned in Scripture the word "harlot" is placed alongside her name as if it were glued to her. When her family members are listed in Joshua 2:13, there is no mention of a husband or children. She was a lady who was involved in sinful pleasures.

When the Israelites sent spies into her city as they were about to begin their conquest of Canaan, she took them in. Interestingly, she had not heard what they had done for God during their march to the Promised Land, nor how well trained their armies had become, but what struck this harlot's heart was what the living God had done for them and through them (Josh. 2:10).

She becomes a beautiful example of how one can overcome her sinful pleasures to become a godly mother. Listen to her testimony in front of the Israelite spies, "I know that the Lord has given you the land, that the terror of you has fallen on us and that all the inhabitants of the land are fainthearted because of you. For we have heard how the Lord dried up the water of the Red Sea for you when you came out of Egypt, and what you did to the two kings of the Amorites who were on the other side of the Jordan, Sihon and Og, whom you utterly destroyed. And as soon as we heard these things our hearts melted; neither did there remain any courage in anyone because of you, for the Lord your God, He is God in heaven above and on earth beneath" (Josh. 2:9–11). Here are the words spoken by one with a repentant heart—"He is God in heaven above and on earth beneath."

There is an interesting insight found a few verses earlier. She took the spies up on her roof and hid them under "the stalks of flax which she had laid in order on the roof" (Josh. 2:6). Why was there flax on this woman's roof, neatly and orderly laid out? In the ancient world flax was gathered by industrious women, dried out and used for spinning and weaving. The presence of such a large quantity of it on her roof may well indicate she had experienced a change of vocation. Interestingly enough, it is said of the Proverbs 31 woman that "she seeks wool and flax and willingly works with her hands" (Prov. 31:13).

Not only did this woman of Jericho repent, but there is good evidence that she placed her faith in the living God (Josh. 2:15–21). When the spies went on their way with a promise to return, they told her to hang a scarlet thread out the window of her home so that when they came to conquer the city, her home would be spared. She replied, "According to your words, so be it. And she sent them away … and she bound the scarlet cord in the window" (Josh. 2:21).

When Rahab said yes to the God of heaven and by faith hung the scarlet cord out her window, an amazing thing happened. God in heaven knew about a coming cross of which she was unaware. The blood was shed on that cross before the foundation of the world. God saw that cross and the salvation it so freely offered and looked down on her faith and saved her by His own blood. And, as a celebration of her faith, she hung that scarlet thread out her window, so that when judgment came and the walls came tumbling down, there was one obvious part of that wall that judgment could not touch because of the scarlet thread. Here is a beautiful picture of salvation tucked away in the Old Testament.

Rahab is listed in the lineage of Jesus in Matthew 1:5 to show all posterity that there is hope for any and all who trust in the living God.

What ever happened to her? Did she ever find a husband? I'll say she did. She lived among the Israelites and fell in love with a prince by the name of Salmon. God blessed their union with a son whose name was Boaz, who became the kinsman-redeemer. This former harlot of Jericho became the mother of Boaz, the Lord of the harvest, who became the husband of Ruth.

Look at Rahab. She is remembered today on this Mother's Day to remind us there is hope for those who may have once lived in sinful pleasures of various types. And today, she lives on in history and in heaven as a good and godly mother who imparted the same qualities to her own family.

Ruth Shows Us How We Can Overcome Societal Pressures

Who is this other mother listed in Matthew 1:5 in the lineage of Jesus? Her name is Ruth. She was a Moabitess. Her obstacle was not that of sinful pleasures but of societal pressures. She was raised in a godless home, not unlike many in the Western world today. She was raised in a pagan, anti-God culture. All the influences of her childhood were against her coming to know the living Lord.

She was a member of a race that actually began in incest (Gen. 19:30–37). Lot slept with his own daughter and she bore a son named Moab. The Moabites did not worship the Lord God. They worshipped the pagan god Chemosh. They offered human sacrifices to him. They were a degenerate people who resorted to all types of licentious behavior.

As a pastor for decades I have noticed that of all the strongholds, the religion of our childhood is the most difficult to break. It seems to have a hold over people. While Satan comes against those in sinful pleasure with accusations, he comes against those with societal pressures with obligations. Ruth is listed here in Matthew 1:5 as a godly mother to show us all that there is hope for those with societal pressures and a sense of false obligations to the religion of childhood.

How did Ruth become an overcomer? She saw her mother-in-law, Naomi, repent and set her face back to Bethlehem and away from Moab. Ruth began to cling to her with these words: "Entreat me not to leave you, or to turn back from following after you; for wherever you go, I will go; and wherever you lodge, I will lodge; your people shall be my people, and your God, my God; where you die, I will die, and there will I be buried" (Ruth 1:16–17). If you want to witness an Old Testament conversion, there it is.

Ruth found a *new determination*. "Entreat me not to leave you." All influences were against her. The religion of her childhood was against her. Orpah's example (she kissed Naomi and "went back to her people and her gods") was against her. Naomi's insistence that she stay in Moab was against her. But faith brought a new determination in Ruth.

Ruth found a *new direction*. "Wherever you go, I will go." Ruth was determined that following the God of Naomi would become her new life's direction.

Ruth found a *new dependence*. "Wherever you lodge, I will lodge." She was saying that she would trust the Lord and Naomi for her basic needs.

Ruth found a *new desire*. "Your people shall be my people." Ruth knew that if she took the God of the Bible to be her God, then she would take His people as hers also. It did not take me long as a new believer to understand that if I was truly going to go God's way, then I had to do so in the company of His people.

Ruth found a *new devotion*. "Your God shall be my God." The interesting thing about this to me is that all she knew of Naomi's God was a God of suffering and sorrow. Naomi's husband had died, her two sons had died, and her heart was filled with grief. But Ruth watched Naomi and knew her and her living testimony brought a new devotion to Ruth.

Ruth found a *new dedication*. "Wherever you die, I will die." Ruth was saying, "This is for life. This is a life decision. I am not coming back if things do not work out just the way I think they should."

Finally, Ruth found a *new destiny*. "Where you are buried I will be buried." I believe Ruth was saying here that "not even death will separate us."

What happened to this formerly godless Moabite woman? Did she find a husband? I'll say she did. Did she become a godly mother? Did she ever! Matthew 1:5 tells us the story. She returned to Bethlehem with Naomi. She married Boaz, the Lord of the harvest. You remember Boaz. He was the son of Rahab. Boaz and Ruth had a son whose name was Obed who had a son whose name was Jesse who had a son whose name was David. Yes, King David, the shepherd, the psalmist, the king. I am sure this trust in the living God was transferred to her great-grandson, for later he would write, "I have been young and now I am old, but I have never seen the righteous forsaken nor his seed begging bread" (Ps. 37:25 KJV).

No more fitting tribute has ever been paid to a wife than when Ruth's husband said, "All the people of my town know that you are a virtuous woman" (Ruth 3:11). Look at Ruth. She stands there in the lineage of Jesus to show us that no matter what our past we can become virtuous through the Lord Jesus Christ.

Yes, if our Lord were here this Mother's Day physically and speaking audibly to us, I have no doubt He would leave the ninety and nine and come to each troubled, lonely, or lost heart in order to impart and impute His righteousness to all who would believe so that it might be repeated that "all the people of our town might know that you are a virtuous woman."

It was not common in the ancient world to list women in a genealogy tree. In fact, in the entire listing of those in the line of Jesus that consumes most of the initial chapter of the New Testament, only four women are mentioned. One might think they must have been some kind of virtuous women. But a closer look reveals an interesting truth. One is Tamar. She dressed as a prostitute, seduced her own father-in-law, and had an illegitimate baby. The next is Rahab, the harlot, followed by Ruth, the Moabitess. Finally, we meet Bathsheba. She is the one who lived in adultery with King David. What do you suppose our Lord is trying to tell us on this Mother's Day? I think He is reminding us all that "if anyone is in Christ, he is a new creation; old things have passed away; behold, all things have become new" (2 Cor. 5:17). The gospel of the Lord Jesus Christ is the good news of hope for any and all on this special day.

PREACHING THE GREAT DAYS OF THE CHRISTIAN CALENDAR

Father's Day

Luke 15:11–32

Dr. O. S. Hawkins

Father's Day... a time for new neckties, family lunches, long-distance calls, and greeting cards. It also affords us an opportunity to examine a model father, the kind of dad every kid deserves.

I had a dad who was very predictable. I remember him as being always there for me. In fact, I can hardly think of a "first" in my life that wasn't marked by his presence. He was there for my first breath... my first word ... my first step ... my first day of school ... my first ball glove ... my first car. My high school graduation, my college graduation, my seminary graduation all had his presence in common. Virtually every memory of my childhood and adolescence from vaccinations to vacations and from ball games to baccalaureates were all memorable experiences for me because of him. Growing up I never wondered or worried if the bills got paid, if the lawn got mowed, or if we would have a roof over our heads. One might think it strange that there are not a lot of pictures of him to be found in the family photo album. He was always the one behind the camera making sure everyone else had a good time and that it was well documented in pictures.

Not everyone on this Father's Day is fortunate enough to have had a father like that. And then, I suppose, some who did might have even taken dad for granted. Some today will be a father someday themselves. Thus, I want to plant a seed in our minds about the kind of father every child deserves.

More and more we are evolving into a matriarchal society. God never intended for this. Today there are too many men who are opting to leave instead of love. Others have virtually abdicated their place of leadership in the home. The presence of a father is an integral key to the success of the home.

Quite honestly, there are not a lot of role models for fathers today. However, there is one who is tucked into one of the parables told by our Lord. He is often overlooked in the story due to the emphasis that is placed on one or the other of his two sons. We call them the prodigal son and the elder brother. I would venture to say that over 90 percent of the messages we hear on this passage of Scripture have one of the two boys on center stage. Yet, the story is really not about them at all. It is about the father. Note how Jesus begins the parable, "A certain man had two sons" (Luke 15:11). Who is the subject of the sentence? The sons? No, the father. He is on center stage here. He is the subject not only of the opening sentence but of the whole story.

Here is a picture of a model father from whom we can all learn some valuable lessons on this Father's Day. Look at him. He is foresighted. He is forbearing. He is forgiving. He is forgetful. And, he is focused. Let's not simply look at him today but learn from him some valuable life lessons.

The Model Father Is Foresighted

> *"A certain man had two sons and the younger of them said to his father, 'Father, give me the portion of goods that falls to me.' So he divided to them his livelihood." (Luke 15:11–12)*

The model father is foresighted. By this we mean that he knows that what he puts into his child at a young age is going to determine what he becomes and how he behaves in later years. Thus, he is an example himself and imparts into his son some absolutes.

The model father teaches the truth to his children from infancy through adolescence. Remember, Jesus was telling this story to Jews (Luke 15:1–2). These were people who had a rich heritage in the Mosaic law with its parental responsibilities well defined. Just before the children of Israel entered their Promised Land, Moses gathered them together and said, "And these words which I command you today shall be in your heart. You shall teach them diligently to your children, and shall talk of them when you sit in your house, when you walk by the way, when you lie down, and when you rise up. You shall bind them as a sign on your hand, and they shall be as frontlets between your eyes. You shall write them on the doorposts of your house and on your gates" (Deut. 6:4–9).

The model father teaches his children the Scripture. He is an example before them in life and lip. He is not merely a "hearer of the Word" but a "doer of the Word" before his family. He has the foresight to know that his actions speak even louder than his words. He gives his children some absolutes. Thus, in the case of the father and his prodigal there are some moral values instilled there from which the son rebels at times.

If we are going to be the kind of father that any child deserves, then we need this type of foresight ourselves. We need to not simply be a material provider (that is important) and not simply a mental provider (and, that is important) but a moral provider as well, instilling Scripture and absolutes into our children.

The Model Father Is Forbearing

"...he divided to them his livelihood..." (Luke 15:12–20)

The model father is forbearing. That is, he is restrained. He lets the boy go when the time comes (Luke 15:12–13). He realizes that some sons seem to have to learn the hard way. This dad could have refused to let the boy go. He could have blackmailed him with the inheritance. He could have played the guilt game, "How could you do this to your mother and me?" There are times when the model father knows what is best but still lets his son go.

I am a dad myself and I have tried to put myself in his shoes. Here is a boy, after all his dad has done for him, who comes and thumbs his nose at his dad. This father could have played the comparison game, "Why can't you be like your older, obedient brother?" There are all sorts of games and innuendos that could have been played at this time.

But here we find a dad who, evidently, was prepared to stand by what he had put in that boy from childhood. He knew the truth of King Solomon's words, that we should "Train up a child in the way he should go, And when he is old he will not depart from it" (Prov. 22:6). The key word here is "train." This promise is not for one who simply sends his child to Sunday school for one hour out of a 168-hour week. This is a promise to the dad who has "trained" his child by life and lip and love and through the investment of his most valuable commodity, his time.

The model father is not simply foresighted, he is forbearing. He restrained himself. He lets the boy become a man. Some dads never learn this. Some continue to hold their children so tightly that they lose them in the very process. This dad let the boy go. He didn't send one of his servants to spy on him. As much as his own heart was breaking and as much as he knew what hard lessons lay ahead for his son, he let him go. I wonder how many of us are willing to forbear, respect our children's autonomy when they have come of age, and are willing to release them. Yes, he let him go. But, he never gave up on him.

Many of us are tolerant up to a point. Then we somehow and so often lose our patience. This father just kept being faithful at home, living with a broken heart at times but never giving up. The boy left home to be free. But he became a slave to those things he thought would give him independence. This generally happens when we get outside the umbrella of authority God has placed in the home and in our lives.

I love the way verse 17 describes what happened. It says the boy "came to himself." All those years of loving training paid off. The boy had been taught better and he knew it. And so, he heads for home hoping to simply become a hired servant.

I can almost see this dad now standing on his porch or perhaps working in the fields but always keeping an eye on the horizon, looking down that road in hopes the boy would come home. And the Scripture says that finally one day, "And he arose and came to his father. But when he was still a great way off, his father saw him and had compassion, and ran and fell on his neck and kissed him" (Luke 15:20). He never gave up.

The Model Father Is Forgiving

> *"... the father saw him and had compassion, and ran and fell on his neck and kissed him." (Luke 15:20)*

Yes, the model father is forgiving. When the boy was a long way down that road, the father started running to him. The boy may have come walking, but dad came running.

The boy began his speech (Luke 15:15–18) but he never got to give it. The father was full of forgiveness. What a dad! He ran to him with a warm welcome. There was no, "How could you have done this to us?" There was no, "Where have you been all this time?" There was no, "What did you do with the money?" There was no, "I hope you are happy now." There was no, "I told you so." There was only a warm, "Welcome home, son."

This dad had "compassion." This word comes from two Latin words that mean "to suffer with." Thus, dad knew what the boy had been through; he knew what was in his heart. The boy had come home hoping to become a hired servant, and dad restored him in forgiveness to his rightful place as an honored son.

Yes, the kind of dad every child needs is not simply one who is foresighted and forbearing but one who is forgiving as well.

The Model Father Is Forgetful

> *"... bring the best robe ... put a ring on his hand ... kill the fatted calf ... this, my son, was lost and now he is found ..." (Luke 15:22–24)*

It is one thing to forgive but quite another to forget. This model father does not hold a grudge. He forgives ... and he also forgets. He allows his boy a place of beginning again. He could have said, "Welcome home, son. I forgive you but you have got a lot of proving to do around here." But he didn't. He put it all behind him.

Now, to say that the model father forgets does not mean that there should be no rules in particular cases of certain prodigals' returns. Remember, we are not seeing a boy here in this story who came home with a rebellious spirit. What is the difference? We are witnessing a boy here who truly repented. He regretted his deed. "He came to himself" (Luke 15:17). He blamed himself for his actions. Hear him say, "Father, I have sinned against heaven and before you and am no more worthy to be called your son" (Luke 15:18). He acknowledged his father's right to be displeased. He said, "I am no more worthy to be called your son" (Luke 15:19). And, he resolved in his heart to not repeat his mistake. "He arose and came to his father" (Luke 15:20).

Repentance involves a change of attitude, which will result in a change of affections, which results in a change of action. This process is illustrated beautifully in this boy's own repentance. First, he changed his mind, his attitude ... "He came to himself." Next, this changed his will, his volition, his affections ... He said, "I will arise and go to my father." And then, this led to a change in action ... "He arose and went home." Here was a dad who could not simply forgive but forget, because here was a son who came home with a truly repentant spirit.

When we forgive, we ought to forget. God does. Aren't we glad He doesn't deal with us "according to our sins" (Ps. 103:10) but according to "His tender mercies" (Ps. 51:1)? The model father is forgetful. And aren't we thankful?

The Model Father Is Focused

> *"...he [the elder brother] was angry and would not go in ... you never gave me a young goat that I might make merry with my friends." (Luke 15:28–29)*

The model father is focused. That is to say that he has his priorities in order and keeps things in proper perspective. Note that in verse 29, the sulking elder brother is complaining about never having been given a young goat as a party feast with his own friends. Think about that. We are talking here about the "fatted calf" (Luke 15:23). To complain about never receiving a young goat at a time like this was sheer folly. This older brother had lost all sense of perspective. How fortunate were these boys to have had a dad who was focused on the right things.

The party is now in full swing. The festivities are at a high. But where is dad? No one can find him. He is outside with his older son helping him to get things in focus and proper perspective. He is assuring the older brother he is "always with him," that "all that I have is yours"; and he is keeping the focus on the fact that it is right to party, for the younger brother had been lost and now was found. The truth is, life goes on and so must we.

Ironically, we are never told how the story ends. The Lord just concludes it without our ever knowing what happened. Did the older brother go in to the party? We simply do not know. Perhaps our Lord left this shrouded in silence in order for you to finish the story yourself on this Father's Day.

This is a beautiful picture of a model father. But the real message on this special day is that this is really a picture of our own heavenly Father. He is foresighted … so much so that He knew that without a substitutionary sacrifice we could never make peace with ourselves or with God. Thus, He gave us not only some absolutes but the gift of His own Son that we might be born into His family.

Like the model father in Jesus' story, our heavenly Father is also forbearing. He lets us go. We are people, not puppets, and the love we can voluntarily return to Him is indescribably valuable to Him. And, He never gives up on us. He is forgiving and forgetful. In fact, He said, "I will forgive their iniquity, and their sin I will remember no more" (Jer. 31:34). And, He is focused. He has everything concerning us in proper perspective.

Isn't it time, on this Father's Day morning, that we complete this story? When we do, we will find Him just like the prodigal son found his father … with wide and forgiving open arms and the promise of a new beginning.

PREACHING THE GREAT DAYS OF THE CHRISTIAN CALENDAR

Independence Day

Jeremiah 8:5–22

Dr. O. S. Hawkins

We are the "prefix generation." We describe many things in our contemporary culture with the use of the prefix. For example, the prefix "mega." We have megabytes, megachurches, even mega-dittos. A prominent prefix today is "eco," as in ecotones and ecosystems. America is presently in the midst of an ecotonic moment in time. An "ecotone" is a technological word from the world of biology that describes a particular place where two ecosystems merge and blend together. I first heard of the word while living in the city of Fort Lauderdale, Florida. There is a particular place where the intercoastal waterway and the New River come together and form an ecotone. The salt water from the Atlantic Ocean flows into Port Everglades and into the intercoastal waterway. From the Everglades, just west of Fort Lauderdale, the fresh water flows through the New River making its way toward the ocean. At the particular place where this salt water and fresh water blend and merge together, an ecotone develops. Ecotones are places of tremendous possibility. Often fish lay their eggs there. Ecotones can also be very problematic to those who are engaged in the battles of ecology.

At this point in time we are experiencing an ecotonic stage in American life. Two worlds are blending and merging together at the same time. One is a modern world and the other a postmodern world. The world in which many of us in the baby boomer generation were educated is history. All the cumulative knowledge of world history will double within the next few years. Our world is transforming at breakneck speed into a postmodern era. This presents a time of tremendous possibility for those of us who can translate the message of our Christian heritage to a world that is in desperate need without changing the heart of its message. It is also a time of tremendous problems for those who are seeking to translate the gospel to our world in the same way we did ten, twenty, or thirty years ago. The Western world is not so much in debate over whether the Bible is true as it is in whether it is relevant. That is, does this Book written in an ancient Middle Eastern culture have any relevancy in a world where we are transplanting organs, going to the moon, and experimenting with genetic engineering. They will never know unless we deal with some of the major questions of our day.

We are living and ministering in a day when the church's influence is waning in a secular society. We are seeing the product of an entire generation that has been reared with virtually no moral absolutes in the home, in many of their schools, and tragically in many of their churches. This past Sunday Great Britain saw less than 5 percent of its population in any kind of house of worship. History records that civilizations that see the collapse of the home and accompanying moral values do not last past one or two generations unless a spiritual awakening occurs. In America we are watching the disintegration of a culture in our own lifetime. We have lost the concept of personal responsibility for our own transgressions, and all of our maladies have become someone else's fault.

When I walked through the Vietnam Memorial in our nation's capital, I saw name after name etched in the granite wall of young people who left their homes and never came back. Some of those names were more than just letters etched in granite; they were personal friends from my high school days. As I looked at that wall, I realized that they would be in their middle age today. If by some miracle they could step out of that wall and go back to their hometowns, they would see a world that is totally different from the one they knew. They would wonder why we have become a nation where over half of our marriages end in divorce. As they walked the streets of their small towns and cities, they would wonder why the Judeo-Christian ethic was but a memory. As they revisited their schoolhouses, they would be shocked to learn that it is now illegal for children to pray in the same classrooms where they were educated. They would be floored to realize that the Gideons could no longer hand them a New Testament on the campuses of their schools, but organizations like Planned Parenthood are often free to dispense condoms at no charge. They would be surprised to discover that in many of their small towns the traditional manger scene was no longer on the courthouse lawn. They would be shocked to see that homosexual lifestyles were legitimized and promoted by much of the rhetoric, appointments, and actions of those who live in high places. As they visited their schools, they would be shocked to pass through metal detectors and see that teenage pregnancy was rampant. Those who lost their lives at such a young age would be appalled to hear that we legally kill 1.5 million babies a year in America today through abortion. As they strolled past the vacant lots and playgrounds of their neighborhoods, they would be shocked at the way they are terrorized by gangs and drive-by shootings. As they looked around, they would wonder what happened to the male leadership that has disappeared from so many of the homes of America.

We should make no mistake about it. The United States is morally bankrupt in large part because we have been led by a liberal philosophy that has made false assumptions about two particular things; the nature of the universe, and the nature of mankind. Liberal philosophy seldom asks "why." It only asks "what." One can take almost any issue. Take the issue of drugs. Few in the liberal establishment are asking "why." Most of them only ask "what." What can we do about this problem? So we dispense free needles to try to clean up the process. This particular point is seen daily with the issue of the HIV virus and the accompanying AIDS epidemic. Not enough people in Washington are asking "why." It does not seem to be politically correct. So we only ask "what." What can we do about the AIDS epidemic? And the answers we are given are more education, how to have safe sex, and the like. We are asking "what" when we ought to be asking "why" about these major moral issues of life. Have you ever thought about why we are called "conservatives"? We are trying to conserve something. We are trying to conserve some traditional moral values that have made America what it has been in the past. These values were conserved by people asking "why" and not "what."

The prophet of old, Jeremiah, lived and ministered in a day much like ours. The nation of Judah had been blessed. They had prospered, but they forgot their roots. They forgot their God. They began to think they were indestructible, and the final result came in 586 BC when they were defeated by Nebuchadnezzar and taken away into Babylonian captivity. Jeremiah was a man who lived with a burden for the way in which his country had turned its back on God. He had seen the blessing. Now he observed the collapse and corruption from within. With a weeping heart he asks, "Where is the Lord, Who brought us up out of the land of Egypt?" (Jer. 2:6). Then he came straight to the bottom line by quoting the Lord Himself, "They have turned their back to Me, and not their face" (Jer. 2:27). As I read these words in this Book of all books, I cannot help but see our own America. I believe God is asking today, "Where is the Lord, Who brought you out of Egypt?" . . . I believe He is asking us, "Why have you turned your back to Me and not your face?" Jeremiah asks four hard questions in chapter 8 of the book that bears his name. Interestingly enough, unlike the liberalism of our day, he did not ask "what." Jeremiah asked "why." These are the four "why's" America needs to be asking herself today. There is a question for the American public, "Why has this people slidden back?" (Jer. 8:5). There is a question for the American pew, "Why do we sit still?" (Jer. 8:14). There is a question for the American politician, "Why have we provoked God to anger?" (Jer. 8:19). There is a question for the American pulpit, "Why is there no recovery?" (Jer. 8:22). Is there a recovery for the Western world?

What would happen if the people, the president, and the pastors of the United States would stand up before the American people and stop asking "what" and begin to seriously probe and ask "why." If the public would seriously ask, "Why have we slidden back?" If the people in the pew would seriously ask, "Why do we sit still?" If the politicians would seriously ask, "Why have we provoked a holy God to anger?" If the pulpits of the land would seriously ask, "Why does there seem to be no recovery?" Let's ask ourselves these questions of Jeremiah's day today:

A question for the American public: Why has this people slidden back?

> *Why has this people slidden back, Jerusalem, in a perpetual backsliding? They hold fast to deceit, they refuse to return. (Jer. 8:5)*

Jeremiah says that the people of his nation "hold fast to deceit, they refuse to return." That is, they and we continue to believe a lie. America seems to be without a knowledge of spiritual things today. We hold fast to deceit and refuse to return. On February 4, 1995, the *Dallas Morning News* carried a guest column by then Mayor Steve Bartlett. He said, "Up until thirty years ago, strong moral values were a part of our daily lives and experiences. They were a part of everything that we did. But in the course of those thirty years we've walked away from those values and put them in a closet. I don't know *why* [emphasis mine] that happened. I only know that it happened." Thirty years ago? Mr. Mayor, you are right. Let us remember what happened thirty years earlier. For one thing the Supreme Court struck down school prayer by prohibiting this simple invocation, "Almighty God we acknowledge our dependency upon you and beg your blessings on us, our parents, our teachers, and our country." That was it! No mention of the Lord Jesus Christ. It was just a simple petition asking God to bless four things—the students, the parents, the teachers, and the country. It is shocking to examine what has happened to those four entities since 1965. The invocation struck down by the Supreme Court called for God's blessings upon "us" (that is, the students). What has happened to the American student? We have the highest rate of teen motherhood in the Western world. Each year one million teenage girls become pregnant. In my own city of Dallas, some schools are equipped with as many as forty nursery beds to take care of the babies that are born from teen mothers who are still in school. Should we be surprised when we have asked "what" instead of "why" throughout these years? We ask "what" can we do about the dilemmas, and so we decided to hand out condoms and forbid groups like Gideons to pass out New Testaments. The petition asked the blessing of God upon our "parents." What has happened to parenthood in America since 1965? We lead the world in divorce. One and one-half million children run away from home every year. Sex abuse seems to be rampant, and the home is disintegrating. But the liberal establishment is only asking "what." The third part of the petition was the invocation of a blessing upon our "teachers." What has happened to the American education system since 1965? In *Stone v. Gramm* in 1980 the court decided, "If posted copies of the Ten Commandments are to have any effect at all, it would be to induce children to meditate upon them and perhaps obey, and this is not permissible. The First Amendment protects it." God forbid that a child obey one of the Ten Commandments. And the result for teachers? School violence, metal detectors, and plummeting SAT scores. The final request was a blessing of God upon our "country." What has happened to the United States of America in the last thirty years? Violent crime is up five hundred times over what it was in those days. It is no longer safe to walk on many of the streets of the cities and towns of America. And, here we are asking "what." The real question is "why?" Why has this occurred? Because so many good people have done nothing.

Jeremiah goes on to say that, "My people do not know the judgment of the Lord" (Jer. 8:7). It seems as though he's speaking of America and not Judah. The judgment of God is seldom heard in any of the pulpits of America any longer. Speak of the judgment of God in the city of Washington, D.C., and you'll be scoffed and laughed out of town by the social elite. But God has not abdicated His throne. He is still in control. As Daniel says, "He still rules over the affairs of men." Ask Israel if this is true. Ask Judah if this is true. Ask Rome or the former Union of Soviet Socialist Republics. Jeremiah says that "Even the stork in the heavens knows her appointed times; and the turtledove, the swift, and the swallow observe the time of their coming" (Jer. 8:7). But Judah did not, nor does America. We have less wisdom than a bird.

Jeremiah continues as though he were speaking to the issues of our own day. Hear him ask, "How can you say, 'We are wise and the law of the Lord is with us?' . . . they have rejected the word of the Lord; so what wisdom do they have?" (Jer. 8:8–9). Is anything more applicable to the United States of America than these words? We have rejected the Word of God for the wisdom of man's own agenda, and we wonder why as the question comes in verse 5, "Why has this people slidden back?" He goes on quoting the Lord Himself, "I will give your wives to others" (Jer. 8:10). Does this sound like America where over half of the marriages end in divorce? Is the judgment of God upon this nation? Jeremiah speaks of those who say, "'Peace, peace!' When there is no peace" (Jer. 8:11). Those in Washington put their spin doctors on every issue saying, "'Peace, peace!' When there is no peace."

Jeremiah speaks to his people and so poignantly to us about the greatest tragedy of all when he says, "Were they ashamed when they had committed abomination? No! They were not at all ashamed, nor did they know how to blush" (Jer. 8:12). This is our greatest tragedy. There seems to be no shame. There is a blatant disregard in much of America for anything that is moral or pure. But we should not blame the politicians for the moral collapse of America. We need to put it where it belongs, at the feet of the church. Biblical moral standards are forgotten in an attempt to appease an immoral culture, and in some ways to "market" the church to a secular world.

It would do us all well to remember that the context of Jeremiah 8 is found in 2 Chronicles 34. In that particular chapter good King Josiah had begun to ask some "why's" instead of "what's." His trusted friend Hilkiah had discovered the Word of God, which had been lost in the house of God. He brought it to the king, and a tremendous turning to God ensued. This is our greatest need, that the church would find this Book and take it to the king. The king led that nation to take a stand on the Word of God, and the country began to prosper once again.

Why is this people slidden back? That's a good question. Jeremiah goes on to quote the Lord Himself. "The things I have given them shall pass away from them" (Jer. 8:13). If God said this of Judah, the apple of His eye, why do you think He wouldn't say the same of any other nation? If America does not start dealing with the "why's" instead of the "what's," judgment is coming. America no longer believes that God controls the created order. We may give Him the occasional tip of a hat at a prayer breakfast or the like, but He by and large has no place in the affairs of men, particularly in the places of power. The question is not "what." The question is "why." Jeremiah continues with another "why."

A question for the American pew: Why do we sit still?

> *Why do we sit still? Assemble yourselves, and let us enter the fortified cities, and let us be silent there. For the Lord our God has put us to silence and given us water of gall to drink, because we have sinned against the Lord. (Jer. 8:14)*

Many Americans have bought into the liberal lies, media manipulation, and public propaganda. The tragedy is the church sits by with a false confidence based on lying words saying, "Peace, peace, when there is no peace." We need to ask ourselves the question, "Why do we sit still?" It has not always been the case.

On a trip to our nation's capital, my wife, Susie, and I walked from our hotel to the Capitol building. After passing through the rotunda, we headed down the corridor toward the House chamber. We entered a rather large room lined with statues of great Americans around the wall, and soon we discovered it was the original House chamber. In that particular room the House of Representatives met for scores of years before the larger chamber was built adjacent to it. While observing some of the statues in that great hall, we noticed a group over to the side with a guide in a red sport jacket lecturing. We moved over near the group to listen. This Capitol guide was in conversation regarding the issue of separation of church and state. He was explaining how that for the first seventy-five years the House of Representatives met in this room, and they opened it on Sunday mornings to an evangelical, gospel-preaching

Protestant church that held services there for seventy-five years. He went on to explain how the First Presbyterian Church (now the National Presbyterian Church) held its Sunday services during those years in the chamber of the Supreme Court Building across the street. As I listened to those incredible truths that have somehow been buried in our nation's history, I asked myself the question—"Why do we sit still?"

Don't listen to those who say that religious principles played little part in the founding of the United States of America. Don't listen to those who say that we were basically not built on a Judeo-Christian philosophy but on more of a pluralistic, deistic philosophy. Forever etched in the charters of the original thirteen colonies is the gospel truth. Rhode Island was established in 1683, and in their charter they said, "We submit ourselves, our lives, our estates unto the Lord Jesus Christ, the King of Kings, and the Lord of Lords, and to all those perfect and most absolute laws given in His Holy Word." Maryland's charter says it was "formed by a pious zeal to extend the Christian gospel." Delaware was "formed for the further propagation of the holy gospel." When the founders of Connecticut wrote their charter, they said that Connecticut was there to "preserve the purity of the gospel of the Lord Jesus Christ." It certainly doesn't sound like Connecticut was too pluralistic in its beginnings. There has been talk of Washington, D.C., becoming the fifty-first state. Can you imagine how their charter might read?

We wonder why in the words of Jeremiah we as a people are "slidden back" and we in the pew "sit still." The answer is in the fact that the salt has lost its savor. Sometime ago I received a form letter from the head of Americans United for the Separation of Church and State in which he was bemoaning the fact that some Christian ministers in America were trying to, in his words, "Christianize America." I am unapologetically trying to Christianize America and the entire world for that matter! This is the commission our Lord gave us before He left. One of my pastoral predecessors at the First Baptist Church in Dallas, the late and great Dr. George W. Truett, stood on the Capitol steps of our nation on May 16, 1920, and gave one of the greatest messages on religious liberty ever heard. In the course of his message, he said, "The one transcending and inspiring influence in victory is the Christian faith. Civilization without Christianity is doomed. Let there be no hesitation nor apology for the insistence that the one hope for the individual, the one hope for society, for civilization, is the Christian religion." That doesn't sound like tolerance to me.

Jeremiah's question comes thundering down through the corridors of the centuries to us today—"Why do we sit still?" America's biggest problem is an apathetic church who has lost her first love. And in losing that first love, we have also lost our influence. We have simply sat still for a generation. When I see certain political leaders with their own agendas contrary to the Word of God coming out of church on Sunday being photographed with Bibles in their hands and waving to the television cameras, the words of Jeremiah 7:9–10 echo in my mind—"Will you steal, murder, commit adultery, swear falsely, burn incense to Baal, and walk after other gods whom you do not know, and then come and stand before Me in this house which is called by My name, and say, 'We are delivered to do all these abominations'?" In the midst of a changing ecotonic world that can go either way, we must stop asking "what" and begin to ask "why." Why are we slidden back? Why do we sit still? Jeremiah continues with another question.

A question for the American politician: Why have they provoked Me to anger?

> *Listen! The voice, the cry of the daughter of my people from a far country: "Is not the Lord in Zion? Is not her King in her?" "Why have they provoked Me to anger with their carved images—with foreign idols?" (Jer. 8:19)*

God asks us another question through Jeremiah's prayer—"Why have they provoked Me to anger with their carved images, with foreign idols?" America did not abandon God. We just made Him one of many others. New Age humanistic thought that exalts man over Christ has taken center stage. It is no wonder those with liberal agendas do not want the Ten Commandments in the classroom. The very first one says, "You shall have no other gods before Me." He is a jealous God. We have supported a pluralism that tolerates a form of Christianity that does not make any demands on a culture. It is a form of Christianity that only asks "what" and never asks "why." Christianity is not just another person's opinion. It is objective truth. We have provoked a holy God to anger in that we have allowed other gods to share His glory.

How did the early Christians engage their culture? What was it about them that caused the Roman Empire to put them to death in the Coliseum and other places of public exploitation and execution? Why the Christians when other conquered peoples of the world did not meet the same fate? The answer is found in one of the ruins of Rome. It is called the Pantheon, the temple of all gods. Some time ago while returning from a trip to Africa, I visited this impressive edifice. As you walk into the temple, you find around all of the walls niches carved in the stone. When the Romans would conquer a certain people who, for example, might worship the god Jupiter, they would bring them to the Pantheon and say here is a niche for Jupiter. You can worship him any time you desire. They appeased their conquered peoples in such a fashion. Perhaps they conquered a people who worshiped the goddess Juno. They would bring them there to the Pantheon and give them a niche for Juno. When they brought the Christians back to Rome in triumph of their military conquest, they took them also to the Pantheon. In effect, they said we are going to give you a niche for Jesus here between Jupiter and Juno. The Christians said no! There is only one Lord, and they gave their lives for that.

Agnostic, apathetic America has no sense that we have provoked a holy God to anger. In fact, we scoff at the idea. He says, "Do not commit murder." And we kill 1.5 million babies a year. He says, "Do not commit adultery." And we live in a sex-crazed society. When Paul wrote the Roman letter, he foresaw Rome's coming collapse, and in chapter 1 spoke of a culture that had been given over to depraved minds.

Is there a recovery? Yes, the most important thing we can do is call upon the name of the Lord in prayer, and then begin to ask some "why's" and elect some leaders with character and genuine moral backbone. It was not the Babylonians who brought Judah low. God only used them. It was God Himself who did it. Why? The answer is in 2 Chronicles 28:19, "For the Lord brought Judah low because of Ahaz king of Israel, for he had encouraged moral decline in Judah and had been continually unfaithful to the Lord."

What did God do? God Himself brought the nation of Judah low. We can blame it on economics, budget deficits, the welfare system, the collapse of moral values, but God still rules in the affairs of men. There is someone in Washington not being factored into the equation. Our leadership is blind to the fact that "the Most High rules in the kingdom of men" (Dan. 4:32). Could it be that behind all the politics is God Himself allowing all of this to happen in America?

What did God do to the nation of Judah? He brought them low. Why? Because their leader, their king, had encouraged a moral decline in the land. Ahaz was personally immoral and unfaithful, and his policies reflected his own character. It is one thing to be immoral, but another to "encourage a moral decline in the land." We have had presidents of the United States in the past who have been known for immoral acts. But it is quite another thing to encourage immorality through people and policies. A leader encourages a moral decline in the land when he takes a pen in hand and signs an executive order permitting the bodies of aborted babies to be used in research. A leader encourages a moral decline in the land when he only asks "what" and seldom ever asks "why."

Leaders of nations bear moral responsibilities, and we do ourselves a tremendous injustice if we do not elect godly men and women to leadership.

America is agnostic toward spiritual things. We seem to have an "in your face" attitude toward a holy God. There appears to be no real sense in the executive, legislative, or judicial branches of government that we are provoking a holy God to anger. So we continue on our way asking "what" when we ought to be asking "why." Why have we slidden back? Why do we sit still? Why have we provoked God to anger? Jeremiah asks the final "why."

A question for the American pulpit: Why is there no recovery?

> *Is there no balm in Gilead, is there no physician there? Why then is there no recovery for the health of the daughter of my people? (Jer. 8:22)*

Is there any answer? Is it too late? People in Jeremiah's day did not repent, and there was no recovery. They were taken into Babylonian captivity and hung their harps on the willow trees of Babylon because they could not sing the Lord's song in a foreign land. Jeremiah asks, "Is there no balm in Gilead, is there no physician there? Why then is there no recovery for the health of the daughter of my people?" (Jer. 8:22). Yes, there is indeed a health care crisis in America today, but it is not primarily physical nor mental. It is a spiritual health care crisis.

Is it too late for us as it was for Judah? Where is the answer? Is there no balm in Gilead? Is there no physician here? Yes, there is a Great Physician. If you go to your personal physician with a physical need, he examines you and gives you a prescription. God gives us a prescription in Jeremiah 3:22, "Return, you backsliding children, and I will heal your backslidings." Yes, thank God, there is still a Physician. The return begins with you and me. Not the politicians. Not the school systems. But with the church of Jesus Christ.

We are living in what has become more and more of a pagan culture not unlike the one with which the early church was confronted. In fact, they were under a tremendous amount of persecution we have really not seen in America as of yet. For example, in Acts 12 the leader of the church in Jerusalem, Simon Peter, was incarcerated by the authorities for his moral stands and for the gospel's sake. Acts 12:5 says, "Peter was therefore kept in prison, but constant prayer was offered to God for him by the church." The church of Jesus Christ has forgotten our primary battlefield. It is very difficult to win a war if we do not know where the battle is being fought. Some of us have forgotten this. That is, while Peter was kept in prison, the church was praying earnestly for him. If Acts 12:5 had been written about the twenty-first century church, it might read, "Peter was kept in prison, but the church picketed City Hall in behalf of him." It might read, "Peter was kept in prison, but the church protested with a mass campaign in his behalf." It might read, "Peter was kept in prison, but the church took over the local precincts in order to make some changes in the elected officials." It might say, "Peter was kept in prison, but the church signed petitions in his behalf." This early church engaged their culture. How? They had the power of God upon them. They knew where the battle was being fought. Go to Ephesus today and walk through the ancient ruins of that first-century metropolis. It amazed me as I did so. As I walked through the amphitheater, down the streets, into the bathhouses and the libraries and the temples of that ancient world, I wondered, how was that city captured for Christ? Paul went there with just a couple of friends and engaged the culture and saw the transformation of a whole city. How? There was no explanation for it but the power of God. The power of God in response to a praying church. If some of us who are called by the name of the Lord would spend as much time listening to God as we do certain talk show hosts on the radio or television, we would be on our way to revival. Some of us do not think we need God because we have a conservative political agenda to follow.

There is a remedy for us. It is the only remedy, and it is not found in the ballot box or on television ads or in curriculum. The remedy is found at the foot of a Roman cross outside the city walls of Jerusalem where the conquering Christ was "made sin for us that we might become the righteousness of God in Him." We are living in the most important days of American history. It is indeed an ecotonic moment in our nation's history. Two worlds are blending and merging together. It is a time of tremendous possibility. It is not too late, if we stop asking "what?" and begin to ask "why?" There is a question for the American public. "Why are we slidden back?" We have forgotten our roots. There is a question for the American pew. "Why do we sit still?" Has an apathetic church forgotten where the battle is being fought? There is a question for the American politician. "Why have we provoked a holy God to anger?" Have we have shared His glory with other gods around us? And, there is a question for the American pulpit. "Why is there no remedy? Is there no balm in Gilead? Is there no physician there?" Yes, the Great Physician is still ready and willing to bless our nation as He did in the beginning. Jeremiah said it best when he said, "ask for the old paths, where the good way is, and walk in it; then you will find rest for your souls" (Jer. 6:16).

What is America's greatest need? Don't blame politicians for the moral collapse. Don't point the finger at the education system. All these are simply fruits of a root problem. We have a generation in America that does not know Christ primarily because the church has not made Him known. What is our greatest need? It is found in 2 Chronicles 34. The church of Jesus Christ needs to find the Book of God in the house of God and take it to the king!

I have tremendous hope in the future of America. I believe we could very well be on the threshold of another genuine spiritual awakening in our land. Could it be that as in the days of Josiah, God is about to give us a reprieve, a revival if you please, before He returns? Do you remember the parable of the unjust judge that is recorded for all posterity in Luke 18? A widow came to him for justice and got none. This was a judge who "did not fear God, nor regard man," and did not fear this woman. But she didn't sit still. She kept coming to his door. Knock, knock, knock, but he didn't open the door. He did not fear God. He did not fear man, and he did not fear this woman. She came again. Knock, knock, knock. But he did not open because he did not fear God, nor man, nor this woman. She continued to knock, but he did not open because he did not fear God, nor man, nor this woman. She kept on knocking, and finally he opened the door. At this point the Lord Jesus said, "How much more will your heavenly Father open the door to you if you keep petitioning Him?" Then He said, "Men ought always to pray and not lose heart." Don't give up on America. Keep on praying, and keep on knocking!

PREACHING THE GREAT DAYS OF THE CHRISTIAN CALENDAR

Sanctity of Life Day

Deuteronomy 30:19

Dr. O. S. Hawkins

"Legal personhood does not exist prenatally." So declared the United States Supreme Court in the now infamous *Roe v. Wade* decision handed down on January 22, 1973. Since that day, millions of babies have been legally aborted in our nation. In its aftermath has not only come the elimination of millions of lives, but tragic trauma to millions of mothers. "Legal personhood does not exist prenatally." Tell that to the lady who wrote me these words:

"Nearing forty years of age and after four children, I found myself pregnant. My husband suggested abortion. I knew in my heart it was wrong. I have suffered supreme remorse ever since. Our home has one empty bedroom—a constant reminder! The doctors could control my problem, but nobody can control my hurt and loss of a very precious life that God Himself created. I carry this around now and for the rest of my life this awful memory, the hurt is all mine. You can tell young women who may be considering abortion that a woman never forgets her baby. The memory lives on and on."

On July 1, 1976, the week of our National Bicentennial Celebration, the Supreme Court expanded its 1973 decision by declaring that abortions may be performed on minor daughters without the knowledge of their parents. It is a strange nation in which we are living where an adolescent cannot get an aspirin in a school infirmary without parental permission, but can have an abortion without such! The 1976 decision also expanded the 1973 decision to allow women to obtain an abortion without the knowledge or consent of the baby's father. While a father must pay child support in other cases (and rightly so), he is often left with no say as to whether his own child comes into the world or not.

Perhaps no other moral or social issue is as many faceted as is the abortion debate. Any serious discussion of the matter will eventually come down to one central issue—when does life begin? This is "the big question." Some say life begins at birth. They contend that until the baby is out of the womb it is not to be considered a human being, simply a "fetus." Others say life begins when the fetus has grown and developed enough to live outside the womb if need be. Consequently, this particular school of thought would say life begins at five to six months. Others say life begins when the baby has a measured brain wave. The argument here is that the secession of a brain wave marks the end of human life, and thus it naturally stands to reason that the beginning of the brain wave would be the beginning of human life. A brain wave can be measured at approximately six weeks after conception. Still others claim that life begins when the baby develops a measured heart beat. Such advocates thus place the beginning of life at approximately three to four weeks after conception. And, others would say that life begins at conception. That is, when the male cell and the female cell unite, thus beginning the life process.

When does life begin? Consider for a moment the argument from science. The nucleus of a human cell is composed of forty-six chromosomes. Twenty-three are furnished by the father, and twenty-three are furnished by the mother. The abortionists argue that during the embryonic stage of development and in the early stages of fetal development, the baby could not survive apart from the mother's body. Thus, their argument is that it is moral to eliminate the fetus if so desired. But the truth is, the same baby could not survive apart from the mother's care after it is born at nine months either. To follow this erroneous concept to its conclusion would be to go ahead and eliminate the baby even after birth.

It is a fact of biological science that the only cell that the mother contributes to the baby is the first one (twenty-three chromosomes) when it meets the father's cell and they combine. At this point conception takes place, and a new person is formed. In the cell structure, the baby is as much a part of the father as the mother. Obviously, during gestation the baby is nourished through the umbilical cord by the mother. But it should be noted that only the baby is nourished. The same baby, after birth, is also dependent upon being nourished by the mother outside the womb. After conception, the child receives no new or additional life from the mother. It is not a part of her body that can be removed like a wart or a tumor. It is an individual person.

It is amazing how abortion activists refrain from using the term "baby" for the unborn and instead cling to the less intimate word "fetus." It is as though this gives more of an appearance that the baby is simply a part of the mother's anatomy like a gall bladder or an appendix. It sounds so much better to say the fetus was extracted than to say the baby was killed. The pro-abortion activist might be interested to know that the word "fetus" is a Latin word. What does it mean in Latin? It is the word for "child." Life is a continual process, and each of us is a part of it. Some of us are newly conceived. Others are developing in the womb. Some are just born. Others are toddlers in the nursery. Some have completed the first day of school. Others are adolescents. Some are adults. Others are elderly. But we are all in a stage of gradual development. Man is no more or less a person at any stage of this development.

When does life begin? Consider for a moment the argument of Scripture. Just because many influenced by New Age persuasions have placed the Bible on the shelf as a worn-out book of antiquity, does not mean it is. Millions of people still hold its truths near and dear to their hearts. Its words and laws have been the foundation blocks for every decent democracy and republic in world history We believe it is revealed truth and our ultimate standard. Jesus stepped into manhood, not at His birth at Bethlehem, but at His conception at Nazareth. The Scripture records, "An angel of the Lord appeared to Joseph in a dream and said, 'Do not be afraid to take to you Mary as your wife, for that which is conceived in her is of the Holy Spirit'" (Matt. 1:20). To Mary, the angel announced, "And behold, you will conceive in your womb and bring forth a son, and shall call His name Jesus" (Luke 1:31).

As many are aware, the New Testament was written in the Greek language. It was the universal written language of the first-century world.

The Greeks have more than one word for our English word "child." The most common word, found over ninety-eight times in the Greek New Testament is the word *teknon*. The word speaks of a child as viewed in relation to a parent. However, there is an interesting word that is found only eight times in the Greek New Testament that throws much light upon what the Bible teaches regarding the unborn. It is the Greek word *brephos*. Note its usage in the following verses:

> *This man dealt treacherously with our people, and oppressed our forefathers, making them expose their babies [brephos], so that they might not live. (Acts 7:19)*

> *Then they also brought infants [brephos] to Him that He might touch them; but when the disciples saw it, they rebuked them. (Luke 18:15)*

> *And that from childhood [brephos] you have known the Holy Scriptures, which are able to make you wise for salvation through faith which is in Christ Jesus. (2 Tim. 3:15)*

> *As newborn babes [brephos], desire the pure milk of the word, that you may grow thereby. (1 Peter 2:2)*

> *And this will be the sign to you: You will find a Babe [brephos] wrapped in swaddling cloths, lying in a manger. (Luke 2:12)*

> *And they came with haste and found Mary and Joseph, and the Babe [brephos] lying in a manger. (Luke 2:16)*

In all the above verses the word *brephos* describes a baby who has already been born. One who is outside the womb! That is, a real live human being. But there are two other verses in Scripture in which the same Greek word (*brephos*) is used. One is in Luke 1:41 where Scripture records, "And it happened, when Elizabeth heard the greeting of Mary, that the babe [*brephos*] leaped in her womb; and Elizabeth was filled with the Holy Spirit." The other is found in Luke 1:44, "For indeed, as soon as the voice of your greeting sounded in my ears, the babe [*brephos*] leaped in my womb, for joy." Note in each of these cases, the *brephos* (baby) is still in the womb. It is blatantly clear that God considers an unborn baby more than simply a wad of tissue. He considers the *brephos* as much a human being as the child who is already born and playing, running up and down the street. In God's vocabulary, the little package of love in the uterus is a *brephos* just as much as the toddler in the play-pen! He uses the same word to identify them both.

There is even a sense in which the issue of life goes back beyond science and Scripture. Yes, back even before conception into the Eternal Councils of Creator God. God deals with us not only after our birth for all eternity, but before our birth and conception and all eternity past. To Jeremiah, God said, "Before I formed you in the womb I knew you; before you were born I sanctified you; I ordained you a prophet to the nations" (Jer. 1:4–5). "My mother might have been my grave" (Jer. 20:17). If an abortion had been performed upon the fetus in Jeremiah's mother's womb, he still would have been Jeremiah. Although his mother may not have known his name, God did! Yes, life begins even before conception in the eternal councils of God. The great apostle Paul put it like this, "Just as He chose us in Him before the foundation of the world, that we should be holy and without blame before Him in love" (Eph. 1:4).

Thus, if life is present at conception, as both science and Scripture certainly reveal, then as a Christian there is no such thing as neutrality. Solomon, the wisest man who ever lived, said, "Deliver those who are drawn toward death, and hold back those stumbling to the slaughter. If you say, 'Surely we did not know this,' does not He who weighs the hearts consider it? He who keeps your soul, does He not know it? And will He not render to each man according to his deeds?" (Prov. 24:11–12).

The main reason convenience abortions on demand are the law of the land is not because of the militant minority of the women liberationists and politicians, but primarily because moral people do nothing and say little as we walk by on the other side of the street ignoring this national blight. Perhaps the thing that is most amazing is the silence of the grand old flagship churches in the hearts of cities across America. Where are all the voices from all the First Baptist churches of our land? Where are the voices from the First Presbyterian churches and the First Methodist churches? Some denominations in recent conventions have even taken pro-abortion platforms and stands. Perhaps Joel asked the question best twenty-five hundred years ago when he cried out, "Where are all the prophets and preachers weeping between the porch and altar over the sins of the people?" (see Joel 2:17).

The church is virtually silent today when a child who by state law is too young to drink alcohol, too young to vote, and too young to drive a car, is at the same time legally permitted to destroy an unborn life and never even notify her parents. What kind of a nation have we become? By and large, the church and synagogue remain silent on the sanctity of life and surrender the truth of the Torah and the good news of the gospel to the lies of the abortionists. Moses' call comes thundering down through the centuries, "I call heaven and earth as witnesses today against you, that I have set before you life and death, blessing and cursing; therefore choose life, that both you and your descendants may live" (Deut. 30:19).

What is the bottom line for you? What do you believe? Is that a human life in the womb? You would not pass by on the other side of the street while men and women were taking two- and three-year-old children and scalding them to death in hot water and simply keep silent. As Solomon said, how we need to "rescue those being led away to death."

Dr. James Dobson has astutely observed that "all the abortion arguments descend to whether one believes an unborn baby is a live human being. If you believe the unborn is a person, then all the peripheral exclusions like rape and incest become folly." Would you kill a one-month-old baby in a crib because he was a victim of rape? Of course not! Then the same baby shouldn't be killed just because he is a few weeks behind in his development still in the womb! Yes, God has "set before us life and death, blessings and curses. Now choose life so that you and your children may live."

When I was a pastor in Florida, a few abortion rights activists rallied at the Federal Court House Building across the street from our First Baptist Church in downtown Fort Lauderdale. I walked across the street to watch their demonstration and listen to their arguments. What amazed me most was the signs they carried. They bore on them the most paradoxical and hypocritical statements imaginable. In fact, our very arguments for choosing life are found in the placards and themes which they promote. They carried such signs as: "Don't impose your morality on me," "Keep abortion legal," "Keep your laws off my body," and "Keep abortions safe." As I watched them and thought about these signs, several thoughts rushed through my mind. Let's think about their slogans for a moment.

At the abortion rally, one lady, attractive and in horn-rimmed glasses, with the obvious appearance of a lawyer or professional woman, was carrying around a sign on a wooden stick which said, "Don't impose your morality on me!" Now, think about that sign for just a moment. If indeed life begins at conception, the fact is plain—abortion is a moral issue! For centuries when medical doctors have obtained their medical degrees they have taken an oath called the Oath of Hippocrates. Many doctors have it displayed on their office wall, framed beautifully and written in flowing script letters. A portion of this Hippocratic Oath states: "I will give no deadly medicine to anyone if asked, nor suggest such council, and in like manner, I will not give to a woman a pessary [instrument] to produce abortion." In listing the things God hates, Solomon says one of the things is, "hands that shed innocent blood" (Prov. 6:16–17). As I looked at that sign, I pictured the bloody hands of a physician who took the Hippocratic Oath promising to never knowingly administer any drug that would injure life. For some medical doctors today it is no longer the Hippocratic Oath but the Hypocritic Oath!

At the rally as I looked at the lady's sign, I also pictured the blood of the innocent victim who never had a chance to "pursue life, liberty and justice" as guaranteed by our Constitution. How long will God continue to bless a nation which is so blatantly oblivious to His Word? Joel, the ancient Jewish prophet, said, "Egypt shall be a desolation, and Edom a desolate wilderness, because of violence against the people of Judah, for they have shed innocent blood in their land" (Joel 3:19). Why did they become desolate? Because they "shed innocent blood in their land." And the woman continues to carry her sign—"Don't impose your morality on me!"

Choice! That is the password for the pro-choice advocates. Their cry is loud and long—"You people who are pro-life are trying to take away my power of choice. Don't impose your morality on me!" Now think about that. We are taking her power of choice? Think about the many choices that are made that lead up to so many convenience abortions on demand. Consider the choices a particular lady has already made. Should I go to the singles bar after hours? And she makes a choice—yes! Should I flirt with that man at the bar or not? And she makes a choice—yes! Should I go out with him or not? And she makes yet another choice—yes! Should I have sex with him or not? And she makes a choice—yes! Should I have sex without any preparation or birth control? And she makes another choice—yes! And then she becomes pregnant! And then she begins to scream that we are trying to take away her freedom to choose. She chose all right, and what is now in her is a live human being, and two wrongs never make a right. She should have the character and integrity to stop saying someone is taking away her choice. She chose. It is not a question of us imposing our morality on her, but her imposing her immorality on us . . . and the unborn, and often asking us to pay for a federally funded abortion at the same time.

The moral principles of the past have given way in our day to situation ethics. From the movie and music industries, and from the public media we hear the selfish cries of a thousand voices calling our children to lifestyles of sexual promiscuity and premarital sex. In our classrooms, modern sex education is perpetrated upon our children, and so often without the basis of a moral standard of restraint. And the woman continues to carry her sign, "Don't impose your morality on me." It ought to have a subtitle, "I'm too busy (with government help and approval) imposing my immorality on you and your children." The same long and legal tradition that acknowledges my right to control my own body, also acknowledges the illegality of harming another person's body.

"Don't impose your morality on me." Do pro-abortionists really mean this? Are they then saying, "I am personally opposed to sex discrimination; however, if others want to discriminate on the basis of sex, that is their right. Don't impose your morality on me. I am personally opposed to racial discrimination. However, if others want to discriminate on the basis of race, that is their right. I don't want to impose my morals on them"? How hypocritical can these men and women be who carry around signs saying—"Don't impose your morality on me!"

Morality is the strength of any nation. If America falls, it will not be the result of a weakened military, but the result of a weakened morality. Of course we need military strength, but more than that we need moral strength and fiber. America's hope is in a genuine repentance. God said, "If My people who are called by My name will humble themselves, and pray and seek My face, and turn from their wicked ways, then I will hear from heaven, and will forgive their sins and heal their land" (2 Chron. 7:14).

In many ways, America has become schizophrenic on the issues of life. What an irony that so often the same ones who hold their signs outside our state and federal prisons promoting life for those guilty of murder and on death row, are the same ones who hold signs at abortion rallies promoting the continual slaughter of millions of innocent unborn babies in abortion clinics. Any society that allows the continual murder of its unborn will not survive indefinitely. Yes, the sign caught my attention ... "Don't impose your morality on me." Can anything be more hypocritical or paradoxical? What we are seeing in our nation is that good and godly people are at last fed up with others imposing their immorality on them!

Another lady carried a sign that said, "Keep abortion legal!" Now let's think about that sign for a moment. There are many who say, "Abortion is all right because it is legal." But just because something is legal does not mean it is moral or right. It is interesting what the pro-abortion people are saying about the unborn. They say that the fetus is a non-person. They say the fetus possesses no soul. They say the fetus possesses no legal rights. The fetus, in their opinion, is simply a piece of property belonging to the mother and can be disposed of at will. And, it is all legal!

Now, that sounds very familiar, doesn't it? It should certainly sound familiar to every black American. Our American history books are replete with the smudge and shame of slavery upon our nation's character. What did slave owners insist about their black slaves? They called them non-persons. They possessed no legal rights. Some even went so far in their stupidity and blindness to say they had no souls. They were simply a piece of property belonging to the master and could be disposed of at will. And, it was all legal! Does that sound familiar?

Abortion advocates are no different from slave owners in the sense that they are fighting for their rights and are ignoring what should be the legal rights of others. Thank God that good and moral people took a stand against slavery! It brought about a civil war, but they stood for what was right. Thank God today that good and moral people are once again making a stand against abortion. Not since the days of the abolitionists and of Abraham Lincoln has the conscience of America raised its voice so loud and long over such a disgraceful national practice.

Once it was legal in this country to own slaves. But that did not make it right! Thank God we came to our senses and righted this dastardly wrong. Today, it is legal to kill babies in the womb, but that doesn't make it right any more than slave laws made slavery right. We went to war in this country to right the wrongs of slavery, and political war clouds are gathering over the abortion question. It is not going to go away! Men and women of conscience are raising their voices over this shameful disgrace.

The late Chuck Colson reminds us of another historical example that offers much hope. "The Christian politician William Wilberforce stood against the deeply entrenched political and economical interest in England's slave trade. He stood as well against the courts that held that slaves were nothing more than property. Despite the overwhelming opposition, Wilberforce and a small band of like-minded Christians persisted. They prayed for three hours a day, circulated anti-slavery literature, mobilized churches and citizens groups, and in the end they triumphed with a glorious victory that stamped out the slave trade. But what was not so glorious was the fact that their campaign took twenty years. They were defeated time and time again in the House of Commons. They were lampooned in political cartoons, and snubbed by society's elite. But they persisted and righted the tremendous wrong."

If abortion continues to remain legal in America, what will be the next class of humanity to be legally and systematically destroyed? Will it be the mentally retarded? Perhaps the handicapped? Certainly, we are already seeing signs that the elderly are next in line. Euthanasia is the Siamese twin of abortion. If the pro-choice advocates argue against bringing "unwanted children" into the world, how long do you think it will be before they begin pushing "unwanted elderly" out of the world?

The next time you see a pro-abortion rally, think about the sign that says, "Keep abortion legal." Remember, just because something is legal does not mean that it is right. Our laws must be changed! One woman who has lived through years of the trauma of an abortion wrote, "If abortion had not been legal, I would not have had to live through those dark years of depression."

At the abortion rally I attended, one particular vocal and vindictive protester wore a sandwich board type of sign that read, "Keep your laws off my body!" Now, that sign sounds right. And, it is. I agree with it! I don't want the government making laws regarding my rights or health care. There are many medical decisions that ought to be personal. Some readers of this book have had plastic surgery. That is your personal decision. Some have desired to donate organs. That is a personal decision. Some have undergone different types of cancer treatment. That is a personal decision. There is nothing wrong with the desire to be free of government intervention upon our bodies. I agree with the sign that says, "Keep your laws off my body." However, for the one who is pregnant, there is no longer one body to think about—there are two!

Those who are influenced by abortion and follow the Judeo-Christian ethic have a dilemma in the fact that in the womb is a person whether they want to believe it or not. Consider these words of the psalmist:

"For You formed my inward parts; You covered me in my mother's womb. I will praise You, for I am fearfully and wonderfully made; marvelous are Your works, and that my soul knows very well. My frame was not hidden from You, when I was made in secret, and skillfully wrought in the lowest parts of the earth. Your eyes saw my substance, being yet unformed. And in Your book they all were written, the days fashioned for me, when as yet there were none of them" (Ps. 139:13–16).

These words teach, without question, that which is developing in the womb is not a blob of tissue, but an expression of God's greatest creation, man!

It is God Himself at work through the creative processes in a woman's body when she is pregnant. What other explanation can one give for two tiny specks of protoplasm coming together and developing into all the intricacies of the nervous system, a circulatory system, a respiratory system, a digestive system, etc. Yes, "For You formed my inward parts; You covered me in my mother's womb" (Ps. 139:13).

A human being exists at conception and not at some later point when he or she begins to look like a newborn. David said, "Behold, I was brought forth in iniquity, and in sin my mother conceived me" (Ps. 51:5). Yes, God's "eyes saw my substance, being yet unformed. And in Your book they all were written, the days fashioned for me, when as yet there were none of them" (Ps. 139:16).

Most abortion advocates describe the unborn as only a blob of tissue. They call the fetus a "conception product." No wonder the lady carried the sign that said, "Keep your laws off my body." But the Creator doesn't see a blob of tissue in the womb; He sees a person. When Rebecca was pregnant with her twins, Jacob and Esau, in distress she called on God and He said, "Two nations are in your womb, two peoples shall be separated from your body; one people shall be stronger than the other, and the older shall serve the younger" (Gen. 25:23).

The abortionists tell us that removing the fetus is no different than removing a blood clot. But God did not see a blood clot in Rebecca's womb. He saw two male children. He doesn't look upon the unborn child as a body part of a mother like her spleen or appendix. In the womb God sees life, individual life. A nurse in our church tells of a turning point in her own experience. When she was working the late-night shift at one of our local hospitals, a young girl was admitted with lower abdominal pain. Two days previously she had had a saline abortion. She requested to be placed on a bed pan. The nurse when removing the pan, among the clots of blood and tissue, saw a fetus of about two months. In her words, "the little heart was beating and the cord was attached as the baby was still alive. I cannot tell you how terrible I felt. I began to cry. That was not just a blob of tissue, but a human life. If only women who are pro-choice could witness an abortion, things might be so different."

Convenience abortions are on the rise today. Consider the following from nationally syndicated columnist George Will, and see what you would decide. Here is the case. "The father has syphilis, the mother tuberculosis. They have had four children. The first one was blind. The second one died. The third one was deaf and dumb. The fourth one had tuberculosis. The mother is now pregnant with her fifth child, but is willing to have an abortion. If you determine she should, she will do it. What would you decide for her? If you chose abortion, congratulations! You have just murdered Beethoven!"

Tragically, for so many unborn, the haunting words of Jeremiah 20:17 have become their epitaph, "My mother, my grave" as millions of mothers' wombs have become millions of babies' tombs. If it is right to fight for equality and civil rights for ourselves, it is hypocrisy not to do so for those who cannot speak for themselves. If it is right to regulate the way animals in our society can be killed, and to ban by law certain kinds of traps, it is sheer hypocrisy not to speak out for those who cannot speak out for themselves. If cattle cannot be slaughtered in ways deemed careless about pain, and if stray dogs and cats must be killed by law in humane ways, it is sheer hypocrisy for those who cannot speak for themselves to be totally ignored by people who call themselves humane.

Until a child is born, a baby is obviously unseen by the human eye. I am convinced that if the womb were transparent, there would be far fewer abortions. If the young pregnant girls who are having abortions could see inside and see the baby being formed, they would seldom abort. One lady wrote of an abortion she had ten years earlier at the age of eighteen. Afraid her parents would be disgraced and disown her, she sought out a doctor to perform the procedure for three hundred dollars. She said, "As I entered the clinic doors, the nurse at the desk took my name and age. She said I was eight weeks pregnant and that it was just a mass of tissue not yet formed. As I lay on the table where the procedure was about to take place, I saw a covered jar on the table close to my feet. Terror ran through me and I asked why this jar was covered up if this thing they say is inside me is just a blob of white tissue? After seeing the jar I knew deep down inside something was not told to me. I felt betrayed and sick. It wasn't until years later when I saw the fetal growth chart, that I realized why they covered the jar. The one thing I lacked was the visual knowledge of what was really happening after conception in my body. The biggest thing I had to get over was to forgive myself for what I had done. The memory will always be there." No wonder the abortionists' clinics do not want to show fetal charts as to what this "blob of tissue" looks like a few weeks after conception.

Children were visible on the steps of the courthouse at the pro-abortion rally that day. One little girl holding her mother by one hand held a sign in the other hand that said, "Keep abortions safe." Now, think about that one. Safe for whom? Certainly not for the baby! Just how is the baby extracted from the womb? There are several methods that are used, and if one carrying the picket sign reading "Keep abortions safe" ever witnessed the trauma and tragedy of the unborn, they would never carry that sign again. Abortion is certainly not safe for the baby.

One method of abortion is commonly referred to as "D&C" (dilation and curettage). The procedure is performed by the physician inserting a spoon-shaped instrument with sharp edges into the uterus. The baby is then cut into pieces and scraped from the uterine wall. And all the while the pro-choice advocates carry the popular sign that reads, "Keep abortions safe." For whom?

Another method is the suction type of abortion. A tube is inserted in the uterus and attached to a strong suction apparatus. This creates a powerful vacuum that tears the fetus from the womb in a mass of blood and tissue. The baby is torn to pieces and sucked into a jar. And all the while the pro-choice advocates carry their sign reading, "Keep abortions safe." For whom?

The third method is used for those farther along in their pregnancy. It is commonly referred to as the saline injection. A long needle is inserted into the mother's abdomen and into the baby's sac. Most of the fluids are removed and a strong salt solution is injected therein. The helpless baby is poisoned by the solution and kicks and jerks violently. He is literally being burned alive! Generally within twenty-four hours, labor sets in and the mother gives birth to a dead baby. However, the abortionist's greatest horror comes true, when this aborted, burned baby sometimes comes forth, still alive and then must be left to die of starvation and neglect rather quietly. A registered nurse in Jacksonville, Florida, describes one such live birth. "There was a baby in this bassinet, a crying perfectly formed baby, but there was a difference in this child. She had been scalded. She was the child of saline abortion. This little girl looked as if she had been in a pot of boiling water. No doctor, no nurse, no parent to comfort the burned child. She was left alone to die in pain."

And all the while the pro-choice abortion advocates carry their signs, "Keep abortion safe." For whom?

Another method is the cesarean section that is generally performed the final three months of pregnancy. Here the physician enters the womb by surgery through the wall of the mother's abdomen and then removes the baby. The baby whose lungs are often not yet adequately developed is left alone to die of neglect. And all the while the pro-choice advocate carries her sign reading, "Keep abortions safe." For whom? Recent debates in Congress include the issue of partial birth abortions for those in their final trimester of pregnancy.

Not only is it not safe for the baby, but what about the mother? Remember, we have more than one facet of our being. We are not simply talking about the physical, but also the emotional and spiritual. The truth is, abortion is never 100 percent safe, whether it is legal or illegal. The constant cry of the pro-choice advocate is, "Don't send us back to back-alley abortions." I have watched them at their rallies carrying coat hangers wrapped in women's bras and undergarments as protest symbols. How degrading to a woman! These women must not think very much of a lady's ability to make a wise choice so as to insinuate that they are going to retreat to some back alley, take some rusty coat hanger, and insert it in their body to abort their baby.

The sign reads, "Keep abortion safe." For whom? As a pastor I have dealt with the aftermath of abortion in many lives. One lady in our congregation had an abortion at the age of twenty as a result of premarital sex with her boyfriend who is now her husband. She says, "It has been over ten years and I still feel the pain and loss of it as if it were yesterday. It was a decision we reached together, one based mostly on preventing embarrassment and shame to our parents and the local church. We simply wanted to get rid of an untimely problem. The college clinic and local planning council simply set up an appointment to have a suction vacuum procedure done. Not once did anyone tell me just how my ten-week-old baby looked, or how it was growing. If only there had been someone informative with the truth from the pro-life perspective. 'If only,' those words I have said a hundred times! When I had my first baby, there was both joy and sadness in my heart. Joy because of the tremendous miracle God had given, and sadness because I fully realized that there really was a baby which I destroyed earlier. It was especially difficult when I began to think how old my child would be and wondered what he or she might have looked like and been like. Time has a way of healing so many emotional scars, but abortion is a scar that is carved on my heart. And I don't think time will ever change it completely!"

Another lady wrote to say, "I became pregnant when I was sixteen. I did not want to have an abortion, but I felt I had no choice. The abortion clinic told me to lie about my age so I wouldn't have to get permission from my parents. As I was in the abortion clinic, I could hear my baby being sucked away during the procedure. I immediately felt the loss and cried. Terrible nightmares started—every night! I became obsessed with wondering what my baby would have looked like and whether it was a boy or girl. I had that abortion in 1975, and until I accepted the Lord Jesus as my Savior, my life and self-worth continued to decline. But after I came to know Christ, I had a hard time forgiving myself. For me, I realized abortion does kill, not only my baby, but in a very real sense a part of me too! I honestly could say, I don't think I would be alive today if not for the Lord's forgiveness and healing." As I read that letter, I thought about the lady who carried her sign that says, "Keep abortions safe." For whom?

Long ago Moses brought his people to decision with these words: "I call heaven and earth as witnesses today against you, that I have set before you life and death, blessing and cursing; therefore choose life, that both you and your descendants may live" (Deut. 30:19).

To the many who have had abortions, please read the following: abortion is not the unpardonable sin! Many live with the haunting, longing that if only that moment could be lived over again. The grief you feel is normal. You should thank God that your conscience is not seared. The good news is that Jesus Christ died on the cross to make a way for you to be free of your failure and saved from your sin. Along with our sins He also bore our sorrows and grief, our mistakes and failures. How beautiful are the words of Paul in Romans 8:1, "There is therefore now no condemnation to those who are in Christ Jesus." God is not mad or angry at you. He hates sin, but He loves you! He stands with open arms to forgive you. "If we confess our sins, he is faithful and just to forgive us our sins and to cleanse us from all unrighteousness" (I John 1:9). If you have aborted a child, God will forgive you right now if you ask Him. Through His forgiveness you can know the true freedom that comes in placing Him as Lord of your life. You can purpose to follow Him, accept His cleansing, and then not call unclean what He has cleansed. You can forgive yourself! Rejoice in the fact that your child is present with the Lord and join Karen Sullivan Ables who put it like this:

In a far away place and a different time
I killed my first child, a most heinous crime.

The state didn't come, and I didn't stand trial.
Judge Blackmun was calm when he said with a smile,
"Killing is legal, say we the High Court.
But don't call it murder. Just call it 'abort.'"

The judge in my heart would not let the case rest.
I had no defense when once put to the test.
Found guilty I was by my heart's Supreme Court.
"You murdered your baby!" they screamed in retort.

With tears on my cheeks it was too late, I knew
To bring back the life of the child I once slew.
The gavel slammed down, and it rang in my head,
"You are guilty as charged, and deserve to be dead."

"We now give you torment to pay for your sin,
Was the sentence passed down from my own court within.
"You will never escape. You're branded. Don't hide.
Your just due is death. You should try suicide."

I was beaten in prison by daily attacks.
I was paying a debt, so I never fought back.
No hope of escaping, and this I knew well.
I cried out to God from my own self-made hell.

That day I met Jesus; He smiled in my face.
He said, "I forgive you. Come walk in my grace."
"Lord, I believe you forgive me and yet,
Blameless you are. Can you pay for my debt?"

"And, Lord, please don't touch me for I am unclean.
I'm filthy with murder; a most wretched being."
I poured out my story. He showed no surprise.
I gazed up with awe at the love in His eyes.

He said, "I paid for your crime, yes, was nailed to a tree.
There's no condemnation if you'll trust in Me.
I took on your blame and your curse on My soul
So you may be free without judgment and whole."

I sputtered, "Dear Lord, where's the justice in this?
I killed my first son, and you offer me bliss?"
Tears blurred my vision, yet there in His face
Were eyes of compassion, blue oceans of grace.

I thought to myself, "Now the past has been buried?
I'm free of the guilt that for years I have carried?"
He said to accept. It's a gift that is free.
This is atonement, not justice for me!

My judge was dismissed, my accusers, and jury.
The truth of His love made them leave in a fury.
He smiled, "Walk with Me and come learn My way,"
And grasping His hand I began a new day.

There is also a word to the physicians who have performed abortions. God's Word says, "Cleanse your hands," (James 4:8). Over twenty-five hundred years ago King David, a murderer, prayed, "Deliver me from the guilt of bloodshed, O God, the God of my salvation, and my tongue shall sing aloud of Your righteousness" (Ps. 51:14). If you repent, God will forgive you and say to you what He has said to another in Scripture, "Neither do I condemn you, go and sin no more" (John 8:11).

Finally, there is also a word to anyone contemplating an abortion. Could you murder your child on its first birthday? Of course not! That would be the farthest thing from your mind, and so should aborting the child while he or she is in the womb. There is a human being inside you. God has already named that child and He is in the process of perfecting him or her. Don't buy the argument that the child is an "unwanted child." There are many couples right now trying to adopt. Please do not do something you will regret the rest of your life. Do not destroy something that is not yours. The child in your body belongs to God, even though it may be in your womb at the present time. One lady who had had an abortion said, "I actually admire the young women in our church, who are very visible, and have had children out of wedlock. They could have taken the coward's way out to avoid the shame of a 'visible sin.' Praise God for their example to other girls that these out-of-wedlock children can be loved and accepted. I cannot look today at an eleven-year-old child without the pain of realizing my child would be that age today. But when I see my baby, I realize how deeply God must love me to once again trust me with one of His little ones." Please do not take an innocent life for your own convenience sake! Regardless of what you may hear at the abortion clinic—abortion is not safe!

And to the silent majority who call abortion murder, it is time to begin acting like it! Solomon warned, "If you say, surely we did not know this, does not He who weighs the hearts consider it?" (Prov. 24:11–12). We must remember that our enemies are not people, but the satanic system and deception behind their practices. "For we do not wrestle against flesh and blood, but against principalities, against powers, against the rulers of the darkness of this age, against spiritual hosts of wickedness in the heavenly places" (Eph. 6:12). Abortion is simply the outward manifestation of the inward problem of the heart. "For from within, out of the heart of men, proceed evil thoughts, adulteries, fornications, murders, thefts, covetousness, wickedness, deceit, lewdness, an evil eye, blasphemy, pride, foolishness. All these evil things come from within and defile a man" (Mark 7:21–23).

Isaiah said it best seven hundred years before the coming of Christ when he said, "Cry aloud, spare not; lift up your voice like a trumpet; tell My people their transgression, and the house of Jacob their sins" (Isa. 58:1). Isaiah was saying, get involved! Write your congressmen. Sign petitions. Warn others that voting for abortion defiles our nation's hands with innocent blood. The real battlefield is the place of prayer. Pray for support organizations that stand for the life of the unborn. Yes, "God has set before us today life and death, blessings and curses. Now, choose life so that you and your children may live!"

PREACHING THE GREAT DAYS OF THE CHRISTIAN CALENDAR

Christmas Day

Luke 2:15–20

Dr. O. S. Hawkins

We've all heard and sung the old Christmas classic "I'll Be Home for Christmas." People go through all sorts of things and jump through all types of hoops in order to "get home for Christmas." Some drive all night. Others fly across the country. They finally get home only to sleep on sofas and floors. But, there's just something about being home for Christmas.

For a lot of us it is simply no longer possible. Some are serving in the armed services across the world. For me we have long since sold the old home place on Crenshaw in east Fort Worth and my mother has now spent over three decades of Christmases in heaven. Like so many I can no longer go home for Christmas physically.

There are a lot of lonely people at Christmastime. We live in a post-modern world where close-knit neighborhoods are things of the past. We come home to shut windows and locked doors in our world. Many of us do not even know our neighbors' names, and for many Christmas is a lonely time. When we are talking about "coming home for Christmas," we are talking about something far more important than coming home physically. We are speaking about coming home spiritually. There are so many who have been away from their spiritual home for so long and there's no better time to "come home" than during the Christmas season.

How can we make the most of Christmas this year? For some making the most of Christmas is simply some warm, fuzzy feeling, listening to carols in the mall that bring back nostalgic memories of days gone by. For others it is filled with such things as decorating our houses and trees or getting the gift we want. For many it's the invitation to a certain party or Christmas ball. But making the most of Christmas involves so much more. Luke 2 tells us how we can truly make the most of Christmas. Here is the account of those who made the most of the first Christmas. These shepherds have so much to teach us today. When they heard the message of Christmas, they didn't go and celebrate it at the local bar in Bethlehem as soon as they got off work. Nor did they gather with all the other shepherds for a company party or even exchange gifts with one another. What did they do? What can we learn from them about making the most of Christmas?

These shepherds provide for us a pattern of how to make the most of Christmas. On this first Christmas we see them calculate it, contemplate it, celebrate it, and circulate it. Let's take this journey with them and "go to Bethlehem and see for ourselves that which has come to pass."

Calculate It

> *So it was, when the angels had gone away from them into heaven, that the shepherds said to one another, "Let us now go to Bethlehem and see this thing that has come to pass, which the Lord has made known to us." And they came with haste and found Mary and Joseph, and the Babe lying in a manger." (Luke 2:15–16)*

Now get this picture. The shepherds are out in the fields of Bethlehem, those same fields where Ruth gleaned in the fields of Boaz and the same fields you can visit and walk in this very day. For the little group of shepherds, that night began like any other night. Their fathers before them had tended the sheep in the same fields and their fathers before them. If you were to journey there this very Christmas season, you would see shepherds in the same fields today tending sheep in much the same manner as they did on that first Christmas Eve.

On this particular night recorded in Luke 2, it was like any other night. The shepherds were not expecting anything out of the ordinary, nor was the topic of conversation about anything spiritual. But then, suddenly, "an angel of the Lord stood before them, and the glory of the Lord shone around them, and they were greatly afraid" (v. 9). And, as though that were not enough, "suddenly there was with the angel a multitude of the heavenly host praising God and saying: 'Glory to God in the highest, and on earth peace, good will toward men!'" (vv. 13–14).

The shepherds then did what all of us ought to do. They said to each other, "Let's go check this out. Let's put it in the calculator. Let's add it up. Let's investigate it. Let's calculate it." So, when the angels had gone away from them into heaven, they said one to another, "Let us now go to Bethlehem and see this thing that has come to pass, which the Lord has made known to us" (v. 15). And thus they began their search.

This is where some of us are today and why some of us gather in church during the Christmas season. This is the wise thing to do and is the first step in making the most of Christmas. That is, to calculate it. Some never really stop to do this. Some are so busy and caught up in the season and immersed in it all. For many, saying, "Happy Holidays" is in reality more close to their hearts than saying, "Merry Christmas." Some of us have heard the Christmas story all of our lives and know it by memory, but for some of us it has never passed from the head to the heart. We begin to make the most of Christmas when like the shepherds we calculate it.

Now, I realize that in our modern world we are separated from this event by two thousand years and for those of us in America by almost eight thousand miles. We don't tend sheep for a living. We don't sleep in shepherds' fields at night. God hasn't sent the angel Gabriel much less a celestial choir to get our attention. However, perhaps He has allowed circumstances or situations to develop in our lives to bring us to the place where we are today. Perhaps a friend has encouraged us. Perhaps we're searching without admitting it. Perhaps deep in our hearts we want to make the most of Christmas this year.

Check it out. Add it up. Like the shepherds, calculate it. This is the first step in making the most of Christmas. Christmas is not just some sentimental story. It is the good news that we have been looking for. It is not a passing fad. The Lord Jesus has been transforming lives for two thousand years and continues to do so today. Begin your own search like the shepherds by saying, "Let us go to Bethlehem and see this thing which has come to pass." And, when you do, you will find Him just as they did. For He said, "You will seek Me and find Me, when you search for Me with all your heart" (Jer. 29:13). The real beauty of Christmas is that He is seeking us. He sent an angel to bring the shepherds. He sent a star to bring the wise men. He sends His Holy Spirit to bring us.

How do we make the most of Christmas? Calculate it. Don't be caught up in only the secular displays and facades. Come and see for yourself.

Contemplate It

> *Now when they had seen Him, they made widely known the saying which was told them concerning this Child. And all those who heard it marveled at those things which were told them by the shepherds. But Mary kept all these things and pondered them in her heart. (Luke 2:17–19)*

I love what it says in verse 18. They "marveled." They were amazed. This is not the kind of amazement that one might have when he sees a magician's sleight of hand that tricks you into believing you see something unexplainable. This is a proper wonder of those acts of God that is beyond comprehension. Once you calculate it, then you will contemplate it. When we see what God has done in so many ways in our lives, we marvel. We stand in wonder. Contemplate it. God has come to us. He has clothed Himself in human flesh and walked among us. He was never contaminated by our sin, and He willingly took our place on the cross. He arose from the dead on the third day, ascended on high, and has promised that He is coming again. Yes, when you calculate it, you contemplate it and marvel as did those who heard the shepherd's message.

We find a very interesting word in verse 19 when we read that Mary "kept all these things and pondered them in her heart." The word "ponder" is a compound word in Greek from the verb "to throw" and the word "together." Literally it means to throw together. One would use this word in the making of a cake in taking all of the ingredients and putting them together. This is what Mary did. She stirred all these things up in her mind. She pondered them all. This story of the manger doesn't mean a lot unless it is linked to prophecy. In the early chapters of Genesis we read the prophecy of this seed of woman, and in Micah, we read that this promised Messiah will be born in Bethlehem. Isaiah foretells that a virgin will conceive and bear a son. Mary was putting this all together. The angel's message to her. The journey from Bethlehem. The virgin birth. Later when she had to flee down into Egypt, she continued to "ponder" those things. When she saw our Lord perform the miracle at Cana, she pondered. When she took Him to Jerusalem when He was twelve years old, the pondering continued. When she stood at the cross, she was stirring these things in her mind. Yes, Mary contemplated it. She thought what all the prophets had said. She put it all together. She stored these wonders in her memory and treasured them up, and note where she did it . . . "in her heart."

When you ponder something, you take all you know about it and throw it together, compare the facts, and consider them. You think through it all and draw your conclusions. Some have discounted the reality and relevancy of the Lord Jesus Christ without ever calculating it or contemplating it. That is not intellectualism. This is an important step in making the most of Christmas. In all the hustle and bustle of the holidays, it is important to pause and contemplate it. It is important to be still and marvel and ponder the meaning and message of Christmas . . . in your own heart.

As Mary took that newborn and as she herself wrapped Him in those cloths, she pondered it all in her heart. She knew those little hands would never wear gold rings or bracelets. They were for something else. She knew they would never touch the finer things of life. They were made to touch lepers' wounds and form spittle for the blind and one day to be the recipient of cruel Roman spikes. As Mary let that little hand clutch her index finger, she "pondered those things in her heart." She contemplated it. As she looked at his little feet, still wrinkled from birth, she could only imagine what difficult steps lay ahead for them. They, too, would receive the Roman spikes and would never walk on lush Persian rugs but on a cobblestone path called the Via Dolorosa. And, millions would follow those steps.

Once we calculate it, it does us good to contemplate it; to put it all together and stir it up in our own hearts.

Celebrate It

> *Then the shepherds returned, glorifying and praising God for all the things that they had heard and seen, as it was told them. (Luke 2:20)*

What is the best way to celebrate Christmas? With our lips and with our lives. These shepherds began to glorify and praise God for all they had seen and heard. And the thing that really caused them to burst out in praise was it was "just as it was told them." When you calculate it and contemplate it, you will find God's word to be true just as it has been told to us, and then you will begin to celebrate it.

Why do you think the spirit of Christmas is so atmospheric? It's in the air and in the environment and in the atmosphere. We walk in the malls and people actually greet each other with smiles and open doors for one another during the Christmas season. Why? All over our secular society the air is filled with music giving praise to the Lord Jesus Christ. Go to the biggest malls in our cities and what do we hear? Christmas carols. Filling the world with the good news of the gospel of Jesus Christ, celebrating it.

Note that these shepherds returned. To what did they return? They returned to what they left. Their homes and their businesses. They returned to their family and friends. What an impact it must have had upon those who knew them best. May God give us the grace to do that this holiday season once we've been home and truly celebrated the season to return to our own homes and our own environment with the good news of Jesus Christ.

Circulate It

> *Now when they had seen Him, they made widely known the saying which was told them concerning this Child. (Luke 2:17)*

The shepherds became witnesses of this great event. They began to circulate it! They "made widely known the saying which was told them concerning this child." They had seen God in human flesh. Their eyes had looked upon the one whom the prophets had foretold for centuries. They had heard the music of heaven. They stopped to calculate it, to contemplate it, and to celebrate it. Now they could not keep from circulating it. This is the way we truly make the most of Christmas.

The shepherds were living in a world of tremendous government oppression. It was a world desperate for some word of hope. It was a world plagued by confusion because men and women had no direction. It was a world plagued by controversy because there was no revelation. The prophets had been silent for four hundred years. It was a world filled with conflict because there seemed to be no hope under the oppression of a Roman government. This was the world in which God stepped that evening in Bethlehem. A world much like our own world today filled with confusion and controversy and conflict. This is why thirty-three years later, eight miles away on Mount Zion and on His last evening, He said, "I am the Way." He is the answer to all of our confusion. He is the one who brings direction in life. He said, "I am the Truth." He is the answer to controversy. He is the one who brings absolutes into our existence. He said, "I am the Life." That is, He is the answer to our conflict and the only one who brings true hope. And, this is what the shepherds circulated that night so long ago.

The Bible speaks volumes to us in these verses. God chose shepherds to first circulate the message of salvation. Oh, there were others in Bethlehem who lived closer to the stable. There were those of importance and prominence in the city square. There were those whose testimonies could carry far more weight. There were obviously men of wealth and wisdom to whom all Bethlehem looked. But God had, and continues to have, a way of confounding the wise. After all, the angels said, "I bring you good tidings of great joy which shall be to all people" (Luke 2:10).

And what the shepherds saw that evening has continued ever since. There are many believers today who never circulate it. Why? Perhaps because they've never celebrated it. And why? Could it be because they've never contemplated it? And once again, why? The answer is because they've never calculated it.

Come home for Christmas. Where does the journey begin? How can you really make the most of Christmas? Calculate it. This is what the shepherds did. Check it out. Add it up. Next, contemplate it. They marveled and were amazed and Mary "pondered it all in her heart." Then, celebrate it. Once you've contemplated this incredible message and Messiah, the best way to give glory to God is to return your life to Him in celebration. And once you do this, you cannot help but speak the things you've seen and heard. You will circulate it. Come home for Christmas.

THE PASTOR—MAJOR PARTNER IN THE WEDDING EXPERIENCE

Jim Henry

Some years ago Ann Landers had a column head-lined with these words: "Clergymen Confesses: They Hate Weddings." There followed a litany of stories from priests and pastors who described some of the horrific experiences they had endured as officiants at weddings. Their reports covered everything from a father of the bride showing up drunk, a best man dropping his pants as he followed the bridal couple down the aisle after the ceremony, to a bride who wanted her dog to walk her down the aisle—and she wasn't blind! One Florida pastor said he had rather have a hemorrhoidectomy than perform another wedding.

I've had my share of unusual experiences during five decades of officiating at weddings. On one occasion, a dog got into the church, proceeded down the aisle, and sat down beside the bridesmaids and observed for several minutes. Another time the heat was turned up instead of the air-conditioning, causing everything and everyone to wilt. At one wedding, the florist forgot to get the bride's bouquet to the church and she refused to walk the aisle. Meanwhile, the organist played every piece in her music arsenal from Beethoven to Wesley. Can I ever forget the night when the pianist playing prelude music, going through her stack of music, began to play "This Old House." Apparently, someone had sabotaged her music repertoire.

There's been the usual dropping of rings, faintings (but never a bride or groom). Then, there's the unusual, like the father when asked, "Who gives this woman to be married to this man?" responded with, "her mother and I and the SunTrust bank." But, I never soured on officiating weddings; I certainly don't hate them. I figure if it was important enough for Jesus to show up at a wedding, it should be important to me. Some pastors refuse to do weddings. I never felt it was optional. I've found that it was a unique opportunity to do several pastoral ministries:

1. It gave me the privilege to lead scores of men and women to faith in Jesus Christ in my personal interview with them or in our marriage preparation classes.
2. At weddings, there are more people in attendance who need Christ or need to return to Him than in most worship services on Sunday. I always worked the Good News in through the couple's testimony or as a part of my message to the attendees.
3. My role as the undershepherd of God's people was elevated.
4. Many in the wedding party or in attendance for the wedding began attending our church and some came to faith and for membership.
5. It opened doors to the wider community, giving me and our church a larger platform of ministry.

No, I never hated weddings. I determined that I would mine them for all the potential good it would mean for the kingdom of God.

I don't consider myself an expert, but the things I share with you in the next few paragraphs may be helpful as you weigh the merits of the investment of time and energy. No, you won't get rich on honorariums. I once received an envelope with no money and a note—"Thank you for helping us. I.O.U." Never did collect! But enough came in through the years to add some to the offering and send my wife shopping.

Premarital Counseling

This wasn't optional for anyone I married or who were married by one of our pastors. In my early years, when the churches were smaller, I did two to three sessions with each couple. In later years, because we offered an extensive Marriage Preparation Class at our church, I did one session with the couples I married. This was usually about one hour in length. Why go to the trouble?

Most importantly, I had opportunity to ascertain their spiritual status. Nothing more critical to their marriage success and eternity than their relationship to Jesus. If one was not a believer and refused Christ after a time of prayer and consideration, we would not officiate for their wedding, as the clear command of Scripture would be violated (2 Cor. 6:14).

We find increasingly many couples who want a church wedding are already living together. When we deal with this, we ask them if they will move into separate housing and be sexually abstinent until marriage. Often they will reply that they live together because of financial reasons, or saving their money for the wedding and honeymoon. We offer to pay the rent until they're married or assist in their wedding expenses. We've had many to opt for the right choice; some have chosen not to and went elsewhere to be married.

If both parties are unbelievers, we seek to lead them to Christ. If they choose not our Lord, we will marry them, believing that our compassion toward them will be a positive witness and bear fruit later, and it has.

Another benefit is the personal angle. As pastor, I come to know the couple at a deeper level. I make notes of our conversation and plug them into the ceremony. How they met. When they came to Christ. Their future plans, etc. This interests the people and adds a personal touch that is widely appreciated.

What are some of the things I ask during my pre-wedding interview? The following is not exhaustive but hits some major points.

a. Their spiritual journey, church membership, and commitment to serving Christ through His church.
b. Biblical roles, the husband as spiritual leader (many don't have the foggiest idea) and the wife as supportive of that role and the understanding of hers (Eph. 5:22–33; 1 Peter 3:1–7).
c. Do you pray together?

d. Do you desire to have children? Are you open to adoption if not able to conceive naturally?
e. What is your financial position? How much debt do you each have? Who will be the treasurer and bookkeeper? Do you tithe? Are you saving money? What are your long-term financial goals?
f. Tell me about your parents and family. Do you bring any emotional or mental baggage into the marriage?
g. What part do your parents play in your life?
h. Do you communicate well? How do you settle disagreements? Is anger or pouting a problem? Can you talk about your deepest thoughts with each other?
i. Who are your friends?
j. What do you mutually enjoy beyond your relationship?
k. Is there anything in your past you have concealed from your partner?
l. Is pornography a part of your past or present?
m. Are you planning or will you plan a wedding service that will glorify God?
n. Are you intimate sexually? If so, would you confess it as sin and abstain until you are one in Christ?
o. Are there any questions you would like to ask me?

Our Marriage Preparation Class is taught by well-trained laypeople and is offered at least twice a year. It lasts for several weeks and includes personality tests, budget planning, etc. Some couples take it before they are engaged. Others have found out that as they work through the classes, tests, and workbooks, they are not compatible for a long-term relationship, and break off engagement or wedding plans, which is far better than breaking up a home. I would encourage you to begin one or send your couples to a dependable church that provides this service. You can design your own prep class as there are many resources to pull from including videos, workbooks, discussions, tests, and helpful books on marriage.

Are the things our church has done or I have sought to do to assist a couple in preparing not only for a wedding but for a lifetime commitment totally successful? No, but our knowledge reveals that our success rate is far above the national average in marriages that last a lifetime. Of the hundreds of weddings I have participated in for over half a century, I only know of less than a dozen that have dissolved by divorce; not perfect, but not bad!

The Wedding Coordinator

Seminary did not prepare me for conducting weddings or wedding rehearsals. I soon learned by experience how to do both. But the growing demands of our growing church and family called for some adjustments; otherwise I was at the church for two nights conducting the rehearsal one night and the wedding the next. I enlisted a godly lady with a tender heart and tough skin to conduct the rehearsals. She observed me for several rehearsals, then she took over the rehearsals without my presence. In time, the scope of her work was enlarged and became an integral part of the wedding process. The following is a list of the benefits and responsibilities of an effective wedding coordinator.

a. She gives you an extra night to be with your family or participate in other activities.
b. She relieves you of the stress of a rehearsal. Between the bride and the mothers, this can occasionally turn into a challenging situation.
c. She coordinates the event with your schedule and the church calendar so that the use of the facilities, parking, etc. does not clash with the rehearsal and wedding.
d. She informs the bride of available resources: kneeling bench, candles, candelabra, musicians, etc.
e. She sets the tone for the rehearsal by opening with prayers,

bringing greetings from the pastor and church, and outlining the rehearsal procedures. She focuses on a Christ-centered event.

f. She has the marriage license in hand to acquire all the necessary signatures, pastor, witnesses, etc.
g. On the wedding day, she runs the show, where attendants dress, restroom facilities, who goes down the aisle at the proper time, seating of guests, lighting of candles, working with the florist and decorators, and a hundred other behind-the-scene details that always occur.
h. She meets with the bride and groom, and the bride and her mother as many times as necessary before the wedding to iron out all of the details, such as mailing in invitations, the program, ushers, and their duties. Will she use a ring bearer, flower girls; or other circumstances that may include assisting handicapped participants, dealing with family arrangements such as stepfather, stepmother, etc.?
i. If the church has a manual, policy, or guidelines for Christ-centered weddings (which I strongly recommend), she can walk through that with the couple so there are no misunderstandings about expectations and responsibilities.
j. Her title can be Coordinator, Rehearsal Director, or Wedding Coordinator.
k. A good practice is to have at least two trained coordinators in case of illness, heavy schedule, etc. Men can also do this job!
l. She should be compensated for her ministry. She is worth every penny and more!

Planning the Wedding Ceremony

This segment is the most important thing we do as pastors. We have the opportunity to exalt Jesus Christ, our heavenly Bridegroom. Therefore, we must pray, plan, and work at this as we would a sermon. For most couples, this is the first, and prayerfully, the only time they will do this. We want it right. They want it right. I've found most couples are responsive to suggestions I may have to assisting them in maximizing the event and glorifying God. Here are some things we can do to be helpful:

a. Remind them of the spiritual significance, the power of the symbol of Christ, the Bridegroom, the Church, the Bride.
b. Ask them to make the music Christ-honoring. Minimize secular music. This can be done at the rehearsal dinner or reception.
c. Make every wedding unique. Add different scriptures, illustrations, anecdotes, and points of interest about the couple. Audiences pay rapt attention to these!
d. Encourage the couple to write their own vows, or part of them. I've had couples who memorized their own vows. Others have sung as the bride came down the aisle or during the ceremony.
e. Have the couple face the audience. This encourages better hearing, and the visual expressions are priceless.
f. Incorporate their testimony. They can share it or you can tell it.
g. Parents should be more than an afterthought, as well as other family members or friends who have impacted their lives in a positive way. Work them into the proceedings in a meaningful way. For example, have the parents come to the front as the couple kneel, lay their hands on their shoulders, and voice a prayer, using a blessings prayer like Numbers 6:24–26.
h. Be sure they get expert photographers and video recorders of the event. They may pay more, but a poor job on this special event has led to heartbreak. This day cannot be a do-over.
i. Urge them not to slap each other in the face with a piece of wedding cake. It's undignified, messy, and can be destructive of hair-do, wedding attire, and is generally unproductive.
j. Encourage them not to have a long, passionate kiss when you come to this part of the service. They can share this later!

k. If they use a trinity candle and someone is singing while they light the candles, be sure the song is short. Standing gazing into each other's eyes for five minutes may seem like a second to them, but eternity for everyone else.

l. Ask if there are any complications that could come up at the rehearsal or wedding (i.e., her father has been married three times, and the mother, former wife, and current girlfriend or wife will be present). How do you want them seated, and who shows at the rehearsal dinner? At the reception, does the father or stepfather get to dance with you? Who goes first?

m. Pray before you begin any time with them. Pray when you conclude. Pray with the groomsmen before you head for the altar.

n. If they are considering a wedding outside, or in a different setting from the church, be sure they are aware of the possibilities of bad weather, uncontrollable noise, difficulty with the sound equipment, electricity, a service crew who are not well prepared to do a wedding, which may be beyond their preparation and capability.

o. Alert them to the reality that young children used as ringbearers, flower girls, etc. are cute, but they can be absolutely disruptive to a wedding ceremony. I've seen them cry, sit down, make faces, run around in between the wedding party and the platform. I encourage them to let them do their thing early and be quickly seated with a parent, relative, or friend. Otherwise, use at your own risk!

p. What about communion during the service? Some couples want to do this with only themselves involved. Others, the wedding participants, and some request it for everyone present. This can be meaningful but also complicated. I don't encourage it, but that's their decisions and yours.

To Sum Up

"Unless the LORD builds the house, they labor in vain who build it" (Ps. 127:1). With an increasingly secular, indifferent, and even antagonistic mind-set toward Christ and His church, we must do everything possible to build the only foundation that will secure a nation and individuals, that is, strong homes. It begins with the proper emphasis on the wedding, but more important, the rest of their lives. One of the traditional wedding vows states: "this union is not to be entered into unadvisedly or lightly, but reverently, discreetly, and in the fear of God. Into this holy estate these two come now to be joined." As "joiners," we must do our best to launch their lives together with preparation for and a wedding ceremony that will not only put a bow on their love but tie a knot in it!

The following are a couple of examples of wedding ceremonies to kindle your imagination and creativity.

Wedding Ceremonies

Example 1

The Welcome

Dear family, wedding guests, and wedding party: it is a joy to welcome you to the celebration of the wedding of ________________ and ________________. This special day has been anticipated, prayed for, and planned with the expectation that it would honor Jesus Christ. ________________ and ________________ believe that He has brought them together. They are grateful to each of you for your love, counsel, encouragement, and prayers that have guided them in this journey. Thank you for your presence in this time of worship and joy. You have multiplied their happiness by choosing to share this memorable day.

The Invocation

Father, Your Word has taught us that where two or three are gathered in Your name, You are present. Thank You for that assurance. Thank

You for Your interest because of Your desire to bless such events as You did in performing Your first miracle during Your visit to earth at the wedding in Cana. We are keenly aware of Your presence. We desire to honor and glorify You. This couple and their families have chosen to actively seek Your blessing and confirmation of Your pleasure in this life-changing day. Would You now bless this joyous occasion as we recognize You are the source of all love, joy, peace, and blessings. In Christ our Lord, Amen.

The Wedding Charge

Do you ________________ and ________________ affirm that you have placed faith in Jesus Christ as your Lord and Savior and you desire to commit your lives to Christ and each other so long as He grants you life? (They respond "Yes" or "We do.")

The Giving In Marriage

It is God who instituted the gift of marriage. It is a gift of His eternal love and plan. Into this intimacy, this mystery of grace, that these two come to commit their lives to living beyond themselves. As they take this step in a new dimension and merge their lives into one, who gives this woman to be married to this man? (Father responds, "I do" or "Her mother and I do.")

The Marriage Statement

________________ and ________________, you are about to make one of the most sacred vows one person can make to another. This is a moment of time that represents accountability for a lifetime.

________________, as the husband, God has given you a clear command: "Love your wife" [Eph. 5:25]. You are to love ________________ sacrificially, "as Christ loved the church." He loved us so much He died for us. He loves us continually. He loves us so completely that "nothing can separate us from the love of God in Christ Jesus" [Rom. 8:35]. Christ's love for us is a sanctifying love [Eph. 5:26]. His "washing" is a cleansing. His goal is our purity. So must your love for ______________ be. You must do nothing that would defile her; nothing that would keep her from being all she can be in Christ. You must love her sympathetically. Paul said, just as a man "nourishes and feeds" his own body, so the husband must nurture his wife and "cherish" her, which means to secure, to build a nest of security and warmth. ______________, you must love ______________ steadfastly. Your love is to be a "united" love, a word closely resembling "untied"! To unite is to be "joined" together, a word that means to glue, to adhere. Yours is to be a lifetime love.

______________, you have responsibilities to ______________, your soon-to-be husband. A man needs many things—appreciation, companionship, intimacy, attention—but one of his primary needs is respect and support. If a man has that, he can handle nearly anything the world may hurl at him. He desires that she is trustworthy, and will be the kind of wife the writer of Proverbs describes as a wife whose husband "has full confidence in" [Prov. 31:11].

One man said of his wife who had stood by him as he navigated a difficult illness, "she did not walk in front of me to rescue me, nor behind me to catch me if I fell; but walked beside me, held my hand supporting me, helping me to stay connected through the most difficult time in my life." That supportive love is an enduring love. You are now ready to share your wedding vows.

The Vows

(**GROOM**): (repeat) "______________, from this day forward I commit all that I am and have to you; through the power of God. By the daily act of my will, I choose to love you as Christ loves us. This means that I will sacrificially lay down my rights and my life for you. I promise to put God first, you second, and myself last. I accept you just as you are, both your weaknesses and your strengths. I will love and respect you as I love and respect myself and God. I will seek to be honest with you about everything, to be understanding and sensitive to your need for love both in my words and my actions. Since God so loved that He gave, I will give to you more than I receive. I will allow you to be an individual and I will encourage you to grow in your relationship to God, to me, and to others. I will treat you as an equal, to be by my side at all times. As your spiritual leader, I promise to teach you by example and therefore to earn your respect and trust. I promise to say the words "I love you" often, to say "I am sorry" when I am wrong, and to say "I forgive you" when you offend me. I promise to be loyal and committed to you only, until death causes us to part.

(BRIDE): (repeat) "From this day forward, I commit all that I am and have to you. I promise to see your needs before my own, to give rather than to take. I promise to put God first, you second, before any other person or object. Even when you are wrong, I will stand by you lovingly. I will seek to make our home a place of rest that you will look forward to coming home to. I promise to work with you and stand side by side with you in your endeavors. I promise to appreciate the material things you provide for me without always wanting more. I will be submissive to your spiritual leadership and promise to be obedient to be loyal and committed to you only until death causes us to part.

The Marriage Rings

The rings you are about to exchange are powerful symbols. They are to be constant reminders of this day, your vows, and your devoted love:

(GROOM):"_______________, this ring I give to you with my joy, love, and thanksgiving that our Lord Jesus has brought you into my life. It is the visible witness of my commitment to you."

(BRIDE): "_______________, this ring I give to you with joy, love, and thanksgiving that our Lord Jesus has brought you into my life. It is the visible witness of my commitment to you."

The Marriage Prayer

Father of eternal love, Faithful Witness, Promise Keeper; You have heard the words and seen the hearts of these two. Now, we pray, that You will seal them with the eternal stamp of Your blessing, grace, and provision for the years of their lives, to Your glory alone in Jesus' name, Amen.

The Pronouncement

Thank you ____________ (groom) and ____________ (bride) for the privilege of officiating at this very special occasion in your life journey. Remember, make love your aim and keeping your vows your watchword. With confidence that you are committed to Christ, to each other, and to building a home centered in the Word and will of God, it is with thanksgiving and praise that I introduce you as Mr. and Mrs. [insert line]. Go now with this blessing: "the LORD bless you and keep you; the LORD make His face shine upon you, and be gracious to you; the LORD lift up His countenance upon you, and give you peace" [Num. 6:24–26].

Example Two

The Invocation

Dear heavenly Father, we bow before You, the Maker of heaven and earth; Creator of mankind; Savior and Lord. We know You are here; our prayer is for us to be aware of Your presence. We know we are fearfully and wonderfully made, and we are in awe of Your greatness. You are the eternal love and You have made possible a taste of that grace in the union of man and woman in marriage; a powerful picture of Your church wedded to You, our forever Husband. You are the builder of the home that lasts, as You have told us in Your Word: "Unless the LORD builds the house, they labor in vain who build it" [Ps. 127:1]. Now, Lord Jesus, lover of our souls with a love that never quits, never remembers our sins, and love that never ends; do honor these two and all who gather for this unique day. May You be well pleased, we pray in the matchless Name of Your Son, our Savior, Jesus Christ. Amen.

The Welcome

Dear ______________ (bride) and ______________ (groom), parents, family, friends. Welcome to this wonderful event in the lives of these children of our heavenly Father. They are grateful for your presence. Your sharing of time to be here is a witness of your affirmation for these two and their families as they begin a new direction in their lives.

For those who are married, may this be a time of reflection and renewing of the vows you shared on a day similar to this one. For those not married, may this day encourage you to trust God our Father for His plan in your life and His unchanging love for you. Since it was God who inaugurated the first home and officiated at the union of Adam and Eve, we can be assured of His intense interest in today's proceedings. We praise and thank the Author of life and love for meeting with us. Let us rejoice together as [insert line] and [insert line] link their lives in this sacred commitment at this sacred hour.

The Giving of the Bride

Believing that _____________ (groom) and _____________ (bride) have sought for and are assured of God's will for them to be husband and wife, and believing that they are committed to building a house built on the sure foundations of God's Word, it is my honor to ask, "Who gives this bride to be married to this man?" (Father, or parents, or friend says "I do" or "We do.")

The Marriage Statement

What makes a good husband? That's a pertinent question to ask in today's environment! A major newspaper had a lead article asking the question "Why Smart Women Make Dumb Choices." A good husband should be marked by several characteristics. He must be willing to leave his mother and father and "cleave to" his wife. Sadly, some men continue to stay emotionally tethered to their mother. The wife feels she plays second fiddle. He should be financially wise with a life reflecting financial integrity. He should have a sense of honor, for that will carry him through some tough days. He should demonstrate courtesy and compassion to his parents, family, and friends, for that is the way he will treat his wife. He must not be lazy, "lazy hands make a man poor," the writer of Proverbs 10:4 reminds us. He will communicate with his wife—listening to her and talking with her. Spiritually, he is a man that's a disciple of Jesus Christ and loves Him supremely. He is a man who is dedicated to obeying God's Word. He is a man who desires the best for his wife and children in a topsy-turvy world. He worships with his family. He is unashamed in his faith. That man will be faithful to death. He will be respected by his family and all who know him. He will raise children for the glory of God. He will, in due time, earn the compliment—"there goes a man of God."

What makes a good wife? The writer of Proverbs states: "a wife of noble character is her husband's crown" (12:4 NIV). A good wife holds the most influential position in our nation. She is the heart of the home. She's the one that every athlete on television says "Hi, Mom" to. She's the teacher, the chef, the enforcer, the referee, the law, love and lover, comforter and counselor, wisdom and instructor, muse and car-pooler, executive and first-responder. Above all, she has a heart for her Lord and Savior. She desires to please Him. She spends time in His Word and prayer. She encourages her husband to be a man of faith. She sees herself as a coequal with her husband, not inferior or superior. She wants her home to be the closest place to heaven a man can find on earth, the place her husband and children run to for renewal, rest, and refreshment. She is so honorable that a man trusts her completely with his children, his resources, his love. She finds satisfaction in meeting her husband's needs and being a partner in reaching out to others and co-laboring together for the glory of God.

The Wedding Vows

Vows are as ancient as time. Archeologists have identified artifacts and texts that are evidence of this timeless practice. In the Bible, vows were always between a man and God. The translation for the Hebrew word for *vow* is "to promise to do or give something to God." A vow was voluntary. It was binding. It was a serious matter. It was often publicly spoken. You come now, to make your vows to God, a promise of your intentions in this relationship.

I, _______________ (groom), love you. I vow to God that as long as I live, I will be faithful to you. I will be one with you and you alone. I receive you as a gift from God. I will treasure you. I will give you my best in all circumstances. Count on me. I will be there so long as I have life. I make my vows to you without reservation. So help me God.

I, _______________ (bride), love you. I vow to God that as long as I live, I will be faithful to you. I will be one with you and you alone. I receive you as a gift from God. I will treasure you. I will give you my best in all circumstances. Count on me. I will be there so long as I have life. I make my vows to you without reservation. So help me God.

The Marriage Rings

We live in a world of symbols that carry value to us: the flag, the colors, the banners, the school, the product; but none more publicly displayed and proudly worn than our wedding ring. These symbols will be a never-failing reminder of this eventful day.

(Groom) I give you this ring as a witness of my vows to God of my commitment to you. I will keep my vows and wear this ring as a public witness of my heart's devotion to you.

(Bride) I give you this ring as a witness of my vows to God of my commitment to you. I will keep my vows and wear this ring as a public witness of my heart's devotion to you.

The Pronouncement

_______________ (groom) and _______________ (bride), today you have made public your convictions that God has brought you together. You have given witness before God and man of your intentions to be husband and wife. You have exchanged rings to physically serve as a public testimony of your desire to glorify God and serve Jesus Christ together for the rest of your lives. It is my joy and privilege as a minister of the good news of our Lord and Savior Jesus Christ to pronounce you husband and wife . . . and may "the peace of God, which surpasses all comprehension . . . guard your hearts and your minds in Christ Jesus" [Phil. 4:7 NASB]. Amen.

The Presentation

On behalf of the _______________ (groom's family), and the _______________ (bride's family), I am happy to introduce for the first time, Mr. and Mrs. _______________. God bless you!

PREACHING ON MORAL AND ETHICAL ISSUES

Dr. Russell D. Moore and Dr. Phillip R. Bethancourt

A few years ago, a man stopped by our church, wanting to talk to me (Russell) about his problems with his wife. He'd started the conversation by asking if I thought the Bible's prohibition against being "unequally yoked together" applied to a couple where the husband was spiritually mature married to a wife who wasn't. He was, he told me, the kind of guy who prayed, read his Bible, and woke the kids up early to go over their memory verses for that week.

She, on the other hand, watched "nasty movies" on television all the time, he said, and was bored by spiritual things. She was so ignorant of the Word of God, he said, that she disagreed with his moderate use of alcohol. He talked about how she didn't even know that Jesus drank wine, even turning water into wine at the wedding at Cana, he said. He went on to talk about the imagery of wine in the Old and New Testaments, and about the apostle Paul's advice to Timothy to "use a little wine for your stomach" (1 Tim. 5:23).

Now, I know Christians are often divided over the issue of alcohol moderation. I know there are churches that can't agree on the issue, and I'm sure there are couples that differ with each other on it too. But it didn't seem natural to me that a woman so "bored" by the Word of God would be that interested in a strictly theological debate over whether the wine at the Cana wedding was fermented or not.

"What does your moderate use of alcohol look like?" I asked. "Sketch that out a little bit for me."

"Well," he said, "every night I'll start drinking a bottle of bourbon and about a twelve-pack of beer until I go to sleep."

Ah, now there was some clarity.

I said it didn't seem to me that his wife's concern here was a "theological debate," as he put it, but rather a real concern for their marriage and for their family. He looked at me quizzically, like I'd veered off from any relevance to our conversation, as though I'd suggested swapping recipes for seven-layer salad. I asked him to look with me at some passages of Scripture that speak about drunkenness, in order to show him why his wife was probably worried. He reached out his hand and held it against my arm, stopping me from turning the page.

"Oh, no," he said, with a smile that seemed to suggest he was embarrassed for me. "I've never been drunk. You're starting to sound like my wife."

Now most of you reading this page right now will immediately recognize that drinking that much alcohol until one passes out, on a nightly basis, is drunkenness. But this man wasn't a liar. He really wasn't, I think, trying to deceive me. He wasn't ignorant either.

He could call Bible verses to mind immediately, and could set them out in their literary and grammatical and historical context. He'd read all the major Christian theological works and could have had a very engaging conversation with me about anything from the pros and cons of elder-led church government to the timing of the Rapture.

He really, honestly, couldn't see what was happening to him or to his marriage. He wanted what he wanted, and he just expected the universe around him to conform to those wants. It had all happened, I'm sure, so gradually that he didn't even notice. It just seemed normal to him. All the rest of us, in his minds, were the crazy ones. I'm like that too—with different issues—and so are you. We just probably can't see where.

Many of us assume, first of all, that gospel preaching and ethical preaching are two different things. That's because we've so often heard preaching done this way. Gospel preaching, in our assumption, is the announcement of good news, the way of reconciliation with God through the shed blood and empty tomb of Christ Jesus. In this sort of preaching, we press the way of salvation and what God has done for us sinners in Christ.

Ethical preaching by contrast, in too many of our minds, is a step after the gospel. It might be practical tips on avoiding temptation, warnings about consequences, or a topical concordance-enabled list of "what the Bible says about" some particular issue or other. At its worst, it becomes a list of rules or a political rally in miniature. Ethical preaching isn't any of that. It is instead the application of the gospel to the whole of human existence, in order to tear down the remaining strongholds of the old order in our lives.

This is what is at stake when preaching on moral and ethical issues. We aren't addressing isolated "issues." We are instead uprooting spots of spiritual blindness—in all of us—that are part of the old devilish empire that is being uprooted by the cross and resurrection of Jesus. And that's why we so often misunderstand what such preaching should look like, and why it's ineffective and, sometimes, even unintentionally satanic.

Preaching and Moral Deception

First of all, what we deem "moral" or "ethical" issues aren't in some "special issues" category to be addressed periodically. These questions fall within the category that the Scripture refers to as the difference between wisdom and folly, the way that leads to flourishing and to life or to misery and to death. The choice of a preacher is not whether his people will receive preaching on questions of right and wrong, justice or injustice. His choice is simply whether they will receive such preaching from him, or from elsewhere.

The devil, after all, is a preacher. Satan opens up God's Word to people, seeking to interpret it, to apply it, to offer an invitation. The first satanic text was explicitly on the question of ethics, whether to discern good from evil on the basis of God's revelation or on the basis of autonomous human decision making. In the third chapter of Genesis, Satan comes to the primeval woman not with a Black Mass and occult symbols but with the Word she had already received from God—with the snake's peculiar spin on it. Throughout the rest of the canon—and the rest of history—he does the same, implicitly or explicitly.

Throughout the Old Testament, the Tempter preaches peace—just like the angels of Bethlehem do—except that he does so when there is no peace (Jer. 6:14). He points God's people to the particulars of worship commanded by God—sacrifices and offerings and feast days—just without the preeminent mandates of love, justice, and mercy. Satan even preaches to God—about the proper motives needed for godly discipleship on the part of God's servants (in, for example, his dialogue with the throne of God about Job).

In the New Testament, the satanic deception leads the religious leaders to pore over biblical texts, just missing the point of Christ Jesus therein. Jesus, instead, announces a coming kingdom that wages war with the powers of darkness. And the battlefield of this warfare is often in the moral and ethical realm. Throughout the New Testament, Paul warns that Satan's way blinds the eyes of unbelievers through the power of plausible arguments (Col. 2:8). Yet the gospel of Jesus Christ shines forth in the darkness to call forth a kingdom life—one that is shaped by an ongoing battle waged, often in ethical ways, through the pursuit of holiness. The preacher finds himself, with every sermon, in the midst of this conflict. The act of preaching is a means by which the Spirit allures people away from the ethics of the kingdom of darkness and to the ethics of the kingdom of light. So there is much at stake in the task of proclamation as it relates to preaching on moral and ethical issues.

Preaching and Moral Issues

When it comes to preaching moral and ethical issues, there are several mistakes that preachers can make. First, preachers make a mistake when preaching on moral and ethical issues if their proclamation is only topical. Now there is a place for topical preaching, especially when addressing complex topics of morals and ethics. But the danger arises when the climate of the sermon creates the appearance that moral issues are disconnected from the biblical text. If a topical sermon on abortion, for example, draws its authority from the latest statistics or political party platforms instead of Scripture, then it could bypass the gospel's power of transformation.

Another danger of topical preaching on ethical issues is distance. Preachers can tend to "preach hard" against moral issues that are distant from their congregation and avoid those plaguing their church. Why? Because the rural preacher in south Alabama has more out-of-the-closet divorced church members than out-of-the-closet homosexuals in his congregation. It's easier for him to preach hard against an issue like homosexuality that his congregation doesn't have to deal with as pervasively as divorce.

Second, preachers make a mistake when preaching on moral and ethical issues if their proclamation is only occasional. The tendency in some congregations is to view preaching on moral issues like using fine china—it's only for special occasions. They fear that if they address ethical issues too regularly, preaching on moral topics will lose its luster. Instead, they save these sermons for preset times established by a denominational calendar or an election cycle. Occasional ethical sermons by the preacher can lead to patterns of occasional ethical concern by the congregation. Of course, there are certainly times when special occasions warrant particular sermons on ethical issues. For example, it is a great thing to see so many churches address the issue of abortion each January during what many refer to as Sanctity of Life Sunday.

However, the occasional approach to preaching on ethics is built on a false premise of what ethics actually is. Ethical and moral issues are not simply the hot-button cultural and political issues of our day. The biblical category of ethics is another way of describing the lifestyle of kingdom citizens. In other words, while it may be appropriate to address specific ethical topics on an occasional basis, the preacher must regularly address ethical living if he is to equip his congregation for the spiritual warfare they face each day.

Third, preachers make a mistake when preaching on moral and ethical issues if their proclamation is only through moral example. Preaching through moral example occurs when pastors hold up particular biblical people and their actions as either a model to follow or a mess to avoid. This is particularly attractive in sermons on the Old Testament. So in a sermon on the ethical issue of adultery, the pastor would point to David's moral failure with Bathsheba as an example of the devastating impact of adultery. Addressing the patterns of holiness and sin in Scripture can certainly instruct the church today.

However, the danger of preaching on ethical issues only through the moral example approach is that it can disconnect the call to moral holiness from the engine of gospel grace that drives it. This risk is particularly significant when moral examples are abstracted from the flow of the Bible's storyline and its fulfillment in Christ. So the reason David's failures with Bathsheba should call us to marital fidelity is not just because of all the bad things that happened to David and his family as a result. In addition, it is because the act of adultery, whether by a forerunner of the Messiah like David or by a believer in the Messiah today, shatters the gospel picture of the one flesh union between Christ and His church.

If those are some pitfalls of ethical preaching, how can preachers rightly address moral issues in their proclamation? First, preachers must recognize the relationship between ethical issues and Christ-centered application. When addressing moral issues, the first step of application the preacher should make is not to show how the biblical text applies to the congregation. Instead, preaching must demonstrate how the ethical issue applies to Jesus before showing what that means for the lives of those who are found in Christ. In this way, preachers can ensure that their application does not bypass the power of the gospel to bring about moral transformation. When preachers address ethical issues, the goal should be to demonstrate how believers should view these topics in light of the resurrection kingdom that is advancing against the stronghold of Satan.

Second, preachers must recognize the relationship between ethical issues and wisdom. Christian ethics is another way of describing biblical wisdom. Wisdom isn't a set of abstract ideas; it's a way of life (Prov. 1:1–7). Indeed, wisdom is a person—Jesus of Nazareth—who is the ultimate reflection of the ethics of the kingdom (Col. 2:3). The task of preaching is to bring the Scriptures to bear on how the believer should walk in wisdom; and this is an endeavor with ethical implications. Preachers should see preaching on moral issues as not just the means by which they can get their congregations to vote the right way. Instead, they must seek to grow their people in the wisdom and knowledge of God so they are equipped to apply the gospel to all of life.

Third, preachers must recognize the relationship between ethical issues and instincts. Most ethical decisions are made at the level of intuitions, not ideas. The man in your church who is thinking about divorcing his wife and abandoning their three kids isn't doing that because he has rationally evaluated the pros and cons of this moral decision. Instead, the satanic powers allure him through an appeal to his appetites for sexual fulfillment and adventure. If most ethical decisions happen at the level of instincts, then the preaching task must seek to form gospel-centered intuitions in the congregation. If our churches can correctly answer the latest polling survey on social issues but don't have instincts shaped to resist the devil's temptation of the appetites, then we have more work to do in the pulpit.

Preaching on ethical and moral issues can seem like a daunting and complicated task. But all proclamation that includes application is fundamentally ethical in nature. The question is not whether preachers will address moral and ethical issues in their sermons. Instead, the questions are when, why, and how will they do it. Will we only preach on ethical issues when convenient? Will we simply baptize our political perspectives with prooftexts? Or will we seek first the kingdom and how to apply it to every area of life, including the moral and ethical issues of our day? Every preacher must face those questions in their sermon preparation and delivery if they want to engage in the battle raging between the kingdoms to shape the moral and ethical lives of their people.

PREACHING THE GOSPELS

Getting the Text Right

Steven Smith

I was sitting in the passenger seat of a Datsun B210 with one of my college professors. This professor was an incredible man. However, he was one of the more socially detached people I have ever met. Sports, fashion, social subjects, and so forth were lost on him. He only knew two things: Scripture memory and soul winning. That was it.

My sophomore year of college I went with him to a speaking engagement and he was dropping me off at my apartment. Before I got out of the car, I asked him how he enjoyed the sermon tape I had given him to critique. The truth is, as a nineteen-year-old, I really wanted to bless him with my incredible exposition. I was waiting for this feedback, which would certainly be a wonderful affirmation of my abilities, when he finally said, "Steven, you need to know one thing. When we get to heaven God is going to evaluate our preaching based upon how much content of Scripture was in it." I was confident he was not listening carefully to my sermon. I loved the Word of God, but I just wasn't sure this was true. Isn't preaching going to be ultimately evaluated by how many people respond? How moved people are? How many downloads? How popular we are? My understanding was that preaching was a means to an end. Not simply re-presenting God's Word and leaving the rest to him.

It took me a period of time, and we are all still on this journey, but I have come to realize that my professor was right. In the end we will be evaluated (James 3:1). And that evaluation will be based upon how faithful we are to the Word of God. Second Timothy 4:1–5 (ESV) could not be more clear: "I charge you in the presence of God and of Christ Jesus, who is to judge the living and the dead, and by His appearing and His kingdom: preach the word."

Nothing could be clearer than the fact that we are to re-present what God has already said, not develop something new to say.

And aren't we glad that this is the case? Aren't you glad that when we stand up we aren't making stuff up but simply explaining what God has said? Nothing is more liberating in the entire world. When we stand before a people, we aren't in the process of inventing; we are in the process of proclaiming. That means I don't have to take on anyone else's personality; I just have to explain what God is saying.

Preaching the Gospels

This desire and motivation is especially true in the Gospels. All the Bible is God's Word. However, the interpretative key to the whole Bible is the Gospels. The New Testament is a working out of what happens in the Gospels. Think of it. The Gospels end, and Acts begins, with the ascension of Christ (Acts 1:6–11). The book of Acts records what happened as a result of the presence of Christ in the Gospels. Romans through Jude is the church's commentary on what happened in Matthew through Acts. The book of Revelation is Jesus Christ the Messiah coming back in physical form to consummate what He began in the Gospels.

This is equally true of the Old Testament! In Luke 24:47 Jesus explains to the disciples that Moses, the prophets, and the Psalms speak to him. The Gospels are the fulcrum that leverages the message of the Bible.

A Case in Point

A couple of years ago I set out to preach what I think is the hardest parable in the Gospels because it would allow me to understand it and be able to teach it. The parable was the parable of the rich man and Lazarus found in Luke 16:19–31. I spent hours and hours with this text. I was looking at the grammar and syntax while aided by the best commentaries. But, after months of study, when I got ready to preach it, the meaning was just as unclear as when I started! While I worked hard, I missed this one simple principle that kept me from the meaning of the text: **The meaning of the text may have less to do with the words of the text and more to do with the author of the text.** So, I knew the words, but I did not know the meaning. I had the translation, but not the interpretation. Let's spend some time with this parable as a way of working out this principle.

This biggest interpretive question of Luke 16:19–31 is whether or not this is in fact a parable. I happen to believe it is, mainly because it fits the parables around it that begin with "there was a man" with slight variations (Luke 15:11; 16:1). Additionally they all have the same basic theme of Jesus' view of lostness. In the end, I personally hope this is a parable. The reason is that if this is just a true story, then anyone could have told it. Peter, or James, or Andrew could simply repeat facts. However, if this is a real parable, then that means that the details of the parable are straight from the imagination of Jesus Himself. Every detail, each nuance, each plot sequence, did not exist before they existed in the mind of God. If this is a real parable, and not just a true story, then we hang on every syllable for this is from the mind of God.

If it is a parable we pay close attention when Jesus says,

> There was a rich man who was clothed in purple and fine linen and who feasted sumptuously every day. And at his gate was laid a poor man named Lazarus, covered with sores, who desired to be fed with what fell from the rich man's table. Moreover, even the dogs came and licked his sores (Luke 16:19–21 ESV).

The Setting

Here Jesus is a sharp picture of contrast. The Pharisees to whom Jesus addressed this parable would have thought that the rich man was extremely blessed. After all, if you had wealth you would not have to work on the Sabbath day. This also enabled one to have the luxury of time to memorize the Law. In the same way, poverty was a sign of a curse.

The First Scene

This first scene is seen in verses 22–23: "The poor man died and was carried by the angels to Abraham's side. The rich man also died and was buried, and in Hades, being in torment, he lifted up his eyes and saw Abraham far off and Lazarus at his side" (ESV). This shows that hell is a reversal of life.

The Second Scene

The second scene is a long conversation.

> And he called out, "Father Abraham, have mercy on me, and send Lazarus to dip the end of his finger in water and cool my tongue, for I am in anguish in this flame." But Abraham said, "Child, remember that you in your lifetime received your good things, and Lazarus in like manner bad things; but now he is comforted here, and you are in anguish. And besides all this, between us and you a great chasm has been fixed, in order that those who would pass from here to you may not be able, and none may cross from there to us." And he said, "Then I beg you, father, to send him to my father's house—for I have five brothers—so that he may warn them, lest they also come into this place of torment." But Abraham said, "They have Moses and the Prophets; let them hear them." And he said, "No, father Abraham, but if someone goes to them from the dead, they will repent." He said to him, "If they do not hear Moses and the Prophets, neither will they be convinced if someone should rise from the dead"(vv. 24–31 ESV).

The three simple affirmations of this text are that hell is a reversal of the life, it is a reversal that cannot be reversed, and the Word of God is the only way to keep people out of hell. Interestingly, nowhere in this do we see the rich man repenting. This is because hell doesn't reform character; it exposes character.

Just an honest reading of this parable clears up so many questions about hell. But even still more questions are raised than are answered. What about the great gulf that is fixed? Is this a parable or a real story? Why did Jesus use the word *hades* for hell? Why is the rich man in heaven and the poor man in hell? Does Jesus have something against rich people? Once in heaven, will we have conversations with people in hell? There are good answers to all these questions. However, I'm convinced that the more you look at those questions, the deeper you drill down into the nuances of the parable, the more you get into the grammar and syntax, *the more likely it is you will miss the point*!

Why? Because the meaning of this parable is not in the parable. The meaning of the parable is actually around the parable. Remember: the meaning of the text may have less to do with the words of the text and more to do with the author of the text.

What then does this parable mean? We explore this in the next chapter.

PREACHING THE GOSPELS

Panning Out

Steven Smith

In the last chapter we were trying to get a sense of what the parable of the rich man and Lazarus was all about. We made the observation that drilling down into the nuances of this parable, the fine details, can actually take us away from the intended meaning. This is because *the meaning of a text may have less to do with the words of the text and more to do with the author of the text.*

By author, we mean the gospel writer. So, how do we get at that meaning? In this chapter we will keep working with the parable in the hope at understanding the way the author uses this parable.

Panning Out

Let's use the language of a cinematographer. A cinematographer can zoom in to get a really close look on a scene. He can also pan out to give the bigger picture of what is going on. Both skills are necessary to understand this text. First, let's pan out to see what is around the text. When we pan out, we see that Luke 15–16 is a group of five parables. Luke's ordering of the parables demonstrates that these are not individual units of thought; rather they each have a place in a sequential progression. Panning out allows us to see this. Let's open the lens to see what is around the parable of the rich man and Lazarus, beginning with the previous chapter.

Luke 15 begins with these words: "Now the tax collectors and sinners were all drawing near to hear Him. And the Pharisees and the scribes grumbled, saying, 'This man receives sinners and eats with them'" (vv. 1–2 ESV). Then He tells them the parable of the lost sheep. The parable has a simple structure: something is lost, found, with rejoicing. This structure is mirrored in the parable of the lost coin that follows, and the parable of the lost (prodigal) son. The sheep, coin, and son are all lost, all found, and all brought home with rejoicing.

However, this third parable about the lost son takes a twist at the end. The first two parables end with friends rejoicing, but the final parable ends with the older brother standing outside—choosing not to rejoice. In doing so he shows that he does not share the father's joy and is therefore no friend of the father. If the Pharisees were paying attention at all they could not miss the message. They were the older brother standing outside showing that they were not friends of God. And this is a setup for the next parable that begins in 16:1.

Luke 16:1–13 is the parable of the shrewd steward. This is a challenging parable in its own right, but here is a quick synopsis. The steward was hired to look over a wealthy man's assets. He was the CFO of a huge estate. When the story opens, he is fired for wasting money. He is stuck. He is too prideful to beg and has no other skills. What he does next is shocking. He goes to all the people who owe his boss money and dismisses their debt. Of course he has no authority to do this, but they do not know this, so they gladly take the reduced debt! So this guy goes from being a poor manager to a liar and a thief. He steals from his boss to win friends who will take him into their homes when his firing is made public.

The effect is that all the money that wasn't his bought him something in his next life—the life he would live when he was no longer employed. It bought him a new place of existence. God is saying, "You are getting fired from this life and I have given a small amount of money to steward, and eternity is going to be different for those who take their financial resources and invest it so that they will have eternal reward." Or said simply, "Take the money you have and invest it in a way that people are saved and those that are saved will greet you one day in heaven."

Here is the connection. Jesus tells three parables that all affirm that He seeks sinners. And then He turns to His disciples and says, "You need to be like me. Don't worry about all this or accumulating wealth in this life. Make the most of the resources you have, that aren't even yours, and spend it on getting people saved. When you go to heaven you have eternal reward that cannot be touched." It is a phenomenally provocative parable that extends the theme of the first three. So far, it looks like this:

Parable	**Main Point**	**Implication**
Parable One: The Lost Sheep	Jesus seeks sinners.	You seek sinners.
Parable Two: The Lost Coin	Jesus seeks sinners.	You seek sinners.
Parable Three: The Lost Son	Jesus seeks sinners.	Don't be like the older brother, who hates sinners.
Parable Four: The Shrewd Steward	Life is short.	Be like the steward: invest your money to win people for the life to come.

The Pharisees are the audience (15:1–2), and they hate what Jesus is saying! Jesus is saying, in effect, "I go after lost people with a passion: I seek them like a shepherd would a sheep, a woman would a coin, or a father would a son, so divest in this life and use your money to invest in the life to come!" This is so radical. They thought money was a personal affirmation of their righteousness that they maintained by staying away from lost people. Jesus said money only exists to get as many lost people in the kingdom as possible. In other words, money is not for you; it is to be employed to win people into the kingdom.

The Pharisees respond: "The Pharisees, who were lovers of money, heard all these things, and they ridiculed Him" (16:14 ESV). Jesus identifies the Pharisees as those who sought to justify themselves before men and then He says, "It is easier for heaven and earth to pass away than for one dot of the Law to become void" (v. 17 ESV). So, Jesus has identified three things that are wrong with them: they hated lost people, they loved money, and they twisted the Word of God by seeking to justify themselves. And so now Jesus tells the parable of the rich man. The rich man hated marginalized people, loved money, and had an extremely low view of Scripture. He was the opposite of Jesus. Now we know why he went to hell. He went to hell for the same reason all people go to hell: he wasn't like Jesus! So, now the five parables look like this:

Parable	**Main Point**	**Implication**
Parable One: The Lost Sheep	Jesus seeks sinners.	You seek sinners.
Parable Two: The Lost Coin	Jesus seeks sinners.	You seek sinners.
Parable Three: The Lost Son	Jesus seeks sinners.	Don't be like the older brother, who hates sinners.
Parable Four: The Shrewd Steward	Life is short.	Be like the steward: invest your money to win people for the life to come.
Parable Five: The Rich Man	Hell cannot be reversed.	Don't be like the rich man and love money more than people.

When I set out to understand this parable, I was frustrated because I began by thinking of this parable as "a tour through hell." But if it is, then it is a bad one because it does not tell us much more about hell than what is affirmed elsewhere in Scripture. It isn't an apologetic for hell, because Jesus didn't need to write an apologetic for hell; His audience already believed it. You could preach this as a "don't-go-to-hell message," but Jesus seems to be saying that the kind of people who go to hell are those who don't love the lost and are only invested in this life. I am not saying that the opposite of those keep are saving works that keep you from hell. No, of course not. We have to read this in light of New Testament theology. Only the atoning work of Christ can keep one from hell. However, once the atoning work of Christ is alive in someone's heart—they stop living for this life and they invest in the next life.

Why would Jesus say it this way? He is trying to turn the Pharisees on their heads. The Pharisees said, "Live rich and separate yourselves from sinners!" Jesus said, "Divest yourself and seek sinners." We learn this from panning out a little bit. But let's pan out a bit further to Luke 17:11 (ESV): "On the way to Jerusalem He was passing along between Samaria and Galilee." Luke intentionally puts this as a marker to fulfill his stated intention in 1:1, namely to give an ordered account to all the things that Theophilus had heard. This fits into the travel narrative that began in 9:51, "When the days drew near for Him to be taken up, He set His face to go to Jerusalem" (ESV). He set His face to go to Jerusalem to give His life for His sheep. This fits within the whole purpose of the travel narrative and moves the story along. Now we understand the parable better. This is not so much about hell as it is about Christ's view of lostness. And we understand this from the macro view, not the micro view. The meaning is found not in zooming in but in panning out. But remember, both skills are necessary.

Imagine someone takes you to the Louvre to see the *Mona Lisa*. Imagine there are no ropes or any other people. Your objective is simply to understand what Leonardo DaVinci has done. So you stand at the back of the room, about one hundred feet away. Would that be the best way to understand it? Of course not. You must move in close so that you can really see it. Then you decide to get so close that you can touch your nose to the canvas. If you did this you would also miss the point again. I have preached sermons that were so far back that you couldn't even see the text. But there are other times when I have gotten in the study and have gotten so focused on the small details that I started to lose focus on what is really going on. The question that this raises is, "What is the right distance?" My response is a bit disappointing, because I don't think that there are any rules about this.

Those of us who are conservative in our theology like there to be rules about everything else, like sermon form. I happen to think that in the sermon process there are times you just start to zoom in. But then I realize that I am so worried about the form of a certain sentence construction that I lost the flow of the passage. So, sermon prep is the art of knowing when to zoom in and when to pan out. If there was one rule it would be that *the proper distance we should be from the text is the one that the author wants us to have.* Each gospel has different themes and uses individual units of thought to move these stories along. But there is a word of warning here: if we refuse to see the individual stories as parts of a book, we will, inevitably, use these stories to teach moral lessons. Wouldn't you rather have seen what Matthew, Mark, Luke, and John want us to see? You can by moving through what David Jackman has called the melodic line.[1] It has a theme woven throughout the book.

How do we do this? We can do it by asking three questions:

1. What does this text say? [**translation**]

   This is working at the text from the paragraph level, to the sentence, then the clause level, and then the word level, in micro-exposition, finding all the nuances of the text. This process yields a translation of the text. Then pan out a bit and ask the next question.

2. How does the author use this text to accomplish his purposes for the book? [**zoom out**]

   This is especially necessary in the Gospels. But how do you find the author's purpose? You read the text, again and again. If you are preaching through a book, then you have already done this. And then ask the last question,

3. What does this text mean? [**interpretation**]

   This is different than question one, because the first is simply a translation of the words. The interpretation is the translation influenced by the author's purpose.

So you translate (1), then pan out (2), then interpret (3). This can look like a diamond:

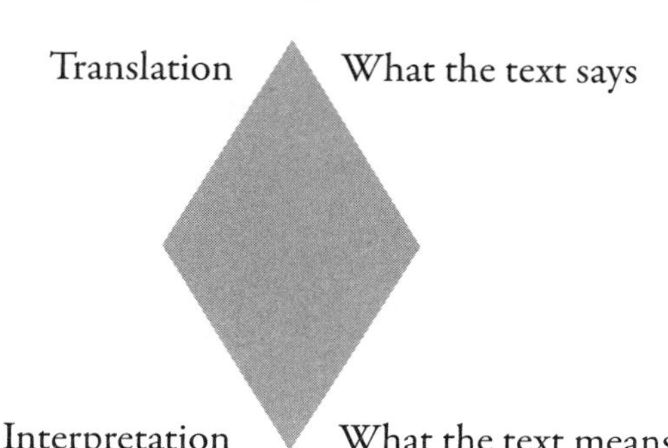

Conclusion

Why is all this necessary?

Well, the first reason is because of the genre. The gospels are not lessons. They are stories. But also because each gospel has its own plot line. All of them are writing somewhat of a biography. Some people think that the Gospels are their own genre because they are biography, but they don't include all the details and they sometimes stop to explain some things theologically. But Matthew is extremely concerned to show Jesus as a teacher of the kingdom. Mark is the most condensed gospel, but he is also centered on the kingdom. Luke is most concerned to show Jesus as Savior. And John has a completely different structure whose purpose is seen in 20:31: "These are written so that you may believe that Jesus is the Christ, the Son of God, and that by believing you may have life in His name" (ESV). Because of this John has more signs and wonders.

This should help us to remember that when we are preaching from a gospel we are not preaching a collection of stories about an event. We are preaching that one text. For example, Matthew 13 is similar to Mark 4. But when I am preaching Matthew 13 I don't have to say, "Mark says it like this." I just preach Matthew 13 because it is a narrative and this is a subplot pitching to the overall theme. I am not preaching an event I am preaching a text. You may compare because it may bring out a nuance in the text you are preaching, but don't preach a composite; just preach that text, because each gospel has its own individual structure.

This is because when God inspired the gospel writers, He did so on the macro level as well as the micro level. I believe God inspired the words of the Bible. In fact, I believe *every* word of the Bible is inspired. If that is true, then I also believe that God inspired the macro structure as well as the micro structure. There is value then at panning out as much as zooming in.

PREACHING THE GOSPELS

The Gospels Include Multiple Genres

Steven Smith

One of the most fascinating things about the Gospels is that they each contain multiple genres. This is because the Gospels are their own type of genre. In the last two chapters we defended the statement that the meaning of a text may have less to do with the words of the text, and more to do with the author of the text. If that is true, then we must ask how the gospel writers accomplished their task. What tools did they use? The answer to the question changes how we preach.

We looked briefly at an example from the parables of Luke, but the gospel writers use many different genres. Imagine if you knew the events in the life of Christ, what literary tools would you use to describe them? First you would need some all-out expositional literature. Just plain explanation. This is the type of literature that explains the doctrine of the very fact that there is an incarnate God—passages such as John 1:1–5. Then, of course, the dominant genre would be narrative. You would need to tell the *stories* that comprise the very life of Christ. Beginning with His birth and childhood, and going all the way to the ascension and commissioning. This narrative would demand sub-genres such as dialogue with others then pure narration where you filled in the gaps with what is going on. And of course you would have to include the teachings of Christ. The teaching of Christ includes short pithy statements and longer sermons such as the Sermon on the Mount. Among the teaching is the genre of parables. The parables consume much of the teaching of Christ, but they are their own genre.

So, the Gospels are narrative, and they are more than narrative. They are really a biography, and a unique type of biography at that. The Gospels really are their own genre. So, in order to accomplish the goal of communicating all that Christ did and said, multiple genres are used in one book. And, in order to re-present that meaning in a sermon, we must understand the differences in these genres. Let's discuss them briefly, then look at some sermon strategies.

Narrative

Character Development

The gospel writers will use clues to show us how a character in the story develops. We know something about the character of Zacchaeus beyond his stature (Luke 19:2–8). Clearly he was curious enough to climb a tree to see Jesus, he was open enough to welcome Him into his home, and he was repentant enough to develop a plan to sell his possessions. However, the most prominent way we understand character development is from the dialogue.

Dialogue

From the dialogue between the characters, we learn exactly what it is that Jesus wants to teach. We also understand a little more of how we can identify with the characters that Jesus is teaching. Think about Jesus' interaction with the woman at the well in John 4. We have a sense of Jesus' way with people: He demonstrates compassion by stopping to talk (v. 4), He is willing to break down cultural barriers to reach her (vv. 7–9), He is incredibly direct (v. 18), and He is ultimately concerned to press her to true worship (vv. 21–26). The woman is incredulous that He would stop to talk (v. 9), knows the party line of her culture (vv. 19–20), is desperately spiritually thirsty (v. 15), and ultimately responds in joy when she understands who He is (v. 39). We know all of this from the dialogue.

Most important, from the dialogue we understand how Jesus responds in certain situations. We learn as much from His strategy from this interaction as we do from His explicit teaching. We know how He welcomed people, challenged people, what He thought of unrighteousness, the law, and the disciple's role within civil government. So, when looking at dialogue, our first question is not one of identification: "Where do I find myself in this story?" Rather it is a question of understanding, "What is Jesus trying to say?" Once we answer the second question, we will understand how to frame the first question when we preach.

Narration

In order to move the story along, the gospel writers include certain amounts of narration. This is most dominant in Acts. For example Acts 15 contains these words: "Some men came down from Judea" (v. 1 ESV), "The apostles and the elders came together to look into this matter" (v. 6 NASB), and "All the people kept silent ... after they had stopped speaking, James answered (vv. 12–13 NASB). This is pure narration, and it is included to give pace and meaning to the flow of events. This is basic, but it's important. The narration provides the linguistic links in the chain of events. The narration is the place where we see most explicitly how the gospel writers felt we should understand these events. So, it is critical to understand. They were inspired by God to write these words in this way, thus why in fact they did write these words in these ways—including some things and excluding others—is very important. We do not need to read too much into them; that is missing the point. The point is that we follow their lead in the communication of them. If a writer pauses to provide a lot of detail (the crowds following Jesus in Luke 14:25 or the physicality of the healed leper in Luke 17:15), we observe that and communicate it. If a writer does not provide detail to things we would really want to know (what happened between the triumphal entry and the temple cleansing in Luke 19:44–45), we can assume the detail is not critical to this writer's interpretation of the story and we can move along. That is, move along while refusing the temptation to supply details where the inspired gospel writer did not give any.

Subplot

In all of this, it is important to remember that the plot to every smaller story in a gospel has a subplot that pitches to the larger plot of the book. It may not be obvious at first. This is because stories are often grouped with other stories, and those groups as a whole pitch to the larger story of the book.

Parables

The parables in the Gospels are more than fascinating. These thirty-eight or so stories of Christ are their own genre themselves. Much has been written on parables. However, let me offer three thoughts as to why parables are unique.

First, the parables are themselves their own genre. Why don't we just lump them with narratives? The answer is, they do not always act like narratives. The parable of the prodigal son (Luke 15:11–32), looks and acts like a narrative. It has narration, character development, and fully orbed scenes. However, the parable of the seed growing secretly is only four verses (Mark 4:26–29). It is simply a lesson from everyday life and does not really function like a fully developed narrative. So even to say the "genre of parables" is to include longer parables, shorter parables, and double parables. Each of these demands a different homiletic approach.

The other reason we treat them differently than narratives is because of their author. When Matthew is recounting the events of a healing or of Passion Week, he is giving us a record of facts. Events that have occurred. However, when Jesus is telling a parable, these events never occurred. They are completely made up! This does not make them less important; it makes them more important. As we stated in the previous chapter, the parables become more important when we understand that all the details of the story are completely from the mind of God.

Finally, the events around the telling of the parable are themselves narrative. This sounds confusing, but think of it this way: when we preach a parable, we are telling a story about someone telling a story. So the setting—the audience, the attending events—in which the biblical writer has placed the telling of the parable is very important. They are clues as to the parable's meaning.

Longer Discourse

Within the Gospels there are some passages that include some longer teachings of Christ. Consider the following passages:

The Sermon on the Mount	Matthew 5–7
The Sermon on the Plain	Luke 6:20–49
The Eight Parables	Matthew 13
The Parabolic Teaching	Mark 4:1–34
The Kingdom Parables	Matthew 18
The Five Parables on Lostness	Luke 15–16
The Instruction and High Priestly Prayer	John 14–17
The End-Time Parables	Matthew 23–25
The Warnings	Luke 12

Jesus is always teaching. And it seems that every narrative is used for the purpose of our instruction, edification, and exhortation. However, these are a sampling of some passages that include longer discourses. These discourses have unique features. Let's look at three of them.

First, they will often include rhetorical markers. These rhetorical markers help us understand how the discourse is bookended. Think about the Sermon on the Mount. It begins with Jesus seeing the crowds (Matt. 5:1), and then after it is concluded the crowds were amazed (7:28). However we interpret the information in the sermon, the context is important to Matthew. He wants us to think about this in terms of the needs of the crowd and the response of the crowd. Similarly, like rhetorical markers, each of the discourses has a unique audience. Often the notation of the audience *is* a rhetorical marker.

Second, the long discourses will have one central theme. This theme may be nuanced differently according to which gospel writer is recording the events. Why this is the case will be discussed below, but for now, it is simply important to know that the gospel's arrangement of similar material may vary from gospel to gospel. This should not be disconcerting.

It's actually helpful. The individual arrangement allows us to understand more clearly what Jesus was trying to accomplish in His writing.

However, while there is one central theme, it may encompass several different issues. The High Priestly Prayer covers many issues, but the essence of the prayer is in John 17:21. Everything that is prayed reflects the fact that the disciples are in Christ and Christ and the Father are one. The visible unity pitches to the goal of John's gospel, which is that all would see this unity and believe.

Let's think about these three features using the long discourse of Matthew 13.

First, note the rhetorical markers. Jesus begins by teaching many things in parables (13:3). Then after He finished the parables He departed (13:53). So from this we deduce that Matthew wants us to see 1:3–52 as one long discourse. However, note the audience. He begins by speaking to the crowds, but this discourse has multiple audiences. At times you have the sense that He is speaking to the whole crowd (v. 3), at other times to the disciples directly (v. 36), and at other times to the disciples with the crowds listening in (v. 10). Matthew wants us to see the difference, and it influences our interpretation.

Within this discourse, every parable He teaches is about the kingdom. That is clearly the theme. He covers many different issues about the kingdom: who will be in the kingdom, what to do about the enemies of the kingdom, and how to respond when we find the kingdom. So there are many issues, but the theme is pretty obvious.

However, there is also another important clue to finding the theme. The first parable, the parable of the soils, is about understanding. Those who are true believers hear and understand. Understanding is not intellectual assent; rather it is understanding that leads to action. After all, the second and third soils know enough to have an initial response; what they don't have is the type of understanding that causes them to endure and bear fruit. They don't have true understanding, because they have hard hearts. Jesus explains all of His parables, gets to the end, and turns to His disciples and says, "Have you understood?"

(v. 51). Their answer is critical. If they do not understand, they cannot respond and obey. They cannot be an enduring and fruitful soil. They affirm that they do, and so He tells them a parable explaining that with this knowledge they should be able to teach others from their storehouse of knowledge (v. 52). So again, the parables are about the kingdom, and more specifically, they are about the blessing of understanding and the peril of not understanding.

Other Genres

Expositional Literature

In the Gospels there is a small amount of literature that is not a part of a story, but simply provides information about who Jesus is, such as John 1:1–5 and Mark 1:1–3. The information is critical and can be somewhat independent of the narrative.

Genealogies

The genealogies in Luke 3:23–37 and Matthew 1:1–17 have unique purposes based upon the purposes of the author. However, they both demonstrate that Jesus is the Davidic King just as has been promised by the Old Testament. The preacher has to decide how to approach this: Should they constitute an entire sermon, or be preached with the surrounding narrative? Like always there is an exegetical concern and a pastoral concern. If they are preached as an entire sermon, the critical thing to remember is that they are a part of the narrative. In Luke they are placed in a way that sets up Jesus' ministry. In Matthew they set up the entire book by showing that Jesus is the Davidic Messiah. So they are important and should not be neglected. And, they should be preached as a part of the larger whole.

So, all we have done to this point is suggest that when we are going to preach from the Gospels, that means we are looking at multiple approaches to a text. In light of the multiple genres of the Gospels, here are some basic sermon strategies when approaching the Gospels.

Sermon Strategies

Timing Is Everything

Since the Gospels are primarily narrative, the preacher spends a great deal of time telling stories. Thus, what is true of good story telling is true of good narrative preaching. This is *almost* always true as we will see. With the rare exception, the preacher should refuse the temptation to give away the point of a story before the story is told. This may seem like an odd practice since we assume that our people know the stories already. However, it's more probable that people don't know the stories even if they think they do. So, when you are telling the story of the rich young ruler (Luke 19:16–22), you must tease out the story. Allow the people to feel the self-righteousness of his posture, and the gentle way Jesus, knowing everything, sets him up to see his own heart. Jesus is not impressed with his self-righteousness, but gives him a chance to change. Jesus always gives hope for the self-righteous. At this point in the telling of the story, there should be a pause. This is a great opportunity for him to repent. And it is a great opportunity for us to repent. The listener should feel their own responsibility in the rebuke of Jesus. We are all given a chance to repent. Then, similarly, they should feel the weight of his refusal when, in stone-cold rejection, he turns to his money and away from Jesus. Again, don't give away the story at the beginning. The story simmers, so allow the sermon to simmer before serving up the full main idea.

Variety Is Essential

Narrative is the primary genre, but as we have seen, there are many types of genre, and many features to the genre of narrative. This means we can have variety in our sermon structure. If you are preaching through Matthew, you will begin with a genealogy, move quickly to some challenging narratives including the temptation narrative, and then on to the Sermon on the Mount. Each of these texts has a different structure, and so can your sermon. The structure will vary.

Also, the length of text may vary. There is wisdom in preaching the whole genealogy in Matthew 1, all seventeen verses. Yet when you come to Matthew 5 you could preach the Beatitudes in one sermon or each beatitude individually. So the sermon structure will vary. This is wonderful because it keeps us fresh and allows for a variety in our presentation.

Fill the Screen

However, one of the temptations in taking a smaller text is that we neglect to tie the smaller text to the broader themes around it. Remember, every conversation, or healing, or teaching, is a part of a narrative. That narrative is a part of a larger group of narratives, and that group of narratives comprises the entire point that the gospel writer wants to make. If we do not understand this, we can isolate individual stories and treat them as if they are individual lessons—like Aesop's fables. However, each story is a sub-plot in a part of the larger story. That is where it draws its meaning. There is meaning in the internal structure, and meaning in the external structure.

Understanding this is a science; practicing it is an art. By this I mean the discipline of understanding a text in its context will allow the preacher to understand the broader themes of Scripture. Knowing that each story in a narrative text points to a larger theme does not mean that we identify that theme the same way in each sermon. For example, if I am preaching through Luke, every time I see Jesus moving toward Jerusalem, this is a good opportunity to teach our people that Luke understands these events as moving Christ further down the road to His sacrifice. This, in a sense, is the ultimate "point" of every narrative. Now, when you are preaching in the travel narrative, say the parable of the shrewd steward in Luke 16:1–13, you may bring that out. It certainly fits in with the story. However, you may have just addressed this fact in a previous sermon on the prodigal son, so it is not necessary. The principle is that we pan out every once in a while to let people see where this individual narrative fits into the larger picture. That we do this is essential. People will not see the big picture without it. When to do this, how often and how long, is a pastoral concern that is dependent on your context.

If God wanted to give His truth as a list of axioms, He could have. He could have made the whole Bible like the book of Proverbs—wise truths to live by. This would have made it easier to preach. And at the same time, it would have made it flat and one-dimensional. The joyous truth is that the Scriptures are full of life. They are full of variety! Therefore, to preach sermons that are true, true to the text, we must consider how this variety informs the sermon.

BABY DEDICATION

Infant's Name: ______________________________

Significance of Given Names: ______________________________

Date of Birth: ______________________________

Date of Dedication: ______________________________

Siblings: ______________________________

____

Maternal Grandparents: ______________________________

Paternal Grandparents: ______________________________

Life Verse: ______________________________

Notes: ______________________________

____

____

____

____

____

____

____

BAPTISMS & CONFIRMATIONS

Date	Name	Notes

FUNERAL REGISTRATION

Name of Deceased: ______________________________

Age: ______________________________

Religious Affiliation: ______________________________

Survivors:

Spouse: ______________________________

Parents: ______________________________

Children: ______________________________

Siblings: ______________________________

Grandchildren: ______________________________

Date of Death: ______________________________

Time and Place of Visitation: ______________________________

Date of Funeral or Memorial Service: ______________________________

Funeral Home Responsible: ______________________________

Location of Funeral or Memorial Service: ______________________________

Scripture Used: ______________ Hymns Used: ______________

Eulogy by: ______________________________

Others Assisting: ______________________________

Pallbearers: ______________________________

____

____

Date of Interment: __________ Place of Interment: ______________

Graveside Service: Yes: _______ No _______

FUNERALS LOG

Date	Name of Deceased	Scripture Used

MARRIAGE REGISTRATION

Bride: ____

Religious Affiliation: ______________________________

Parents: ____

Groom: ____

Religious Affiliation: ______________________________

Parents: ____

Date of Wedding: ____________________________________

Location: ____

Ceremony Planning By: ______ Minister ______ Couple

Others Assisting: ___________________________________

____

Maid/Matron of Honor: _______________________________

Best Man: ____

Wedding Planner: ____________________________________

Date, Time, Location of Rehearsal: __________________

Reception: ______ All Wedding Guests ______ Invitation Only

Reception Location: _________________________________

Photography: ______ During Ceremony ______ After Ceremony

Date of Counseling: __________ Date of Registration: __________

Miscellaneous: ______________________________________

____

____

____

____

MARRIAGES LOG

Date	Names of Couple	Scripture Used

SERMONS PREACHED

Date	Text	Title/Subject

NOTES

The Gospel of the Servant King // Daniel L. Akin

God Sent His Son and We Killed Him: Mark 12:1–12

1. C. H. Dodd, *Parables of the Kingdom* (New York: Charles Scribner's Sons, 1961), 93.
2. C. S. Lewis, *The Last Battle* (New York: Collier Books, 1970), 140–41.

Two Great Commandments/Two Great Loves: Mark 12:28–34

1. James R. Edwards, *The Gospel According to Mark* (Grand Rapids: Eerdmans, 2002), 371.

A Sacrifice of Extravagant Love: Mark 14:1–11

1. D. A. Carson, "Matthew," in *Matthew, Mark, Luke, with the New International Version (The Expositor's Bible Commentary, Vol. 8)*, ed. Frank E. Gaebelein and J. D. Douglas (Grand Rapids: Zondervan, 1984), 593.

Great Moments in Great Places // Mark L. Bailey

The Hill of the Beatitudes: A Life Well Worth Living: Matthew 5:1–12

1. R. G. V. Tasker, *The Gospel According to St. Matthew* (Grand Rapids: Wm Eerdmans, 1961), 61.
2. C. S. Lewis, *Mere Christianity* (New York: Macmillan Publishing Company, 1952 edition), 118.

A Spring in the Valley of Jezreel: The Development of Courage

1. William Shakespeare, *Julius Caesar* 1.2.140–141.

The Garden of the Olive Press on the Mount of Olives: A Commitment of Obedience

1. Billy Graham, *Answers to Life's Problems: Guidance, Inspiration and Hope for the Challenges of Today* (Thomas Nelson, 1994).

An Altar at the Top of Mount Carmel: The Need to Make a Decision: 1 Kings 18

1. Swindoll, Charles, *Today in the Word*, Moody Bible Institute, (August 1991), 16.

The Gospel Project // Steve Dighton

A Final Farewell: Acts 20:17–32

1. Rheta Grimsley Johnson, *Good Grief: The Story of Charles M. Schulz*, 2nd ed. (Kansas City, MO: Andrews and McMeel, 1995).

Growing in Grace // J. D. Greear, Ph.D.

Eight Principles for Sacrificial Giving: Exodus 35–36

1. J. Strong, *Enhanced Strong's Lexicon* (Bellingham, WA, 2001); N. D. Osborn and H. Hatton, *A Handbook on Exodus*. UBS Handbook Series (New York: United Bible Societies, 1999), 698–99.

Five Lessons about Prayer from an All-Night Wrestling Match with God: Genesis 32

1. Martin Luther, as quoted by David Steinmetz, "Calvin and Luther on Interpreting Genesis," Beeson Divinity School podcast, Oct. 9, 2012.
2. The name "Jacob" means "grasper" or "deceiver."

Faith Is Action: Hebrews 11

1. C. S. Lewis, *A Grief Observed* (New York: HarperCollins, 1961), 34.

Five Lessons about Following God in Crisis Moments: Genesis 12:1–4

1. John Calvin, *Commentary on Genesis* (trans. Alister McGrath; Wheaton, IL: Crossway Books, 2001), 203 (paraphrase).
2. C. S. Lewis, *The Screwtape Letters* (San Francisco: HarperCollins, 2001), 155.

God Does Not Need Your Money: 2 Samuel 7

1. David Jeremiah, *Giving to God* (San Diego, CA: Turning Point, 2001), 117.

Jesus' Sovereignty Does Not Keep Him from weeping With Us: John 11

1. Charles H. Gabriel, "I Stand Amazed in the Presence."

"The Five Core Gospel Truths from Jesus' Genealogy": Matthew 1:1–17

1. From Tim Keller's message on Matthew 1:1–17, "The History of Grace." Delivered at Redeemer Presbyterian Church, December 14, 2008.
2. William Hendriksen, *Exposition of the Gospel According to Matthew*, vol. 9, Baker New Testament Commentary (Grand Rapids: Baker Academic), 110.
3. Again, I am indebted to Tim Keller for pointing this out.

Life in a Healthy Church // Dr. Jeff Iorg

Jesus Is Lord: Philippians 2:5–11

1. Richard Melick, *The New American Commentary: Philippians, Colossians, Philemon* (Nashville: Broadman and Holman, 1991), 95–109. All lexical insights in this message are found in this excellent analysis of Philippians 2:5–11.

Preaching the Authority of the Word of God // Dr. James MacDonald

Promise #1: God Is Always with Me (I Will Not Fear): Deuteronomy 31:6; Hebrews 13:5–6

1. Compiled using WordSearch 9 Bible software.
2. J. F. Hurst, *John Wesley the Methodist* (Kessinger Publishing, 2003), pp. 297–8.

Detours, Dead Ends, and Dry Holes // Dr. Adrian Rogers

Sermon Date: July 9, 2004: Exodus 13:17–22

1. Joseph H. Gilmore, "He Leadeth Me: O Blessed Thought."
2. Fanny Crosby, "All the Way My Savior Leads Me."
3. Ibid.
4. Oscar C. Eliason, "Got Any Rivers?"
5. Joseph H. Gilmore, "He Leadeth Me Beside the Still Waters."

A Walk Through the Psalms // K. Marshall Williams, Sr.

Refuge: Psalm 23:4

1. C. H. Spurgeon, *The Treasury of David*, vol. 1 (McLean, VA: MacDonald Publishing Company), 355, 365–70, 373.

Rescue: Psalm 23:5

1. C. H. Spurgeon, *The Treasury of David*, vol. 1 (McLean, VA: MacDonald Publishing), 370–73.

Revival: Psalm 23:6

1. C. H. Spurgeon, *The Treasury of David*, vol. 1 (McLean, VA: MacDonald Publishing Company), 356, 370, 372–73.

Blessed by the Best: Psalm 103:1–5

1. C. H. Spurgeon, *The Treasury of David* (McLean, VA: MacDonald Publishing Company), 275–277, 284–90, 299.

Funeral Service for Bette Sibley // Dr. O. S. Hawking

1. Fanny Crosby, "Someday the Silver Cord Will Break."

Preaching the Gospels Part II // Steven Smith

Panning Out

1. See David Jackman's helpful comments in the video curriculum *Preaching and Teaching New Testament, Gospels and Acts* (London: PT Media, 2008).

INDEX

A

B

C

D

E

F

R

S

T

U

V

W

Y